Lisa,

We hope you enjoy reading the book as much as we did writing it. Thank you so much for all of your support. You're wonderful!

Tiffany

Seriously... It's Not You; It's Me!™

By Marjan Fariba and Tiffany Lyon
as members of
Impish Nymph Productions LLC

Seriously... It's Not You; It's Me!™

by Marjan Fariba and Tiffany Lyon

©2009 Impish Nymph Productions LLC

ISBN: 978-1-935125-62-4

Cover design by: Jeff McKinley Artworks Inc.
Logo design by: Jon Robertson, 1-800 ProColor, Inc.

Printed in the United States of America on acid-free paper

For additional copies of this book go to:
www.rp−author.com/seriously

Robertson Publishing
59 N. Santa Cruz Avenue, Suite B
Los Gatos, California 95030 USA
(888) 354-5957 • www.RobertsonPublishing.com

Impish Nymph Productions LLC

FORWARD

DEDICATION

This book is dedicated to all who are, have been and will be in the dating and relationship scene.

GRATITUDE

We owe a debt of gratitude to our families for putting up with all the time away from home while researching and writing our book. We especially thank our husbands for being amazing sounding boards and for their support of this project and our future projects to come. We also thank our boys, Kamron, Kia, Alex, and Jack for being patient throughout the process. Thanks go to our parents, siblings, uncles, aunts and cousins (and Dante, the dog) for always being there; we couldn't have done it without them.

Special thanks to Kamron Fariba who served as our intern and helped us interview the college crowd. He made many exciting and intuitive contributions to our book. We thank our friends on the courts, in the neighborhood, and in our lives for their immeasurable support and continuous curiosity about our book – they kept us going through the difficult periods.

We thank all of our contributors for their time and for sharing their stories with us. While the people who have supported us are too numerous to specifically mention, a few contributors took a special interest in the book after being interviewed and they went to great lengths to support us in our endeavors. We give a very special thanks to Billy Daly of Los Gatos, CA who offered valuable insight and a deep understanding of human relationships and the world of dating. We have watched him work miracles with individuals in need of dating and relationship advice. We would also like to thank Bill Iammatteo for his humorous catalogue of dating stories, Jeff McKinley for his artistic eye and his support of the redeeming value within our book, and Jeanne Butler who supplied us with a continuous stream of interviewees.

QUESTIONS ANSWERED

There are a few questions that have been frequently asked of us. First, how did you decide to write this book together? We were working on our independent projects and thought it would be great fun to work on a project together. We have so many crazy friends and family members who have experienced a menagerie of dating escapades that it was a natural subject and the timing was right. Our contributors, friends and families have continually commented on the dynamic energy between us. They have pointed out that, together, we seem to bring the best out in people. We truly enjoyed each other and had a great time working on our project. We look forward to many more ventures together. Our friendship grew deeper and stronger throughout this process. The most important thing we learned is that having a great friend in one's life as an adult is priceless.

Second, why did people give you interviews about their intimate and detailed relationship information? We don't know for a fact why they were willing to do it, but many of our contributors needed to talk about their own stories without being judged. While we gave no advice, we played the role of the listener and allowed them to be comfortable when pouring their hearts out to us. Many self-revelations occurred during our long interviews. At the conclusion of their interviews, many contributors recommended that we interview their friends and family. While we interviewed many people, we selected only the most relevant interviews to our particular characters for inclusion in our book.

Third, did you tell your contributors how you were going to categorize them? No, we did not know ourselves until we collected all of our data. Surely, some contributors will be disappointed when they see their information within a particular section. We can only say to those individuals that it is just another perspective and a potential avenue for self-discovery.

Fourth, given that there are so many dating books out there, what is different about yours? Ours is not a dating book. It is a book about self-discovery and simply provides a humorous guide to the characters who are out there in the dating world based upon our research. We provide information for the buyer to take or leave. We offer very little advice other than to love yourself, get to know yourself, and to accept others as they are.

Fifth, where did you get the explicit sexual content that is in the book? The sexual content in the book was derived from our contributors' interviews. Verbatim sexual texts and email conversations have been included in some of the stories. **We do not recommend this book for minors; it is a book for a mature audience. The explicit content is only a small fraction of our book. If your sensibilities are offended by the explicit nature of a story or interview, please skip the section and move to the next.**

TABLE OF CONTENTS

I. Introduction

As the saying goes, make big decisions with your heart; make little decisions with your head. Following your feelings was an important lesson Oprah shared with her goddaughter's graduating class at Stanford in June of 2008: "And how do you know when you're doing something right? How do you know that? It feels so. What I know now is that feelings are really your GPS system for life. When you're supposed to do something or not supposed to do something, your emotional guidance system lets you know. The trick is to learn to check your ego at the door and start checking your gut instead. Every right decision I've made – every right decision I've ever made – has come from my gut. And every wrong decision I've ever made was a result of me not listening to the greater voice of myself."[1] She told them: "So, lesson one, follow your feelings. If it feels right, move forward. If it doesn't feel right, don't do it."[2] This lesson is particularly relevant in dating. We were inspired to write this book after watching friends and family who continually allowed themselves to be guided by their heads rather than their hearts in their dating and relationships.

We began the process of writing our book by researching today's dating patterns. We must emphasize that all research, information, and deductions are non-scientific and we are not licensed psychiatrists, therapists or any kind of shrink tank. Our information was gathered first by observation and through our own personal experience. Next, we sought outside input from our circle of friends and family and then through interviews of others. Over the past year, we interviewed many people worldwide from the ages of 19 to 70 years in order to learn about their experiences in relationships and the dating world. We spoke with both single and married men and women. Understanding that we would not use names of the participants, individuals eagerly shared their most intimate and personal dating and relationship information. Surprisingly, the list of those who were interested in participating in our research exploded in concentric circles. We never could have imagined the magnitude of the need and demand to share and to learn about the world that lurks behind the scenes in the dating game.

---

[1] http://news-service.stanford.edu/news/2008/june18/como-061808.html
[2] http://news-service.stanford.edu/news/2008/june18/como-061808.html

While the data we gathered is not scientific, it is real and it reflects reality. It reflects the who, what, when, where, why and how of relationships and dating today. We have discovered that dating and relationship stories are common across the world. What was most intriguing to us was the discovery of universal commonalities including what people desire, the characters that are found out there on the dating circuit, and the games that are played. We found the manipulations, games, and shenanigans occurring in the dating and relationship world to be funny, eye-opening, exciting, and mind-altering.

We begin with the characters that exist in men and women's fantasies. We examine the difference between reality and fantasy in terms of who is out there in the marketplace. While fantasy is alive and well, refusal to face reality may mean a lonely future. Not that there is anything wrong with fantasy. It is simply what it is. It is usually intangible. In the rare cases where fantasy is tangible, it is temporary at best.

We next explore the game and show that, while there doesn't have to be a game, there is plenty of gamesmanship going on in the dating world. The funny thing is that there is no one game; each character is playing his or her own game. The various games are explored throughout the character chapters in the book.

Through our research, we found that there are some universal characters in the dating and relationship world. We analyzed those characters and grouped them loosely into categories of takers, givers, or somewhere in between. We developed the characters through their own words in our interviews with them and through stories about them. Sometimes, the interviews speak for themselves. Some interviews contain interesting contradictions. In many cases, we merged the information gathered in our research so that no character or story reflects one individual. In other cases, we fictionalized the information included from our research.

We have not made a judgment as to whether a character is good or bad because that depends on your own perspective and whether that character is right for you. For example, we examine the ubiquitous Player as he presents himself in his environment. We found four types of Players: the Diplomat, the Magnet, the Forever Bachelor, and the Sportsman. We have included descriptions, interviews and stories about each type of Player. Some readers may find one, some, or all of them to be reprehensible; others may drool or marvel over them. It is all about perspective.

We had a great time working on some of our characters and had a difficult time writing about other less exciting or interesting personalities.

2

Takers like the Players and the Divas are thrilling, but givers like Intellectuals and Nurturers are not as enthralling. However, they are all out there in the dating scene. A book about dating and relationships would be incomplete without both the fascinating and the less titillating. We must point out that some character stories are very graphic and explicit. We felt that these particular characters could not be fully developed without exploring the lurid side of their lifestyles.

In light of the above, it was always a breath of fresh air when we spoke with genuinely funny, light-hearted people. While they really didn't fall into one specific character type, they were just fun or interesting. We have thrown in three Breath of Fresh Air sections to give a look at some regular people out there. We broke the Breath of Fresh Air sections up by age. The first Breath of Fresh Air section is located after the Takers section. It includes interviews of a male and female in their twenties. The second Breath of Fresh Air section is located after the section titled, "It's a Give and Take." It includes interviews with two males and two females spanning the ages of the thirties and forties. Finally, the last Breath of Fresh Air section is located after the Givers. This last section includes interviews with a man in his late sixties and a woman in her seventies. Look at these fun and interesting interviews as palate cleansers before you move onto the next course.

After thoroughly studying each of our defined characters, we determined that, for the most part, they become highly predictable in their actions in dating and relationships. People are who and what they are. They may evolve, but their basic character will never change. While general characteristics like a sense of humor or a short fuse are patent and may be spotted quickly by even the unobservant and obtuse, the deeper qualities and characteristics that make a person who he or she is may take more than one date to discover.

To be successful in the dating and relationship world, all you have to do is figure out who you are and then what type of character is right for you. We created a Gravity Wheel that depicts in a graphic form the magnetic pull between certain characters. The Gravity Wheel is included in the Appendix. If the readers recognize themselves in our characters, we hope that they will learn about themselves. We hope that our readers will discover that they are not alone out there and that their experiences are not unique. We have touched upon issues that are not usually spoken about, but are in the forefront of many daters' minds. We hope our discoveries

3

will help you find the Yin to your Yang by giving you a leg up in the world of hidden meanings.

Falling in love is not the same as being in love. When you are in love, you have made an intelligent choice. Contrarily, when you fall in love, you are experiencing a purely emotional and physical response without analysis for long-term potential. If you have found someone who you respect, he or she has qualities that are compatible with yours, you can see yourself spending a lifetime with him or her, and you can imagine having children with him or her, you may come to love the person for who he or she is. One can fall in love many times over with the same person – it is purely emotional. Mutual respect and communication is the key to long-term happiness.

When dating, keep an open mind and an open heart. We hope the information and stories in this book will help you to learn about yourself, figure out who is out there, and discover the secret to finding a life-long partner, if that is what you desire. If you are in the dating market, you may not be looking for the right type of person. Don't blind yourself with pre-conceived ideas. Often, we don't know ourselves so how can we come up with a litmus test for our future partner? Genes, society, family and our environment shape us. We become victims of our own circumstance. In determining with whom we end up, we need to learn who we have become. We need to know ourselves first.

II. Fantasy vs. Reality

Both men and women have fantasies about their ideal mates. The trick is to realize the difference between fantasy and reality. Love is born out of reality. Love is taking someone with his or her inherent faults and not trying to change him or her. Love is acceptance and respect.

The link between reality and love was eloquently discussed in a quotation of the <u>Velveteen Rabbit</u> in Osho's book <u>Maturity: The Responsibility of Being Oneself</u> on pages 80-81.

> There is a beautiful definition of realness through love in Margery Williams's beautiful book The Velveteen Rabbit.

> "What is REAL?" asked the Rabbit one day. "Does it mean having things that buzz inside of you and a stick-out handle?"

> "Real isn't how you are made," said the Skin Horse. "It's a thing that happens to you. When a child loves you for a long, long time, not just to play with, but REALLY loves you, then you become Real."

> "Does it hurt?" asked the Rabbit.

> "Sometimes," said the Skin Horse, for he was always truthful. "When you are Real you don't mind being hurt."

> "Does it happen all at once, like being wound up," he asked, "or bit by bit?"

> "It doesn't happen all at once," said the Skin Horse. "You become. It takes a long time. That's why it doesn't often happen to people who break easily, or have sharp edges, or who have to be carefully kept. Generally, by the time you are Real, most of your hair has been loved off, and your eyes drop out and you get loose in the joints and very shabby. But these things don't matter at all, because once you are Real you can't be ugly, except to people who don't understand . . . once you are Real, you can't become unreal again. It lasts for always."

Love makes you real; otherwise you remain just a fantasy, a dream with no substance in it. Love gives you substance, love gives you integrity, love makes you centered.

Once you have gotten beyond the fantasy, reality will reveal that love and relationships are hard work. If you are willing to put in the work and effort, the payoff is great. If all you seek is a one-sided fantasy, enjoy remaining lonely in love.

A. Fantasy Characters

We have developed the fantasy man in the following section on Prince Charming based upon what women have told us in our research. The fantasy woman is later described in the section entitled "Eve."

1. PRINCE CHARMING

Prince Charming is the knight in shining armor that every girl dreams of finding. Some fantasize about settling down with one Prince Charming; others might prefer a new and different Prince Charming for every night of the week. Whatever the preference, Prince Charming seems to have some common characteristics. Prince Charming sweeps her off her feet and takes her breath away. He is as close to perfection as a man can be. He is charming, tall, and handsome. He is well endowed and knows how to please a woman. His body is sculpted and defined; he is physically fit. He offers both a physical and a mental orgasm. He is as magnificent as his white magical horse. He exudes animal magnetism, charm and electric energy. His cheeks are chiseled and his jaw is square. He melts the hearts of all women. His piercing eyes shoot arrows into her heart as he admires her, fluttering his gorgeous think eyelashes. The heat and energy surrounding Prince Charming is combined with a cool breeze that comforts her and puts her at ease, preventing her from melting into a puddle on the ground.

As he walks toward her, his swagger and confidence takes her breath away. The closer he gets to her, the more her heart flutters. He holds her hand with his large, warm, firm, strong hand. He loves women – he gives her the feeling that she is the only woman in the world and he wants her. He is so confident and secure in himself that she is free to want him or leave him. Surely, she wants him.

Prince Charming respects women and makes them feel fantastic about themselves. He is the ultimate lover of women. He listens and catches details that most men let slip by. He makes a woman feel good without shallow complements. He is quiet and soft-spoken, but there is no doubt that he knows what he is talking about. He is worldly and extremely intelligent. He is up for life and loves life. He is a magnificent dancer and can dance in any style, including Salsa, Ballroom, and Tango. He is a wonderful dresser. He is immaculately clean and always smells fresh. Most importantly, Prince Charming has a keen sense of humor.

When Prince Charming is engaged in sex with a woman, he is in tune with her every need. He is slow and deliberate, taking his time to make sure that he first pleasures her in every way possible. His lips are divine, deliciously plump, perfectly moist, and he uses them to their full advantage. He enjoys the process of pleasing.

BEWARE: Although every man would love to be Prince Charming to his woman, too much of a good thing can be asphyxiating. Fantasy is good as long as it does not displace reality.

A FANTASY DATE WITH PRINCE CHARMING

You feel privileged when Prince Charming invites you to enter his sanctuary. His place is warm and real with beautiful, vibrant, and exciting colors. It seems that each piece of furniture was individually customized and created for his space. His uplifting and charming personality shows through in every room. The kitchen reveals that fabulous and exotic food, drink and merriment abound. Without words, Prince Charming makes you feel beautiful inside and out. He validates you as a person and allows you to love yourself. Prince Charming makes you feel as if you are the best lover in the world.

After experiencing relaxing music and soft touching in the main area, he gently sweeps you off your feet and lifts you like the air into his strong muscular arms. He nudges your cheek with his and then bends toward your lips and gently kisses you. He glides toward the bedroom and you have no idea where you are; you are in the clouds without gravity, feeling as if you are riding a white unicorn into ecstasy.

He carries you into the love suite and places you on his beautiful bed with white, crisp and soft linens. He sits next to you and caresses your hair, while looking into your eyes with his deep, passionate, sensual, look of desire. He sweeps your hair away from your neck, and begins to kiss the nape of your neck. As his beautiful and graceful long strong fingers gently caress from your neck to your breasts, he unbuttons each button and sweeps his hand against your skin as he goes to the next button.

Then, he unbuttons his own shirt while sitting next to you, leaving it unbuttoned, but showing his beautiful bare chest and abs. Your heart is beating heavily. He removes your shirt and bra, placing them carefully away. He bends down and kisses your stomach and gradually reaches around to remove your skirt. The skirt is placed with your other garments. He looks at you, knowing that you are his for the taking. Kissing your shoulder and moving toward your breasts, he wets his lips and kisses around the nipples, gently sucking on them.

He kisses lower and lower and lower until he gets under your belly button. He gently removes your underwear and places it near your skirt and blouse. He pleasures you with his steamy breath, lips, tongue, and long warm fingers. You are in ecstasy and breathing heavily; your head is spinning. He kisses you gradually up to the navel and back up toward your mouth. You are numb with pleasure and have not been able to lift a finger to do any pleasing for him. He expects nothing and needs nothing other than to please you.

His perfectly sized penis is beautiful and erect. You want him so badly, but he is taking his time ravishing you. He is giving you more than you can imagine for yourself. The moment comes when he knows you are ready for him and he makes love to you while continuing to caress your neck, your lips, and your breasts with his lips. He completely satisfies you; you are in ecstasy.

After enjoying one another in a warm and loving embrace, he kisses you on the lips and excuses himself for a moment. He leaves the room and comes back moments later with two glasses of ice cold water with lemon. He hands one to you and sits next to you as he takes a sip from his. He leans over, putting his water on the night stand, moves your hair away from your ear, and gently caresses your ear with his fingers. He slowly and gently lifts your chin toward him and asks you what you would like for breakfast in the morning.

The next day after you have returned home, Prince Charming sends a lovely bouquet of flowers to you with a message card that says, "It was a night to remember forever. PC."

2. EVE

Men are different than women; they do not dream about finding their mate as little boys. Where most women dream of their wedding day from the time they start playing dress-up, boys play policeman, firefighter, and hero. Whereas women have very specific ideas about their Prince Charming, most men don't know what they want. In fact, some men say they want nothing from women. Others say they simply want a woman who is not bossy, bitchy, rude, snobby, or mean.

Eve represents the woman for everyman, whatever he desires. Eve is the love of his life, the lover, the mother, the wife, the live-in girlfriend, the slut, the nurturer, the forbidden fruit, the vamp, the goddess, the coquette, the gullible, the temptress, the friend, the breadwinner, or the necessary evil.[3]

While Eve's characteristics are as varied as the men who are fantasizing about her, common desired traits would make her a woman of unequivocal character. She has a beautiful face and a gorgeous body with feminine curves, smooth skin, thick long hair, alluring eyes, and luscious lips. Her breasts are perky and her warm soothing breath beckons him to want her. Her soft and sensual voice is music to his ears.

Eve's energy is magnetic and positive, making her irresistible at first glance. She doesn't need to do anything to attract him. The attraction is natural and easy. She is a no-maintenance kind of woman. She is a giver and a pleaser; he will become the apple of her eye. She makes him feel as if he is the only man in the world for her. She will follow him to the ends of the Earth and will bring him joy and ecstasy at every turn. She will nurture every need and listen with baited breath to every word. She makes him feel secure and strong.

NOTE: It is possible for a woman to be the Eve to her man. However, her emotional and physical needs must be met in order to give her the strength to fulfill that role.

---

[3] Lynn Elliott Letterman, a Los Gatos artist, created <u>The Story About Eve</u>, a graphic art piece that incorporates all of the adjectives used to describe Eve in the Bible.

A FANTASY DATE WITH EVE

Eve is wealthy, cultured, and intelligent. She is well versed in litera-ture and current events, talented, and confident within herself. She is men-tally and emotionally balanced; therefore, she is able to bring simple and innocent happiness and pleasure. Eve is sensual beyond belief.

She invites you into her home, opening the door wearing a long silky white gown that is open all the way down her back and exposing her cleavage in the front. Her thick, long hair glistens in the sunlight and is draped over her shoulder. After greeting you at the door, she walks away, beckoning you with her eyes to follow her. You admire her gorgeous toned back as you follow her into the room. She has exotic drinks pre-pared and brings one to you.

No words are necessary. You hear the soft sensual Celtic music in the background. She comes closer and stares into your eyes, licking the foamy drink off her lips, preparing her lips to touch yours. She gently leans in and tickles your lips with hers. Her breath reveals sweet nothings and smells of passion fruit. She gently touches your arm with her fingertips and brushes down until she holds your fingertips, pulling you toward the bedroom.

You walk together into a room fit for a queen. The bed is positioned in the center of the room away from the walls. It is beautifully draped from top to bottom in elegant silks and other rich fabrics. She takes your drink, putting it on a table next to hers. She goes behind you and touches your shoulders and back, gliding her hands under your shirt. She moves to your front and undoes each button with a kiss. She takes off your shirt and tosses it to the floor. She unbuckles the belt, undoes the button and unzips your pants, pulling them down and removing them. She then has you sit on the edge of the bed while she undresses you completely.

She kisses you passionately, holding the back of your neck tightly, pulling it towards her. You can feel the strength in her hands and arms. You are in under her control. You let go and want her to take you under her spell.

She pushes you back onto the bed and she has you watch while she undresses herself. She slowly slips out of her dress, revealing that she is wearing nothing underneath. Her beautiful curved body is exposed and her nipples are hard and pink. She gracefully comes over to you on the bed and leans over you; allowing you to kiss her breasts. She kisses your chin and then moves down to your navel. She kisses your navel and slowly licks down from there until she is pleasuring you with her lips, tongue and hot, steamy mouth. She gives you the ultimate pleasure.

Eve then changes her position and you make passionate love to one another. She pleases you for hours without wanting anything in return. She has mastered the art of pain and pleasure, knowing how to delay your ecstasy. At the end, she releases you from your pain and the fireworks fly. You have experienced pure ecstasy and pleasure.

Eve steps out of the bed, slips into a sheer robe, offers you a cold drink of water, and invites you into her multi-jetted, steam shower. She excuses herself to prepare an exotic, delicious, and decadent meal while you relax and enjoy the shower. When she invites you over to the dinner area, she sensually feeds you. The food and wine are incredible. After the meal, she invites you to spend the evening together where you enjoy more passionate sex.

The next morning, you wake to see her dressed beautifully and you marvel at the wonderful breakfast table waiting for you. She feeds you like a god. After breakfast, she has a surprise for you. She puts her hands over your eyes and guides you back into the bedroom. You gladly close your eyes and look forward to her surprise. You feel Eve's hands still over your eyes, but you feel more hands caressing you all over your body. The feeling is unreal and heavenly. Eve has you open your eyes and you notice two other beautiful women caressing you while Eve gently kisses your lips, reassuring you that your pleasure is her desire.

B. Reality

While it is fantastic to have dreams and fantasies, attempting to live out a fantasy is only temporary and you are fooling yourself in the long run. However, it is possible for a woman to find her true prince and for a man to find his true princess in reality. If you work on figuring out who you are and analyze who and what you truly need, you will find your prince or princess.

THE PRINCE AND PRINCESS

Whereas Eve is the every woman for man and Prince Charming is the ideal mate for every woman, the characteristics that men and women look for in a mate are as varied as the men and women that we find in the world. While some men and women in the dating world find what they are looking for easily, others find it impossible to attain their preconceived ideal. Some men look to find a woman who mirrors their mother. Some women look to find a man who mirrors their father. Still others hold out for the mate who is as elusive as the Holy Grail.

It appears that most men initially look for a good time and the physical package while most women from an early age look at the whole package. Men and women have different needs at different stages in their lives. Accordingly, the type of person needed to fulfill their needs at any particular stage is dependent upon where they are in life. As Jacqueline Kennedy Onassis stated: "The first time you marry for love, the second for money, and the third for companionship."[4]

When men are young, they focus on fun and physical fulfillment. It is all about having a good time. As they mature in their late twenties, they begin to look for stable, reliable women who will be good and nurturing mothers. The potential wife should be supportive, loving, respectful, caring, a competent mother, and the glue that holds the family together. The men spend their thirties working hard to support their families and have little time to do anything else. In the forties, some men tend to look back longingly at the young frivolous days and may find themselves looking for excitement. Some look for a lover to bring peace, excitement and discretion with no strings attached. Men view this as a time to have new beginnings; the kids are heading off to college and many marriages cannot survive the new empty nest. This is when men rethink relationships and realize that the Princess of yesterday no longer satisfies their need in the Princess of today. In looking for their Princess of today, they take a more relaxed view of dating, having no expectations of immediate or future commitments. They are more mature the second time around, understanding that it is all about being real, having fun, and finding a romantic partner that is in the same place in life as they are.

Throughout their lives, some men view a one-night stand as a necessity to fulfill their animal desires, nothing more. As the man enters his fifties and sixties, he looks back at his wife for companionship and a mature relationship. If the marriage did not survive the turbulent middle age years, he will look for a new companion with whom to grow old, travel, share enjoyable moments, and laugh. They want to live, laugh, and love.

Similarly, women look for different men as they grow and mature. The difference between women and men is that women are on a faster

---

[4] http://www.brainyquote.com/quotes/quotes/j/jackiekenn126998.html

speedway toward marriage than are men due to their reproductive clocks. Like men, young women want to have fun and frivolity. However, by the early twenties, women are looking for a mate that will be suitable as a husband and a father of their children. As with men, the thirties are the work years and all emphasis is on the family and rearing young children. Once the forties hit, women also find themselves needing excitement and wanting a sexual partner who fulfills their needs. This is also a time of new beginnings for women. The forties are a struggle; a woman's body is changing and she is now faced with the end of her fertility. Unlike men, though, there is not a relaxed view of dating and future commitments. Women, generally, like to be secure in their relationships and are more panicky in dating than men because they are feeling insecure at this stage in their lives. This is why many women in their forties begin to look better than they ever have before. They focus on health, beauty, and fitness. They need validation of their beauty and sexuality. They can become phenomenal lovers at this stage. In order to do so, however, they need a man who is interested in passion and sex. Like men, women want to grow old with a companion so that they may enjoy the golden years.

Prior to finding their Prince or Princess, most participants in the dating world learn about themselves and what they are looking for through their dating and relationship experiences with the various characters discussed in the following chapters. You must kiss many frogs and jump over many hurdles before you can appreciate the real deal. While no one is perfect, there are certain characteristics that most people think a Prince or Princess must possess. At the top of the list is respect. Next to that is trust. Communication is the key to trust. After that, the idealistic characteristics are in the eye of the beholder. While no one will possess all of them, the Prince and Princess should have some of the following qualities: honest, good communicator, sensitive, intelligent, sweetheart, good manners, sincere & genuine, giving, generous, spontaneous, uplifting, social, pleasant, good parent and role model, active and athletic, loving, humorous, great sense of humor. light-hearted, well-rounded, worldly, non-judgmental, nice, great smile, balanced, great lover, supportive, nurturing, self-secure and confident, financially secure, a good earner, from a good family, warm and caring, healthy, good cook, competent to run the household, and/or loving companion.

III. The "It" Factor

Hard to define, the "It" factor is just there, part of a character's energy and space. You are either born with "It" or you aren't. This is the quality that makes others want to be part of your life. "It" makes others want you to succeed. "It" makes things come easily for you, where others who do not have "It" must work much harder to accomplish the same things in life.

This quality allows people from oblivion to become stars. "It" has nothing to do with physical beauty. Look at Hollywood. There are many stars that are not classic beauties, but they are very successful on screen, in television shows, or on the red carpet. People want to know about them. "It" is charisma and magnetism.

This special charisma and magnetism allows certain politicians to achieve stardom and fame above their political positions. Take President Obama as an example. He had throngs of people showing for his grand events during the campaign, for his victory party, and for his inauguration. Both he and his First Lady, Michelle, have graced cover after cover of magazines and people are really interested in reading about them. In fact, it hasn't been since Jacqueline Kennedy that the First Lady and her fashion sense has garnered such respect and awe. The two have become a power couple – not all residents of the White House have achieved such fame.

Outsiders envy and aspire to emulate persons with the "It" factor. That is why the paparazzi are able to sell their pictures for great sums of money. People are interested in the "It." We want to know what they are wearing, what they are eating, what they are talking about, where they are going, with whom they are socializing, etc. People just want to know and, if they are able, they want to be just like them. This is why Target, Wal-mart, and Kmart create lines of clothing for the masses that copy what the stars have worn.

The stars start trends and fads because people want to do what they are doing. Diets are created by others watching how and what they eat. Material items like cars, purses and watches become the trend of the moment if a star has been seen driving or wearing one. Children's names become popular by who is popular in Hollywood at the moment. The media loves the "It" factor – "It" makes people excited and curious to watch the news shows to see what is happening. "It" is the hook.

From the outside looking in, a star has it all together. Things should come easily. However, not everyone with the "It" factor effectively utilizes "It" to his or her advantage. In order to spin the "It" into gold, one must know and understand that he or she has something very special and be confident in himself or herself. Some "It" people simply haven't internalized their gift and "It" may be squandered. That's okay. Once they mature and appreciate the gift, things will continue to fall in their laps.

In dating, some characters have "It" and some don't. The Players and the Divas have "It." People want to be around them. People like them. People want to date them even though a happy ending isn't likely. Others like the Responsible Adults, the Socially Awkward, and the Nurturers don't have "It" and they have to work hard to achieve happiness in the dating world. Others might be able to fake "It" temporarily. The Gold-diggers and the Home Wreckers have a charisma or appeal in some shape or form because they can get what they want in a calculated way. When not born with "It," becoming comfortable and confident in your own skin goes a long way toward attracting others in the dating world. Over and over, the people who interviewed with us told us that they were attracted to confidence. Over-confidence and cockiness was not attractive, however. The best way to gain the right amount of confidence is to like yourself and be who you are.

IV. The Game

What is the dating game? Everyone we've spoken with seems to know that there is a dating game being played, but no one knows the rules. They all have different rules and seem to be playing a different game. No wonder no one likes the dating scene. It is very confusing. What we have found is that no particular rules apply to every situation. Waiting to call two days after a date may be too long in some circumstances. An immediate text after the date might be just the ticket for some, but too clingy for others.

There are, of course, traditional protocols for dating. However, people don't seem to have manners anymore. The protocol has been stretched into a game that no one knows how to play. It might be better to treat dating like a business. When you go for a business interview, you don't wait two or three days to send a thank you note to let the company know you are interested. You hop right home and get it in the mail or email it. Why don't we treat our dates, whom we are interviewing for a potential personal partnership, with the same respect? Wouldn't you rather know that someone is excited to spend time with you? Why is it taboo to express your feelings?

We think too much. We overanalyze. We let our emotions clutter our minds and create drama where there really isn't any. People who are insecure create imaginary dating games. Fear of rejection breeds insecurity. On the first date, most people are on their "best behavior" and they are afraid to show their true selves. Some wait for eight dates before their true selves are revealed; others wait years before the reveal and then they end up breaking up because their partner is disappointed with the big lie. Do you really want to waste your time, effort and money pretending to be someone else? You have to come out sometime. Why not begin as yourself on the first meeting?

There should be no game. Why go out and waste money on an expensive dinner with two pretenders sitting across from each other saying fake things? If you are going to drop your bad habits for party manners on your first date, you better drop them for good. You are setting up expectations with your first impression. Instead of wasting your time and money on a dinner, you could get a cup of coffee or tea at a local coffee house and then go on a long walk. Talk and walk and get to know one another and then decide whether you want to go on a date when you feel comfortable being yourself.

The younger you are, the more real you are. The older you are, the more baggage you carry behind you and the more you think there is to hide. The older people get, the more they obsess. The older they are, the less able they are to let go of the past. The younger live for tomorrow; the older live for yesterday. Few seem to be living for today. That's what is wrong with dating. If everyone would be real and focus on the here and now, dating might actually be fun.

If you are real on day one, regardless of how old you are, then there is no need for a "reveal" later on. If you don't trust yourself and you really don't like who you are, then you have only one alternative to faking it. Focus on loving yourself first. Work on yourself before you go out there to find a partner. The more confident you are and the happier you are with yourself, the less you will have to search for that Prince or Princess. He or she will find you. The more you go with the flow, the easier it is.

Girls, let's use your dress size as an analogy. Let's say you are a size 10, but you really want to be a size 6. If you are a 10 today, then buy a 10 today – don't shop for a size 6 and try to squeeze into it. You cannot force it, the zipper will pop, and you will be very uncomfortable wearing it. When you become a size 6, then shop for a 6. Figure out your current size and be happy with it and buy what fits you today. Alternatively, if you are not happy and want to be a 6, don't buy a dress today. Instead, work on yourself, exercise, and eat less. When you get down to a legitimate 6, then buy your size 6.

If you want to play a game, create your own game and make sure the players know what they are playing. If you are playing "Monopoly," make sure your dates are not playing "Sorry." If you want to create a game, cre-ate a game for the particular character in mind. If you are dating an egotis-tical god-like character, like a Player, tailor a game suiting his characteris-tics. Likewise, if you are looking to have a good time with a Diva, create a game suiting her unique qualities. But understand that the game should only be played with the temporary relationship in mind. Games end with a winner and a loser. Such games may help you get to know yourself so that you may ultimately be the true you.

V. The Takers

Some people are givers and some are takers. Others fall somewhere in between. Takers come in all different shapes and sizes. Some take emotionally; others take mentally; others are financial takers; some are spiritual takers; and still others are material and physical takers. The takers tend to be selfish and self-absorbed. They have little consideration for others. They are the game-players in the dating arena. They play their own game with their own rules. Dating is about a happy ending for them; it is not about the journey. They play to win.

A. The Players: Take your self-respect.

The most ubiquitous character in the dating scene is the Player. Most everyone knows or has encountered a Player at one time or another. The term generally includes all of the self-serving, sex-seeking men out there.[5] We have found that the Player falls into one of four categories: The Diplomat, The Magnet, the Forever Bachelor, or the Sportsman. The Diplomat and the Magnet are typically married, but continue to play the field. The Forever Bachelor rarely marries. The Sportsman may marry, but the marriage won't last. The Diplomat has "It" and more; the Magnet has status and wealth; the Forever Bachelor has "It" only, and the Sportsman has skills in bed and is really a one trick pony.

The Players all have one goal in mind. They want to get laid and be the object of the woman's desire, leaving her wanting more – even when they have no desire to give the woman any more. In their minds, sex is all about the guy. The woman is there to please the man. Unless there is a connection, this character cannot wait to get away from the woman after he has cum; in fact, he may be planning his exit before the deed is done. Knowing this fact, if a woman gets involved with any of the Players, she must realize the short-lived relationship is what it is and nothing more.

If the woman unwittingly allows herself to get emotionally involved with a Player and it doesn't work out, she should not kick herself. She must go easy on herself and allow an ample amount of time to go through the stages of letting go. She will first be confused, angry, and disillusioned. After those stages, she will understand and accept what has happened. If the woman is lucky enough to go through this experience, it can be viewed as a right of passage in the world of dating and relationships. The experience will add tremendous value and insight to her life. The process of letting go may take up to a year; sometimes more, sometimes less. The woman should embrace this experience and understand that many others go through the same experience, regardless of the length of the relationship. Whether it was a one-night stand or a five-year relationship, you need time to feel and to heal.

---

[5] The female version of the Player is the Diva and she will be discussed at the end of the section on The Takers.

To wrap things up, find a great friend to talk to who will truly listen and not judge you. If you can't find a good friend, keep a journal of your thoughts and read, read and read.

1. THE DIPLOMAT

We call the ultimate Player "The Diplomat." He has a high sex drive and is an adrenaline junky. Like Bill Clinton, The Diplomat possesses charisma, power, status, etiquette, politics and the keen sense of relationship. He is articulate and a charismatic communicator, leaving people eating from the palm of his hand. He has prestige, magnetism, and class. He loves women. This character has an in-born sense of entitlement that is nurtured by his mother from birth. He can and will have his cake and eat it, too.

He has a loyal and strong support network of people who genuinely like him. That network has been created from all sorts of prior and present relationships, both business and personal. He has a high sense of social grace and etiquette that leaves others feeling good about themselves. He adds value to people's lives in any relationship. Even his prior conquests worship and adore him forever. They will come to his rescue at a time of need. He is worth having even for a minute and he will end things on a positive note. While in his company, you feel as if the world has been handed to you for that one moment in life. You are lifted to a higher plane for a lifetime after spending one moment with this character. Other Players admire the Diplomat. He is not threatening to others, but rather, he is viewed as a role model.

INTERVIEW OF A DIPLOMAT

1. *Age: 40's*
2. *Gender: Male*
3. *Education Level:* Graduate Degree
4. *Profession:* Owns a successful law firm
5. *Personal Status:* Married. I have been married for many years and, during that time, I have had many memorable encounters with beautiful women.
6. *Interests/hobbies:* I enjoy listening to and playing jazz music, golfing, racing cars, occasional family boating trips, politics, and making money. I love the water and boating.

7. *What initially attracts you to the opposite sex?* Being attractive is the key. If they are more mysterious, you want to learn more about them. I am looking for spontaneity. The same old, same old can get boring; you want to do fun things with them that you cannot do with your spouse. I love to try new things.

8. *What do you find appealing in a woman?* It takes two to Tango. I am drawn to women who are fun and exciting. The main attraction is when you immediately know that she wants you.

9. *What do you find to be a turn-off in a woman?* I don't enjoy a woman who is boring, who has no sense of humor, and who doesn't understand witty intellectual remarks. The biggest turn-off is the woman who cannot go with the flow. I need to be able to call the shots so that our meetings fit into my life.

10. *Where do you meet women?* Yacht club, work, traveling, friends' parties, sporting events, horse races, tennis clubs, country clubs, etc...

11. *When you are out with your friends and you see someone who catches your eye, what do you do?* I approach them with a witty line.

12. *Have you ever had trouble moving on from a past relationship?* No. [Laughs.]

13. *Where do you take women when you go out with them?* I take them to my boat and show them the time of their lives. If I am sure that the beach house is available, we will go there for a little romance.

14. *What are you looking for in a relationship?* They must always be entertaining, new and fresh. I want to be excited to talk to the person and I want to feel that I really want to be with that person. No matter how long you have been with them, you should always feel excited to be with them. I want to be treated sensually by my woman. The man should treat the woman with respect.

15. *Would you have a sexual encounter with a married woman?* Of course. I don't see the down side. It spices up my life and makes me a better man.

16. *What type of clothing do you prefer your women to wear when you go out with them?* I love classy clothing that is easy to remove or get under; designer clothing seems to fit women better. I don't like them to be too overboard in their dress or labels.

17. *What is your preferred body type and shape for a woman?* I like tan, slender, tall women with long legs, smooth skin, a good complexion, a pretty face, sexy eyes, and silky hair.

21

18. *How do you feel about perfumes and colognes?* I like fragrance. It gives me something to recognize her by.
19. *How important is the first kiss?* Very important. I leave a good impression with a passionate first kiss. It is an art and I believe that I have mastered it.
20. *Would you have sex with a woman if she were drunk?* Yes. A little alcohol takes the edge off and things usually are much smoother.
21. *Do you wear boxers or briefs?* White briefs.
22. *How do you make sure a new sexual partner is free of STD's?* I have to trust her.
23. *Where would you be willing to have sex with a woman if you were hot and horny?* In my office or somewhere private and unexpected.
24. *Where is your favorite place to have sex if you had a choice?* In my bed or on the yacht.
25. *Do you use protection and, if so, who provides it? If you don't use protection, how do you stay safe or is it an issue?* I try to have it available most of the time. If not, I will not penetrate. There are many ways to have fun with a woman.
26. *What do you think of one-night stands?* In my opinion, most men have them, if they are lucky. Most women have them because they can.
27. *How do you break off a one-night stand or short relationship without being hurtful?* I have had problems with breaking off the relationship. I try to give the woman her time to talk to me after our short time together so that she may understand why we cannot continue the sexual relationship. It is important for women to be validated and to know that they are not being used, ignored or disregarded. I treat the short relationships as a foundation for future respectful encounters.
28. *How do you characterize yourself?*

     Positive attributes: Positive thinker, optimistic, happy, respectful, love women, honest, intelligent, driven, compassionate, entitled, a great communicator.

     Negative attributes: I love women too much and want to have them all!
29. *How do you think others see you?* The same way I see myself.
30. *What is your personal philosophy on monogamy and monogamous relationships?* It is a good thing at the moment.
31. *Do you believe there is a game people play when dating?* Yes. It is the game of hard to catch. That is attractive. A man loves to pursue a woman. The woman loves to be pursed. But once the woman is cap-

tured, the game is over and it's on to the next. Even unattractive women can play this game and get the men interested.

Below the Belt:

1. *Is sex an important factor in deciding whether you will continue to date someone?* I would say yes. It is very important.
2. *Do you enjoy it when your date wears lingerie?* I like a woman who takes care of herself from top to bottom, under and over. It gives me pleasure to take care of her in the same regard.
3. *Have you ever experienced ménage à trois?* Yes, I have. I believe it is God's way of saying that you have been very good, "Enjoy yourself; you deserve it." I would stay with the combination of two females and myself.
4. *What is sexy to you in a woman?* Being a woman and wanting to be treated and taken care of like a goddess. Her eyes and lips.
5. *Does the size of her breasts matter?* Bigger is better.
6. *How much make up is too much?* I like women to be more natural, but yet, made up.
7. *Long hair or short hair?* Long, any color.
8. *Do you prefer a particular pubic hair design?* Baby bald is scary to me, I feel like a pedophile. Partial Brazilians are a real turn on. You know, it really doesn't matter when you get right down to it!
9. *How many sexual partners have you had in your life?* Too many to share with you.

HOW TO MASTER BREAKING UP: LET IT BE THE GIRL'S IDEA.

They were young and in college. They met in the dorms and dated for six months. They spent their days and nights together, partying and having fun. She loved him and he was into her. Wherever they went, he had throngs of girls hanging all over him; he was a girls' man. She didn't like it, but loved being the one who had him at night. At the end of six months, he was feeling antsy and needed his space. He was feeling smothered by her. He began to call less often and had other things to do during the day. He had to study at night. He was paying less and less attention to her, but, when they were together, his attitude toward her did not change. He was the same loving, charismatic guy that he had always been. He paid less attention and apologized more for not paying more attention to her.

She became frustrated and missed him. She demanded more of his time. He made excuses, but always responded to her calls; he never ignored her. She asked him to meet for a talk. They met and she told him that, if he couldn't meet her needs, they would have to call it off and go their separate ways. He told her, "I understand and I want to do what is right for you." She was sorry that he didn't argue about it, but she couldn't say anything because it was she who broke it off. He then surprised her by kissing her on the cheek and saying, "I'd love to still spend some quality, friendly time with you." She was so thrilled and she thought that was a fantastic idea. She felt respected and loved. They remained great friends and he moved on to another girl from the pack.

TOUCHED BY THE DIPLOMAT

I have been the CEO of many successful start-ups. I achieved success at a young age. At 44 years of age, I have in my power and at my disposal women of all sorts, politicians, other CEO's, and other high-powered individuals. Therefore, I have seen it all and am not easily impressed. However, the following story left an impression upon me.

After the Clinton presidency, I was attending a fundraiser for his wife. I was in the queue for a picture with Bill Clinton. Rather than taking an opportunity to get a picture with the former president, cocky as I am, I chose to turn my back to the photographers, look Clinton in the eye, and invite him to join my start-up's board of directors. Rather than snubbing me, Bill Clinton suggested that we go ahead and have a picture taken and that we could talk about it at another time. I thought I was being brushed off at that point, but took the picture and moved to the next portion of the event.

Near the end of the fundraiser, while I was standing and socializing with others, Bill Clinton made an effort to find me. Bill approached me, addressed me by my first name, and put his arm around my shoulders. He smiled warmly and leaned in so that I could hear him. Looking into my eyes, he told me that his focus was on Hillary's campaign at this time, but that he would love to discuss the opportunity at a later time. Bill thanked me for the opportunity. I was blown away and felt like I was on top of the world. I felt as if I had been touched by one of the greatest masters of relationships. I never had that suit jacket dry-cleaned after that event; in fact, it is framed on the wall of my closet to remind me that the master graced me with his presence.

2. THE MAGNET

The Magnet is the most dangerous of all the Players. He achieves his status as a Player through wealth and animal magnetism. He also has a high sex drive. He has mastered the swagger. Unlike the Diplomat, the Magnet thinks only of himself and shows a genuine disregard for others. The Magnet ultimately turns people off and burns bridges behind him. Unlike the Diplomat, the Magnet is nothing without his wealth. He has no sense of entitlement and is weak and insecure. In fact, the Magnet lives in constant fear of losing his status and wealth. Subconsciously, he does not believe he is entitled to his success. He ends up sabotaging his life through careless and risky business and personal behavior.

He is highly self-conscious about his appearance, attention seeking, pretentious, and loves to show off his possessions. He seeks attention and drama in his life, but like a politician, he does not want to be exposed. In the end, any attention is good attention for him; this is why he keeps the women in his life on a string, pouring on flirtation and charm to keep them interested, and then ignoring them once he has captured their attention. He is a heavy texter, likes to talk on the phone, and is witty and quick with his responses. In spite of the above, he is not a good communicator. Unlike the Diplomat, he is not discreet about his indiscretions. Often emulating his father, the Magnet has learned this behavior.

The Magnet lacks social intelligence and is so self-absorbed that he is either unaware or does not care about the social repercussions of his behavior. When dealing with women, the Magnet uses and abuses them for temporary boosts to his ego. Contrary to the Diplomat, the Magnet is not a lover of women. Where an encounter with the Diplomat is a net-gain game, leaving women feeling empowered and richer for knowing him, an encounter with the Magnet is a net-loss game, leaving them feeling confused, used, abused, and angry. He is often surprised by the negative reaction resulting from his inter-personal interactions.

He intends no harm; he believes he provides those around him with temporary pleasure and enjoyment by gracing them with his company for a very short and exciting moment in time. The problem with the Magnet is that he does not communicate his intentions up front. A woman falls under his spell and allows him to rapture her, often expecting a continued romance. He typically has no intention of having a long-term relationship; in fact, most are one-time deals. He is unfaithful by nature and very fickle.

He likes everything on his terms and he likes to be worshipped by many. Where he sees himself as socially appropriate and polite, the reality is otherwise.

Some have given the Magnet a nickname of "Slut Machine" because he sleeps around, but when one of his lays ends up causing trouble for him, he pays her off to be quiet. Pull the lever and it pays off big time. He can get away with his promiscuity because he has purchased a strong support group through business dealings. However, while these people are dependent upon him, they are not loyal to him and, at a first chance, they will turn on him because they envy his toys and his ability to break the rules. He prides himself on being incorrigible and un-trainable. He can become delusional, thinking that he is untouchable. His socially unacceptable behavior eventually catches up to him. And lastly, to his wife or significant other, he can be emotionally abusive by flaunting his lays in front of her.

DANGEROUS MAGNETIC FIELD BETWEEN A MAGNET AND A DIVA

Here is an example of the no-win, no holds barred competitive game played between a Diva and a Magnet. Both parties are in need of control (and help). There are no winners in this game. The story of this Diva, who was accustomed to being treated like a queen, began when she was accidentally caught in the net of a Magnet who treated her like all of his other inconsequential conquests. She didn't like his game and decided to play her own game of anticipation with him. She messed around with him to the point where he feared her and what she would do next. Here is her story:

I had known this person for years, working together in the same company in San Francisco, California. We were both happily married, but we were both known to be open to outsourcing. There was never anything more than a friendship between us and I was never physically attracted to this man.

After the end of a very tough and exhausting fiscal year, I went to a wine bar in the City with some girlfriends. I had a few drinks with appetizers. We were a bit tipsy and wild that evening. All of my girlfriends were flirting with my long-time friend. He happened to come over to where I was sitting and we shared a laugh, another glass of wine, and talked about our families. Although I had no intention of any kind of interlude with this man, I spent the rest of the evening talking with him.

We were having a wonderful conversation when our attention was called to another woman sitting at the bar. She was sloppy drunk. She said something that I could not hear. I asked him what she said and he told me, "She said, 'I hope she goes for you.'" I didn't think anything of it and before I new it, "Hummm," was coming out of my mouth. It was out of character and I don't know what came over me. One thing led to another and he took me to a nice hotel near the Financial District. We had a drunken sexual interlude that was not memorable.

What I remember is that, after we arrived at the hotel, he gave me the key to the hotel room and told me to go up and make myself comfortable. He was obviously excited about the potential encounter; he seemed a bit flustered. I asked him, "What room number?" He said, "Oh, yes, of course." He then told me the room number and I went up to the room and made myself at home. I sat on the couch and kept waking up with drool on my chin. The next thing I remember is hearing the door open and seeing him walking through the door. In a flash, his face was in my face and he was telling me how sexy I looked. He was smothering me with passionate kisses that didn't seem to end. I couldn't breathe.

We sat on the edge of the bed. He started to undress and I reached over and grabbed his penis over the top of his pants, feeling to make sure it was worthy. I then unzipped his pants, pulled it out, and put it in my mouth. He really did have a beautiful penis; in fact, I had never seen one like it before and I have never seen one like it since. He was still unbuttoning his shirt and I believe I shocked him with my move. That wasn't the end of my shocking moves.

I continuously barked orders at him. I told him to take my clothes off, which he did. Then, I noticed that I was intensely thirsty and asked him to go get me some water. Cottonmouth was setting in. He got me the water and then we got into bed. He was being coy with me and wouldn't tell me what he wanted me to do. So, I asked him what he liked, making sure that he knew it was going to be our only night together. He told me that his favorite thing was a hand job. I stuck out my palm and told him to spit. He spat once like a girl. I told him to spit again. The second time, I got some real spit. I moved my hand down to his penis and gave him a hand job, rubbing his spit all over. It was mechanical and robotic. We were conversing about his sexual likes and dislikes while I rubbed him.

I was bored very quickly and clouded by the alcohol. I told him to go take a shower after the hand job, which he did. I did not join him; I stayed on the bed and took a quick nap. When he came back, I gave him a blowjob and sat on him. He mentioned that I liked to be in control. I agreed. But then I said, "No one is holding you back from making suggestions." At that time, I was really getting bored. There was no passion; there was no excitement; there was nothing. So, I told him to finish it off and cum. He did. I got up and put my clothes on. I said, "Thank you," and left. He offered to take me home, but I took a cab. As I mentioned, it really was not memorable.

The next morning, I thought about what I had done and had a great deal of remorse. I could not believe that I had jeopardized this long-term friendship with a silly night of meaningless sex. That day, I happened to see him again. I wanted to approach him and talk about what had happened. I thought we should forget that it ever happened. To my amazement, I got the cold shoulder. He completely ignored and disregarded me when he saw me. I gave him the benefit of the doubt, hoping that he was thinking along the same lines that I was thinking. I let this awkward moment go, thinking that he might be embarrassed.

The next day I ran into him again at the office. I approached him and he again ignored me. This time I persisted and I approached him, asking him, " Why are you ignoring me? Are you bipolar or schizophrenic?" He replied, "No (with a smile); we did it once, it was fun, and we'll do it again." I did not know what to say to that and said, "Hum. Great. Okay. Then we are fine." I left feeling really shitty about putting myself in that position. I was not used to being treated that way and I did not like it.

A week later, I saw him around the water cooler and was happy that things had gone back to normal. He said, "Hello," to everyone around me, but ignored me again. This time, I felt like he was disrespecting me in front of others in my place of work. I wondered who he thought he was. I went over to him and whispered in his ear: "Are you hiding cause I can see you?" He wrinkled up his face and stuttered, "No, no," turning his back. I leapt over to his other ear and playfully said, "I am still here." He said clearly annoyed, "I know." I squeezed and patted his shoulder and left feeling bewildered. For me, the war began at that point. It was now a battle for the upper hand.

Two months went by without contact other than a casual nod in the hallway. I simply was not okay with being treated like a bimbo. I saw this as a mutual opportunity for the two of us and we really needed to return to our friendship as if nothing had happened. It was getting very uncomfortable for me at work. His image was shattered in my mind and I found myself left with two choices. I could leave it alone or I could mess with him for a while and have fun doing it. I chose the latter.

During the next two months, I had an opportunity to observe him and I realized this was his pattern with women. I felt even more degraded, realizing that I was part of a group with which I would rather not be associated. The women by in large were all physically fit, but were socially inept. Most had poor self-esteems and continued to lurk around him, making it clear that they were available on his demand and whim. He would never demand a second rendezvous with any of them. He treated them like shit and they all stuck to him like mud.

Understanding that I could only engage him in my game by allowing him to think he was playing mind games with me, I dumbed myself down. Through my gamesmanship, I learned more about him. I learned that his ego was always getting in the way of his success. He was highly insecure. He portrayed an image that he was not capable of being. He wanted to be thought of as a James Bond type, but he lacked the class and social intelligence to continually engage in sexual encounters without leaving a trail of angry women behind. He typically went after easy bimbos that he could discard easily. I was the exception to the rule.

My game was to confuse and frustrate him by peaking his interest and crushing his ego. I had time, energy, and money to focus on my new play toy. It was a game of power. Knowing that he liked naïve and unintelligent women, I played the role. I suggested that he could teach me a thing or two and played up to his ego. I suggested that he could mentor me. He said, "Don't take this the wrong way, but you are full of shit." I knew he was interested in my game. The next day, I sent a text at 10:00 a.m.: "Do you want to play?" At 10:15 a.m., he replied, "What do you have in mind?" We were both bored at separate board meetings. I texted, "Poker, of course." He replied, "What kind?" I texted, "The good kind." He replied, "Oh... I figured." I texted, "How about next Thursday." He texted back, "I'll see." I responded, "We need a few people to play." He again texted, "What do you have in mind?" I replied, "Bring a friend." He asked, "Male or female?" I said, "Male, of course." He wrote, "Oh." The conversation died at that point. I was testing him to see how deep his ego was. He believed that he was the king and was turned off by the potential of competing with another man.

I ran into him the next day and said, "So Thursday?" He said, "I don't know" in a nonchalant manner. I said, "Are you going to bring a friend?" He said, "Maybe, maybe not." He left. He was completely turned off. I was coming on too strong and realized that I had to act like a bimbo to bring him back into the game again. I was enjoying playing with him at this point.

Thursday morning arrived and I texted him with a "?." He responded back, "I am sorry. Busy with family. Can't meet Thursday." I let it go for the time being. Some time passed and I texted him with another "?." He responded, "What do you need?" I texted, "I don't particularly need anything. I like to go with the flow." He replied, "Excellent answer. I like to go with the flow." I texted, "How about we meet this Thursday night?" He wrote, "I'll let you know." I saw him the next day and I asked him: "Are we on for Thursday night?" He said, "I am thinking about it. Most probably." It seemed like he enjoyed leading me on. I next replied, "Don't forget to bring your friend." His mouth dropped open and he stood there in disbelief. My game was to batter his ego as many times as I could at this point. It seemed as if I was succeeding. My intention was not to meet with him outside of the office again. In fact, the game was verging on providing me with a mental orgasm.

The next day I texted another "?." He texted back saying, "Sorry. No can do. Busy with family." I expected that and texted back, "Oh well."

I saw him a while later and noticed that he was wearing an ugly gray colored tie. That was the perfect opportunity to penetrate his ego by commenting on how unattractive he looked. I told him, "Gray is not your color. Who buys your clothes?" Snippily, he said, "I do. Can you do better?" I laughed and said, "Maybe."

A couple of days later, I sent him a shirt and tie anonymously. To my surprise, he wore it and strutted like a peacock in front of me. I commented to him, "Nice shirt and tie." He responded, " I know." He was receptive to my game. So, I continued sending anonymous gifts and waiting to see his reactions. My gifts were very clever and each had hidden meaning. The gifts started simple and were designed to feed his ego. They were designed to remind him of our friendship and make him comfortable around me again. The gifts were humorous and inexpensive. After the receipt of each gift, I made sure to see him and get his reaction. I would talk with him about the gifts and have him walk me through his experience with each gift.

Because of his insecurities, he was not able to take negative comments of any kind. I would make little comments and professional suggestions that would help him to look better and more refined. For instance, I suggested that he change his tailor and wear more fitted designer suits. He would get his feathers ruffled and respond by saying, "What, do you think I need to look better?" This particular man was very conscious of his looks, money and demeanor. While he seemed to reject my comments at the time, he would show up the next day and week wearing new fitted suits and shirts. He would strut in front of me in his new outfit and I would raise my eyebrow. He appeared to take my comments to heart.

He seemed to be enjoying the game as no other woman was playing the game like this. I happened to see him at happy hour at the wine bar and indicated to him that if he wanted me to continue playing, he had to give a little. He needed to initiate more to show that he was interested. I said, "You are making this game very difficult to play, and what you need is a slap on the face and smack against the wall." He agreed, saying, "You like it that way." I laughed. He said, "Let's meet tomorrow," and winked. I said, "Don't disappoint me again. Knowing your character, that is what you do, you disappoint people." He said in a firm voice, "No – tomorrow." I had nothing to worry about because I knew for a fact that there would be no meeting tomorrow. I said as I turned on my heels to walk away, "I won't hold my breath."

I knew that he did not like demands put upon him and he liked to be in charge. So, to get a reaction, I pushed him. If I had really wanted to meet with him, I would have waited for him to text me with the details. However, I took it upon myself to push him to commit to a time and place. The next morning I texted a "?." He immediately responded with a text: "Flirtations can stop. I cannot deliver what you want." I could predict his behavior by now. He was indecisive and I knew that his character would say and do things differently when under the influence of alcohol. I felt like I was beginning to understand him very well.

The next day, I cornered him in the conference room. I told him: "You are my captured audience. Are we cool." He exasperatedly said, "YESSSSSSSSSSS." I told him, "I love to play and I hope you don't take me too seriously." He put his head down and said, "Oh yah, we're cool, we're cool?" I enjoyed watching the emotional oscillation and knew that he was a little concerned about me and began to feel frustrated with me. I asked him whether he hated me and he responded, "It is all in your head."

Knowing that I had pushed him a little too far, I ignored him for a while. The more I ignored him, the more he paid attention to me. He tried to catch my attention by making silly hand gestures and goofy remarks or flirting with other women in front of me. The more he acted goofy, the more bored I became with him. I saw him as an old toy that no longer interested me. However, I wasn't done messing with him yet.

I still had some work to do. He was wearing a gorgeous red tie and I mentioned to him that red was a good color on him. He smiled and started showing up in my space again wearing red. When he thought the game was over, he would egg me on to start it again. He seemed to enjoy thinking that he was controlling my emotions and wanted to be in my thoughts. People in his circle noticed that he was friendly with me at this point, which peaked their interest. They saw how confident I was around him and that I wasn't cowering in the corner whispering about him like the rest of them. They thought that I had an inside track to him and held the key to dealing with him. I provided a listening ear and it validated me in knowing that I had correctly assessed his character.

He began to worry when he thought that we were all sharing notes about him. The city of San Francisco, although large, is a small community. Our office is even smaller. The circle around me grew bigger and bigger and both men and women seemed to seek me out, trying to get at him through me. He had left a wake of angry bitter people behind him the size of a title wave. I was surprised, wondering why all of these people were coming to me for friendship and advice. But, I was shocked to hear some of their professional and personal stories about him. However, I had no intention of befriending any of them or sharing any information with them. In fact, I was feeling a little nervous about how messy his life seemed to be getting and wanted nothing to do with him anymore. The game was no longer fun for me.

I decided to end it when he texted me, begging for mercy. He texted: "I've tried to be polite and even play along with this. But I've heard from at least five people that you are talking about me to others. This threatens my family and my career. I sincerely hope that you do not participate in conversations about me. Thank you for understanding." He appeared so weak and pathetic at this point; he was not the strong and entitled game player that he portrayed himself to be. He was mistrusting and paranoid.

Although I had intended to make him sweat a little, I would never have jeopardized my career or position by exposing him. The funny thing is that all he needed to do from the beginning was not to be an asshole or jerk and take a few minutes to talk to me about where we stood. Respect is very important in these matters. While he had done all the damage possible to his own reputation and name by his own deeds, he was seeking someone else to blame for the inevitable fallout that was on its way. He was afraid. He was feeling vulnerable and exposed. His only alternative was to move to a new pool of women where his ways were not known. He requested to move to the office on the other coast. Game over. I was happy to close this chapter of my life!

THE MAGNET FLAKES ON A PSYCHO DRAMA

I was so excited that, after months of flirting, he finally initiated a romantic meeting between us. I knew he was married, but I didn't care. The chemistry between us was incredibly electric. We planned a getaway in Napa for a weekend when his wife was scheduled to be out of town.

In preparation for our romantic rendezvous, I bought new outfits, lingerie and luggage. I was beside myself with excitement. I prepared myself from head to toe. I got a manicure and a pedicure, I had my hair colored and cut, I had my teeth bleached, and, lastly, I shaved "the girls." I was ready for a good time with the ultimate catch.

He was to pick me up from my house at 7:00 p.m. I had food and very expensive wine opened and ready to go. I knew he was used to the finer things in life and that is why I didn't spare any expense in preparation for our meeting. I wanted to be worthy of him.

It was 6:30 p.m. and my heart was pounding from the anticipation of spending alone time with him. I had fantasized about this very evening over the last month.

It was 6:59 p.m. and I stood by the door, waiting for the doorbell to ring. From there, I watched out of the front window for his beautiful expensive automobile to pull into my driveway. The clock chimed 7:00 o'clock and no car and no doorbell. I started thinking the usual. I wondered whether he was lost because my place was on a windy hillside road. I wondered whether he had a flat tire or had been stopped by the police for speeding to my place. I poured myself a glass of wine and didn't eat any of the cheese for the fear of having cheese breath. I looked at the clock and it was 7:30 p.m. My cell phone rang.

I picked up my phone and saw his number on the display. My heart sank. He said, "Sorry, I just can't, thanks for understanding." I was so disappointed and the tears were running down my cheeks. I didn't want him to hear it in my voice, so I quickly said, "Sure, no problem, I'll see you next week." He said, "Great, see you then." I couldn't believe it; I shaved, racked up my credit card, and waited like a fool for the asshole. I drank the whole bottle of wine and ate the cheese.

I saw him the following week and asked him what happened. He told me that I was different and not like the others. He had too much respect for me, considering what I had gone through in my life, with health and family issues. He told me that he couldn't commit to me and he knew that is what I wanted. I told him that if he had that much respect for me, he would have told me sooner before I spent a ton of money on him.

He asked what he could do to make it up to me? I shrugged and walked away. I was still furious with him. The next day, I received a package full of cash with a note saying, "Sorry. This should cover your expenses."

INTERVIEW WITH A MAGNET

1. *Education Level:* College
2. *Age:* 30's
3. *Profession:* Executive
4. *Personal Status:* Married
5. *Interests/hobbies:* Beach volleyball, working out, fast cars and fast women, spectator sporting events, and hanging out with friends.
6. *What initially attracts you to the opposite sex?* Looks. Love blondes, they are outgoing. Brunettes can be beautiful, too. Blondes like to have fun and are ready to go.
7. *What do you find appealing in a woman?* Someone who I can talk to and I don't get bored with, someone who can stay on the same level with me. Someone who keeps my adrenaline flowing and, when I'm with her, I won't be looking forward to the end of our encounter.
8. *What do you find to be a turn-off in a woman?* Someone who is stupid and dumb and doesn't care about what is going on in the world. Past being pretty, I like a woman who I can stand being with on a short-term basis. The clingers make me feel good, but they make me nervous and I ultimately have to be mean to them – it is sort of like clipping the nails of an animal that are digging into the cliff for dear life. It is horrible and wonderful at the same time.
9. *Where do you meet women?* Wherever I go.
10. *Where do you hang out?* Sports bars, sporting events, my athletic club, my country club, work, friends' houses.
11. *Have you ever had trouble moving on from a past relationship?* No, never.

12. *Where do you go/what do you do with a woman?* I take a woman to a nice place that is out of the way or we go to her place. I pay for everything.

13. *If you were a candy, what would you be?* Mr. Good Bar because I'm that good.

14. *What frustrates you with relationships?* I get frustrated with the ones who become obsessed with me and can't accept a one-time relationship for what it is.

15. *What are you looking for from a woman?* Someone with whom I can have fun. Someone with whom I can be myself and be comfortable. It's cool to hang out with a new woman once in a while.

16. *Would you go out with a married woman?* Yes, it is a great game. I love that game. I get off on married women. If your marriage gets to a certain point and the excitement is gone, adding a little excitement from the outside might actually help your marriage. If you need a one-night stand or quick pick-me-up to keep it going, then it should be okay to have it.

17. *Do you smoke?* I love a good cigar.

18. *What is your preferred body type and shape for a woman?* Not too skinny. Love curves. Not on the heavier side, though. Skinny with curves is perfect.

19. *How do you feel about perfumes and colognes?* I like perfume on the woman. Smell is very individual and unique.

20. *How important is the first kiss?* Very important, another first impression.

21. *Will you have sex the first time you meet a woman?* Yes. Absolutely. You have to be in the mood. I am a bit kinky.

22. *Would you have sex with a woman if she were drunk?* Yes. By that point, I have usually been drinking as well.

23. *Do you wear boxers or briefs?* Boxers.

24. *How do you make sure a new sexual partner is free of STD's?* I definitely care. In the heat of the moment, I trust, but sometimes don't wear a condom. People are having a lot of sex. Now, I will never do a virgin, but when I was younger it was a way to make sure they were safe. However, doing a virgin was too much work, a lot of stop, go, stop, go, stop. It is not a nice thing. They always became too clingy and dependent.

25. *Where would you be willing to have sex if you were hot and horny?* Anywhere. On the front of a speedboat. In the car. In the parking lot. Love the shower.

26. *Where is your favorite place to have sex if you had a choice?* The bed is my favorite as you can do the most things. I love variation.

27. *Do you use protection and, if so, who provides it?* No, I try to pull out unless I know the woman is on birth control.

28. *What age range do you date?* No preference -- over 25 to 49.

29. *What do you think of one-night stands?* A lot of people do it. Humans are sexual beings and need to have many partners. I know I do.

30. *How do you break off a one-night stand or short relationship without being hurtful?* I am not great at that. I am kind of terrible. I ignore them. I figure they'll get the message once they don't hear back from me. I tell them that I love them as a person and say, "Honey, it's not you, it's me." I will say anything to get rid of them after the fun is over.

31. *What was your parents' status when you were growing up?* Married. My father had his share of women on the side.

32. *How do you characterize yourself?*

> **Positive attributes:** Confident, good-looking, happy, I enjoy everything I do. I love life. I try not to be very arrogant. I want people to judge me on me and not what I have. I provide a positive experience to women and those around me.
>
> **Negative attributes:** I can be kind of a dick. I can ignore people and not call back. I like to mess around with them. It's fun.

33. *How do you think others see you?* Hopefully, the same way I see myself. Someone who has a lot to offer and is just out for a good time.

34. *Please include a detailed description of your ideal encounter with a woman.* I see her at the bar. All the guys are hovering around her. I break into the crowd, introduce myself, and stand right next to her. Knowing that the guys are watching me, I know she is impressed. We engage in small talk and I whisper sweet nothings into her left ear. The left ear turns women on sexually. I take her to a hotel room and we have two hot hours of passionate, exciting sex. She thanks me and leaves. I never see her again.

35. *Do you believe in "love at first sight"?* Yes, in a way. I definitely believe in love at first attraction; I can tell the woman is interested by the way she twists her hair and points her toe towards me. If a woman

touches her hair and crosses her leg with her toe pointing towards the guy, she is interested and ready to roll.

36. *What is your personal philosophy on monogamy and monogamous relationships?* Hmmm. I want my wife to be true to me.

37. *Do you believe there is a game people play when dating? If so, describe the game.* Yes. Cat and mouse. The woman wants to be pursued. Both want to have the upper hand and be in control. You want to keep the interest, but not struggle for the upper hand. It's a give and take. It is the stronger personality that controls and dictates. The issue becomes who is going to concede more. It never ends till you get married. After that, you lose the mystery, and it is clear who has the stronger personality.

38. *Is the dating game a mystery or are the rules clear? If clear, what are the rules?* People are very good at the dating thing. I learned from my father. Be confident, but not cocky. If you can support it, then be it. Dating is a boasting game. I don't bull shit. I want to keep the excitement going.

39. *Have you ever gone out with a woman who turned out to be a bitch?* I like bitches. I like sassy girls with attitude. They make me crazy and excited. I don't want them to be too easy. I like to play that game. I'll be an asshole. Younger women love the ass hole thing. Treat them like dirt and they will stick to you like mud. When playing their game, don't be mean; just be jokingly mean and witty. It is fun to mess with them. Make fun with them. When it is time to get out though, sometimes you just can't be polite; you have to be mean to get out. When doing so, I make sure to let them know that I've been trying to be polite.

Below the belt questions:

1. *Is sex an important factor in deciding whether you will continue to date someone?* It is almost the most important factor. I consider myself to know what I am doing. I have a lot of experience. There are certain sensual spots that are typically ignored; for example, there are many sensitive spots around the shoulders and the neck. The breasts are highly sensitive to touch. Foreplay is huge, practice makes perfect. I pick up on what they like. I like to begin by standing behind her, gently pushing her hair away from her neck and caressing her neck. I then kiss all the way down her backbone. Then, I turn her around and kiss

her stomach and go back up to her lips, where I can passionately kiss her and have her melt in my arms. In one-night stands, I go for it aggressively. In the heat of the moment, we skip forward and go straight to it. Usually alcohol makes you more uninhibited.

2. *Do you enjoy it when your date wears lingerie?* Yes. I like to take it off very quickly. I prefer it to be sexy. Nothing is fun also.

3. *Have you ever experienced ménage à trois? If not, would you consider it? If so, what combination of male/female?* I have a couple of different times. The first time, I was in high school. I was messing around with two girl friends; we got into it and before I knew it, we all went for it. That was how I lost my virginity when I was 15. It was quite a confidence booster.

4. *Does the size of her breasts matter?* I love big breasts. The bigger, the better. As long as they are not too small, I am happy.

5. *Do you prefer a particular pubic hair design?* Baby bald. Maybe a little hair.

6. *How many sexual partners have you had in your life?* Hundreds.

3. THE FOREVER BACHELOR

The Forever Bachelor will take from those women he can have, but will give to the one he can't have. Typically thinking of himself as an upstanding citizen and a "good guy," this character goes through the years dating, living with women, and failing to commit for one reason or another. The Forever Bachelor is a charming, smooth talker who looks great. He loves to hear himself talk; he often has many theories on dating and considers himself a professional in the areas of dating and relationships. He is attractive and usually dresses well. He is confident and content. He is so content with his life and himself that he has no burning desire or need for a wife. He lacks ambition. He needs constant excitement and is high-energy. He is both afraid of commitment and leery of love. Although he lacks the animal magnetism of the Magnet and Diplomat and he may not be well to do, women gravitate toward him because he exudes self-confidence and he is a great communicator. He has a great sense of humor. He has "It."

Taking care of oneself is of the utmost importance to the Forever Bachelor. This character is most apt to be the "metro sexual" with manicured nails and waxed eyebrows. He works out to be healthy, not to be buffed. He eats well and is always trim. He expects his women to look after themselves in a similar manner. The Forever Bachelor insists that his women practice "good personal hygiene" which includes professional manicures and pedicures, waxing, and a pubic area that has been groomed. She must be healthy and fit. She must eat healthily because "bacon cheeseburgers are not a good recipe for longevity."

This man falls back on what is easy and convenient, knowing that his relationships are not long-term, but he will keep his relationships going and lingering. Often unfair to the women in the relationships who want a long-term commitment and perhaps a family, this character is selfishly and knowingly wasting the woman's time. His mantra includes the line that if you are truly in love, you don't need a marriage certificate to prove it. If and when the woman asserts herself, finally demanding commitment, this character will hit the road. He is rarely faithful to those with whom he is living. He doesn't feel fully committed and, therefore, doesn't think having relationships outside the co-habitation is a true "cheat." While he will often date several women at the same time, he will rarely engage in one-night stands.

Like a Diplomat, the Forever Bachelor makes you feel good while in his presence; he adds value to everyone who becomes involved with him, but he will not commit to a dating relationship. He knows he will break the hearts of his women and enjoys this power over them. This is what he finds so appealing in the Apple; she is the ultimate challenge for him. He wants her heart on a platter, but he doesn't understand that she has no heart. He chases the heartbreak that will never be.

He has usually grown up in a family that practiced religion, but the Forever Bachelor has rejected the group dynamic of the religion and often refers to himself as non-religious, anti-religion, an atheist, or going it alone. As this character moves into his forties, he often realizes, with chagrin, that he has missed his opportunity to settle down and have a family. Sometimes, he becomes bitter about the area in which he lives, claiming that the statistics are bad for the men due to the male-female ratio. This Forever Bachelor will go to foreign lands to play and party with young, free women. The Forever Bachelor typically stays single for his life, but, in the event he ultimately finds and allows himself to succumb to true love, he will be an older groom.

AN INTERVIEW WITH A FOREVER BACHELOR
MARRIED TO HIS GAME

1. *Education Level:* College
2. *Age:* 30's
3. *Profession:* Sales and Marketing
4. *Personal Status:* Single
5. *What initially attracts you to the opposite sex?* Looks and appearance. Past that, I look for good communication to keep the interest level up and I hope to have fun.

   The first things that any human being is attracted to are the physical attributes. Sometimes, you don't get past that. However, I have noticed that the best sex seems to be with girls that are not the prettiest. For example, I dated a girl that was drop dead gorgeous. She was immature; she had put all her eggs in one basket, completely relying on her beauty. At first, it was cool, but it wore off quickly. She was boring in bed. We dated four weeks and then she became a top model on a show. When she was on the show, she referred to me as her boyfriend, even though we weren't exclusive as far as I was concerned.

6. *What do you find appealing in a date?* From every angle and stage, you should enjoy your date. You should enjoy the way she dresses and behaves as well as her etiquette and how she talks about her background. My criterion for a woman is her physique, personality and level of energy. Women are attracted to a man who is escorted by two other women.

7. *What do you find to be a turn-off in a date?* Lack of attention. I cannot stand a date that is not focusing on me, someone who is always looking at her phone. I won't date people who are bad listeners.

   There are thousands of turnoffs: a girl who tries to play the masculine role in a relationship. I like to open the door for a lady. I enjoy people who take care of themselves. Eating poorly is not a plan for longevity.

8. *Where do you meet women?* Everywhere. Clubs, restaurants. I look for the opportunity to meet people everywhere. Work is not the best place due to sexual harassment policies. However, at work you can be yourself and not hustle or be superficial. People put up walls and are not themselves when they are out looking for a date, but at work, people are generally themselves.

Friends, I meet people everywhere I go, bars. I like people so it is easy for me to interact with them. Bars are bad. I have rarely slept with girls I meet at bars. Work is the most successful place for a relationship to blossom. People are more themselves at work. A lot of times, I lower the volume of my personality and watch for the body language. I have incorporated my dating lessons into my work life and have found that the same rules that work for dating work well for me in the business world. You can tell when people are interested and when they are not. Don't waste your time.

9. *When you are out with your friends and you see someone who catches your eye, what do you do?* I smile. If she is receptive, I move to the next step. "Hello, how are you?" If there is a smile, I communicate more. If I don't see a smile, I stop.

10. *Where do you hang out?* San Francisco, restaurants, bars (wine bars), elegant places and cafes.

11. *What are your thoughts about online dating?* I don't do it. It is so frustrating hiding behind the screen. I'm not sure what you get out of it. People who do it have no time or patience. The on-line dating sites put you in a category that might not even fit you. It is all marketing. However, international on-line women are more receptive and honest. They are not afraid of coming out to meet you as they are. They are real. I have not tried it. I don't have to. If it turned out to be huge dry spell, maybe.

12. *Have you ever had trouble moving on from a past relationship?* Yes. I got stuck. It's an investment that you lose. Hurt, pain and disappointment. It took me one month to get over the person. I immersed myself in sports.

My heart was broken in high school. She went out on me because I refused to go all the way with her. I was afraid of getting a girl pregnant. This happened to my older brother and it ruined his life. I don't let people in very easily, maybe because of my early experiences in dating. I rarely cut off a relationship. I find the familiarity of going back to the old comfortable relationship and not cutting it off completely to be comforting.

13. *What are your rituals for preparing for your date?* [He answered, snapping and twirling his arms in a disco-like motion.] I dance around and get my energy up.

14. *Where do you go/what do you do on a date?* I like to go for drinks or coffee. If the woman is uptight, I suggest drinks. Dinners or sports

make great dates. Perhaps a hike. I try to find out what they like and do that. The less formal of a date the better. Casual. The more you build it up, the more nervous you will be. I send a message that says, "Let's go and have a good time and not worry about a love at first sight."

15. *If you don't know your date well, do you meet at the designated place or do you pick your date up?* Meeting is always beneficial.

16. *Would you be interested in going for coffee and a walk instead of a dinner date for the first date?* Yes!

17. *How often do you have a boys' night out?* I go out with my friends seven days a week. No special place; we are workaholics.

18. *What frustrates you in the dating scene?* The mindset of girls in this area frustrates me. They want security, a guy with good looks (like Brad Pitt), excitement and more. They mostly want someone to pay for their plastic surgeries.

It seems that I date a wider age range the older I get. I date young 20's and rarely late 30's, my own age. I don't find enough attractive available women in my age group. Many women my age have families and kids. I find myself dating from a younger and younger age group. The older women are more mentally attractive and hold my thoughts more. But there are not many quality 30's to pick from. The Bay Area is tough for guys, the ratio of men to women is two to one. When you have a lop-sided equation, you rarely see the ugly duckling with the super model. The women have their pick from the top of the litter. The average guy would have a better chance of finding someone of his caliber in another area.

Definitely the ratio and the pool of quality women are lacking. I relate dating to fishing. A guy who doesn't know how to cast his line comes back empty. The one who knows how to cast can fish even if the fish are not hungry. I do respect the guy who goes over and talks to the girls and can make a move. I love the girl who doesn't mind approaching the guy. The other pretty girls get angry at her because they are just sitting there and looking pretty. I rarely approach a girl that has a flippant attitude. You'll never beat her at that game. The more you talk to her, the more she will turn her back. If you ignore her, she will come to you. If you want to distinguish yourself from rest of the pack, then don't do what they are doing. My way of going about it is not paying any complement, glance, or stare. I am pretty confident and wait for them to come up to me. They usually do.

19. *What are you looking for in a relationship?* I want someone who is nice, someone who is in my position, someone who understands how to be herself. I want a real and authentic woman from the ages of 27 to 35. She has to be attractive and take care of herself. I would much rather have an older woman who takes care of herself than a younger woman who doesn't. If she is too nurturing, I can't play my role that well.

    If I find a woman that I fall in love with, I will drop all my dates immediately. There is no substitute for the real thing. I am not a one-night stand guy. I am cautious. I try to be upfront with them, but they hear what they hear. I like to have my cake and eat it too, but it doesn't always work very well.

    When the guy pulls back and begins putting anything less than 50% of the effort into the relationship, the woman often tries to make up the difference. Then it landslides and the woman gives more and more. This violates the tenets of male-female relationships that have been established from the dawn of time. The role of the woman is to be chased. The masculine role is that of the chaser. Then you have a relationship where the correct polarity is created.

    I also think that being best friends in the relationship just kills the passion. If they are best friends, there is no passion. When people say they don't fight, it is either a perfect relationship or a dull one. Make up sex is worth fighting for.

    I see a lot of women testing the guys. The woman sometimes fights for control, not because she wants it, but because she wants the man to assert it. She doesn't want to win the fight; she wants to feel comfortable that you are man enough and she can count on you. If the guy is a push over, how can she possibly relax and know that every-thing is going to be all right.

    You can't change a man. It is easier to change a woman than a man.

20. *Would you go out with a married woman?* I have. Something I shouldn't have done, but I was fine with it. It was just sex. Sometimes it is a turn-on, but, in this case, it wasn't. I have had so many years of being a player, that I have become passé and careless about it. I don't think I will burn out. A more likely scenario is that I will fall for someone.

21. *Would you date someone who had a child from another relationship?*
Yes, with restrictions – I do not want to take the second place in her
life.

22. *If you were to live with someone, how long would you be willing to live
with her without a permanent commitment?* Depends on the goal.

23. *Would you consider financially supporting your partner?* No. It is a
tricky one. It depends on the circumstances. If she is a homemaker
and doing her job, then no problem. Absolutely, if she was taking care
of the children, yes. That might be a temporary thing, though. If I get a
feeling that they would be happier doing something else, I would help
them get there. If they saw how much was coming in on the paycheck
and they were out buying Gucci bags, I would not be happy.

24. *What makes an impression on you regarding your date?* Whether she
is in the moment and not whining; how she treats others; whether she
smiles and is in a good place in life.

25. *What type of clothing do you prefer your date to wear when you go out
on a date?* Simple, but elegant.

26. *Do you wear boxers or briefs?* Both. Boy shorts.

27. *What is your preferred body type and shape for a woman?* Slender,
athletic, under size 10 max, no fake things -- all natural.

28. *How do you feel about tattoos and piercings?* Not preferred. It is self-
mutilation and shows insecurity.

29. *How do you feel about perfumes and colognes?* A light scent is fine.
Good hygiene is critical. This can make you and break you. Bad breath
is a deal breaker. Every time I smell a great perfume on a girl who
passes by me, I go up to her and let her know how nice she smells.

30. *How important is the first kiss?* Ahhhh!!!! Very important in that it
shows her comfort level with her sexuality.

31. *Do you want to pay on the first date? And after the first date?* I pay
and need her to appreciate that fact. Gratitude is important.

32. *What are the most appealing things a date can do?* She drops her napkin under my legs and disappears for a while!

33. *Will you have sex on the first date?* Sex on the first date is taboo. If it
happens, it is a good thing for a guy. It is more problematic for a
woman. In the U.S., women feel guilty about it, but internationally,
women do it without feeling guilty and it happens more often.

34. *How do you protect yourself from STD's?* Condoms are something
that you stop wearing after you are dating the same person long
enough. I have not been tested for the last five years. I don't think

AIDS is a real threat to me. If I had one-night stands or girls of a lesser caliber, I would be worried. I normally don't date unless I am very familiar with the person. That is why I date from work more often. Currently, I am in a sexual relationship with only three women. Maybe one of whom I would not be using a condom with. She asked me if I was practicing safe sex with the others. I simply said, "Yes." I don't volunteer much information to any of my dates about any of the others, but I will answer if asked directly. I won't lie.

35. *When on a date, where would you be willing to have sex with your date if you were hot and horny?* Anywhere. Somewhere where you least expect. In an elevator of a law firm.

36. *Where is your favorite place to have sex if you had a choice?* All the places that are least expected. On the hood of a car. Outdoors, the car is unbelievable. One time, I gave up my body for lent. Five of us boys agreed not to ejaculate, including masturbation. I survived forty days of no orgasm, but having sex was great. I gave my word to my guy friends that, if I were to lose, I would put $100 in the pot. I had a girlfriend at the time. When we had sex, I found that I could go on forever without ejaculating. It was an amazing exercise in self-discipline. It taught me about the woman testing the man. She wanted me to cum; she tried to get me to lose the bet. It was more pleasurable for her to see me suffer.

37. *What do you do if protection is not immediately available?* I don't know. Don't do it. It is foolish to have sex in the heat of the moment with no protection. I had a heat of the moment sexual encounter with a nurse in Thailand. I immediately regretted it. I got tested and I was okay, but I was very nervous before the results came in.

38. *What do you think of one-night stands?* Drunks participate in them. No control of your mind. If it happens, it is okay.

39. *How do you break off a one-night stand or short relationship without being hurtful?* Be tactful and say, "I have to go on a trip." I don't have one-night stands very often. I have a friend who has them frequently. He has told me that, in the middle of the sexual act with a woman, he starts planning his exit. He knows that he will want to get out of there the second he cums. He thinks, "What the fuck am I doing here?" Gone. Over. Done. He says that there is a chemical change upon cumming. It doesn't matter if he was into the girl for the whole evening; as soon as he completes the sexual act, he can't wait to get out. He told me about a time where he was taking a girl to her car.

45

She wanted him to stop so she could give him a blowjob. He pulled over, she did it, and, as he was cumming, he turned on the ignition. Her car was over twenty blocks away and all he could think about was having her open the door and pushing her out to the curb. The difference between the panicky feelings of wanting to get out immediately and wanting to stay for the night is the connection.

40. *What was your parents' status when you were growing up?* Married.

41. *How do you characterize yourself?*

    Positive attributes: Positive mental attitude; smile a lot; high energy; health conscious; sure of myself; I love my life and, if someone comes along, I'll share. Self assured. I am compassionate to people. Open minded. I entertain others' beliefs, but I still come away with my beliefs. I am very good at advice and knowing what to tell people. I am very perceptive.

    Negative attributes: Emotional, pickier as I get older, impatient, higher expectations, I know what I can have and want it. I go with the flow too much; sometimes the bills don't get paid on time. I am not a planner. I am a procrastinator. I am easy going. I am a last minute kind of guy.

42. *How do you think others see you?* I think they see me as polite, a good guy, and a good advisor.

43. *Please include a detailed description of your ideal date.* I pick her up dressed to the hilt, I feel good, I worked out and we're going to dinner followed by a club. She has made herself up, taking care of herself from head to toe. Great positive energy, we do not expect anything and go with the flow. Lots of gentle touching gestures, babe. Older, attractive, depth, interesting. More important than the venue, I would much rather get along with the person and show her a good time.

44. *When you meet someone new, how long does it take you to know if the person is "the one" or has the potential to be "the one"?* I know within the first five minutes.

45. *Do you believe in "love at first sight"?* No.

46. *What is your personal philosophy on monogamy and monogamous relationships?* Monogamy is important if you want to have a serious relationship. Again, it depends on the goals. On the guys' side, they always think about having sex with other women. They won't necessarily do it, but I guarantee they are thinking about it. Don't talk about it. Just accept it; that it is they way things are. Don't ask, don't tell.

47. *Do you believe there is a game people play when dating? If so, describe the game.* Absolutely. I don't think it is negative. They just don't understand the dynamics of courtship. The game of being cool and cooler and going home alone is retarded. There is an art to courtship and it is a game that has existed since time began.

Many times people don't want to know the truth. As an example, there was a girl who was dating a guy for two or three months. He suddenly stopped calling her. The choices are: A) the grass is greener, or B) he lost interest in her. My advice to her was to be more compassionate toward him by pulling back and giving him room rather than picking up the slack and chasing him to the dire end. Give him a break and let him go. If we are honest with ourselves, we realize that he is now chasing someone else. If we take that as being the truth, then having her chase the situation will not help. Once you have compassion for the other person, it is so much easier for you move on to the next relationship. If you have a chip on your shoulder, it shows and becomes emotional baggage. Emotional baggage adversely affects a woman's beauty. Let him off the hook. Men love to chase; not to be chased.

Everyone plays. You appear to be someone more appealing, hiding your flaws. It's a hide-and-seek game. Men open up sooner than women.

The women in my age group have huge hang-ups and money expectations. There was a huge change after the ".com-bust." It was all about career. Dating changed; before, it was easy going. Women have many more choices in men than men have in women now. Most men around 35 to 50 complain about the dating scene. Between ages 18 to 25, girls are free-spirited. Between 26 and 30 years old, something happens to the women and between 30 to 36 years old they are desperate. After 36 years old, all bets are off; they are set in their ways and use what they have for temporary fixes. Women always use their beauty to get what they want up to age 36. In the U.S., we are in the dating bubble. The worst is California and worst yet is the Bay Area and the worst of all is Silicon Valley.

48. *Is the dating game a mystery or are the rules clear? If clear, what are the rules?* It is a mystery. No one knows what the game is. Everyone has his or her own game. There are too many hidden thoughts. Timing in unknown, people should follow their instincts. If I like the woman

and she calls right away after our date, I LOVE IT. I believe women are too sensitive.

49. *On average, how many dates are required before you consider your-self to be in a relationship? What qualifies as a date?* It varies. Sometimes a month or two. If a woman is too mysterious, it means she is too complicated. A date is going out to dinner with gentle touching gestures. When you date for a certain amount of time, the woman tends to think it is a relationship. I am upfront with them. It really doesn't matter what conversation has taken place; they hear what they hear. My logic of sleeping with one and going out with another isn't always easy. No matter what kind of a discussion you have had, they still get clingy.

50. *Have you ever been on a date with a girl who turned out to be a bitch?* Yes. Disgusting. Rude. Inconsiderate. Obnoxious. Someone who only thinks about herself. Conceited. I knew after a few minutes in the car together and suggested that we go home immediately; I turned a 180 on the road to take her back home.

51. *If interested in your date, how long do you wait to communicate with her?* I will tell her before the date is over. I send a light text the next day, something to let her know that I had a good time and that I would want to go out again.

52. *If you were not interested in dating her again, would you let her know? If so, how do you let her know?* I will communicate and let her know I am going to be busy for the next life. All jokes aside, I have rarely told a woman that I am not interested. Normally, I might see her again, but it would be on a different plane. We might go out as friends in the future.

Below the belt questions:

1. *Is sex an important factor in deciding whether you will continue to date someone?* Yes, I am a physical person. If she is not sexual and passionate, it is a no-go. But sex itself without the connection will get old. Just the physical part of sex will get you into a robotic mood. Sex is much more than the motion of it.

2. *Do you enjoy it when your date wears lingerie?* I like it natural; don't force it. Sexy to me is something that is not planned. Lots of sponta-neity is good. When you plan your outfit for sex, it is not spontaneous.

3. *Have you ever experienced ménage à trois? If not, would you consider it? If so, what combination of male/female?* I have, yes. All combinations, but I like more female to men, of course.
4. *What is sexy to you in a woman?* The way she carries herself, confidence of being a woman. Be comfortable with herself.
5. *Does the size of her breasts matter?* I like them athletic so I don't want DDD. She can't run if they are bobbing up and down, hitting her in the eyes.
6. *Do you mind surgical enhancement of breasts, lips, teeth, etc?* Anything beyond natural is not good.
7. *How much make up is too much?* Just enough to be subtle is perfect.
8. *Are skimpy, body-fitting outfits a turn-on or a turn-off?* They are okay if the woman has a nice body and can wear it in a nice classy way. It depends on the body. I would much rather see the woman dress her age. Aging gracefully is being comfortable where you are. A forty year old should not dress like a twenty year old.
9. *What do you think of coffee houses as a place to meet someone?* Not too much. Coffee nerds are no good.
10. *What do you think of the work environment as a place to meet someone?* It is dangerous for the companies, but better for the individuals.
11. *Do you prefer a particular pubic hair design?* Brazilian. I do not want to have to pull out my weed-wacker and put on my goggles when I am down there. [He rubs his mouth like he's pulling hair off his lips and chin.]
12. *How many sexual partners have you had in your life?* 20.

THE FOREVER BACHELOR LOOKS FOR GAME

There was a really good-looking tall guy at work that I had been watching over the last few months. He had girls with him all of the time. At lunch, the large round table in the cafeteria would have this guy sitting with six or seven women, all laughing and having a great time. I wanted in on it. I had tickets for a ball game and asked him to go with me. When I asked him, he smiled and agreed to join me. We agreed to meet before the game at a bar near the ballpark.

When I met him, he was already having a drink with another guy from work. I joined them. We finished our drinks and then walked to the game. On the way there, I had a great conversation with the other guy who happened to be from my hometown. As we were walking, my date got a phone call from a girl and he talked to her while he walked next to me the whole way to the game. It was unbelievably rude.

When we sat down, I sat down next to him. I asked him with whom he had been talking and he said it was an old friend, "Just as you were talking with an old friend." I didn't know what he was saying, so I shrugged. Maybe this was a good indication that this guy had a problem and that he created drama in his own head. But, we were there for the next few hours and I decided to make the best of it.

The game was great. He bought us hotdogs and beer. We had a great conversation and I have to admit that I was very attracted to him. After the game, he suggested that we go to his house. I followed him there and we had an amazing time in bed. Around 1 a.m., there was a knock at the door and another woman appeared. He invited her in and offered her a drink. I got dressed and came out of the bedroom. He introduced us to one another. My mouth was hanging open. Again, I should have known better.

I said, "Maybe this is my cue to leave," and I started walking out the door. He hugged me and said good-bye. I was laughing on the way out; I couldn't believe that someone could be such an ass.

The next day at work, he told me that he had a great time with me. I asked him, "What was the story with the girl?" He told me that when I had been having such a good time with the guy on the way to the game, this girl called and set up a date for later that evening. He said that he had no idea that we would hook up because I seemed to be enjoying the other guy's company more than his. My mouth dropped open.

Wow. Imagine that – he was setting up a date with someone else while on a date with me. What an insecure, rude, asshole! He knew he was having another girl over when he invited me into his bed. He just wanted to have sex with me so that he could prove to himself that I was into him. I told him that a guy had never treated me so rudely and that he needed help. I told him not to expect to go out with me again.

He was shocked and didn't like the fact that I didn't want to see him again. He said, "Call me if you change your mind."

AN INTERVIEW WITH A CONTENT AND HAPPY BACHELOR

1. *Gender:* Male
2. *Age:* 30's
3. *Education Level:* College
4. *Profession:* Entrepreneur
5. *Personal Status:* Single
6. *Are you looking for a long-term relationship or a meaningful one-night stand?* Yes. I have male desires. I have been with a lot of women; at least 200. I am looking for a long-term relationship. I am very selective when it comes to long-term relationships. There is a saying that I live by: "It is better to be alone than to wish you were alone." I have been with a girl over six years and we lived together. I knew she wasn't the one, but it was easy and convenient. Over time, she became bitter due to my passive aggressive behavior. We stayed together out of habit. The last year was tough. I was not dating, but was having heavy petting with other girls during the time we were together. In fact, I had many encounters with other women during that time. Men are very visual; of course, I became attracted to women during the time I was living with my girlfriend. Heavy petting is my way of staying safe, not completely cheating, and still having a happy ending with another woman.
7. *What initially attracts you to the opposite sex?* Aside from the obvious, my hierarchy of importance is for the girl to have a great smile, sexy eyes and a nice figure. I expect to have a good dialogue and an intellectual discussion regarding politics, current events, business or just sex. I want a woman who can get into the conversation. I hate a complainer, a "Debbie downer" who complains about everyone and talks badly about everyone. Bad hygiene is bad. I love a woman that is manicured.
8. *Where do you meet people?* Everywhere. I have never Internet dated. I have friends who say it is like shooting fish in a barrel and it is great for one-night stands.
9. *If married, would you cheat?* I would get married, saying that I would never cheat and I would believe it deeply when I said it. But would I be capable of it? I don't know. The engineer, the geeky guy that brags he has never cheated may be able to brag because an opportunity for him to cheat has never come up.   But when the right opportunity

comes, it would be hard. I would like to say that I would take the high road. As I get older, I see fewer opportunities coming my way and that might make it easier for me not to cheat.

10. *When you are out with your friends and you see someone who catches your eye, what do you do?* I look for the opportunity to initiate a meeting.

11. *Have you ever had trouble moving on from a past relationship?* The last one was very difficult. After you break up, everything reminds you of the person. You hear your song on the radio, pass by the restaurant where you dined together, and remember the habits you shared together. All of those things make it very difficult to move on. She gave me an ultimatum – she told me to shape up or ship out. She told me that she didn't like my friends and that I had to drop them; she didn't like my business and I had to change it; she didn't want me to hang out so much with my family; and so forth. She drank too much and became a mean drunk. There's a story called "The Trunk Story." Every couple starts off the relationship with a big trunk. They start off loving each other. Every time they have a difficult time they put a brick in the trunk till it gets too heavy to carry. She gave me the list of things to change and a timeline to respond. The last day to adhere to the list, I didn't. I moved out. She couldn't believe it and she began compromising on her list, but I left anyway. That was the best thing I did. I only stayed with her for as long as I did because of habit and familiarity. She opened the door and I ran out as fast as I could.

My first love was in high school. Her mom didn't like the fact that we were sleeping together. I remember telling her mother that she should allow her sixteen-year-old daughter to make her own decisions as to whether to be intimate with me. Now that I look back, I see how crazy and foolish I was. I am shocked at my behavior back then. We went our separate ways for college. When I graduated from the university, I received a letter from her saying, "You deserve to know that I still love you." I called her and we went out. We did some heavy petting, but I didn't feel anything. It was puppy love in high school; after college, it just amounted to a roll in the hay with no passion. I have always been poor with communication when I have not had feelings for the person. The night ended without any fireworks and I wanted it to end sooner. She called me a couple of times, but I didn't answer. This is my passive aggressive nature; I don't like confrontation so I stop contact. The texting era makes it so much tougher. They just text and text. I can't get away.

12. *If you were a candy, what would you be?* I would be a Hot Tamale. I am very sexual.

13. *What frustrates you in the dating scene?* No frustration, no obstacles. I am pretty happy go lucky. Cocky. Very secure with myself. I feel that I can have any girl I want and they want me. I have been very fortunate that girls love me.

14. *Would you go out with a married woman?* I have in the past. Yes, but only for a quick role in the hay and nothing more. In my early thirties, I was with a girl who was married. I was in her house, in her bed, with all her husband's pictures all over. After the act, I looked at the photos, felt very uncomfortable, and I left. I never saw her again.   Typically, if I am with a married woman, she must be very attractive and highly desirable, otherwise I don't need the headache. I don't want to be a home wrecker and I don't like people who are either. This is a slippery slope and needs to be approached with caution. If you see anyone too long, emotions get in the way.

I think this texting thing gets people connected. There is a lot more communication today than I would have participated in before. A couple of years ago, my cousin showed me how to use my text and, ever since then, I have become a texter. It is a great tool for flirting and talking dirty. Women are literal and you have to be very careful what you say in your texts.

I dated someone that I was fond of, but she was not the one for me either. I knew it would devastate her to call it off, but it was getting to that point. I wanted to be respectful to her, as she deserved someone good in her life. Normally, I just quit communicating; she deserved better. I broke it off with a text. I like my time with me. Ideally, I am looking for a fantastic, out of this world person to take my breath away . . . if there is such a woman.

15. *Would you consider financially supporting your partner?* Sure, of course.

16. *What type of clothing do you prefer your date to wear when you go out on a date?* What a man is attracted to when he is younger, he will be attracted to when he is older. I like a short skirt, sexy attire, hair up. I wouldn't want my mate to dress sexy without me.

17. *Do you think women try hard to please you?* All women think they are good in bed. They have the look and make the sound. They think

they can make the man cum. The man will cum with or without their effort. Italian's have a saying: "Do you know why women pretend that they are cumming? They think the men care." The greatest title for a future book can be "All Women Think They Are Good In Bed." The women who are looking for a one-night stand want the men to perform. There has only been one woman in my life that took my breath away both in bed and out. I loved her the first time I laid eyes on her. But, she was emotionally unavailable. I will always remember our time together.

What about men who try to please girls? Heidi Fleiss said "Viagra is the worst nightmare for the hookers." If you take Viagra and don't need it, you become a rock star. You last forever and can go and go.

There was this other time with an older woman. The only time I had my hands cuffed was when I took ecstasy. She handcuffed me, she was 40 and I was 33. She took control of the situation; she took a duffle bag out of the closet and then tied my hands to the bed with Velcro handcuffs. She did it so fast that I didn't know what she was doing. She started dancing in front of me and got on top of me. It was a wonderful experience; she gave me her best game. I was with her three other times and she was a good lover. I took E with her on each of the other times.

18. *What is your preferred body type and shape for a woman?* Face, smile, nice legs and breasts. A hand full of 36C+ is the perfect size.
19. *How do you feel about tattoos and piercings?* No.
20. *How do you feel about perfumes and colognes?* Perfumes are nice.
21. *How important is the first kiss?* It is important just to feel the connection. As long as they smell nice and taste good.
22. *Do you want to pay on the first date? And after the first date?* Yes. Absolutely.
23. *Will you have sex on the first date? If so, would you talk to your date about your preferences freely?* Yes. I prefer for the girl to tell me what she likes. I am open to instructions. I like to please her.
24. *Would you have sex with your date if she were drunk?* Yes. I am probably going to be drunk myself. I love champagne and sex.
25. *Do you wear boxers or briefs?* Boxers now. I remember being in another town with a few girl friends. We were all having a great time in our hotel room and we started getting comfortable in our jammies and undies. We were only friends and no hanky panky was going on be-

tween us. I walked out in my "tighty-whities" and the girls started laughing at me. They told me to get rid of them. I immediately started wearing boxers. I am very gifted down there and I like to be snug, but I understand that girls like boxer briefs or boxers better than briefs. I like my girl to wear a lacy thong.

26. *How do you make sure a new sexual partner is free of STD's?* Hence me saying, "I would much rather have heavy petting." I would much rather have the "happy ending" for both without the risk to either. I don't do condoms. I don't like them. It doesn't feel good.

Herpes story:

There have been 3 or 4 times when a woman has told me that she has had Herpes. I bolted on each occasion. The first was when I was 17 and I did this girl on the river. We were standing in shallow water and we did it. A month later, I brought my buddy to her house so we could do a double date. I was in bed with her and she told me she had gotten Herpes since we last saw each other. She said, "I just got this thing. I got it from my girlfriend. She had a real outbreak; I got it from the sheets." Her friend who had the disease was out there in the living room with my buddy. I jumped out of the bed with one goal in mind, saving my buddy. I ran out there and told him that we had to get out quickly. After we got into the car, I told him what was going on. He rolled down the window as we raced away and he spat out the window the whole way home, thinking he could spit away the Herpes germs. I went to the nurse's station the next day and she explained that you get it within ten days of exposure. Those ten days were Hell, but I was happier than ever on the eleventh day. My buddy was good, too.

On a second occasion, a woman told me that she had Herpes after we had been to a couple of movie dates. After she told me that, I stopped seeing her and I never saw her again.

The third time, I was in my thirties, and she took me out to meet her family. We had been on five dates and she told me the story about how she had Herpes. She said, "I really like you and I need to tell you something." She told me that she had it. I said, "It's no big deal." I told her that I had dated a girl with Herpes before to make her feel better. She said "I'm going to make love to you like no one ever has before." She told me that she could tell when the Herpes blisters are

55

coming because it is really painful. I made an excuse to end the evening early and I never talked to her again. She said some guy gave it to her and he never warned her.

When I find out they have a disease, I run like Hell. The trouble is, not everyone is honest about it. I resent people who knowingly pass diseases to their sexual partners. I've been very fortunate so far.

27. *When on a date, where would you be willing to have sex with your date if you were hot and horny?* On the plane. We made love in an outhouse once. It was so sick; it was hot and gross. It was just disgusting and smelly. Won't do that again. Well, probably won't.

28. *Where is your favorite place to have sex if you had a choice?* My favorite place is a nice, nice bed, my bed. The fever makes it hotter. I get the fever when the woman is seducing me and she is getting into my head. The fever comes when she has the power knowing that she can have me and I can't have her. I love this feeling. It has only happened to me once in my life.

29. *What if you liked your date and she did not return your call the next day or week? What would you think and do?* I would call once or twice max. It has never happened; no one has ever broken up with me. They all want me. I don't usually break up either; I just leave and drop them. I don't like confrontation and I don't like hurting people.

30. *What age range do you date?* 35-45. I was recently with a 48 year old. A few months ago, I was with my friend at a bar. This 33 year-old-girl came over to us. We got drunk and closed the bar down. She was going to be the maid of honor at a wedding the next day and I asked if she had a date for the wedding. She said she didn't and asked me to go with her as her date. I declined, but told her that I would come for a brief visit. She didn't believe me. The next day, I showed up at the wedding. I looked good and her friend pointed me out to the girl. I stayed for few minutes and, after the reception party, we stayed at the hotel and had sex. She was so into me. She called me that weekend from the airport. When she got home, I texted her, but she didn't respond. Later, she said she was looking for a long-term relationship, but that she was currently in an abusive situation. She said that she had to work it out with her boyfriend first. Later, after two weeks, I sent her a text saying, "Don't you miss my kisses?" She said, "I do, but my boyfriend is tired of reading your texts."

I love women. I am honest and straightforward. Sometimes, I am too honest.

31. *How do you break off a one-night stand or short relationship without being hurtful?* In the past, I simply didn't communicate with them further; I didn't respond if they contacted me. I figured that they aren't stupid; they have to know. I recently began to tell them that I am emotionally unavailable. Most recently and for the first time ever, I had enough courage and respect for the woman that I was dating to express my fears and thoughts when breaking up with her. It was heartbreaking to sit there and listen to her pouring her heart out to me and telling me how much she loved me. I felt really badly about the whole thing, but I was relieved that I was able to let her go and have her move on with her life. She deserved to find someone who wanted the same things out of life and who would appreciate her and love her.

32. *What was your parents' status when you were growing up?* Happily married.

33. *How do you characterize yourself?*

    Positive attributes: Loving, caring, decent; I am considerate of other people's feelings. I am cute, sweet and cuddly. I can be the girl's best friend. All the women fall in love with me and I warn them ahead of time that I am not there for the long-term. I have a great sense of humor and I have low expectations of others so that I rarely get disappointed. I am my own security blanket; I am very sociable; I have friends from all walks of life. I maintain my friendships forever.

    Negative attributes: I am a procrastinator, my sense of urgency is lacking. I am too comfortable with myself. I find that most successful people are insecure with themselves; that is what gives them their drive to be successful. I have been very fortunate. People categorize me as a ladies' man or a player; I don't think I am because I really enjoy being with women. I am a poor communicator when it comes to ending relationships.

34. *How do you think others see you?* Nice, considerate, charming, I have a huge sexual appetite. I am insatiable and naughty.

35. *Please include a detailed description of your ideal date.* I drive up to her house, she asks me in and has a bottle of wine open. I pour us each a glass of wine and check out her house, looking at her pictures. As we get into my car, I open the door for her, and I take her to a nice restaurant. We sit by the bar, watching people. Being alone at a table for the first date is not exactly cozy. I chat with her and I get to know her. If I like her, I ask her my favorite questions: 1) do you listen or do you

wait to talk? 2) On your hierarchy of values, which is higher, honor or loyalty? These are typically great conversation starters. We have a great conversation and hopefully there is a connection. If she is enjoying herself, I extend the evening to a place with good music, or a piano bar. There are so many different ideal dates for different situations. There is a different one for one-night stands, long-term relationships, and so forth. I am very aggressive. I know guys who have had a crush on the girl and when they go out, they have so much invested in the date that they forget to kiss or make a move. I never forget to make a move; I make it early on. I kiss girls on the first date. Period. How it starts out is how it is going to end up. The guy who waits to kiss the girl after four or five dates blows it. A one-night stand is not a planned thing; it is a random occurrence.

We then go back to the girl's place. When you kiss the girl in front of her house, she will almost always invite you in. Or, if you don't have a place, just get a room. I love kissing; I would kiss her a lot. It is very intimate. When you are in a relationship for a while, you forget to kiss. People who are in relationships for a long time actually have sex without kissing. Sensuality is lost over time. This is why people look outside their commitments; they yearn for the lost sensuality and excitement.

36. *Do you believe in "love at first sight"?* Yes. But it has never happened to me. During the first six months, you never know the real person. You meet the representative of the person. The more genuine the person, the less the representative. In reality, people will show you as little as possible. Slowly the person's bad habits are revealed.

37. *Is the dating game a mystery or are the rules clear?* The dating game is a mystery because everyone is different and every situation is different. I don't play games.

38. *What is your personal philosophy on monogamy and monogamous relationships?* I believe one should be monogamous once in a committed relationship. However, one can also slip, not because he or she wants to, but it is Mother Nature. We are social animals and love intimacy.

Let me tell you the story of the frog and the scorpion. They come across a big body of water and the scorpion asks for a ride. The frog said, "You'll kill me." The scorpion says, "Why would I sting you? Then, we'll both die." The frog was afraid, but figured if the scorpion stung him, they would both drown. Half way into the body of water, the scorpion stung the frog. The frog looked at the scorpion and the scorpion said, "Sorry, it's my nature."

I wish I had been in your chairs during all of your interviews. The plethora of knowledge you gals have gained must be amazing.

Below the belt questions:

1. *Is sex an important factor in deciding whether you will continue to date someone?* It must be. When I was young, I would say sex was key. But now, I think it is great sex that is important to keeping a relationship interesting.
2. *Do you enjoy it when your date wears lingerie?* Yes. I love a black bra and black lacy panties.
3. *Have you ever experienced ménage à trois? If not, would you consider it? If so, what combination of male/female?* Yes, I was living with my best friend who is now happily married. I was a bartender out of college. While bartending, I had met a couple of girls who were sitting together at the bar. One was blonde and the other was brunette. I went out with the brunette a couple of times. A couple of months later, I ran into the blonde and her redheaded friend at another bar and we were drinking. We started talking about how the redhead's boyfriend wanted to have a threesome. I told her to try it out on me first. She and the blonde came over to my apartment. When we got into my bedroom, the girls were on the bed kissing each other. Clothes started coming off. I got on top of the redhead and I didn't take things slowly. I wasn't very good at it at that time. While I was doing her, she was kissing the blonde. I was so bad and sucked big time. The redhead went down on the blonde girl. I put my drink down and got behind the redhead once again. The blonde started crying and saying, "You don't want me here." She told me that I was awful in bed. She got up and got her clothes on and left. I realized that I had picked the brunette over her the first time and then I had done the redhead twice and ignored the blonde again. The moral of the story is, make sure you share yourself with both girls.

   Today, I would do it differently. Here is the story of the old bull and the young bull. Up on the hill, they look down and they see beautiful cows in the pasture. The young bull says, "Let's go down and fuck one." The old one says, "Lets fuck them all." If I were to do it differently, I would take one of those purple pills to make me a rock star and I would take care of them all.

The hottest woman that I have ever seen in my life was when I was 14; she was 23. She was driving me home from some school event. I was so horny for her, but I didn't know what to do with her. She came onto me and kissed me. I asked her if I could touch her thigh and she said, "Yes." I touched the side of her thigh with my fingertip and said, "Thanks." I got out of the car and went into the house. I have kicked myself about the lost opportunity many times. It's funny how perspective changes as you get older.

4. *What is sexy to you in a woman?* Hair, nails, dress, calf muscles, and a woman who likes sex.

5. *Do you prefer a particular pubic hair design?* Shaved is good. Landing strip is popular. I love to give oral sex, so I would prefer less hair.

6. *How many sexual partners have you had in your life?* Well over 200.

7. *At what point would you consider turning a committed relationship into a monogamous relationship?* Most women would say a committed relationship is a monogamous one. They are the same to me. Commitment is committed.

8. *How does a man like to be treated by a woman?* With respect. I don't believe men should be treated like kings; I don't need a woman to get my beer or cook my food or such. In order for any relationship to work, it needs to be win-win for both; both parties need to put in 100% of their effort.

9. *What do you want in a woman?* I want black bra, black panties, hair up and lots of love.

10. *Any rules on swapping between friends?* No. People with money seem to do it more. There is a taboo about dating a friend's girl.

11. *What is your opinion about women?* I love women. I could not live without them.

12. *Describe your standards for a woman?* Smart, sassy, sexy, the three sss's.

13. *Anything else to add?* Have you heard this story? I love it. There was an old Italian couple in their 80's who had been married for 60 years. Once a week, he walked into the town to buy a fresh loaf of bread that was meant to last a week. He always made a sandwich for his wife out of the first cut from the heel of the bread. Every single time, he gave her the heels. After sixty years, the wife said, "Honey, I hate the heels of the bread." He said, "But Honey, that was my favorite part all

along." When two people love each other, they give the other their favorite thing.

THE FOREVER BACHELOR EATS THE APPLE

He was comfortable with his status and relationships. He had just gotten out of a five-year relationship when his girlfriend gave him an ultimatum to either get married or move out. He moved out. She was disappointed, but not surprised. He was back on the market as a free man. This time, he was truly free.

At a friend's barbeque party, he met a woman who was astonishing, breathtaking, secure, confident and gorgeous. They hit it off well. She was a very successful entrepreneur and he was financially secure and doing well in his own businesses.

She wasn't looking for a long-term relationship and, knowing his background, she was confident that he wasn't looking for a long-term relationship either. At the barbeque, he excused himself to go to the restroom. She followed him and walked right in with him. She closed the door behind her and locked it. He was shocked in a good way, not knowing what to do. She grabbed the back of his neck and planted one right on his lips. Then she took his hand and put it in her underwear. He couldn't help but probe around. Then, she put her hand on his hard penis to see if it was worth the trouble. She found him to be gifted and she knew that he would be worth her while. They went back to the party and he texted her while watching for her reaction. He wrote, "I will never wash my finger again. I can still taste you. Yum, yum. You are so sweet." She blushed and smiled at him, knowingly.

They communicated later that night. She told him that she was looking for a good time and wanted it her way. If they were to meet, she wanted him to wear a white crisp dress shirt with black slacks and black boxer brief underwear. He responded with his own fashion requests. He wanted her to wear a short skirt, black sheer lacy panties, high heels, and hair up. He told her that he was sexually gifted and that he would do things to her that no man had ever done. She rolled her eyes and told him that she'd heard that many times before, but she was interested to find out what he had to offer. She told him to take care of the logistics. She tipped him off that he could ask for the half-day rate at a nice hotel. (Nice hotels have a hush, hush, half-day rate from noon-6:00 p.m. Typically, you have to ask for the manager to get this special rate.)

The day came for their first encounter. He had arranged for their first date to take place in a hotel on neutral grounds. He had successfully arranged for the half-day rate. He was all ready for her, or so he thought. He had red roses, chocolate, champagne, and romantic music playing in the background. She knocked on the door and said, "Room service." He opened the door and handed her a red rose. She was dressed in a tight fitting, short, black skirt with a tiny, little, black, form-fitting top that cupped her breasts. She walked in, put her purse down, and tossed the flower on the bed. She ripped the chocolate box open and helped herself to the chocolates.

He was a bit offended by the way she cast the rose away and gobbled up all of the chocolate without offering him even one. As he would find out, she wasn't there to be considerate of his feelings; she was there to enjoy herself. There were many more unexpected moves to come. He followed her instructions to a tee. He poured champagne into the glasses and handed one to her. The Sinatra played in the background. He sat on a chair. She danced her way over to him and sat on his lap, sipping her champagne. He looked as if he had been hit by lightening. He couldn't move his limbs. Her beauty and the anticipation of being with her paralyzed him. He was staring at her and didn't know what to do.

She loved it, knowing that she had to take the lead as usual. She would take the bull by the horn. He was not accustomed to allowing the woman to take the lead; in his mind, he was the master in the bedroom. But she was too much to handle and gave him stage fright. All he could do was pat her arm and play with her hair. He had completely forgotten his moves. He lost his groove. She was looking forward to his making good on all his talk about being the man. She reminded him about what he had told her after the barbeque. She asked, "Do you remember how you told me that you were going to do things to me that no man has ever done before?" He responded confidently: "You will fall in love with me and want me more every day like all the other women." She said, "I have heard that before, but I am looking forward to seeing what you have in mind." She was waiting for him to deliver and hoping it would be soon. She said to him laughingly, "I am waiting."

She could tell that he was nervous; he had been nervous for the first fifteen minutes of their encounter. She sat on his lap and he went for a kiss. She turned her head because she didn't like the way he was kissing. There was too much tongue, not enough sensuality. She wanted to start off gently, using all her senses and enjoying the moment. She thought there was nothing worse than a sloppy kiss. She knew that there is a formula to kissing. You don't just kiss with your lips, you start with your hand behind the neck; then you move your face close to his and touch his cheek with your lips and gently move your lips toward his until they touch. Start the kiss with just the lips for two to three seconds; wet his lips with your tongue; and push a little of your tongue into his mouth; and then, go for it.

It took four takes before he got the kiss right. On the last take, she directly told him: "Do nothing, don't turn your head. Just sit still; I'll show you." He followed the directions and then enjoyed the best kiss of his life. She wanted the kiss to be a certain way. He thought that she would want things fast. Maybe that was his wishful thinking; he was projecting because he couldn't wait to be inside her. She wanted to climb into the bed and relax a little. She wanted to enjoy the moment. They started kissing again. He couldn't wait to be inside her. He forgot about foreplay. He begged her to let him inside. She humored him, thinking that if he took the edge off, he would relax a little. After he came the first time, he was more relaxed and ready to please her. After they freshened up, they went back to bed for the second round.

This time he took over and was able to please her. However, a little instruction was required. Just like the kissing, when he first went down on her, he was all over the map. She stopped him and told him to be more sensual and gentle. She told him that there were many nerve endings down there and that he needed to relax his tongue and use his finger delicately like an artist with a paintbrush. She told him to gently use his tongue as if he was licking an ice cream cone rather than poke at her clitoris like a lizard. She explained to him that it was just like French kissing. While French kissing her vagina, he used his finger to further pleasure her. He thought that she had the most beautiful vagina he had ever seen. He told her that it tasted like vanilla candy. They continued on for another few hours of fun conversation, laughs, hot sex and relaxing together.

He thought it was an amazing experience; she found nothing amazing about it. She asked him when he was going to do the things that no other man had ever done? He looked disappointed and asked if he was gifted enough for her? She said he was not below average. He was devastated, but quickly came back with the comment that there are tiers to his relationships and she would have to wait until next time. She told him that there wouldn't be a next time and that he should have put his best game forward because you never a get a second chance for the first impression. She told him that she enjoyed his sense of humor and great energy.

He thought she wanted certain things from him. She thought she was teaching him. He thought he could fulfill her sexual fantasies. She was simply bored with him and had already moved on in her mind. She was always looking for excitement. She was in love with herself. He was in love with her. When they were lying in bed, she said, "I want you and your friend together here now. Bring a friend next time." He said that he was hurt and jealous by her request and that he would never mention another woman while in bed with her. He thought it was incredibly insensitive of her.

She told him their encounter would be the last and she wanted him to enjoy his day. He was beginning to feel as if she had put a spell on him and he couldn't be without her. He was becoming obsessed with her. She was confident, aloof, attractive, successful, honest, forthright and fun. For the first time in his life, he was falling in love. "This must be what love is," he thought. When she was getting ready to leave, she asked, "Is there anything else I can do for you?" He responded, "You can tell me you love me." So she did. And she left.

He had butterflies in his stomach every time he saw her thereafter. For her it was over. For him it was anything but over. His sensations were heightened when near her, his cock was always hard for her because he was always thinking about her. The trouble was, he knew that she was emotionally unavailable. He thought that he could change her availability overtime. In her mind everything was temporary and freedom was her game.

He sent the following letter to her expressing his feelings about her.

THE FEVER

Dear Apple,

You are one of a kind. Sexy, seductive, enticing, captivating, alluring, intelligent, witty, but so very, very, very dangerous.

When it comes to sex and romance, I consider myself the best of the best, I have no equal. And yet I know I am no match for you.

Throughout the ages, there are tales of women so seductive that countries go to war in the pursuit of attaining her.

But no one man nor country or thing can contain Apple. Yet countless men will attempt this impossible task.

*Your never aging beauty is only surpassed by your incredibly
strong spirit. I say "never aging beauty" because Mother Nature
wouldn't dare blemish you for even Mother Nature fears your wrath.*

*For Apple only answers to the gods. I would never cross you;
you will always be on my team.*

*Once a man has been inside you, he is forever a prisoner to his
own desire of returning to that frenzy of ecstasy.*

*No man can be warned or cautioned of your ability to place
them in the seductive fever, for men don't choose you, you
choose them.*

*Forever yours,
Forever in the Fever*

She loved the letter and appreciated his ability to express himself. He requested to see her again. She obliged as she truly enjoyed being in his company. He asked what he could do to prove his love for her. She said, "You can get a friend to come join us next time." He surprised her and called her bluff. He arranged with a married friend to join them at a time of her choosing. When he told her, she didn't believe him. He put his friend on a conference call and she was caught off guard. After they got off the phone, she realized that he really was a player and he knew how to play her game and maybe even beat her at it. She told him that all she really wanted was him and that she didn't need his friend anymore. She knew there was a lot more to him that she wanted to explore. Where he initially portrayed himself as weak and playable in order to get her attention, he turned out to be a lot more than she expected him to be. They became friends with ongoing benefits and he remained a Forever Bachelor.

NOTE: The difference between the Magnet and the Forever Bachelor is that the Magnet comes on strong with all of his might and possessions when he is actually weak and empty inside. The Forever Bachelor comes across as needing nothing and wanting nothing – he acts as if he will go with the flow and appears to be bobbing around in the water. He is actually a lover, a friend, and someone a woman wants to have in her life for the long-term. Where the Magnet takes value from the woman, the Forever Bachelor adds value to her life.

4. THE SPORTSMAN

Finally, the Sportsman is the weakest type of Player. The Sportsman has no magnetism, charisma, entitlement, status, or "It." The Sportsman is indiscriminate in his sexual partners. He is a self-centered, egotistical rabbit who simply wants a lay and a notch on the belt. This character is selfish in the sack. Although he prides himself on his sexual prowess, he is all about pleasing himself. He usually has a tight group of sleazy male friends who participate with him in the life style of sex, parties, and drinking binges. This is the character that many people think of when they refer to a "Player." He is similar to Don Juan in his sexual behavior, but he is no Don Juan. Where Don Juan is intelligent, pretentious, good-looking, well groomed, and seeking to impress the ladies at all times, the Sportsman doesn't much care about impressing anyone other than his friends and himself. He is confident and knows how to pour on the charm to catch a woman's interest. However, immediately after the encounter, the woman will realize that she served nothing other than an animalistic need. In spite of his reputation, women still want to be involved with him, mistakenly thinking they will be able to change him into a committed fellow. He is known in some circles as "the Banger [BangHer]." The Sportsman is often found on fraternity row and in college. However, the true Sportsman is a grown man who has failed to outgrow the "hooking up" that is rampant in today's college life.

INTERVIEW OF A YOUNG SPORTSMAN IN COLLEGE

1. *Gender:* Male
2. *Age:* 20's
3. *Education Level:* College
4. *Profession:* student/model
5. *Personal Status:* Single
6. *If single, are you looking for a long-term relationship or a meaningful one-night stand?* I am looking for a fun fuck body. I want a friend with benefits with NSA [no strings attached].
7. *Interests/hobbies:* Working out, reading, partying.
8. *What initially attracts you to the opposite sex? Past the initial attraction, what keeps you attracted?* Definitely looks and body first. And past that, I notice a nicer body. A person who is down to fuck (DTF),

66

go with the flow and is chill and cool about it. I don't like girls that stress about everything.

9. *What do you find appealing in a date?* Obviously past physical beauty and attractiveness, if we were to go out and if she had a nice ass, you would want her to show it off in a tight skimpy dress and have everyone look at her. I don't want the date to be forced to go to the next level. You want it to go the direction of sex on its own. Being on a date, you want it to actually be fun. I would like to have a nice conversation as well.

10. *What do you find to be a turn-off in a date?* Sometimes on a date, I don't care much about what they say; I just hang with it. Sometimes they talk and gossip. I hate it when they gossip about people and complain the whole time. I like a positive attitude and outgoing girls. An over-achiever kills. A women's rights activist is just a no go. They try to be too masculine to be equal, rather than chilling. There is a place for everything and when you are on a date, you just want to chill.

11. *Where do you meet people?* Everywhere and anywhere.

12. *When you are out with your friends and you see someone who catches your eye, what do you do?* I tell my friends I am going to approach her. Then we judge her physically as a group. The question before the judges would be, "Would you?" The first would say, "I would." The second would say, "I definitely would." Then, I would go for it. A big time criterion is how a woman carries herself -- like her swagger and knowing she is the shit, even if she's not. There are a lot of girls that can be potential, but are snobby and don't have it. If the girl is by herself or with another girl friend, it's easier to approach. If she is with a bunch of girls, it's harder to approach. For instance, if there are a few girls that might interest us boys, but there are one or more guys hanging around with them, we just don't approach. That takes the wind out of the whole thing. The ironic thing is that you wonder why the girls don't come and approach us. The best way to approach girls is to have them be with another girl friend without a guy around.

13. *Where do you hang out?* Beach, school, frat.

14. *What are your thoughts about online dating?* It's for losers. It's a half-assed attempt at dating when you are afraid of rejection. You can't have a fear of rejection and hide behind the screen. I think it's for much older people; it's for people over 60 who have lots of time on their hands and don't really know where to meet their own kind.

15. *Have you ever had trouble moving on from a past relationship?* It is always hard to break off a relationship and to get over it. For that reason, you should never make the other person the center of your life. You must have yourself be the center of your attention and have hobbies, friends, and activities that are part of your being. Of course, if you invest time and effort in a relationship, it is always harder to get over it. But you should look at it as people come and go, but the only one who stays is yourself. If you love yourself and you are well rounded with good morals, you can pick up and go. You can learn from it and evolve or repeat the same scenario over again.

16. *What are your rituals for preparing for your date?* Shower, shave, pregame dump and, if you don't want to be horny before the date, you do a pre-game beat-off.

17. *Where do you go/what do you do on a date?* If you don't know the girl, the best place would be the movies. Movies are a fail safe. You don't know if you are going to hit it off with the girl or not. When I took a girl out for the first time, we hit it off so well that, in the middle of the movie, we got up and left to neck. A movie is a safe bet if you don't know how you can mingle with her. You go out on a date with a girl to get in her pants sometimes with or without dinner and they are okay with it. The girl that you think is more worthy and needs a little more nudging, you spend time and money to get into her pants. The next time you just do a booty call.

18. *If you don't know your date well, do you meet at the designated place or do you pick your date up?* I usually pick her up at her house. In college, people hang every Thursday and Friday night. Having a girlfriend in college for the first few years is pretty hard. It's not a cool thing to do.

19. *How often do you have a boys' night out? Where do you go with your friends?* Mini golf, action movies, order in pizza and watch t.v. Sometimes hanging at home with the boys is really nice.

20. *What do you hope to happen when out with the guys?* Act silly and goofy.

21. *What frustrates you in the dating scene?* I don't like the expectations and the emotions. Sometimes you just want to have a girlfriend with benefits (fuck friend). Sometimes you just don't want to go with girls that require work. In school, you are constantly surrounded by alcohol, girls, and parties. It is so hard to be with one person and if you are

with one person, you end up cheating and breaking up. So, it is much easier to just not date or have a relationship.

22. *What are you looking for in a relationship?* Spontaneity. It can't be forced. You put in time; they put in time. It is good to take care of and to be taken care of. I want someone who surprises me and keeps life happening. She must be sexually compatible. It would be nice if I did not have to be the initiator all the time.

23. *Would you go out with someone who has a boyfriend?* Yes. It is so much more kinky and sexual. Humans suck. A lot of times guys cheat on their spouse or girlfriend with girls who are usually less attractive, less desirable and less classy because it adds a little kinkiness to things. If someone is older than you, it can be kinky and gives you an adrenaline rush. I did cheat on my girlfriend and the feeling was good while I was doing it, but after the fact, I felt guilty . . . but not that guilty.

24. *Do you mind if your date smokes?* Yes, smoking is a big/huge turn off for me.

25. *Are you hoping to find a woman who is financially secure?* If she were already rich, it would be total turn-on. Money is always a turn-on.

26. *Would you consider financially supporting a woman with whom you happen to fall in love?* I am not much into supporting the woman. It is not a turn-on at all.

27. *How does it make you feel if your date flaunts her assets?* You really don't want her to talk about it, but rather to have it without saying anything. You want them to be classy about it, not trashy about it.

28. *What type of clothing do you prefer your date to wear?* Cocktail dress. It could be slutty. Something to show skin. If they got it, flaunt it. High heels. No underwear preferably.

29. *What is your preferred body type and shape for a woman?* 5'8" ish, skinny, fit with boobs. A butt is a plus.

30. *How do you feel about tattoos and piercings?* Body piercings are hot on the belly. Tattoos can be a turn-on in the lower level.

31. *How do you feel about perfumes and colognes?* Odor can kill. Too much perfumes sucks.

32. *How important is the first kiss?* Really important because it shows you how compatible you are sexually. However, you can learn how to kiss.

33. *Do you want to pay on the first date?* I'll pay.

34. *What is your preference and philosophy on who should pay the bill on dates with you?* The guy should pay the dinner bill and, if the girl wants to pay for dessert, that would be fine.

35. *What are the most appealing things a date can do?* Turning her phone off before dinner is okay, but if your phone doesn't ring during your date, it means you're not popular.

36. *Would you have sex with your date if she were drunk?* It depends on how drunk. At parties you are usually drunk and that is what you do.

37. *Do you wear boxers or briefs?* Boxer briefs.

38. *How do you make sure a new sexual partner is free of STD's?* If you are drunk at the parties, it doesn't matter. The word gets around if a girl is a slut and sleeps around and has some kind of a disease.

39. *Once you have decided to have sex with your date for the first time, are you free and uninhibited in the act or more conservative and reserved than normal?* If drunk, you go all out, but if normal, you kind of keep it less aggressive.

40. *Where would you feel comfortable having sex with your date?* Car is fine. It is not very formal. Home makes it too formal. Car is easy and fast.

41. *Where is your favorite place to have sex?* My bed.

42. *Do you use protection and, if so, who provides it? If you don't use protection, how do you stay safe or is it an issue?* I do. I do.

43. *What do you do if protection is not immediately available?* Never happened.

44. *What if you liked your date and she did not return your call the next day or week? What would you think and do?* I will call once or twice and drop it.

45. *What if your date called you a month later? What would you say and do?* You go along with it. Whatever.

46. *What age range do you date?* 18+

47. *What do you think of one-night stands?* They are very common in college. If you are keeping your standards high and doing it for fun and it's mutual, then it's cool.

48. *How do you break off a one-night stand or short relationship without being hurtful?* I say, "I gotta go workout." Then, I gradually call less and less, hoping she gets the message.

49. *How do you characterize yourself?*
    Positive attributes: Good looking, nice body, good personality, sense of humor, nice smile, and smart.
    Negative attributes: Talk too much, narcissistic.
50. *Please include a detailed description of your ideal date.* Club, dancing, hotel, roses, champagne, dinner and breakfast.
51. *When you meet someone new, how long does it take you to know if the person is "the one" or has the potential to be "the one"?* I know right away.
52. *Do you believe in "love at first sight"?* No. I am not a firm believer in love at first sight.
53. *What is your personal philosophy on cheating?* Cheating is bad, but once in a while, if you have to do it, it means something in your relationship is missing and you're looking elsewhere for it.
54. *Do you believe there is a game people play when dating? If so, describe the game.* Some girls play hard to get. If a girl is way into you, it's scary. Like she laughs hysterically at every stupid joke you say, texting continuously and shit becomes a turn-off and, when they stop texting, then you want to text them again. I like the chase; it makes it more exciting.
55. *Is the dating game a mystery or are the rules clear? If clear, what are the rules?* Don't be too over interested, keep your cool. Timing is important, don't ever overstay your welcome, leave some room for imagination, don't share it all at once.
56. *Do you believe emotions interfere with the dating process?* Yes. People can get attached too fast and that can create problems.
57. *Have you ever been on a date with a girl who turned out to be a bitch?* Yes. She pretended to be detached and not into the conversation, like too mature. Why was she even out with me if she was going to be such a bitch?
58. *If interested in your date, how long do you wait to communicate with her?* A day.
59. *If you were not interested in dating her again, would you let her know?* No, she'll figure it out.
60. *Would you mind if your date contacted you immediately after the date?* No, not if I liked her.

Below the belt questions:

1. *Is sex an important factor in deciding whether you will continue to date someone?* Great sex yes. It is a plus.
2. *Do you enjoy it when your date wears lingerie?* It's cool.
3. *What is sexy to you in a woman?* The way she carries herself.
4. *Does the size of her breasts matter?* Yes. C is nice.
5. *Do you mind surgical enhancement of breasts, lips, teeth, etc?* I don't mind as long as I don't notice it.
6. *Are skimpy, body-fitting outfits a turn-on or a turn-off? Turn*-on!
7. *What do you think of coffee houses as a place to meet someone?* It's really cool. It is a lot more intellectual.
8. *Do you prefer a particular pubic hair design?* No hair.

THE SPORTSMAN PLANS FOR ESCAPE

At the yacht club we were hanging with the friends. We were drinking, laughing, flirting and having a good old time. Around closing time, we all paired off. The club has been our weekly hang out for years and most girls coming to the club have known us in more ways than one. I took a new girl home with me that night. She was hot and ready to party. It was about 1:00 a.m. when we arrived at my place. We had a couple more drinks and then started fooling around. We ended up having mad, passionate sex. Around 5:00 a.m. that morning, she was still there in my bed and I had to get rid of her.

I got out of bed and put on my old high school tuxedo with ruffles. After I was fully dressed, but still unshaven, I woke her up and told her that I had a very important meeting to attend that morning and she had to go. She looked at my attire and said, "It must be a very important function so early in the morning as you are wearing your ruffles." She got up and left. Right after she left, I took off my tuxedo and crawled back into bed.

BYE-BYE LARD ASS

We were fraternity brothers and we lived the life of the fraternity. We went to a bar near the local university and got in with our fake ID's. There was a knockout thirty-year old professional woman at the bar. We did a quick Roe Sham Bo and he won. My friend made his moves and the woman went for it. He ended up going home with her in her car.

She lived at least twenty minutes from campus. They had drunken sex. He dozed off, but woke up in a fright. He realized that she was not as attractive as he thought; the beer goggles had worn off. She was not bad enough to qualify as coyote ugly so that he would have to eat off his own arm to get away, but he had an urgent need to get out. He woke her and asked her to drive him back to campus.

She told him that she would take him back in the morning. He kept waking her every half hour, insisting that she take him back. Every time, she looked more ugly. He told her that he had an exam first thing in the morning and he still needed to study for it. She said dismissively, "You college boys always worry about your exams when I have important work in the morning. I need my beauty sleep." He kept pestering her until she blew a gasket. She refused to drive him home and assured him that she would get him back to school in the morning. She threatened him not to disturb her again.

Panicked, he rifled through her purse and found her car keys. He got into her car and turned on the ignition. He honked the horn to get her attention and he saw her looking out of the window. She opened the window and yelled at him, asking what the hell he thought he was doing.

He yelled back at her as he stepped on the gas, "Bye-bye lard ass!" He floored the gas pedal, peeled out, and drove himself back to campus. He parked the car and left the keys in the ignition. We never heard how long it took her to find her car.

TOO MANY GIRLS, TOO LITTLE TIME

He was a freshman in the fraternity who was finding it very difficult to manage his old life with the new life of too many girls and too many parties. He had a girlfriend, but found that he simply could not remain faithful with all of the temptations. He did not want to lie to her so he figured the only thing he could do was to break up with her. He took advice from his older fraternity brother as to how to break off his relationship. He texted his high school sweetheart as follows:

> Dear Bear,
> Being in a frat is so much fun. I'm sure that you are
> having fun in the sorority as well. It must be hard to
> remain faithful to me and not hang with other guys 'cuz
> it is certainly hard for me to not hang with other girls. I love
> you too much and I think it would be best for us to be free
> while we are at different schools. I hope you understand.
> Love,
> Bear-Bear

He felt really good about himself for being honest with his high school love. A few days later, he received a large envelope in the mail. He opened it to find an 8X10 picture of her giving a blowjob to some guy. He was heart-broken and devastated. He really did love her and couldn't believe his eyes.

He went ballistic and reacted without thinking. He did the only thing he could think of – he sent the picture to her parents.

THE BABY DOLL BLANKET

I had a friend and we used to go clubbing together. He was a player. He got a girl pregnant and ended up married and divorced. I moved in with him after his divorce. His daughter was around eight years old at the time.

While living there, I picked up a girl for a one-night stand. I took the girl back to our place and I lit a nice romantic fire in the fireplace. She was begging me to do her in the ass. I'll lick ass, I'll do ass, but nobody is going to touch my ass. She kept begging, so I agreed to do her like she wanted. We were there in the living room, pretty drunk. I was hitting it and hitting it and all of a sudden, it ripped and shit was spraying out everywhere. It kept coming out. I didn't know what to do. The girl started crying. I quickly grabbed a baby blanket that was on the floor to try to clean things up before my roommate came down the stairs. It turns out that I had grabbed his daughter's doll blanket – I threw it into the fireplace and it exploded, sending liquefied smoky shit all over the house. When the smoke cleared, the girl was hysterical and my roommate was standing over me shaking his head, saying "Howie, Howie, Howie," in disappointment, disbelief and despair. He said, "Oh, how could you do this to me?" He has never let me live it down. Every birthday since, he has given me a doll and a blanket.

BACK IN THE SADDLE AGAIN! AN INTERVIEW WITH A FIFTY YEAR OLD SPORTSMAN

1. *Contributor age:* 50's
2. *Gender:* Male
3. *Education Level:* College
4. *Profession:* Entrepreneur
5. *Personal Status:* Divorced
6. *How is dating different for you today?* Single life is not much different than it was when I was in college. The only difference is that now girls mean "yes" when they say "yes" and they mean "no" when they say "no." They are more open about sex and what they want. The key is to be honest with everyone about what you want and how many people you are seeing at the same time. I date women from the ages of twenty-nine to forty-nine. Some are dumb as doorknobs; they are obtuse about what I am really after and what dating is about. But most women understand the logic of dating. I am most comfortable with girls around the ages of thirty-six to forty-two. It is most important for me to find someone who can keep up with me. I love to party all night long.

   If my wife had not asked for a divorce, I would eventually have asked her for one. After my divorce, it took me three months to get back in the groove of things. I quickly learned that girls could be as deceiving as guys in dating.

   The first girl I went out with after my divorce played me. She lied and she was deceiving. I learned that the girls who are really interested in you want to see you on Thursday, Friday and Saturday. The other ones see you as a filler between Sunday and Wednesday. Thursday and Saturday are the most prestigious nights for date nights. She made me believe that she loved me and I was the only guy in her life. I helped her move out of her ex-husband's house. After I spent my entire day helping her move, she said she was tired and wanted to rest. I found out that she actually went out with another guy that night.

She would ask me to buy her stuff. I found out later that her Sunday through Saturday guys were all buying her expensive stuff. I eventually caught up to her lies, broke it off, and got smart. I didn't get attached to anyone for a long time after that.

I did eventually get emotionally involved with this girl who I met on Yahoo Personals. She was a thirty-seven-year-old model. On our first date, we went to a restaurant in town. There, I saw an old acquaintance who sent a bottle of wine to our table. Before I knew it, he was sitting at our table and horning in on our date. He literally sat there with us, enjoying the wine, for an hour. The owner of the restaurant finally took pity on me and asked him to leave us alone. After our date, I walked her to her car. We hugged, but she wouldn't kiss me. The next day she called me; she didn't like to text. She preferred the phone. She asked if I could go to the restaurant to look for her sunglasses. I did and the owner and I spent three hours looking for them, but we couldn't find them. I called her to let her know that I couldn't find them and she told me she thought I was very special to spend three hours of my time looking for her sunglasses. She later told me that she fell in love with me at that point.

On our next date, I took her to Monterey for a day. We had a lovely day. When we drove back to her house, we had a few drinks. She thought that I was too drunk to drive home and she insisted that I sleep on her couch. I agreed to stay on the couch if she would sleep on the couch with me. She agreed, but made it clear that we were not going to have sex. She drove me crazy!

We got naked and engaged in heavy petting on the couch, but she wouldn't have sex. I went home the next morning and returned to her house later the next day. That day, we did it at her house. I made love to her. The difference between sex and making love is that sex is fun, passion, passion, passion, and you know there is no connection. Making love is having a connection with chemistry.

She knew that I was dating two other gals at the same time. After four weeks of dating, I started seeing her on Saturdays and Sundays. We were spending our weekends together. She became my main girl. At that point, she asked me to choose between her and all the other girls. She asked me where our relationship was going because she was getting emotionally involved. She needed a commitment from me. She asked me to make a decision. I committed. I bought a $65 thousand dollar diamond ring and proposed to her.

After two months of engagement, she changed. She saw that I had a life insurance policy that would benefit my kids and she wanted me to put her name on it instead. I told her that we were not married yet. She started wanting more and more. She became a money grubbing woman. We started fighting over small things. She turned out to be a total bitch. I told her that I thought she was just in it for my money. I decided that, if we were going to stay together, I needed her to sign a prenuptial agreement. She got upset and walked out. After she walked out, she called me every fifteen minutes. I told her to stop calling me and I told her that we were over. I asked her to return the ring to me.

I went to her place to talk to her about it. She said, "Do you really think it is all about the money?" She punched me in my face with the big old rock. I told her she was a psycho bitch. My eye was bleeding profusely. I went into the house, cleaned up my eye, and took a picture of my wound. I told her that we were over and that I would call the police if she kept bothering me. She gave me the ring and I left. I seem to have lost the ring somewhere; I haven't seen it since. She called me a year after our break-up. We had sex again, but I didn't feel anything for her – it was only sex. There was nothing there; it was over.

7. *What do you think about online dating?* I love online dating. It is a constant source of dates. At least you know you can always get some for cheap. Everyone lies about his or her age and weight. I always ask how current the photo is. I only do coffee dates with the on-liners; I go to Starbucks. I met this one girl on-line and asked her if the picture was current and she said that it was current within three months. I arrived at the coffee shop early and was working on my phone when a girl sat at my table. I didn't recognize her. It was crowded and I thought she was just waiting for another table. Then she said, "So, are you disappointed?" I couldn't believe it was the same woman that I saw online; she had to be 50 pounds heavier and a good ten years older. I told her she didn't look like her picture. She acknowledged that the picture was old and explained that she didn't think I would go out with her if I had seen her current picture. I got up to leave and told her that if she thought I was going to start a relationship with someone who lied at the beginning, she was crazy.

8. *What initially attracts you to the opposite sex?* Eyes first, then hands, and finally boobs. They need to take care of themselves and be active.

9. *What is a turn-off?* A foul mouth and no loyalty to friends; a woman who stabs her friends in the back is the worst. A woman who doesn't like kids is a no-go; they must want to have grandkids. I will never date a woman who never had kids. I can't stand women who are late all the time. It is disrespectful.

10. *Where do you meet people?* Everywhere. I look at their hands to see if they are married. If they are, I know they are looking for NSA (no strings attached) fun and that can be fun. The married girls pay in cash for hotel rooms. These days you have to be careful with STD's. 90% of time the girls ask for protection. You have to watch out for the other 10%.

11. *If married, would you cheat?* No. I am not looking to get married again. I don't believe in love at first sight, I believe in attraction and lust.

12. *When you are out with your friends and you see someone who catches your eye, what do you do?* I go over and meet her if she has been looking my way. I go over to her and say things like, "You have been looking over my way all night. Are you interested in me or my friends? You can have any of us; it's your choice." Sometimes, I'll go up to a woman and say, "You deserve me." That always gets a laugh. Other times, I'll say, "Here is my phone number, do you want to go out or not?" In a bar, 75% of the women appreciate the fact that you go up to talk to them. The other 5% are scared to death that the guy is a rapist. 70% react positively when you approach them.

    When the girls are going to the bathroom, I stop them and tell them, "I just wanted to see what my future wife looks like." I might ask them, "What nationality are you? You have no Italian in you? Would like some?" If I ask a woman whether she would like to dance and she declines, I will respond with, "I suppose that means a blow job is out of the question?" They laugh and then dance with me.

13. *Have you ever had trouble moving on from a past relationship?* No. When I say it is over, I am done. Later in the interview, he shared this story: I got a girl pregnant and her parents found out. They basically wanted us to get married. The father asked her to get an abortion. I fell in love with her, but she moved away. I got over her after a couple of weeks. The best thing to do is to find another girl immediately. Be with your friends. I saw her again years later and she had let herself go.

14. *Do you wear boxers or briefs?* Boxers now.

78

15. *Tell us about one-night stands.* You don't tell people that you are going to have a one-night stand. You have to see where the date goes. There is one gal who I met in a bar. We had what would typically be a one-night stand that night, but I still hang out with her. She became a fling and has become a good friend. I don't want a relationship right now. I am busy at work.

16. *Is there swapping of dates between friends?* That depends on the friends. If it was just a one-night stand, we ask if the other guy minds. There are some guys who think nothing of doing your last girl.

17. *What kind of people do you see in the dating scene?* Single girls who want to create an image for themselves; they are looking for a high roller. They are gold-diggers. Married ones are looking for a champagne good time. There are guys who don't spend money like crazy, but are high rollers. The ones who spend a lot of money want to look rich, but they are often not.

    There are certain girls who you just know are gold-diggers. I met one gold-digger at the park. This girl was all over me. We went out to dinner. The drunker she became, the more her personality came out. She started asking me about my money, my house, my job and I told her she needed to take a Valium. I told her that I wasn't interested. She was the ultimate gold-digger. She wore a short mini skirt showing off her great legs. She wore a low cut top showing her cleavage. She was very attentive, taking care of all my needs from blowing my nose to blowing my hose.

    Dallas is the number one gold-digger town. They all look like expensive call girls. The girls look for rich dudes. They know how to play the game. They even take sex lessons. They dress to the hilt and have tons of cosmetic surgery. They are well versed in whatever they need to be; they know just enough. They know when to open their mouths and when to shut up. They know how to be proper in front of people.

    Laguna beach is also a high roller singles' place.

18. *Describe your ideal date:* I would like to go with a girl for a weekend in Venice.

19. *How does a man like to be treated by a woman?* A man wants to be treated with respect; I want to cherish the woman. The woman should value the guy in all aspects. The man cherishes the woman by treating her well; he does everything to make her feel good.

20. *What do you want in a woman?* I want a best friend who is a sexual animal. It might not last forever. I lost my chance with a couple of girls by not moving fast enough. I'll get my chance when they break up.

21. *What is your opinion about women?* I love women. I can't live without them. I don't think women give themselves enough credit because they know that this is a man's world. My daughter is a go-getter -- she is not going to take any shit from anyone. I want her to be strong.

22. *What frustrates you about the dating scene?* Peoples' misconceptions. Most people think that single people are just hanging out and having sex without having meaningful conversations. The truth is that single people bond with each other and depend on each other. We all build good friendships to help one another. And we have sex. This reminds me of a funny story:

    We all went to a Shoreline concert. There was a pre-party at my house at 2:00 in the afternoon. The concert started at 6:00 that evening. We were blasted by the time we got to the concert. There were seven girls and six guys. We went to the bar and bought more drinks, looked for a spot on the lawn and, during the next three sets of musicians, I started kissing all the girls around me on the lawn. It was a big orgy. Then we went back to my house. We drank more. The girls slept on my couch. I took them to my bed and we all kissed.

23. *How would you describe yourself?*
    Positive: Amicable, I am romantic, generous, ambitious, aggressive in a positive way, I think I am very self confident and egotistical. Social butterfly, loud and obnoxious. It is a situation where the good can also be the bad; it is the Yin and Yang. **Negative:** I can be considered to be egotistical, abrasive, politically incorrect, and aggressive. If I want something I will get it. People like me better today than they did when I was younger and married. I am probably known as a partier.

24. *Describe the dating game.* There is a game that people play. Women play more than the men do. When you get a woman sexually and emotionally aroused, they are honest with you. The Internet dating game is the same bullshit where it is easier to play the game and lie about yourself.

25. *Anything else?* Yeah. You do have to be careful out there. I went to this party with my friends. We caught a ride with another guy. We were drinking and dancing and having a great time. My friend and I

woke up at my house the next morning and neither of us could remember anything from that night beyond 10 p.m. We have wracked our brains and we have asked around, trying to figure out how we got home. We have concluded that someone slipped us a "mickey." Never leave your drink unattended!

Below the belt questions:

1. *Is sex an important factor in deciding whether you will continue to date someone?* Absolutely. If the first kiss sucks, it is over. When you kiss, the lips and the tongue need to fit together right. It can't be too slow or too fast. After the first kiss, you should want the second. I have been disappointed when I found great girls who were bad kissers. In fact, one was so hot that I asked her to try again. I had to tell her that I wasn't feeling it. She literally sucked.

2. *Do you enjoy it when your date wears lingerie?* Yeh. It is not a big deal though. I prefer sexy clothes over lingerie.

3. *Do you have any preferences as far as pubic hair is concerned?* I prefer clean versus bushy. I like a landing strip. Most women manicure. Back in college, most didn't manicure.

4. *Have you ever experienced ménage à trois?* Twice. Two guys and one girl. I have two girls who have been asking to do something together with me recently. One is married and the other one is single. I want to go with the flow. I haven't said "yes" or "no."

5. *What is sexy to you in a woman?* Minimum bra size of C. I love a woman who can dance well and who can actually have a conversation with me. I want her to show me a little PDA [public display of affection], I like her to touch me when we are together. I love to sex text. A nasty text is sexy. As an example, she writes, "How is your cock?" I respond, "Hanging around right now in a meeting." She texts, "How do I get his attention? I am getting wet thinking about you." I write, " How would you make it worth my while, are you a sure thing? Will you do your job well?" She replies, "I want to do my job well for you." The girls love acting out. If we are going out that night, we work up to it all day with naughty texts. Once we see each other, she rapes me. I like the woman to be aggressive.

6. *How many sexual partners have you had in your life?* Close to 1000 in college. We had a contest in our fraternity where we wanted to see

who could do the most new girls at each sorority house for the semester. We called this sport fucking. I won semester after semester.

We also had an annual party known as the Box Party. We had a four-story house. We would get all the pledges to get refrigerator boxes and then we would make a maze out of them. We would put mattresses here and there in the maze. The maze was pitch black. We would hand out maps of the maze to the guys so that we would know where to take the girls. One night, I was with 7 girls at different times. It was like an orgy; you could hear moaning and groaning all night long. Looking back, it was really disgusting; the mattresses were filthy.

B. The Gold-digger: Takes your money and runs.

The ultimate user of others, the Gold-digger climbs the rungs of the socio-economic ladder to fulfill himself or herself with material goodness. However, the Gold-digger is lacking something inside and will never be satisfied, no matter how high up the ladder he or she is able to climb. Never satisfied, they swing like Tarzan from one wallet to another. They usually hold out for the wealthiest mate in the area. While they hope to marry their victims, they are willing to be kept in luxury. A Gold-digger is a perfect fit for an affluent individual with sexual and emotional needs.

Flaunting their sexuality and their physical beauty at the potential victims, Gold-diggers offer themselves in a planned and controlled fashion, ultimately capturing an emotional attachment from their victims. They understand that their victims are attracted to shy, innocent and naïve persons. Accordingly, the Gold-digger acts the part. They treat their search like a job, seeking a lucrative resulting affair. They are skilled, detail-oriented, and good planners in their mission of catching the big fish. They have the uncanny ability to find the biggest fish in the pond. They can spot another Gold-digger a mile away and they tend to give one another a wide berth. Gold-diggers cannot succeed unless they are good people persons. They are typically sociable and pleasant to be around. They are always ready, very well dressed, and they appear to be completely enthralled with their potential conquests. They will make their victims feel desired and wanted by showing the victims the time of their lives.

They are smooth operators. Having completed their research prior to acting, they know their subject matter well, appear financially secure, and pretend to be very generous with their money. They act amiably, agreeing with whatever their potential conquest says, not offering their own opinions until after they have tied the knot. They drive expensive cars, but may not own them. They wear designer clothes, but their credit cards are often maxed to the limit.

Once they have captured a mate, Gold-diggers go back to their old routines and let their bodies go until it is time to search for their next conquest. They will not commingle their funds earned from their prior conquests; they will insist upon living off of the new conquest's money. Gold-diggers suck their victims dry. They start with small items like clothing, jewelry, personal goods, and small luxuries. They then move on to club memberships, cars, and houses. They make sure they are set up for the future before they move on to the next wrung of the ladder. They leave their conquests broken and confused.

The Gold-digger is raised to be what she or he is. It is not that they are bad people; it is that they have never learned any other way. Like everyone else, they are a product of their environment. Typically coming from a family that has emphasized the value of material goods ahead of everything else, they are pretentious and have lived a façade from a very young age. They have not lived within their means and have kept up with the Jones' at whatever cost. Lacking self-respect, Gold-diggers rely upon appearances and the material bounties of others to make them who they are. The lessons in materialism continue from generation to generation. The children of the Gold-digger follow the lead of the parent, making the proper connections in life and befriending only those children who will lift them into a higher social circle.

Many Gold-diggers have had trouble throughout their youth with a parent of the same sex and have grown to dislike and distrust others of the same sex. For example, a female Gold-digger will have serious issues with her mother and will dislike most other women. She needs other women in order to climb the ladder, but they are only a part of her life to serve a means to the end. Gold-diggers are the quintessential leaches as they will, without compunction, use whomever they can, male or female, to better their social standing and circle of friends. The "friends" are often manipulated into arranging meetings, communicating desires, and creating introductions for the Gold-digger. After the inroads are made, the Gold-digger jealously guards the new source of wealth and will not share new connections with the old "friends."

BEWARE: These individuals can be extremely manipulative and financially draining. If you are a person of wealth and find yourself to be in need of companionship, it would be cheaper to pay for an escort service than to get hooked up with a Gold-digger. Once in the clutches of a Gold-digger, you will be sucked dry. Be aware and be careful out there. One large clue that you may have come across a Gold-digger is the clothing he or she wears. They wear head to toe labels and want you to think that they have money. Typically, self-assured people do not need to wear labels continuously. Continuously and conspicuously wearing labels may indicate that they are on the job and in their uniform.

THE GIGOLO

Coming from a lower middle class background, she fell in love and married into a higher socio-economic class. With the marriage, all of her material wants and needs were met. She gave birth to two children and the servants took care of the children: the chefs and daytime nannies dressed the children and fed them. The nighttime nannies helped the kids with their homework and read them nighttime stories before tucking them into bed.

She spent her time decorating the home, attending high-society functions, and running the household staff. She began to resent her husband for his continuous business travel, leaving her alone for weeks or months at a time. She surrounded herself with people who made her feel really good about herself. She needed constant affirmation and validation.

The marriage ended in a high-profile divorce. After the divorce, her new status became a millionaire divorcee with two kids. All eyes in the high-society singles' scene were on her. She enjoyed having everyone look at her as she entered the room. Her insatiable need to be the center of attention drove her to organize speaking engagements for herself, posing as a fundraiser/philanthropist. This put her on the map for others who may not have known of her available status. She was still in a vulnerable emotional state and was in danger of being swept off her feet. Knowing what to do, a man with the right moves would be able to capture her by validating her, by affirming her beauty, and by playing into her insecurities.

Here is my story:

I was a forever bachelor for good reasons. I held a professional job, selling medical equipment, and made a good living. I owned a beautiful co-op in Manhattan. I was considered to be good looking – tall, dark and handsome. I had women at my disposal on my whim. I had tons of friends. I enjoyed life immensely.

My longest relationship with a woman was six months. Once the excitement was gone, the relationship became a bore and the woman offered nothing of value to my life – I needed excitement. It would have taken an extraordinary situation to ever consider being tied down for the long-haul.

However, as I was getting older, there were times when I contemplated marriage as a means to having children, who could then carry on my legacy. But, then again, the thought of being permanently stuck with one woman in my life made me cringe.

What do you know – one night I was at a bar with my friends and they were discussing the latest high profile high-society divorce. I listened and they all laughed and joked about their own desires to move into the mansion. I got into the conversation at that point and I proposed a challenge for all of us. I suggested that we race to capture the heart of the newly available high-society divorcee. They laughed and accepted the challenge with one caveat – the game would be won by the one who married her. The caveat caught me off guard and I had to catch my breath. I thought, "What do I have to lose? I could have a family and live in the lap of luxury. Maybe this is the only way I can be temporarily committed."

The game was on. After some research, I was able to locate her whereabouts. She would be attending a fundraiser for a children's hospital. I bought a table and invited prominent doctors that I knew from my medical equipment sales business. I talked the organizer into setting my table up next to hers. The night came and I dressed to kill, wearing my expensive watch and my best shoes.

Luck had it that our tables were even closer than I expected. I browsed the room, located the tables and went off to find my group during the cocktail hour. I felt the entire room pause when she walked in. Whispers started. Unlike everyone else, I left and walked to the bar as if she did not impress me – I made sure she saw me walking away – our eyes met as I turned and walked out.

While at the bar, I caught a server and arranged for an exotic drink to be sent to her. I instructed the waiter to point me out to her when he handed her the drink. After talking with the waiter, she looked over and nodded with a smile, but rejected the drink. I nodded back, raising my drink to her. Strike one, but I captured her attention.

I waited to see where she would sit at her table before I chose my seat at my table. I wanted to be face-to-face from my table to hers. She saw me interacting with my guests all evening. I did not look her direction one time. During the auction after dinner, she bid for a trip for two to Italy. I bid against her. She really wanted the trip and I knew that she would keep bidding. I took the chance and kept bidding against her. We were laughing together throughout the bidding competition. I bid over the limits of my bank account and she let me have it.

There was laughter and excitement in the room and she said, "Maybe I should split it with you?" That was my cue. I said over the din of the crowd as I stood up, "I'll do one better. This is my gift to you. As long as you take me with you."

We had a captivated and mesmerized audience – waiting on her response. She smiled and said, "We'll talk later." There were whistles and oohs and ahhs. That was my lucky night and the audience helped me out.

As I went up to empty my bank account to pay for the trip, she was there paying for other items, one of which was a diamond necklace. I told her that the piece was beautiful, but not as beautiful as she. She smiled and blushed.

I told her that I could clear my schedule to accompany her to Italy on the following weekend. To my amazement, she agreed and we went to Italy. The romance began. I put on my best game. I called my friends and family, asking them not to contact me until I was sure that I had her. I could not believe my fortune – she was beautiful, filthy rich, and fun to be around.

This was no longer a bet – it was my future and fortune. It was a lottery ticket handed to me. The bet was as good as won. We dated for five months and I proposed to her. She declined the first time. I continued to romance her and, the second time, I made it a very special proposal in Paris under the Eiffel Tower. She accepted. We set the wedding date.

All I could think about at that point was the yacht, car, houses, private islands, and other luxuries that I was going to have. But I needed to seal the deal. I wanted her to give me a child to carry on my legacy and hold my spot in society.

She didn't want any more kids. She already had her two kids. I told her we were in love and we should have a special love child. We left it for future discussions. She then wanted a prenuptial agreement. I convinced her that love trumped all and she agreed. She succumbed to all of my manipulations and married me without a prenuptial agreement and with my baby in her uterus.

Our wedding was beautiful and my son and I would live in the lap of luxury forever after. She became clingy, insecure, needy and abusive, demanding too much of my time. I had too much money, too much fun, and too many beautiful women to be stuck in the house with her. Now, when I go out with my friends, we enjoy the new life of the rich and famous and all of the incumbent perks.

Trust me . . . when you marry for money, you earn every penny.

SECRETS OF A GOLD-DIGGER

1. *Contributor age:* 40's
2. *Gender:* Female
3. *Education Level:* College
4. *Are you financially secure?* Yes
5. *Profession:* Real estate agent
6. *Personal Status:* Divorced
7. *If married, how many times have you been married and for how long?* Three times.
8. *Interests/hobbies:* Shopping, traveling, entertaining and going out to restaurants, working out, girls weekend get-aways and girls' nights out.
9. *What initially attracts you to the opposite sex?* How they dress and carry themselves, what car they drive and what kind of watch they are wearing. A watch tells you a lot about a man.
10. *What do you find appealing in a date?* How generous they are with their money.
11. *What do you find to be a turn-off in a date?* Tight wads.
12. *When you are out with your friends and you see someone who catches your eye, what do you do?* I look at them and smile. If they look at me, I giggle.
13. *Where do you hang out?* Where I know good potential will be. I hang out at a few of the local exclusive bars where a lot of my fellow real estate agents hang out. That is a good feeding ground for clients as well as potential dates. I am always working the situation, wherever I go. If not a potential dating relationship, there is always the possibility of a potential client. Are they selling or looking to buy?
14. *What are your thoughts about online dating?* I have only looked at the most prestigious sites, as I don't want to waste my time by trying to figure out whether the person is worth my while. They prescreen for

me as far as financial potential. Then, I can screen for the rest of the package. I'm not sure about the whole on-line dating thing, though. You cannot really get a feel from people when they are hiding behind the screen; I am very good at reading people and I prefer to meet them in person.

15. *Have you ever had trouble moving on from a past relationship?* Not really, I move on when I am ready. Men usually don't leave me; I leave them.

16. *What do you think of one-night stands?* Someone who hasn't done her research or somebody who is very horny. You should never give it away if you are looking for a long-term relationship. That is all you have to work with; your body and your sexuality is your primary weapon and asset in love and relationships. You want to make sure that your mate appreciates you.

17. *How do you break off a one-night stand or short relationship without being hurtful?* I don't do one-night stands.

18. *What are your rituals for preparing for a date?* I take very good care of myself and I am always ready to leave the house looking fantastic. Your next husband could be waiting around the corner when you go to pick up your mail.

19. *Type of lingerie you would wear on a first date? And the following dates?* I am a true lingerie person. I show my man what a real woman should look like. In fact, I have an entire armoire dedicated to my lingerie.

20. *Where do you go/what do you do on a date?* I prefer the man to plan for a very nice night out, preferably at a very expensive restaurant. I enjoy dining with good company. I enjoy it when he looks at me and admires me.

21. *If you don't know your date well, do you meet at the designated place or does your date pick you up?* I expect him to pick me up in his beautiful car. If I don't trust him to do that, I won't go out with him.

22. *Would you be interested in going for coffee and a walk instead of a dinner date for the first date?* Coffee is stupid. If they want me to go out with them, they should fork it out. I am worth more than a cup of coffee.

23. *If you were a candy, what kind would you be and why?* I would be a box of Godiva chocolate. Savor my rich taste over time.

24. *How often do you have a girls' night out? Where do you go with your girlfriends?* Often enough and we go to very nice nightclubs and bars.

25. *What do you hope to happen when out with the girls?* I hope to meet someone with a lot of potential for a future relationship.

26. *What frustrates you in the dating scene?* Men pretending to have money when they don't. There are many men who are frauds – they dress well and wear expensive shoes and watches, but they have their credit cards racked up to the sky.

27. *What are you looking for in a relationship?* I am looking for a man who can support my spending habits and who adores me enough to do so without complaining. I am worth every penny. I will work hard to make him happy as well.

28. *Would you go out with a married man?* It depends on the circumstances. If he can afford both of us, sure . . . I don't mind. I've been a kept woman in the past and it really isn't so bad. However, I would much rather have him to myself.

29. *Would you date someone who had a child from another relationship?* If I find the right guy, I can deal with the kids. I would prefer not to deal with them though. They take attention away from me and I won't play second fiddle.

30. *If you were to live with someone, how long would you be willing to live with him without a permanent commitment?* I won't live with a man without a permanent commitment. He either commits or he doesn't.

31. *Are you hoping to find a man who is financially secure? Is financial security more important than love?* Yes, of course. I am old fashioned and I expect to be taken care of by my man. I will take care of him in other ways. In fact, my mother made sure that I knew how to take care of a man. She taught me a great deal in that area. For my 21st birthday, my mother sent me to a school in Dallas where I learned how to please a man sexually. It was a fantastic experience; I was able to get over my inhibitions and I learned how to drive a man crazy in bed. I learned both technique and the mental magic of a satisfied man.

32. *Would you consider financially supporting a man with whom you happen to fall in love?* No. I don't believe women's lib is all that it is cracked up to be. It leaves women doing three times the work; we not only have to take care of the kids and take care of the house, but now we are expected to make the bacon before we fry it up in the pan. It's getting easier and easier for the man in the relationship.

33. *How does it make you feel if your date flaunts his assets?* Love it. Love it. Love it.

34. *What type of clothing do you prefer your date to wear?* Very expensive, tasteful, and classy. I want his shoes to be shined; scuffs are a real turn-off. So are worn down heels. A man should also make sure he is nicely groomed. Clean and filed fingernails are important.

35. *What is your preferred body type and shape for a man?* Fit would be nice, but it is not required. In an ideal world, he would be fit and able to keep up with me.

36. *How do you feel about tattoos and piercings?* I don't like them, but they are not a deal breaker. Typically, the men I am attracted to don't have them. If they do, they got them when they were young and foolish.

37. *How do you feel about perfumes and colognes?* I don't mind either way.

38. *How important is the first kiss?* It's fine. I have learned to work with whatever I am given. I can always turn a kiss into one that he will never forget, no matter how good he is.

39. *Do you expect your date to pay on the first date?* Of course, and on every date thereafter.

40. *Will you have sex on the first date? If so, would you talk to your date about your preferences freely?* I will not have sex on the first date. I don't want to be a slut or just give it up for nothing. But I can guarantee that, once I get them in bed, they do not want me to go.

41. *Would you have sex with your date if he were drunk?* Of course. Alcohol is the best lubricant on the market.

42. *How do you make sure a new sexual partner is free of STD's?* I am very careful as it can affect my life forever. I make sure I take condoms with me, just in case he doesn't have them.

43. *Where would you feel comfortable having sex with your date?* His bed or my bed or a very expensive, well appointed hotel. Luxury is a turn-on. I like whatever bed we are in to have gorgeous linens. A nicely appointed bed can make you feel like a queen.

44. *Would you date a wealthy man who has a venereal disease?* Hummm!! I have never been in that situation. He would have to be very rich and use double condoms at all times. I might also have to use a female condom at that point, but . . . I don't think you are supposed to use both together. Yeh, that is a tough one.

45. *What if you liked your date and he did not call you the next day or week? What would you think and do?* I would care if I was interested and would want to know what happened. But if he doesn't call, I'll call

him to find out where he is with things. At a minimum, he can always be a potential client for my real estate business. I never cut a string if I don't have to.

46. *What if your date called you a month later? What would you say and do?* I wouldn't let a month go by -- I don't like to leave things swaying in the breeze.

47. *What age range do you date?* Age is irrelevant. It is attitude that dictates.

48. *What was your parents' status when you were growing up?* My parents divorced when I was eleven and my mother married three times after that. I lived with my mother and learned a great deal about people because we moved many times. Each of my mother's husbands was wealthier than the last. I guess money begets money.

My father was devastated by the divorce; he really loved my mother and I believe he still does, despite all that she put him through. Ever since the divorce, he has told me that I need to marry someone who can make me happy financially; he always felt that he couldn't support his family in the manner that we deserved on his public servant's income. He worked really hard and had an important job with the police department. He was proud of his job, but regretted that he could not be a better provider for his family. My mother never let him live it down. Before they married, he promised her that he would go to law school and that he would become an attorney. He always said the police job was a means to an end and that it was not permanent. My mother became pregnant with me and I suppose life happened and law school became a distant dream. The joke is, after all this time, my dad is now going to law school at night and he is dating one of his professors.

49. *How do you characterize yourself?*

   Positive attributes: Attractive, good body, beautiful face, good sense of fashion and style, great in bed.

   Negative attributes: I can't really think of anything.

50. *Please include a detailed description of your ideal date.* Ideally, a handsome rich man shows up in a limo to take me to the opera with private box seats, champagne is waiting for us chilled and ready to go. After the opera, we go to the most exclusive restaurant in the city and then to his house for a nightcap, but no sex. He wants me, but respects my body at the same time.

91

51. *When you meet someone new, how long does it take you to know if the person is "the one" or has the potential to be "the one"?* I know immediately upon looking and talking to him.

52. *Do you believe in "love at first sight"?* No. Money can buy love many times over. You can be in love and poor for the rest of your life. You can be content and satisfied with a man of means without being in love.

53. *What is your personal philosophy on monogamy and monogamous relationships?* It is required for me while in the relationship.

54. *Do you believe there is a game people play when dating? If so, describe the game.* Of course, put your best foot forward.

55. *If you were not interested in another date, would you let him know? If so, how would you let him know?* Yes. I will let him down gently and tell him that we can keep our relationship as friends and professionals. If he doesn't get it, I won't mince words.

56. *Would you mind if your date contacted you immediately after your date? No.*

57. *How much attention is too much or too little after the first date?* Never too much.

58. *On average, how many dates are required before you consider yourself to be in a relationship? What qualifies as a date?* If I am having sex, I am in a relationship with the guy.

59. *Is the dating game a mystery or are the rules clear? If clear, what are the rules?* It is clear to me. Find your potential mate and make sure he fits your requirements up front. They won't change for the better over time; they may change for the worse.

60. *Do you consider yourself to be a game-player in the dating arena?* No.

Below the belt questions:

1. *Is sex an important factor in deciding whether you will continue to date someone?* No. Some men can lose their interest in sex when they get older. I just want to pleasure them in whatever way they want to be pleasured.

2. *Do you enjoy wearing lingerie?* Yes!

3. *Have you ever experienced ménage à trois? If not, would you consider it?* No. Never.

4. *What is sexy to you in a guy?* The way he dresses and carries himself.

5. *Does the size of a penis matter?* Not really. It can be a bonus.

6. *Will you kiss and tell your friends or do you keep it private?* No, I keep my personal life pretty close to my vest. If I need help connecting with a potential suitor, I will surely ask my girlfriends for help. Sometimes, you need a girlfriend to set up the first introduction or to set up a situation in which you can meet and get to know the guy.

7. *What is your opinion about surgically enhancing your body? How much enhancement is too much?* I believe that it is up to the individual. Technology has gotten to the point where we can all look our best much further into our future. I have no problem with it so long as I don't end up looking like a cat.

8. *How many sexual partners have you had in your life?* I don't feel that I want to disclose that answer.

C. The Smotherer: Takes attention, your ring finger, and your space.

The Smotherers are attention-seeking and often find themselves rushing to love and pressuring their mates to the altar. They are needy. Smotherers pride themselves in the value they add to their mates' lives, working hard to be the best spouses imaginable. In fact, Smotherers can be very good spouses for those who don't mind providing continual love and affection. However, without getting to know their mate prior to marrying, the Smotherer often ends up in divorce court.

A Smotherer's identity is wrapped up in the couple and his or her role within the couple. The Smotherer has rarely been without a boyfriend or girlfriend and has never been able to stand on her or his own two feet. The Smotherers find validation through their dates and mates. There is very little time that elapses between the end of one relationship and the beginning of the next. Due to their continual and serial relationship status, the Smotherers never get to know themselves or to love themselves as individuals. They are afraid to be alone with themselves.

This type is often mistaken as a Gold-digger. There are some similarities, including the rush to the marriage and the appeal for wealth. The Smotherer is attracted to someone who can make him or her materially comfortable. The difference between the two is that, once married, the Smotherer is content and not looking to climb the next higher rung on the ladder.

The Smotherer is insecure and jealous in his or her relationships, often worrying that his or her partner will be looking for the next best thing.

The Smotherer will work very hard to make it work, but is often controlling at home. They make up for their lack of self-confidence with control. The Smotherers rarely cheat while in a relationship, but they are very flirtatious and love attention from the opposite sex. They are very conscientious about their physique. Growing old is poison to them. They like to think of themselves as perpetually physically young.

The Smotherer is ambitious and often academically intelligent. He or she can be a good earner and successful professionally. Unlike a Gold-digger, the Smotherer lacks social intelligence. The Smotherers love to talk about themselves, telling the same stories repeatedly to the same people. They rarely allow others, including their mates, to get a word in edgewise. They often become a drain on social occasions. They have a way of making it all about them. They are not good listeners and are extraordinarily opinionated, seeming to have an opinion about every subject under the sun.

Smotherers are fighting against the tide of loneliness; they repel others with their overzealous antics. While they seem to have a collection of many friends, the friendships are often superficial. Their few true friends tend to be even more needy than they.

BEWARE: What's the rush? Slow down. Don't declare yourself exclusively committed to one relationship until both parties have had a chance to assess their feelings.

INTERVIEW OF A SMOTHERER

1. *Contributor age:* 40's
2. *Gender:* Male
3. *Education Level:* Graduate Degree
4. *Profession:* Self-employed
5. *Are you financially secure?* Yes.
6. *Personal Status:* Divorced -- Once married for 4 yrs. One son. Looking for a long-term relationship and wants to get married.
7. *Interests/hobbies:* Work out, beach, ski, underwater scuba, surf, bike, black belt in Karate, writes novels, and loves to grill.
8. *What initially attracts you to the opposite sex?* Smile and then being a nice person with no insecurities.
9. *What characteristic is most appealing to you in a date?* Personality, sexy but not flaunty, good conversation.

10. *What characteristic is not appealing to you in a date?* Mean-spirited, conceited, or flirting with others while on a date with me.
11. *Where do you meet people?* Workout club, friends' houses, child's school, restaurants, but not bars.
12. *When you are out with your friends and you see someone who catches your eye, what do you do?* Nothing.
13. *What are your rituals for preparing for your date?* Shower, shave, and show up.
14. *Where do you go/what do you do on a date?* Dinner.
15. *If you don't know your date well, do you meet at the designated place or does your date pick you up?* Meat at the place.
16. *Would you be interested in going for coffee and a walk instead of a dinner date for the first date?* Yes.
17. *Do you treat dates differently when set up by a friend or relative?* I am much more courteous.
18. *How often do have boys' night out?* I'm not scanning when I'm out with the boys. We usually go to dinner after golf or a sporting event.
19. *What do you expect to happen when out with the guys?* Nothing, just having a good time with the boys.
20. *What frustrates you in the dating scene?* The lack of nice, available women.
21. *What are you looking for in a relationship?* A best friend and a lifetime partner.
22. *Would you go out with a married woman?* No. It makes me mad when they don't wear a ring.
23. *What about separated, but not divorced?* No way, they end up getting back together.
24. *Would you date someone who had a child from another relationship?* Yes. I have a child so I hope she would not have a problem with it either.
25. *If you were to live with someone, how long would you be willing to live with her without a permanent commitment?* I would be okay with living with someone for one year. I do not date anyone under 40.
26. *What type of clothing do you prefer your date to wear?* Nothing!
27. *What is your preferred body type and shape for a woman?* Lean and fit.
28. *How do you feel about tattoos and piercings?* Not big on either, but I can live with it.

29. *How do you feel about perfumes and colognes?* I do not want to smell her from twenty feet away. I have zero tolerance for body odor!

30. *How important is the first kiss?* Big time important; it gives me a taste of how comfortable she is with her sexuality.

31. *What if you liked your date and she did not call you back the next day or week? What would you think and do?* I would call her and, if she didn't return my call, I wouldn't bother any further.

32. *What if your date called you a month later? What would you say and do?* I would say, "What kept you?" If she had a reasonable explanation, then I would be okay with talking to her further.

33. How do you characterize yourself?

    Positive attributes: Gentleman, old school, proper, good manners, sweetheart, sensitive, forgiving, pleaser, considerate, understanding.

    Negative attributes: I can't think of any.

34. *Please include a detailed description of your ideal date:* A surprise trip to somewhere warm like Hawaii; surf, sand, dinner and drinks under the sunset.

35. *When you meet someone new, how long does it take you to know if the person is the "one" or has the potential to be the "one"?* Not very long.

36. *Do you believe in "love at first sight"?* Yes. Someone I connect with; someone whom, after the first date, you know you'll be with for a long time.

37. *What is your personal philosophy on monogamy?* It is a good thing.

38. *Do you believe there is a game people play when dating? If so what is the game?* Some people play. I don't like to play the game. Games have to go away. It is like hide-and-seek. It is good to be straightforward.

Below the belt questions:

1. *Is sex an important factor in your dating life?* Yes

2. *What do you think of sex talk on the first date?* Fine with me.

3. *How important is lingerie to you?* Not high on my list. Sometimes, it's okay.

4. *Have you ever experienced ménage à trois?* Yes. I will not consider it again.

5. *What is sexy to you in a girl?* Great eyes, smile and looks.

6. *Will you kiss and tell your friends or do you keep it private?* I never tell. I am very private.
7. *Do you treat dates with long-term potential differently than fun quickies?* Yes. No quickies for me.

A NEEDY MAN

He was married and is now divorced with a young son. His wife came and went several times before he finally drew the line and told her that he wouldn't take her back. She had never been sure about their relationship. He had proposed to her within weeks of meeting her and, while she liked him very much, she had allowed herself to be pressured into marrying him before she was ready. They quickly ended up pregnant.

After the divorce, he tried online dating, but he didn't like the feeling that his date would be able to go home and look at the fifteen or so other possibilities on the computer. It made him insecure to think that any of the others might be better than he. He couldn't shake the feeling that the on-line dates were looking for the next better person.

He met a woman for coffee on the suggestion of a friend. The woman was recently divorced and attempting to get back into the market, but she had that wide-eyed look that a deer has when looking into your headlights. She was nervous about the whole dating situation; she had only dated two men since her divorce and that made a total of three guys she had ever dated in her life.

The two seemed to hit it off right away; they majored in the same subject in college and they had an easy conversation. They laughed. They ran into friends at the coffee shop. It was light-hearted. At the end, he gave her his card and told her to call him. She went home and texted back within hours: "I enjoyed meeting you this morning; my number is ##########. Give me a call." That afternoon, he called her and they talked for hours. They set up a date for the next evening. He was going to cook for her at his home. She was very excited about their date.

They had a wonderful time at his house; he cooked an amazing meal and they shared wonderful stories into the evening. They kissed and he told her that he could easily fall in love with her. That night, he made it clear that, if he was kissing her, she could not be dating others. They set another date for the next evening.

She thought about what he said. She really liked him, but could not agree to an exclusive relationship at that point. She was not ready to

97

commit, and, frankly, she did not know him well enough to know whether she wanted to be in a relationship with him yet. The woman told him that there was a friend with whom she had previously set up a date and she wanted the opportunity to follow through with it.

He told her that he could not be with her if he was wondering whether she was looking for the next best thing. He told her to go find herself. She asked him whether he would still be interested in her if she explored a little and then called him back when she was ready. He indicated that he didn't want to be second choice.

She really liked him and decided that she didn't want to let him go. He introduced her to his son and they got to know one another, sharing dinners and evenings at home watching television and movies. They spent weekends at his house. She read bedtime stories to the little boy. She tucked him in at night. The man started hinting around about getting married after only three weeks. Afraid, she pulled the plug, indicating that she really did need to date some other people before she tied the knot again. He sadly let her go. She went off to pursue other dates and experiences, relieved.

D. The Home Wrecker: Takes your mate.

The Home Wreckers befriend you and slowly move in on your mate. They are usually attractive, cunning, and looking for a long-term relationship, but for some reason, they are unable to find love on their own. The Home Wreckers pretend to have no agenda other than friendship. They learn about their target over the years and slowly make their move. It is easier to move into an already established, familiar, and comfortable situation than to create one from scratch.

For instance, if it is a female executive secretary that is moving in on her boss, she will befriend the boss's wife and provide a listening ear when the husband is away on business. The Home Wrecker ingratiates herself with the wife by helping the boss to choose fabulous gifts for the wife; gifts that the Home Wrecker secretly desires. The wife will ultimately share with the Home Wrecker her frustrations and stories about the boss, which the secretary will tuck away for later use. At the same time, the boss ends up sharing his frustrations about his marriage with the secretary. The secretary knows all the cracks in the relationship. She will then use this information at the opportune moment to move in on the boss. This is the typical story of the "executive secretary wife-to-be."

BEWARE: There are many Home Wreckers out there. They are insecure and admire what you have, but they have no idea how to create and build it for themselves. They only know how to steal it. Be aware of the single friends who only hang around families and married people. Do not allow unrelated singles to infiltrate your family; singles with no agenda are usually more comfortable with other singles. This is why you'll hear a single person say that they have grown apart from their married friends. If you encounter a Home Wrecker in your relationship, remember that it is your marriage that is threatened. Do not fall into the trap; marriage is hard work; it takes patience, understanding, forgiveness, and trust to be success-ful. Before abandoning your ship to the Home Wrecker, think about all it took to build it and realize there are many pirates out there who want to take it over. They are only pirates. They go from ship to ship. Hang in there and protect your crew.

A RIDE HOME

It all started in the cheer classes. As the affluent mothers of the teen-aged daughters enrolled their girls to take lessons for upcoming competi-tions, the instructor befriended the families. She participated in their BBQ parties and was invited to birthday parties as well. Being young, attrac-tive, single, and available, she captured the eyes of the husbands. She had her pick.

The wives did not see her as a threat; instead, they viewed her as part of the family and enjoyed her exciting life and the company she provided. She was very good with the wives. When shopping with the wives, she would listen to their stories. She traveled with them for cheer competi-tions, keeping their secrets, offering to be the copilot on their naughty ad-ventures when necessary. At the same time, she befriended the husbands. She went shopping with them to help select the wives' birthday or anniver-sary gifts. She listened to the husbands' stories.

Gradually, she made her choice as to which husband she wanted. She chose the most powerful man amongst the group. She began subtle flirta-tions. After spending an evening with the family enjoying wine, watching movies, and playing cards, she mentioned that she had a little too much to drink. The wife invited her to stay over. The instructor said, "Thank you, but I'll just get a cab." The wife said, "Don't be silly, my husband will drive you home." That's where it all began.

The instructor had expected this answer. She and the husband got into his sports car and flew down the road to her house. As they drove up to the house, she put her hand on her forehead, claiming to have an awful headache. The husband walked her to the door. She pretended to be wobbly and he held her firmly. As he unlocked the door for her, she rested her head on his shoulder and looked up with adoring puppy eyes. Their lips met for the first kiss.

The kiss was long and passionate. He was taken by her at the first kiss; she had fallen in love with him long ago. He had been holding back for some time and now all bets were off. He asked to come in for a while. She declined and said, "Bring me coffee in the morning." She wanted him to be sure and to have no regrets. He went home and thought about what had happened. He was looking forward to his trip to Starbucks in the morning.

When he showed up at her door the next morning, she opened the door in her tiny, short jammies, already clean, showered, and made up. Her long blonde hair was draped around her little pert breasts. She looked like the little bad girl that he had been fantasizing about for a long time.

They did not waste a moment drinking coffee. They went straight into the bedroom and, two hours later, he left for work with a smile on his face. He couldn't stop thinking about her and texted her at noon on the same day. He texted, "How about coffee this afternoon?" She replied, "Come on over when you are ready. I'm waiting for you!"

This was most convenient for him. She had her own place and knew he was married. He thought that, since she knew the family, she would understand that he would never leave his wife. Little did he know, she thought that she could have him for herself and that he would leave it all for her.

The encounters went on several times a week, sometimes twice a day. He thought she was a fun toy to have on the side. He showed up every afternoon for sex when he was supposed to be going to work out. He wore his work out clothes and he worked out there. This went on for months and she began to hint to him that she wanted more of him. She pushed him to give her more. She threatened to end the affair if he could not provide more time for her. He made it clear to her that he would never leave his family. She began dating others, trying to make him jealous.

Meanwhile, she started working on the wife. When the wife shared a meaningless complaint or frustration about her husband, the instructor agreed and made it a bigger deal that it was initially. She started seeing the husband less and less and spending more and more time with the wife. When they went out together, the instructor introduced the wife to single men. The wife was not interested or comfortable with that. However, with the instructor's help, the wife gradually started feeling that her husband wasn't giving her the attention that she deserved. They started to grow apart.

The instructor's plan was working. The husband and wife began arguing frequently. The husband wanted to see the instructor more and more. She knew exactly what he needed at this point because she had orchestrated the rift between the married couple. She fulfilled him emotionally and physically where his wife was failing. They texted continuously throughout the day. She sent texts complementing his private parts. He texted back, "Thinking of you; missing you; wanting you; wanting to be inside you." She responded, "I'm thinking of kissing your cock." He then asked, "What do you want to do to me you dirty little girl?" She replied, "What do you want me to do to you?" He wrote, "Lick my lollipop until it pops!" He wanted her to treat him like a piece of meat and take control. She played the sleazy, dirty little girl that he wanted. That's all he really wanted.

One night, he texted her from home while in his bedroom. He accidentally left his phone on his nightstand while he went to take a shower. The instructor texted, "Bring me coffee in the morning. I'll suck your lollipop." The wife leaned over to look at the phone and saw the text, but there was no name with the text, only two stars. Her heart sank. She texted back, asking what the person would like in their coffee. The instructor responded, "The same as usual, silly." The wife asked, "Anything with the coffee?" The instructor replied, "Only your beautiful dick." The wife tried to find out who it was by asking her name. The instructor did not respond, now fearing that she was texting with the wife. She did not want to be found out. She replied, "Wrong number, sorry."

The wife was devastated. She walked into the bathroom and shook the phone at her husband while he was taking his shower. He couldn't see as his face was covered with soapsuds. The wife stood there with the shower door open, allowing the cold air to come into the shower. He rinsed off quickly, panicking and thinking how to respond. He asked her, "What are you doing?" She read the text to him. He said, "I don't know what is going on. I don't know who that is and there is nothing going on." She said, "Let's be real. We've been together too long for you to lie to me. Who is it?" He denied everything and they left it for the night. He slept on the couch.

The next morning, the wife called the instructor and told her what had transpired. The instructor came over to comfort her. The instructor told the wife that he must be having an affair with a text like that and she should think about leaving him. The wife had no intention of leaving him. The instructor didn't understand how the wife would want to stay when it was so obvious that he was cheating on her. The instructor did not realize that bimbos come and go, but the real wife and matriarch of the family is in ultimate control and will rarely abandon her post. She may not like it, but the family depends on her – she is the pillar of strength for the family unit. She may be put upon, but she will not abandon her post lightly. The husband won't leave either, unless the wife kicks him out into the hands of the bimbo. The instructor worked hard on the wife, but to no avail. The wife gave her husband an ultimatum to stop the affair or she would leave with the children. He was guilt-ridden and remorseful. He agreed and ended the affair with the instructor.

To the instructor's chagrin, the affair was over. She was devastated. She was desperate to have him. Having no other weapon available to her, she started spreading rumors about their affair and sacrificed her standing with the wife. The wife heard the rumors and could not believe that she had allowed herself to be manipulated by the "little tramp."

She confronted the instructor who denied everything. The wife told the instructor to stay away from her husband, home and family or she would make sure that the instructor would never have another client again for her business. The wife, in some way, felt sorry for the instructor as she had had a very hard life and was young and foolish. The wife advised the instructor to search for true love of her own and not to wreck another's family.

INTERVIEW OF A GULLIBLE HOME WRECKER

1. *Contributor age:* 30's
2. *Gender:* Female
3. *Education Level:* High school drop out
4. *Are you financially secure?* Yes
5. *Profession: The* arts
6. *Personal Status:* Single

7. *Are you looking for a long-term relationship?* Yes, that would be nice, if I find the right guy.

8. *Interests/hobbies:* Gambling in Vegas. I used to go when I was younger. I would go once a week. I wanted to do it professionally. One year, I won $40 thousand at one of the higher-end casinos. Most gamblers are from New York and Newport. The villa is where everyone wants to stay. I had a connection with my gambling friends who hooked me up with a villa one time. The dealers get to play with other peoples' money at other casinos. I was used as a pinch gambler once. They always trust the guy to play for the high-end gamblers, rather than the girl. They want to party with the girl; they don't trust her to do the job. There are not very many girl gamblers who are high rollers. I always take my girl friends with me and I pay for them, but I want them to leave me alone while I am gambling. I am taking up golf and tennis. I love watching the Food Channel.

9. *What initially attracts you to the opposite sex? Past the initial attraction, what keeps you attracted?* Their swagger and how they carry themselves. I want my guy not to be the normal guy in our area. I like guys that are not caught up with the scene here. This town is full of players. I like intelligent guys. I like sports and the stats that go along with them. They keep me intrigued. I like to watch all kinds of sports. My current boyfriend is perfect. He loves to watch sports. He is a "good guy." He has character. He cares about others; he is strong and honest even when he feels insecure.

10. *What do you find appealing in a date?* Insecurity is a turn-off. Guys say I make them insecure and that I am too good or too good-looking for them. Players are turn-offs. I tend to date older guys. My last boyfriend and I went out for two years; he was two decades older than I. After a year of being miserable, we broke it off. The ex-wife was the cause of most of our problems. There was a lot of jealousy from her. He and I had started dating before their divorce. I am friends with all my ex's. If the guy has children, I cannot plan my life around the kids' schedules. I want to see my men more than a couple of nights a week, regardless of the kids. I need to have my total freedom to go and come as I please.

11. *Where do you meet people?* I don't date a lot. I met one guy in Vegas. I met my ex at a car-racing event. It was a whole weekend thing. I met his kids. We found this dog on the racetrack and tried to find its owner; we liked each other immediately. I don't want to get married

and have kids. Most guys want to have fun with me; they treat me like a toy. For me, men and dating is very confusing. My life is crazy. Crazy things happen around me all the time.

12. *Have you ever had trouble moving on from a past relationship?* I have been dumped many times. When I was younger, I dated a man for two years. He was a wild bad boy. He would go out and party all the time. He and his friends would take off and go to Vegas. I found him in bed with another girl. I always forgive them and end up being their friends.

13. *What do you think of one-night stands?* They are a lot harder to get than you think. I have tried to have a one-night stand, but the guy always wants more from me. I thought I was going to have one with a wealthy businessman from Los Angeles. I met him in Vegas. He was the "Well" (the high roller). I thought he was super cute. We went to a boxing match. We ended up hooking up that night and I thought it would only be for that night. He surprised me later when he invited me to come visit him in LA. He was so L.A. – he surrounded himself with people who could only talk about money. I couldn't stand it. I didn't go down to see him any more after that.

Another time, I was at a sports bar and I met a man who was married. He captivated me with the first glance. He had magnetic powers. We hung out for a few hours. When we were outside, he offered me a cigar and taught me how to smoke it. He thought I was really cute and that I didn't know how to smoke. I had a little too much to drink and couldn't drive. (This seems to work well. Drink too much and have a rich guy take you home.) He offered to drive me home in his very expensive car. We kissed in the car and it was passionate. I was electrified. He asked if he could come in and I said. "No." I said, "Good night," and he reluctantly went home. I don't think he could believe that I was sending him home.

He texted me the next morning and asked if he could come for a visit. He came over and we had sex. He didn't use protection. Around 4:00 p.m. that same afternoon, he came over again and we had wild sex again. The first few times we had sex, he pulled out. After he found out that I was on the pill, he came inside me. We were mentally connected.

He told me he was doing this because he and his wife were growing a part. While he did tell me that he would never leave her, I didn't believe him; we were so good together. Our affair went on for three months. He made me feel like I was good in bed.

He sent texts to me like: "Thinking of you, missing you; wanting you; wanting to be inside you."

I would respond: "Thinking of your cock."

He would then write: "What do you want to do to me you dirty little girl?"

I would reply: "What do you want me to do with you?"

He would end it with something like: "I want you to lick my lollipop until it pops."

He wanted me to treat him like a piece of meat and I did. I was not myself when I was with him. I was a sleazy and dirty little girl. He wanted me to only want him for sex. He had a beautiful cock. He was actually very controlling and jealous if I dated anyone else.

We stopped seeing each other after people starting talking about us. But it was he who spread the news about us more than anyone else. He started hanging out with me in front of his wife. He would have his arm around me when she was across the room. He was not subtle at all.

He couldn't give me what I wanted from him, which was more of his time and commitment, but, at the same time, he was bothered when I went out with others. I told him that I needed to continue to date others if he wasn't going to leave his wife. I was honest and would tell him what I was doing even though I knew he wouldn't like it. He continued sleeping around with other women as well. His own son tried to hook up with me. Somehow, his teen-aged son knew about us, but he didn't care.

We are now openly friends. In the beginning he texted me twenty-four hours a day. I think he got emotionally attached to me. I don't want drama in my life. I don't trust him. If I go with him, he will continue sleeping around with others. He is very insecure. He wants attention from me. He is too cocky and doesn't think his wife would do anything like he does. He is very controlling. I care about him. We love each other. He told me that he loves me as a person. He is very lonely. He is looking for a woman's companionship because he isn't getting it at home.

I knew that I could never have him and tried not to get emotionally close to him. He would have loved to see me fall in love with him. I tried not to.

I get checked every time I change sex partners.

14. *How do you break off a one-night stand or short relationship without being hurtful?* I haven't had a one-night stand. I look for long-term. Once they have been with me, they want more. Women normally don't want to be the one-night stand; it is only when the men don't call that they end up being a one-night stand.

15. *What are your rituals for preparing for a date?* I buy new designer clothes that the guy has not seen me wear before. I like to keep it new and exciting. I wear a sexy thong and bra.

16. *Where do you go/what do you do on a date?* I don't date. I go to a bar where I know a man will bring me home if I have had too much to drink. If I like the guy, I'll invite him in.

17. *Would you be interested in going for coffee and a walk instead of a dinner date for the first date?* No. I want them to wine and dine me.

18. *If you were a candy, what kind would you be and why?* Taffy. I stick with you for days or months or years.

19. *How often do you have a girls' night out? Where do you go with your girlfriends?* My friends all seem to be married. We go out when they can get away from their obligations.

20. *What do you hope to happen when out with the girls?* I want my friends to leave me alone so I can do my thing. I like them to be around; I like to know they are there for me. I will pay their way, but they need to let me be.

21. *What frustrates you in the dating scene?* Players. They only want to have fun with me. They don't take me seriously. Just like the casinos. They don't take a beautiful woman seriously. They don't think a woman can be a "well."

22. *What are you looking for in a relationship?* Long-term security. And someone who can let me be free. I don't want kids. So it is better if I find someone who has his own. That is why I like older men who have been married before and already have their kids. Hopefully, the wife has custody of them.

23. *Would you go out with a married man?* Yes, but I would feel guilty for a while till he leaves his wife. They usually are not looking outside of their marriage unless there is something already wrong with their relationship. I can help by being a good companion. The wives and the ex-wives usually hate me. The daughters don't like me too much, either.

24. *Would you date someone who had a child from another relationship?* Absolutely. I prefer it. The only problem would be time constraints. I

don't want to be bound to the point where we can only do things two or three times a week.

25. *If you were to live with someone, how long would you be willing to live with him without a permanent commitment?* I will never give up my own place until I am married. I am too independent.

26. *Are you hoping to find a man who is financially secure? Is financial security more important than love?* Absolutely to both.

27. *Would you consider financially supporting a man with whom you happen to fall in love?* No.

28. *How does it make you feel if your date flaunts his assets?* Love it.

29. *What type of clothing do you prefer your date to wear?* Doesn't matter when we are at my place. But I like us both to look good when we are out.

30. *What is your preferred body type and shape for a man?* Athletic.

31. *How do you feel about tattoos and piercings?* Not for me.

32. *How do you feel about perfumes and colognes?* Don't care.

33. *How important is the first kiss?* Very. It could be the hook.

34. *Do you expect your date to pay on the first date?* Yes.

35. *What is your preference and philosophy on who should pay the bill on dates with you?* The man should pay. I want to be taken care of if they are coming to my place after the date. I take care of them in other ways.

36. *What are the most annoying things a date can do?* Nothing annoys me. I am pretty easy going.

37. *Will you have sex on the first date? If so, would you talk to your date about your preferences freely?* Yes. I like to befriend the person before sex. Usually married, they love me and they can't get enough of me. I listen to them and give them companionship after sex. Sometimes they like to come over and not have sex. Oral sex is an important necessity. I have them do me first. They are happy to please me. I make sure they are happy, too.

38. *Would you have sex with your date if he were drunk?* Yes, 'cause I am usually drunk the first time.

39. *How do you make sure a new sexual partner is free of STD's?* Oops. I should be more careful, but I do get tested between sexual partners. Usually every two months. I am on the pill so I don't worry about pregnancy. Most married men I am with are very reckless and don't use a condom. However, most of them have only been with their

107

wives. The older ones, if worried at all, only worry about pregnancy. They don't think about STD's. This must be a generational thing.

40. *Once you have decided to have sex with your date for the first time, are you free and uninhibited in the act or more conservative and reserved than normal?* Completely uninhibited, wild and crazy, as I know they will desire me more. I act as the person they want me to be -- a bad little girl. This makes them feel powerful and naughty; something their wives have never given them. I provide their ultimate fantasy and they can't live without me once they have had me.

41. *Where would you feel comfortable having sex with your date?* My bed, hotels and the pool.

42. *Where is your favorite place to have sex?* My bed.

43. *What do you do if protection is not immediately available?* If they seem safe, I still do it.

44. *What if you liked your date and he did not call you the next day or week? What would you think and do?* Has never happened to me. But, if they don't call, I guess it would be considered a one-night stand.

45. *What age range do you date?* Older than myself. At least 10 years older.

46. *What was your parents' status when you were growing up?* Messed up completely. I had a very hard childhood. No real parents. I moved out when I was 16 and dropped out of school. I did what I had to do to make it through. I think I did pretty well, looking at where I am today and considering from where I came.

47. *How do you characterize yourself?*

> **Positive attributes:** Easy going, beautiful, great body, good in bed, fun to be with, free and outgoing. Men love me.
>
> **Negative attributes:** Women, wives and ex's don't like me. Their daughters don't like me either. The sons do.

48. *Please include a detailed description of your ideal date.* I would like to fly in a private jet to Monaco. Stay on the yacht. Play poker and win. And then have sex all night long.

49. *When you meet someone new, how long does it take you to know if he is "the one" or has the potential to be "the one"?* I know right away.

50. *Do you believe in "love at first sight"?* Yes, there needs to be a magnetic chemistry right away. And, it must last.

51. *What is your personal philosophy on monogamy and monogamous relationships?* It just doesn't happen. People have different needs at different times. I wouldn't trust any guy to be monogamous.

52. *Do you believe there is a game people play when dating? If so, describe the game.* Yes. There are too many people playing the game. But I know what men want and I can give it to them. They all want me and want to have fun with me. But they don't understand that I can be contagious. Men are very insecure and easy prey.

53. *Have you ever been on a date with a guy who turned out to be an ass?* Of course. I was having an affair with this married guy; I ran into him at a bar where he was sitting with a group of friends. I had one too many drinks that night and I sat on his lap and massaged his neck. I made a comment that he didn't like. I commented on how hard he can get. He was furious with me to have said such a thing in front of his hoity-toity friends, as he didn't want to be exposed. He grabbed me by the arm and threw me onto my butt. I was embarrassed and hurt. He told me to leave and never show my face again. I couldn't understand why he was treating me that way -- we had been together for the last two months and most people knew of our affair. I was almost sure that he was ready to leave his wife for me. But I guess I was wrong. I left in tears and anger. The next day he sent flowers and apologized for his behavior. He explained that I had over-stepped my bounds and had put him in a tough situation with his friends who knew his wife. He would never leave his wife and therefore the affair had to stop. It turns out that this person had been sleeping around town for sometime. One of the women who saw what had happened approached me later and confided in me. She was a one-timer with him and was still obsessed with him. She pumped me for information about him. I told her to get over him and that he would never leave his wife for us girls. She needed to face the fact that she had been a one-night stand with the guy. She needed to move on. For some girls, it is really hard to accept.

Below the belt questions:

1. *Is sex an important factor in deciding whether you will continue to date someone?* Yes, sex is <u>very</u> important to me.
2. *Do you enjoy wearing lingerie?* It depends on what the guy is into. I don't wear it for me.
3. *Have you ever experienced ménage à trois?* Yes. All combinations.
4. *What is sexy to you in a guy?* His swagger and confidence.

5. *Will you kiss and tell your friends or do you keep it private?* I do tell my friends.
6. *Are the men who you meet in a bar a potential long-term relationship or are they a one-night stand?* Only long-term, I hope.
7. *When you go to a bar, do you hope to find someone?* Yes, of course. I hope that they will drive me home when I have had too much to drink.
8. *What do you think of athletic clubs as a place to meet someone?* They are great; I can look my best and very sexy in my workout attire.
9. *What do you think of the work environment as a place to meet someone?* Yes, it is a good place, too.
10. *How many sexual partners have you had in your life?* I have lost track.

E. Psycho Drama: Psychologically drains you.

Psycho Dramas can be identified as early as junior high school. They are shit disturbers. They talk behind your back; they burn bridges, seeing no value in relationships beyond the present moment. They are users and energy zappers. Some are sexually "easy," trading sex for "popularity." They are often raised in dysfunctional families where they have been demeaned and mentally abused by one or both parents. Ultimately, they put themselves first in every relationship.

Psycho Dramas are selfish characters that love to play the victim, enjoying any kind of attention and drama. This character is quite adept at making a scene where he or she will confront others with hurtful, appalling and irrational words. They are pain seekers and complainers. Having no social filter, they freely discuss their past tragedies to anyone who will listen. Unaware of social boundaries, they appear to be oblivious of the impact of their actions on others. He or she can be gruff and rough, loud and obnoxious, and act in disregard of social etiquette. They bully themselves into social gatherings where they create a stage for their drama. Twisting the truth to keep the drama going, they contradict themselves and forget their stories. Their aggressive and tenacious personalities may be used as an asset in certain fields of employment.

The Psycho Drama personalities repel others due to their mean-spirited nature. They have names for others around them and are highly judgmental of others. Accustomed to being treated badly by important persons in their own lives, they have learned to treat others in a similar manner. Looking for pity, they blame others for whatever has gone wrong in their lives.

There is no accountability for their actions. The lonelier they are, the more they act out. The more they act out, the more they repel people. They often die alone because they have alienated their families, they have no true friends, and they have burned all of their bridges.

The Psycho Dramas are confused and, while they appear to be overly confident on the outside, they have low self-esteems. They look to others for validation. They work hard on their outward appearance so that they will be noticed. They keep in great shape. They strut around so that others will look at them; however, others generally don't pay much attention to them.

While Psycho Dramas are often attracted to people with money, these characters do not possess the social skills of the Gold-digger. They cannot slip into a relationship with the needy, gullible, and wealthy because they are obvious, abrasive, unapproachable, and very easy to spot. The male Psycho Drama often finds himself looking up to the Magnets in the dating scene, knowing that he lacks the natural charisma, animal magnetism, and self-learned swagger that a Player exhibits.

The bruising Has-been is a fiery match for the Psycho Drama because they like to stir things up and the Psycho Drama will feed on the fire. However, a Nurturer or a Stepped Upon Nobody may be better able to keep things on an even keel over the long-term.

BEWARE: Once a Psycho Drama, always a Psycho Drama. There will be no reform. They can provide great entertainment at parties and in the work place; things are never boring around them. They are good to look at and fun to listen to when spewing their viewpoints. However, this character may become a stalker if mistreated. If you romance this type, you will find yourself in the midst of constant turmoil and you will have to work hard, consoling and reassuring the Psycho Drama.

WALLET STORY:

From his perspective:

I met a hot girl at the sports bar. She had a great body, great smile, great long hair, great teeth and a great tan. She was in her late thirties. I am almost 50, single, and have never been married. I was hesitant about approaching her, but I had a wingman with me. He offered to buy her a drink and asked her to join us at our table, telling her that I was very interested in her.

She happily came over. We had great conversations about sports, trucks, boats and engines. She seemed to be very informed about these subjects for a woman. I thought she was interesting. I found out that she worked in promotions for a professional basketball team. She told me she had an in for second row seats for all of the basketball games and that she would be happy to arrange tickets for me. She didn't realize that I had my own box. I asked her out to dinner for the following Saturday. I knew the perfect place to take her.

She didn't know me well so we agreed to meet at the restaurant. When I first saw her as she walked into the restaurant, she looked hot and I couldn't wait to get to know her. She was wearing a short, tight-fitting, low cut, leopard print dress with sexy heels. Her hair was long and smooth. Her eyes sparkled. I had arranged for a special table in the back where we could get to know one another. We sat and enjoyed some champagne and appetizers.

After asking her permission, I took the liberty of ordering the main dishes. She seemed to really enjoy my selection. I ordered a phenomenal bottle of wine and we spent three hours talking about her and her interests. I wasn't really listening as her beauty mesmerized me. The waiter brought the bill and I realized that I didn't want the night to end. I reached into my pocket to get my wallet, but it wasn't there. I remember changing my pants at the last minute because I spilled a glass of wine on myself on the way out. I was so nervous about the date that I had been trying to calm my nerves. I accidentally left my wallet in the first pair of pants.

I have never been so embarrassed in my life; I didn't know what to say. She was very good about it and offered to cover the check; I told her that I would pay her back and thanked her for not thinking badly of me. I didn't want the evening to end, but we had driven separately and I had an early plane to catch in the morning. We shared a fabulous kiss that made me weak in the knees. We went our separate ways and said we'd be in touch.

I had to be at the airport to get on the plane at 5:30 a.m. and I had no time to call her while I was away because there was one emergency after another with the business. She was on my mind and I figured I would catch up with her within a few days. I never imagined she would turn out to be such a drama queen. Maybe it was a blessing in disguise that I couldn't get in touch with her fast enough. I saw her real personality before I got too involved with her.

She started sending me texts that were unbelievably rude and unnecessary. She panicked easily and over-reacted in no time. I must have received over 50 disturbing texts from her calling me names and threatening my well-being. I couldn't wait to get home to pay her off. When I finally got a hold of her and paid her back for the $500 dinner tab, I felt that it was the best investment in my future that I could have ever made. Forgetting my wallet that night saved me from getting involved with a psycho-bitch!

From her perspective:

They met while partying at a sports bar. They agreed to meet the next night for a dinner date. He suggested an expensive and exclusive restaurant for which it was next to impossible to get reservations on the spur of the moment. He took care of the reservations. They met in the lobby and were escorted by the hostess to a wonderfully romantic and quiet table.

He proceeded to order the most expensive champagne to complement their appetizers. He next ordered a bottle of the best red in the house to go with the fillet mignon he ordered. They had wonderful conversation and continued their dinner over dessert. The waitress brought the bill and he reached down to pay. He checked in his jacket pocket and then his pants. He kept fumbling around.

He looked very embarrassed and then told her that he had somehow forgotten his wallet. He apologized over and over. She believed him; he looked as if he really was sorry and had not planned this. She told him not to worry about it and pulled out her credit card. She told him that they could settle up later.

He walked her to her car and they shared a wonderfully warm and electric kiss good night. She did not want the night to end, but they had brought their own cars and it was a natural end to the evening. She texted him the next day to let him know how much she enjoyed the dinner. He did not respond. She texted him a few days later saying, "I hope everything is okay. I haven't heard from you." There was no response.

Feeling that she had been duped, she again texted him saying, "Hey. I don't care if you want to talk, but you owe me $500. You better pay up." No answer. That evening, she texted him: "I should not have paid; I should have made you wash dishes. I want my money." As she expected, there was no response.

On the fifth day, she texted him again: "I don't know who the fuck you are or where the fuck you live, but I'm going to find you. I'm going to track you down like a dog and get you." Again, there was no response from him.

On the sixth day, she received a text from him. He said, "I'm so sorry. I had to fly to Paris on my private jet to take care of an emergency with the company. I could not contact you before now. I would love to meet you and get the money to you." She didn't believe him and half-heartedly suggested that he fly his private plane to meet her at a coffee shop in town. He agreed to meet her at the suggested spot and they selected a time.

She was waiting there and he was a minute late. She began packing her bag to leave and then noticed that he was driving around the parking lot looking for parking. He was driving a black Diamond Series Bentley. He parked and came over to her, carrying a bouquet of flowers and a card. He greeted her with a big smile and said, "I am so sorry; I know what you must have thought. I have never forgotten my wallet before and I hope to never do it again. Here is the entire amount of the bill with tip in cash. Please forgive me." He handed her the flowers with a card apologizing again. He then looked at her and said, "Have a nice life." He walked back to his Bentley and drove away.

She sat there with the flowers upside down and her chin on the ground. She thought to herself with a tear in her eye that she had just kissed off her chance for a lifetime of happiness by showing her true dramatic nature.

INTERVIEW WITH A FEMALE PSYCHO DRAMA

1. *Contributor age:* 40's
2. *Gender:* Female
3. *Education Level:* High School
4. *Are you financially secure?* Yes.
5. *Profession:* Business owner.
6. *Personal Status:* Single/Divorced & Widowed
7. *If married, how many times have you been married and for how long?* Twice. Once for 12 years and then divorced. Another for 10 years and widowed.
8. *Are you looking for a long-term relationship or a meaningful one-night stand?* No one-night stands for me. Bad girls like the one-night

stands and it is not going to happen in my life. A long-term relationship is what I am looking for.

9. *Interests/hobbies:*   Working out and physical fitness. Gardening.
   Reading mysteries and romance.

10. *What initially attracts you to the opposite sex? Past the initial attrac-
    tion, what keeps you attracted?* They have to be attractive to me ac-
    cording to my taste. They have to possess a high intuitive tap into the
    universe and a good vibe. Their eyes have to be good. They have to be
    attracted to me. They have to be fit. I want a man with whom I can
    workout.

11. *What do you find to be a turn-off in a date?* Even if not attractive, I
    would go on a date with someone if he were a very nice person. The
    biggest turn-off is a bragging man. They oversell themselves to catch
    the girl. The more attractive I am to the guy, the more he tries to sell
    himself. They tend to be insecure when they brag more. The good girl
    doesn't care about possessions. I can figure out about the guy all by
    myself without him over-selling himself. In on-line dating, the line
    about "physical fitness" is where I always get disappointed – they al-
    ways show up with a big gut. They lie about their physical shape even
    though I make a big deal about it before we meet in person. I guess
    they think I won't notice! If they are going to lie about their physical
    appearance, then they should only date blind women.

12. *Where do you meet people?* I used to go out and chase it. I don't want
    to meet them in places where you don't normally go. I have decided to
    leave it to the universe and the gods. I occasionally go out and, if I
    happen to meet that guy, then so be it.

13. *When you are out with your friends and you see someone who catches
    your eye, what do you do?* Make eye contact. I only go so far. I think
    a man can determine when the woman is interested. I have to wonder
    why they can't be smart enough to read us.

14. *Where do you hang out?* Home, work and the gym.

15. *What are your thoughts about online dating?* It doesn't work for me.
    The ability to lie is too easy. People hide behind the computer screen.

16. *Have you ever had trouble moving on from a past relationship? If so,
    what did you do to finally get over it?* I have had that. The more infre-
    quently I date; it is harder to get over it. Not knowing what I did
    wrong and why it didn't work out is the hard part. You just need time
    to go over it in your mind. I always go back into me and work from the

inside out. What was my stake in it? What was his? And, who was responsible? I self-analyze the situation.

17. *What do you think of one-night stands?* They will not work for me. They are for needy and lonely people. People think I look like a bad girl, but I am not. My friend has more fun and rides a different horse. I remind her that what you look for in the dating world is often what you end up getting. Don't give it all away on the first date. If you can get into my head, my vagina goes with it. I am holding out for the right guy.

18. *What are your rituals for preparing for a date?* Sometime ago, I would put all my effort into my dates. Now, I simply try to be myself.

19. *Type of lingerie you would wear on a first date?* Nothing fancy because who would see it? I know I am not going to have sex until the fourth or the fifth date.

20. *If you don't know your date well, do you meet at the designated place or does your date pick you up?* Designated place. Better safe than sorry.

21. *Would you be interested in going for coffee and a walk instead of a dinner date for the first date?* Yes.

22. *Do you treat dates differently when set up by a friend or relative?* No.

23. *How often do you have a girls' night out? Where do you go with your girlfriends?* Not as often as we used to. We go to bars around town.

24. *What do you hope to happen when out with the girls?* I just want to have a good time. I no longer have any expectations.

25. *What frustrates you in the dating scene?* Perpetual lying and selling.

26. *What are you looking for in a relationship?* Somebody who gets me. I think the majority of people have the wrong perception as to who I am. I am more than that. I am a very grounded, intuitive, life-experienced person. I know what I know and I am comfortable with myself. I have done my work to get here. They are intimidated by my front, outside physical appearance, and directness. I don't waste time or beat around the bush. Some people seem to be afraid of me; I just don't get it.

27. *Would you go out with someone who was married?* No. What's in it for me? Not unless his wife knew or she was coming along on the date. One time, I decided that I was going to do it. I thought, "Screw it." He was begging me to just give in to him. My little girl (vagina) said, "Go for it. This date, this time we are on, get your hall pass because it's going to be a freaking crazy night." At the last minute, he said, "I am sorry; I cannot deliver on what you want." I thought,

"Don't mess with me like this, you chicken shit." I never entertained the idea of doing a married man again.

28. *If you were to live with someone, how long would you be willing to live with him without a permanent commitment?* Not long.

29. *Is financial security more important than love?* It matters.

30. *Would you consider financially supporting a man with whom you happen to fall in love?* I would be dating him, but not living with him. He needs to support himself if I am going to live with him.

31. *What makes an impression on you regarding your date?* His listening skills, honesty, integrity, and his actions.

32. *How does it make you feel if your date flaunts his assets?* Over-selling his stuff is not good.

33. *What type of clothing do you prefer your date to wear?* Occasionally appropriate – I mean appropriate for the occasion.

34. *What is your preferred body type and shape for a man?* Fit.

35. *How do you feel about tattoos and piercings?* Not really good.

36. *How do you feel about perfumes and colognes?* Light side. Body odor is only okay if I stink, too.

37. *How important is the first kiss?* The first kiss is important. It sets the standard for chemistry; it sets the tone.

38. *Do you expect your date to pay on the first date?* I don't expect it, but wouldn't it be nice?

39. *What is your preference and philosophy on who should pay the bill on dates with you?* My preference is that the gentleman behaves as a gentleman. I am old fashioned in thinking that he should pay for the first couple of dates and then I cook for him.

40. *Would you have sex with your date if he were drunk?* No.

41. *How do you make sure a new sexual partner is free of STD's?* Knowing is important.

42. *Once you have decided to have sex with your date for the first time, are you free and uninhibited in the act or more conservative and reserved than normal?* Free and uninhibited and he is probably a dud. When I am free, I eat them up alive. Many of them suck in bed.

43. *Where would you feel comfortable having sex with your date?* Home. In the heat of the moment, who's to say?

44. *Where is your favorite place to have sex?* Bed.

45. *Do you use protection and if so who provides it? If you don't use protection, how do you stay safe or is it an issue?* I like to think I have,

117

but not as often as I should. Someone should always provide it. I hear it in my head. I have my own condoms at home.

46. *What if you liked your date and he did not call you the next day or week? What would you think and do?* That would hurt my feelings. I start blaming myself. I re-remind myself that the experience is not about me. I question what I did. Re-remind yourself that everything you think is not always true. Don't assume anything.

47. *What if your date called you a month later? What would you say and do?* I would remind myself about not assuming anything. I would be cool and take one step back.

48. *What age range do you date?* 42-47 range.

49. *What was your parents' status when you were growing up?* Married and then divorced when I was 13. My mother cheated on him and re-married and divorced that man. The apple rolled really far from that tree.

50. *How do you characterize yourself?*

> **Positive attributes:** Coping skills, being able to digest and rightfully file things that are actually in my control and for those that are not, to let them go. I am responsible for what I say and what I do. Honest, sense of humor, witty.
>
> **Negative attributes:** I can't think of any.

51. *Please include a detailed description of your ideal date.* A charismatic, intuitive, insightful, witty, charming, endearing, and twinkly gentleman picks me up on time from my house, dressed appropriately for a charming quiet restaurant. I want to listen, talk and be heard. Great conversation, taken home with a nice kiss and no tongue in the mouth.

52. *When you meet someone new, how long does it take you to know if the person is "the one" or has the potential to be "the one"?* By the second date.

53. *Do you believe in "love at first sight"?* Yes.

54. *What is your personal philosophy on monogamy and monogamous relationships?* I'm a one trick pony. I do them one at a time.

55. *Do you believe there is a game people play when dating? If so, describe the game.* Definitely. The game is: "It's all bout me. Deception." Pretending to be something they are not. It is all about them. In most instances, there is a front. Lies and more lies. Guess who I am? I don't date that much for all those reasons. I am learning to be more patient. I don't jump anymore. I am willing to work for it. It feels like

they are not totally upfront on who they are in the beginning. You just have to wait and see if this is the real behavior or if they are different. They lack confidence in being themselves.

56. *Have you ever been on a date with a guy who turned out to be an ass?* Yes. He got very accusatory and confrontational till I started to cry. Mean and nasty. Mean and controlling.

57. *If you were interested in a further date, would you wait for him to call you or would you let him know?* Because I can't hide my feelings well, I would use words like: "Let's see; I'll check my schedule." That way, I wouldn't appear too eager.

58. *Would you mind if your date contacted you immediately after your date?* That wouldn't bother me at all. It is true honesty. I would be very impressed.

59. *How much attention is too much or too little after the first date?* Coming on too strong is constantly checking and calling. But if you are off the chart with the guy, it is never too soon.

60. *Do you believe emotions interfere with the dating process?* Yes. Both emotions and perceptions.

61. *On average, how many dates are required before you consider yourself to be in a relationship? What qualifies as a date?* The old school train of thought. A good solid week. You can see the same person for a month and they can say, "We are not in a relationship." Now, you have to verbalize and secure it before it is official. You have to communicate and clarify.

62. *Is the dating game a mystery or are the rules clear? If clear, what are the rules?* It is both. The rules of engagement are vast and wide.

63. *Do you consider yourself to be a game-player in the dating arena?* No.

Below the belt questions:

1. *Is sex an important factor in deciding whether you will continue to date someone?* If intimacy were below par, I would talk to him about it.

2. *Do you enjoy wearing lingerie?* Yes, it is okay.

3. *Have you ever experienced ménage à trois?* No, but I almost did it as a gift for a friend of mine. Two girls and a guy. I would want to be the focus and reciprocate.

4. *What is sexy to you in a guy?* Their level of confidence and truly believing in themselves.

5. *Does the size of a penis matter?* Please . . . yes. If the guy knew where to put his hands and how to do the right thing, size would not matter so much. But most guys don't have the know how and don't care about figuring it out. Maybe if a guy were teeny-tiny, he would gather the necessary knowledge because he would have to.

6. *Do you prefer more or less hair on a man?* I like a little hair on the chest. Too much hair will kill me. I like a man to be groomed and trimmed. I want what I give; I am groomed.

7. *Do you prefer tanned or natural skin?* Not a preference. Tanned means he likes to be out in the sun.

8. *Will you kiss and tell your friends or do you keep it private?* I will only go so far. I keep it private.

9. *Is spirituality important to you?* Absolutely. As long as they will not try to mess with my spirituality, I am okay. They can think and believe what they want; just leave me alone!

F. The Has-been: Takes attention, irritates and emotionally bruises others.

The Has-been achieved success at an early age and now has a dimming star. He or she may have been a child actor, a professional sports player or a jock in high school. People rallied behind him or her while successful in the field or stage of choice, but after losing the spotlight due to the aging process or an injury, the Has-Been has lost his or her allure. They miss being in the limelight.

The Has-been often surrounds himself or herself with others who look up to his or her past exploits. This person loves to have groupies. The groupies may be people that admired him or her along the way and who never had a shining star of their own. As long as this person's ego is being fed and boosted by the groupies, he or she is happy. The happiness, however, is temporary and he or she often ends up lonely. When not feeling the adoring crowd, this character may become mean-spirited and seek drama so that he or she is at least the center of attention for a brief moment. This character can be a bruiser to those around him or her. If there is no positive attention coming his or her way, he or she will make a scene to create attention. They will fabricate information to make the people around angry and cause turbulence so that they can then smooth things over and look and act like the good guy or gal. The Has-been is highly manipulative.

This character lives in the past and does not know how to move forward. He or she is unable to look to the future. Delusional and lost, the Has-been is unable to move forward and commit in relationships. The Has-been has never truly grown up and is intensely selfish. He or she is not a good friend; he or she will be a friend as long as it's good for him or her. For example, he will have no compunction about stealing a "friend's" date or girlfriend. He will kiss his friend's date. He will play footsy under the table with a friend's date. He likes to have a good time – even if it is at someone else's expense. The Has-been has a wicked sense of humor. Their circle often includes the Psycho Dramas as these characters will keep the fire fueled around them. The Has-been may be thought of as a "shit-disturber." He or she sits back after making a few calculated comments to see how people react.

BEWARE: Don't take what this character says to heart; get corroborating evidence before allowing yourself to get upset over his or her fabrications.

DATING HISTORY of a HAS-BEEN

Over the year 2008, I was the most hated man in town. I guess I am just too honest to be successful in the dating market; I call it like I see it. Girls seemed to be attracted to my honesty; they were attracted to me when I acted like an ass-hole. For some reason, it seems like girls want to be with a jerk. If a woman came up to me and was acting like a gold-digger, I would tell her to her face that she was a gold-digging bitch. She would huff out of the joint and then, minutes later, come back and buy me a drink, trying to prove to me that she wasn't what I thought.

One time in a bar, a girl came up to the group I was in and looked at me with a cute little smile. She was hot, but then she asked how old I thought she was. I added about seven years to how old I thought she really was just to get a rise out of her. She then stripped off her leather coat to show me her beautifully cut arms and body. She then said, "Now what do you think?" I shrugged and said, "About the same." The girl was so mad that she tried to get my attention by hitting on one of my friends who was sitting next to me. She came over and sat in his lap and then started making out with him. I sat back and enjoyed my beer . . . and the show.

I often went out with this group of friends; some of whom were married and some who were single. When things got a little boring, I brought up something that was told to me in trust so that I could create a little excitement for the evening. One married man and woman were out with us and I mentioned to the guy in front of the wife whether or not he remembered meeting the hot chick over at the bar counter. The wife, of course, got all jealous and the evening was dominated by the guy trying to defend himself and the wife imagining that her husband was looking at all the other women in the bar.

Another time, I saw one of my married friends making out with another married man in the alley behind a restaurant. I brought this up in front of some other friends and the woman went ballistic, defending her honor by denying that it ever happened. Later, I mentioned to the woman that I heard someone else talking about the incident in the alley. The woman called the person, yelling and accusing him of trying to ruin her reputation. I texted the guy while he was receiving the ranting phone call, asking whether the woman was giving him shit. He replied, "You guys are demented and you deserve each other; leave me out of this." I apologized and told him that I always had to do clean up for her because she ruins her own reputation with her diarrhea of the mouth.

A FREE FOR ALL FOR THE HAS-BEEN

The Has-been went out with the guys on a Thursday evening. They texted as follows beforehand:[6]

> **3:00 p.m. on Thursday**
> HB (Has-Been): hay are we meeting at the bar?
> F1 (friend): I'll be there around 8.
> HB: cool, I'll bring the girl.
> F1: bring one for me
> HB: we'll get a few over there

> **4:00 p.m. on Thursday**
> F2: Hey HB, what's going on tonight?
> HB: we're hooking up at the bar at 8:30 p.m. I am brining the girl and we'll pick up a few there
> F2: who's the girl?

---

[6] Spelling and punctuation in texts is in the form given to us by the contributor.

HB: some girl

F2: what's her name?

HB: I don't remember. Big boobs, tanned and thinks she's all that shit. can't really understand her, but ok to hang with

F2: wow cool. Is she hot, available for us all?

HB: I guess

F2: see you at 9:00

8:45 p.m. on Thursday

F1: where the hell are you? I've been here for the last half hour. It's dead.

HB: where are you?

F1: shut up dumb fuck. I am at the bar.

HB: oh, I am on my way. The girl got mad cause I called her the wrong name when we were in bed, had to make it up to her

F1: get me some of that

HB: will do

Later that night at the bar, the scene is as follows:

The three guys and the angry girl are there; she is a Psycho Drama to the max, thriving on the fact that he forgot her name and she is making him pay. Some of her girl friends come over to join them; they all get free drinks on Has-been. The guys all pair off and dance with the girls. Somehow, on the dance floor, they all switch partners.

Has-been disappears into the bathroom with a girl wearing a tube dress. She had previously flashed them on the dance floor, showing off her new boobs. In order to get a closer look at them, Has-been takes the girl into the women's bathroom and gets busy with her. When he comes back to the table, the Psycho Drama asks him where he has been. Has-been tells her that he was making a long-distance business call. She points to his phone on the table and arches her eyebrow with a scowl. Has-been shrugs, saying, "Oh! Oh well." She storms off. Has-been and his buddies all laugh and enjoy their evening. Has-been takes the tube dress girl home with him that night.

INTERVIEW OF A HAS-BEEN

1. *Contributor age:* 40's
2. *Gender:* Male
3. *Education Level:* Jr. College
4. *Profession:* Ex-professional sports player
5. *Personal Status:* Divorced
6. *If divorced, how many times have you been married and for how long?* Married once for 14 years and I have three kids.
7. *Are you back on the market?* Yes, I'm BOM, but I'm not looking for a long-term relationship. I'm not looking to get married again.
8. *Interests/hobbies:* Sports, basketball, and working out.
9. *What initially attracts you to the opposite sex?* Sense of humor, looks, personality and the connection between us.
10. *What do you find appealing in a date?* Looks and personality.
11. *What do you find to be a turn-off in a date?* Triangle maker, someone who wants to create jealousy, someone who thinks she is all that shit.
12. *Where do you meet people?* Wherever, in a bar or at clubs.
13. *When you are out with your friends and you see someone who catches your eye, what do you do?* I feel the vibe and then make a move.
14. *What are your thoughts about on-line dating?* I don't use it and don't know how to use it.
15. *What are your rituals for preparing for your date?* Put on clothes.
16. *Where do you go/what do you do on a date?* Go out to dinner.
17. *How often do you have a boys' night out?* Four nights a week. Bars and clubs.
18. *What do you hope to happen when out with the guys?* Get laid.
19. *What frustrates you in the dating scene?* The game.
20. *What are you looking for in a relationship?* Don't know.
21. *Would you go out with someone who was married?* No.
22. *What about someone who is separated or has a boyfriend?* No/yes/I don't know.
23. *Would you date someone who had a child from another relationship?* Yes.
24. *If you were to live with someone, how long would you be willing to live with her without a permanent commitment?* For a long time.
25. *What type of clothing do you prefer your date to wear?* Jeans, t-shirt, casual.

26. *What is your preferred body type and shape for a woman?* Fit.
27. *How do you feel about tattoos and piercings?* Don't mind them.
28. *How do you feel about perfumes and colognes?* I like cologne on women. No body odor.
29. *How important is the first kiss?* Very important. A bad kisser is not a good thing.
30. *What is your preference and philosophy on who should pay the bill on dates with you?* I like to pay.
31. *Will you have sex on the first date?* Yes.
32. *Would you talk to your date about your preferences freely?* Yes.
33. *Would you have sex with your date if she were drunk?* Yes.
34. *Lights on, off or dimmed?* Depends on what she looks like.
35. *What do you require prior to engaging in the sexual act?* I always protect myself.
36. *Once you have decided to have sex with your date for the first time, are you free and uninhibited in the act or more conservative and reserved than normal?* Always uninhibited.
37. *Where would you feel comfortable having sex with your date?* Anywhere. I have done it in the restrooms of most restaurants/clubs in the area.
38. *Where is your favorite place to have sex?* Bedroom.
39. *Do you use protection and, if so, who provides it? If you don't use protection, how do you stay safe or is it an issue?* I provide it. Yes, it is an issue.
40. *What do you do if protection is not immediately available?* Nothing. Can't do it.
41. *What if you liked your date and she did not return your call the next day or week? What would you think and do?* Game playing - come on, that's so dumb! I hate that.
42. *What if your date called you a month later? What would you say and do?* Pick up the phone and talk.
43. *How do you characterize yourself?*
    Positive attributes: Low key, nothing bothers me, honest, get along with people, none judgmental, flexible, and generous.
    Negative attributes: Call it as I see it. Too opinionated.
44. *Please include a detailed description of your ideal date.* Go out to dinner and dancing.

45. *When you meet someone new how long does it take you to know if the person is the "one" or has the potential to be the "one"?* I know right away.

46. *Do you believe in "love at first sight"?* No.

47. *What is your personal philosophy on monogamy?* It is important.

48. *Do you believe there is a game people play when dating? If so, describe the game?* Yes. And that bugs me the most. You're not sure if they like you or not. You're not sure if you are coming on too strong or not. I like to call the girl the next day and let her know I liked her. I don't want to worry if it is too soon to call.

49. *If interested in your date, how long do you wait to communicate with her?* I'll talk to her the next day.

50. *Would you mind if your date contacted you immediately after the date?* No.

Below the belt questions:

1. *Is sex an important factor in deciding whether you will continue to date someone?* Yes.

2. *Do you enjoy it when your date wears lingerie?* I don't care one way or the other about it.

3. *Have you ever experienced ménage a trios?* Yes. It was awful and it was with two guys. He kept hitting it and I was missing it.

4. *What is sexy to you in a woman?* A woman who is confident, not bitchy and doesn't brag about her teeth, looks, and that all the guys want her.

G. The Socially Correct: They take your time pretending to be someone else.

The Socially Correct care what others think of them above all else and will give up the privilege of being true to themselves in order to appease the image and expectations that others have of them. The Opportunist pressures him or herself to conform. The Circumstantially Correct is pressured from the outside to conform.

1. OPPORTUNIST

Sometimes known as Opportunists, they look for others who will make them look good. They enjoy a date that is arm candy. They enjoy a mate who fulfills the preconceived notions of their families and friends.

The Opportunists wear the most up to date clothing; they are clean-cut, well groomed, and well tailored. They will follow the trends, not wanting to seem out of touch. They are in good shape and care about their appearance, not to be healthy, but to be attractive to others.

They live in the shadow of what others think of them. They have a low self-esteem and are insecure. They are not good friends. They won't be there for you in the tough times; they won't have your back unless it will make them look good. They keep their opinions to themselves until they take a poll of what others think. They sway with the breeze.

The Opportunists may fall prey to unscrupulous financial schemes; they will jump on the bandwagon if everyone else is doing it. Even if it is against their better judgment, they go with the masses. They are afraid to be left out. They don't want to miss the greatest deal or investment.

They think everyone else is interested in what they are doing. If sitting at a restaurant, they will whisper, paranoid that all other guests are listening in on their conversations. They feel that people are watching and listening.

It is rare for them to find a successful long-term relationship because they look for someone who will please the outside people looking in. If a relationship doesn't work out, they will talk badly of the other party and blame them for the failure. They cannot accept fault or blame. They are the ultimate chameleons, not knowing or caring who they really are, but only trying to fit into the "in" group of the moment.

While Opportunists are often cheap, they do not want to be seen that way. They down the drinks as long as they are free. They pretend to be classy and hope to date only classy individuals. They love to talk about others in a negative way in order to make themselves shine. They attach themselves to VIP's and mooch off of them and ride their coat tails.

The Opportunists only put out if they can get something in return. They love online dating because they can make themselves look however they want to look. When behind a computer screen, they can be whomever they choose to be for the moment. They are great actors. They can tell you everything you want to hear, but it might not be true. In the long

127

run, you may never discover who they really are – you will only find that they are not who they originally portrayed themselves to be.

This character can be a dangerous date because he or she is usually hiding something. They have not permitted themselves to be truthful in who and what they are and in whom and what they are looking for in a date. They are not looking deeply; they are satisfying only their immediate need and pleasure.

BEWARE: If you are in a relationship with this type, it is always going to be about them. You cannot win with this character. Invite them to your parties as fillers; they are usually a good time.

A SOCIALLY CORRECT INTERVIEW

1. *Contributor age:* 40's
2. *Gender:* Male
3. *Education Level:* College
4. *Profession:* Real Estate Developer
5. *Personal Status:* Single
6. *Interests/hobbies:* Anything in aviation and outdoors
7. *What initially attracts you to the opposite sex?* First is physical; next is personality.
8. *What do you find appealing in a date?* "Me!" I like a fun sense of humor and a smart woman.
9. *What do you find to be a turn-off in a date?* Chewing nicotine gum.
10. *Where do you meet people?* On-line. It is addicting and ego-boosting. It is an alternative to meeting people at grocery store.
11. *When you are out with your friends and you see someone who catches your eye, what do you do?* I will send a drink to her and, depending on the number of drinks I've had, I will then approach.
12. *Where do you hang out?* Bars in nice restaurants where there is always a crowd.
13. *Have you ever had trouble moving on from a past relationship?* Yes, I was with a Persian girl for about six years and then she left me. She put all of her focus and energy on family and friends, leaving very little attention for me. She ultimately left me, telling me that the relationship wasn't working for her; she said it wasn't my fault. It took me one whole year to get over her.

14. *Where do you go/what do you do on a date?* Dinner and sporting events.

15. *If you don't know your date well, do you meet at the designated place or do you pick up your date?* Pick them up.

16. *What frustrates you in the dating scene?* The superficiality. The gold-diggers that are always around wanting free drinks. They want to be kept women. I call this a Tarzan effect because they swing from one man to the next; from one wallet to another.

17. *What are you looking for in a relationship?* Sense of humor, stability and smartness.

18. *Would you go out with someone who was married?* No. Well, it depends on whether she was very rich.

19. *Would you date someone who had a child from another relationship?* Yes.

20. *If you were to live with someone, how long would you be willing to live with her without a permanent commitment?* I did it for six years; next time I want a commitment fairly soon.

21. *Are you hoping to find a woman to share your life with who is financially secure?* Yes.

22. *Would you consider financially supporting a woman with whom you happen to fall in love?* I am a romantic; I believe in love. However, I need someone who can contribute to the household.

23. *How does it make you feel if your date flaunts her assets?* I don't like it.

24. *What type of clothing do you prefer your date to wear?* Depends on the date. Sexy and classy.

25. *What is your preferred body type and shape for a woman?* Proportionate, 5'4" - 5'7", brunette, and fit.

26. *How do you feel about tattoos and piercings?* One tattoo is okay. No tramp stamp.

27. *How do you feel about perfumes and colognes?* Perfume is okay. No curry.

28. *How important is the first kiss?* Nothing is worse than a bad kiss.

29. *Do you want to pay on the first date?* I pay.

30. *What is your preference and philosophy on who should pay the bill on dates with you?* I'll pay till the third or fourth date. Then she needs to pony up.

31. *Will you have sex on the first date? If so, would you talk to your date about your preferences freely?* I would, but I don't like to. I prefer to wait for three or four dates.

32. *Would you have sex with your date if she were drunk?* She usually is.

33. *Do you wear boxers or briefs?* Briefs.

34. *How do you make sure a new sexual partner is free of STD's?* I ask if she has any STD's. I use protection -- Jimmy's. I keep them in the glove compartment.

35. *Once you have decided to have sex with your date for the first time, are you free and uninhibited in the act or more conservative and reserved than normal?* More missionary.

36. *Where would you feel comfortable having sex with your date?* Home.

37. *Where is your favorite place to have sex?* Bed.

38. *Do you use protection and, if so, who provides it? If you don't use protection, how do you stay safe or is it an issue?* Oral it is. One way.

39. *What if you liked your date and she did not return your call the next day or week? What would you think and do?* Move on.

40. *What if your date called you a month later? What would you say and do?* I'd say, "What's the story?"

41. *What age range do you date?* 32-48 years.

42. *What do you think of one-night stands?* The women control the tempo. The women pick the men rather than the men choosing the women. Lots of guys will participate in them if the opportunity is there. Players do it. They tend to be charming and do two or three different girls at a time. They tend to do one-night stands. They screw anything that wears a skirt.

43. *How do you break off a one-night stand or short relationship without being hurtful?* I am big on communication.

44. *How do you characterize yourself?*
    Positive Attributes: Optimist, fun loving, humorous, committed.
    Negative Attributes: I can't think of any.

45. *Please include a detailed description of your ideal date.* Around water, restaurant, walk on the beach, champagne, blanket, drive home with the top down.

46. *When you meet someone new, how long does it take you to know if the person is "the one" or has the potential to be "the one"?* Four to five months.

47. *Do you believe in "love at first sight"?* No.

48. *What is your personal philosophy on monogamy and monogamous relationships?* Commitment is important.
49. *Do you believe there is a game people play when dating? If so, describe the game.* Yes. Talking about what doesn't matter. It reflects immaturity and it is a waste of time.
50. *Do you believe emotions interfere with the dating process?* Baggage prevents moving forward.
51. *On average, how many dates are required before you consider yourself to be in a relationship?* Women know.

Below the belt questions:

1. *Is sex an important factor in deciding whether you will continue to date someone?* Yes.
2. *Do you enjoy it when your date wears lingerie?* It is so 80's.
3. *Have you ever experienced ménage à trois? If not, would you consider it?* In my college years, I did it with both 2 girls and 1 man and 2 men and 1 girl. I would definitely do it again, either way!
4. *What is sexy to you in a woman?* Her hair.
5. *Does the size of her breasts matter? If so, what is the preferable size?* C to D.
6. *How much make up is too much?* I don't like too much.
7. *Are skimpy, body-fitting outfits a turn-on or a turn-off?* Depends.
8. *Do you prefer a particular pubic hair design?* Landing strip, Hitler mustache and baby bald.
9. *How many sexual partners have you had in your life?* Refused to answer. He knew a woman at the other table, appeared nervous, and stopped the interview.

2. CIRCUMSTANTIALLY CORRECT

Another type of Socially Correct is the Circumstantially Correct, individuals who have been caught in a social or religious trap that does not allow them to be true to themselves. The Circumstantially Correct are not strong enough to stand up for themselves, especially when young. They will succumb to pressures applied by family, culture, or religion that limit and restrict who they may date or marry. They rarely are free to marry the person of their own choosing. While they may know who they really are, they repress their true selves.   Ultimately, however, the Circumstantially Correct will yearn to be free to be themselves.

There are many examples of Circumstantially Correct people who marry and later decide they need to be true to themselves. Some are gay and are afraid of what their families will think, so they marry. Others were born in the wrong body and wake up next to their spouse with a burning desire to transform into the opposite sex. Still others marry the wrong person when they are really in love with someone else. Prince Charles is a famous example of a character ensnared in familial and social obligation. Obviously in love with Camilla from the beginning, he was forced to marry another who suited the royal litmus test. In the end, after having been forced to live a lie for years, he went back to his true love. As history has shown, all parties suffered in the relationship that was built upon lies.

The lesson here is that passing judgment on others and making others tow your line is not a good way to achieve health in relationships and dating. People are who they are and they need to be left free to be what and whom they are without feeling imprisoned by the expectations and desires of family, friends, and society. Acceptance and allowing others to discover for themselves who they are is the key to long-term happiness for many. This way, other innocent victims will not be brought into a charade that may have an unhappy ending for all involved.

BEWARE: The truth will come out eventually; it is better to deal with it sooner rather than later. The truth will set not only you free, but also those who are ensnared in the lies with you.

MARRIAGE IN THE CLOSET

They met in college. They were both from good families with traditional Baptist sensibilities. He was a prized catch, handsome, and sought after by all the girls. He was 25 and his family was pushing him to marry a girl from the hometown. At that time she was an undergraduate in college and he was in graduate school. He caved into the family's pressure and married her. She was young and beautiful and had been raised to be a good wife. She had never dated anyone else; he was her boyfriend in high school.   While he knew that he did not want to get married, he could not tell his family why. He knew he was not attracted to women. He was afraid that he would be disowned by his family and cut out of the family business and money.

They married and immediately had two children. After the birth of their children, they rarely had sex. He never kissed her. He never offered foreplay. He cringed when she touched him. She did not know things should be different. He became exceptionally critical about her physique and made sure that she followed a limited calorie diet and worked out every day. He thought that, if he made it clear that she didn't look good enough for him, she would not push him to make love to her. He ravaged her self-esteem.

The marriage lasted for about fifteen years. He couldn't stand her anymore. He resented her. While he resented her, she began to resent him, realizing that there should more to a marriage than just children and taking care of the house. She was missing affection and needed more TLC. She noticed that he spent a lot of time away from the family; he was always with single men. She couldn't figure out why all of his friends were single; there was never anyone for her to talk to when his friends came over to the house. He tried to let her know that he was gay with subtle signs. She ignored the signs and lived in denial.

She finally accepted the situation when he started spending the night at one particular friend's home. She was dumbfounded and devastated, feeling that her whole life had been a sham. In reality, both of their lives had been a sham due to the societal pressures that he had felt as a young man. He had waited forty years to be who he really was. He had stolen fifteen years from her.

While he was relieved, she was angry. The children were devastated and did not understand. For the sake of the children, the wife and husband worked together to muddle through. Through it all, the two became best friends. In reality, that is what they had always been. They ended up having a better understanding and love for one another than ever before. Although his family rejected him, her family still considered him to be their son.

H. The Diva: Takes whatever she wants.

Usually intelligent and funny, the Diva is accustomed to getting her way. In the dating world, she is the ultimate female player. Regardless of socio-economic class, her parents have made every effort to make her comfortable and happy. They have built their daughter's self-esteem, leaving her with a great deal self-confidence. Groomed to be successful in their social and educational environment, Divas are given tools in etiquette, social protocol, athletics, languages, communication, deep understanding of people, and articulation. They have been taught to be prim and proper, but may sometimes deviate and rebel when young. Either way, they have been given the tools for success from a very young age and are well trained to excel in all areas of life.

The Diva never gossips because she is not concerned with others, she is internally focused. She is so into herself that she has no room for anyone else. She does not waste her time gossiping because it serves no purpose other than to surround herself with negative information.

The Diva is very spoiled and expects all around her to cater to her needs. She does not understand the word "no" and will keep at it until she gets her way. She does not understand that there is any other way than hers.

Surprisingly, people do want to be around the Diva. Because she is self-assured and confident, she is a lot of fun. She has no need of anything from anyone. She has so much confidence in what she does that others volunteer to be involved in her endeavors. The Diva is wise to the ways of the world. People like to see her happy because she is not pleasant to be around when she is not happy. The dark times are very dark and can be contagious. The Diva influences those around her. People generally enjoy being around her because life is exciting and things happen.

Rules do not apply to Divas. They will create their own rules as they go along. They will twist the truth, bending it to support their own interests. They don't break the rules; they bend them. In the rare event that things don't go their way, they completely disregard the situation and quickly move on, flipping their hands back, saying: "Whatever." They do not carry the burden with them. They do not dwell on the past, even if it was yesterday. Every day is a new day and things in the past are so yesterday.

The Diva's basic needs must be met. Her home must be comfortable and her needs must be attended to. She will do what is necessary to make herself happy with her appearance. Plastic surgery of this type or that is a valuable tool to this character. She never follows fashion trends, but she may set trends. She knows what she feels good in and wears what makes her feel good. Contrary to the name, the Diva is not pretentious. She does not wear too much makeup. She is traditional in dress. She marches to her own beat. When she walks into a room, she attracts attention.

The Diva is always herself and real. She lays all of her cards out on the table at the get go, even in business dealings. People, however, are so used to hiding the ball and playing games, that they rarely believe all of her cards are face up. After dealing with the Diva for a while, they will realize that she was upfront, honest, and correct. The Diva is extremely decisive and does not waiver once a decision has been made. She has the power to make things happen. She knows people, she knows how to maneuver, and people want to help her achieve her goals. She has "It."

She is emotionally detached, but warm and appealing to everyone. She develops contacts wherever she goes and keeps good relationships with most everyone she meets. The Diva will not hesitate to call in a favor when she needs it and she expects compliance. The Diva will do a favor without asking for anything in return. If she can do it, she will. However, she knows that a favor is owed to her at some point in the future. It may not ever be collected, but she rests assured that she has left the deposits in the account for future withdrawal, if and when necessary. If the other party waivers or waffles when asked for a return favor, he or she is dropped completely from the circle and will often come back begging to be included again, offering much more than what the Diva originally re-quested. Accordingly, she is an incredible fundraiser.

In dating, the Diva portrays many similarities to the Player. Like Cleopatra, she will rarely be exclusive to one man for her life, but will commit to only one man throughout her life. In matters of love, she is wild and untamable. She is highly confident, knows how to use her body and charm to attract her sexual partners, and she only goes after the most dominant male on the scene. From the beginning, her rules are clear. In the first encounter, she goes with the flow; the second time is planned; and from then on, all encounters are on her terms whenever, however, and wherever. She has an unusually high sex drive and can handle many men at one time. She loves to be with two men at one time.

She enjoys giving pleasure and will accept pleasure in return. Men who are fortunate enough to be involved with a Diva remember her forever and she becomes a permanent chapter in their books of love and lust.

When they enter into her world of fantasy, they experience true ecstasy. She can easily move from one man to another and once her conquest becomes dependant or emotionally attached, she cuts the ties, instantly separating from and releasing him. However, she never ends her relationships; they are simply altered in the type of relations. The sexual game ends, but she keeps him in her circle of friends. She views all relationships, whether sexual or not, as contacts for the future. In this regard, she is similar to the Diplomat.

An encounter with a Diva is rarely a one-time event, but it will never be a long-term relationship. She normally keeps two or three games going at the same time. Unlike the Player, she is highly protective of her family; she will not risk humiliation by bringing the game close to home. However, she does enjoy flaunting her playmates to one another as it heightens sensuality and results in a competition for her affections.

The Diva is the queen of elegance, class and charm. Once caught in her net, men become addicted to her sexual being. They can't get enough of her. They want her everyday thereafter. She becomes an obsession for them. The Magnet, however, seems to be able to resist her spell – the Diva and the Magnet repel and attract each other in a magnetic relationship. He is the hunter and needs continual boosts to his ego and validation of his masculinity by playing the game of chase, catch and release. His ego seems to be threatened by the Diva and her need to control the game.

The following are things men have said about the Diva:

1. How can one woman be so beautiful and sexual all in one package?
2. You have brought joy and ecstasy into my life.
3. You are the picture of a perfect woman: sexual, beautiful, sensual, strong, and lovely.
4. I want to have you with me all the time. I think of you when I am with anyone else but you.
5. You are the ultimate woman.
6. I desire you with all my heart and, knowing that I can't have you, I would much rather be in your arms for a moment, knowing the risks I take by doing this, than be in the arms of another for a lifetime in comfort.

BEWARE: If you fall prey to a Diva in the dating world, she will take you into her arms and capture you, giving you the ultimate ecstasy while with her. Enjoy, but do not become emotionally attached. She will soon tire of you and will dispose of you. Take her at her word when she warns you not to fall for her, as there will be no happy ending for you.

A DIVA TALKS ABOUT HER WAY

1. *Contributor age:* 30's
2. *Gender:* Female
3. *Education Level:* Graduate Degree
4. *Profession:* Entrepreneur
5. *Personal Status:* Single. I am not looking for anything. If it finds me, I will definitely enjoy my time with a new and exciting person.
6. *Interests/hobbies:* Having fun; watching my business enterprises succeed; developing connections with people. People watching, puppeteering, tennis, exercise, partying and socializing. Never camping -- I care too much about my comfort and surroundings to put myself in that situation. The only camping for me would be in the Ahwahnee hotel in Yosemite.
7. *What initially attracts you to the opposite sex?* I am initially attracted to a man's looks, the way he carries himself, and the way he is dressed. Tall and handsome. Lean and mean. Bad boy look. Distant and delicious like candy. Past the initial attraction, I look for a sense of humor, a level of confidence, and the way he makes me feel when he looks into my eyes. I have to feel the excitement from the way he looks at me or there is simply nothing there to pursue. Strong big hands and arms. Intelligence, sexual prowess and confidence. Easy going and catering to my desires and needs. Their long-term financial potential.
8. *What do you find appealing in a date?* Sense of humor and adventure. Exciting and spontaneous, their ability to communicate their thoughts. Their mannerisms and manners. Generosity and worldliness and a conversationalist. No pretentiousness. I like a guy who can enjoy both expensive and inexpensive restaurants. A cheeseburger and fries are great once in a while. Non-political, non-religious, and non-judgmental. He will have your back in an emergency. Strong and manly, but yet sensual and genuine. How relaxed they are around me. I don't much care about the topic or the content of the conversation as much as the delivery. I find a man who is articulate and who speaks

slowly quite appealing. Of course, taking care of the bill before it even gets to the table adds extra points.

9. *What do you find to be a turn-off in a date?* Egotistical and self absorbed. Bad taste in everything. Foul language, opinionated, judgmental, dismissive, condescending, hot temper, pouty, overly sensitive, weak, insecure, short, know-it-all, anti-social, sports fanatic, big drinker, smoker, drug user, tattoos, show off, in general someone who is classless and yucky. Turn-offs for me would include someone who becomes clingy, someone who is sloppy, and someone who wants to talk and complain about their spouses or life. I want my time with the person to be productive and efficient with the focus on me. Sometimes the focus can be on sex and nothing else. In those cases, it needs to be passionate and it is helpful if there is little conversation.

10. *Where do you meet people?* I don't particularly look for people. They find me and I decide if it is a go or not. I love to play and my game requires a man who is extremely confident with himself and his manhood.

11. *When you are out with your friends and you see someone who catches your eye, what do you do?* I summon him over with a not-so-subtle gesture of some kind. If I am with a friend, I will introduce the two of us to him.

12. *Where do you hang out?* Home, work, sports club, coffee houses and bookstores.

13. *What are your thoughts about online dating?* Not interested; it is for much older, desperate people who need to hide behind the screen. I think the older you get, the more help you need to find a date. There are sites for married people of all ages who are looking for sex, companionship and the like. I think it is more fun to find people the organic and natural way.

14. *Have you ever had trouble moving on from a past relationship?* Yes. I have had trouble getting over a game that did not go the way I intended it to go. I like to be clear about what I am doing, what game I am playing, and I like to understand exactly what is going on. When there is confusion and I have no control over the outcome or where it's going, I get bothered and try to make sense out of the situation. I guess you can call it the game of control. I have always been in control and this time, for the first time in my life, I didn't have the control of the game or its outcome. It was a good experience for me to go through. I learned something new about myself. I learned to get out fast if the

game is not played my way. I do not like to waste my time on people who won't be there for me later in other capacities. You can't win them all and that is okay. Take the loss gracefully and play again with a different player.

15. *What do you think of one-night stands?* First of all, you never know what will be a one-night stand. You'll have to wait until tomorrow to see. I love one-night stands. I think people who are looking for adventure and newness look for one-night stands. There are those who like to have emotional, lovey-dovey sex and there are others, like me, who are only looking for fun and exciting moments in life.

16. *How do you break off a one-night stand or short relationship without being hurtful?* Sometimes, you thank the person and get up and leave. Most of the time, there is no need to break anything off. People make the mistake of cutting things out of their lives for good. Communication is the key. Just because two people have sex doesn't mean that there needs to be a next time or an ongoing sexual relationship. As long as neither of them is an ass about it, they can maintain a friendship afterwards. It is important to have communication the next day or sometime soon thereafter to clear the air and shoot the breeze without making anyone feel badly. Humor is very important here. The discussion should be as follows: "I had a great time. It was fun. How many drinks did I have? Do you know? I am feeling that it must have been quite a few because I had a major hangover the next day. [This is assuming you did drink. If not, just say that you felt as if you had lots to drink.] How are you feeling about our encounter? It was a crazy night. Well, I am glad we both had fun. It was a night to remember. I have to go now; I have a heavy schedule for the next couple of weeks and need a lot of sleep and concentration for work. Thanks again. It was fun."

17. *What are your rituals for preparing for a date?* New outfit. Shave, pluck, and shower.

18. *Where do you go/what do you do on a date?* Go to a party or out to dinner. Occasionally, I go to the movies.

19. *How often do you have a girls' night out?* All the time. We go out to a restaurant or bar. We go to parties. We go to an occasional movie.

20. *What do you hope to happen when out with the girls?* Flirt and laugh all night. Have fun and bother the guys.

21. *What frustrates you in the dating scene?* Not much other than people who are not upfront with what they are looking for in a dating relationship.

22. *What are you looking for in a relationship?* Ultimately, I would like to find an intelligent, loving man with good genes. For now, I would like to have a quickie with someone who is spontaneous, loving, caring, spicy, and who has a great sense of humor.

23. *Would you go out with a married man?* Of course, it is only about sex. The married guys are safe for me; they won't want to disrupt their own families by clinging on to me.

24. *What about someone who is separated or has a girlfriend?* No. They are in limbo and it is a gamble either way.

25. *Would you date someone who had a child from another relationship?* It depends where the person is in his life. I would not date a married man with young children; things are too difficult at that time and I would not want to cause a permanent rift in his relationship with his wife. I want families to stay together. I would be fine with it if the guy was single with children.

26. *If you were to live with someone, how long would you be willing to live with him without a permanent commitment?* I never lived with anyone other than my parents. I like my own space and I probably would not live with a man unless I was married. There would be no reason to do so.

27. *Are you hoping to find a man who is financially secure? Is financial security more important than love?* I want a man who has the potential to be and who has ambition to be someone. I am looking for emotional and mental security and care very much about my basic needs and comforts. I don't need a man to support me financially, but rather to support my wants, needs and who I am.

28. *Would you consider financially supporting a man with whom you happen to fall in love?* Yes. I have enough ambition for the both of us.

29. *How does it make you feel if your date flaunts his assets?* As long as it's bigger than the average size, I don't mind him flaunting his personal asset. Seriously though, I do not like a show-off; it is a turn-off and draws too much attention. What is he trying to prove?

30. *What type of clothing do you prefer your date to wear?* Clean cut. I love a crisp, white, buttoned shirt and jeans for the casual look. A man in an expensive, well-made suit is exquisite for a more formal look.

31. *What is your preferred body type and shape for a man?* Athletic with big arms, long fingers, and strong legs. I like them tall and handsome with dark hair.
32. *How do you feel about tattoos and piercings?* Not good.
33. *How do you feel about perfumes and colognes?* If very mild, smells are okay. I do not like to smell like another person after they hug me.
34. *How important is the first kiss?* Important. My stomach has to twirl.
35. *Do you expect your date to pay on the first date?* Of course.
36. *What is your preference and philosophy on who should pay the bill on dates with you?* Whatever is right. For me, whoever invites pays. If I pay, I can be in control and not indebted that way. I look at it as if they are providing my entertainment.
37. *Will you have sex on the first date? If so, would you talk to your date about your preferences freely?* Yes. I am always happy to show the man what I like. I want him to be comfortable and secure when he is with me and I want him to know that he has pleasured me.
38. *Do you prefer your date to wear boxers or briefs?* Boxers.
39. *How do you make sure a new sexual partner is free of STD's?* Communication. Trust. In the heat of the moment, I have not thought about it.
40. *Once you have decided to have sex with your date for the first time, are you free and uninhibited in the act or more conservative and reserved than normal?* Completely uninhibited. Time is golden.
41. *Where would you feel comfortable having sex with your date?* Not in a restroom; anywhere else that is private from others.
42. *Where is your favorite place to have sex?* Bed. You can do more on a bed than anywhere else.
43. *Do you use protection and, if so, who provides it?* He does.
44. *What do you do if protection is not immediately available?* Oops.
45. *What if you liked your date and he did not call you the next day or week? What would you think and do?* Oh well. I don't care. I like to initiate and end as I please.
46. *What age range do you date?* 20 to 50 years.
47. *What was your parents' status when you were growing up?* Married. I had my father wrapped around my little finger from the time I was born. He had a pet name for me and always made me feel special like a princess.

48. *How do you characterize yourself?*
> **Positive attributes:** Fun, funny, exciting, smart, beautiful, lovely, happy, trouble, humorous, lively, vivacious, horny, curious, wild and untamable.
>
> **Negative attributes:** Judgmental, choosy, no patience at all -- especially for stupid people, no empathy, no limits.

49. *Please include a detailed description of your ideal date.* Prince Charming comes to my castle on his white horse to pick me up. I ride on his lap facing him. We escape off into the horizon where we have mad passionate sex all night long. We wake and have breakfast on the porch overlooking the ocean with light jazz playing in the background and then we return to bed for the day.

50. *When you meet someone new, how long does it take you to know if the person is "the one" or has the potential to be "the one"?* Immediately.

51. *Do you believe in "love at first sight"?* Yes. I love myself. Parents love their children from the time of birth. Other than that, I don't believe in love at first sight. I cannot give up the control long enough to be swept off my feet.

52. *What is your personal philosophy on monogamy and monogamous relationships?* If I am completely happy and satisfied, there is no reason to go somewhere else.

53. *Do you believe there is a game people play when dating? If so, describe the game?* Yes. People don't really know who they are and are afraid to discover who they are. The sad part of the game is that people allow others to define them. It is the game of come and get me or I am coming to get you. But, no one ever wins the game. That is why it is called a game. Once they get together, the game is over.

54. *Have you ever been on a date with a guy who turned out to be an ass?* I went out with bad boys who are by definition asses. However, they would try to hide who they were to impress me, which didn't impress me a bit. I went out with them because they were serving my needs for fun and games.

55. *If interested in a further date, would you wait for him to call you or would you initiate further communication?* I let my feelings be known right away before I change my mind. I don't expect others to read my mind. I initiate.

56. *If you were not interested in another date, would you let him know?* Absolutely. I don't want to leave them hanging or be pestered later.

One time, I did not do a very good job with communicating my lack of interest. At a wild and crazy party, I had met this guy who was cute and interesting for the moment. We had a quick one-night encounter. Nothing more, nothing less. A month later, I saw him again at another wild and crazy party. He approached me by the bar, referenced our night together, told me how much fun he had, and asked me why I hadn't hooked up with him again. I was not thinking clearly and I was under the influence of alcohol. I brutally told him that our night together meant nothing and gave him a nasty example. I said, "When someone is hungry, even if you put shit in front of them, they will eat it." He looked at me and wilted. To this day, I feel badly about how I handled that situation and will never again treat anyone as badly. It was totally uncalled for. What I should have said was, "We had a great time together and I will remember it fondly. However, it can't happen again."

57. *Would you mind if your date contacted you immediately after your date?* I love it, love it, love it when that happens. It shows how confident the person is with himself. I like to be appreciated.

58. *What form of communication would you prefer from him?* It doesn't matter. A phone call is the best because it shows self-confidence and self-assurance.

59. *How much attention is too much or too little after the first date?* Never too much. The more, the better. Attend to me. That being said, too much enthusiasm is too much. Relaxed is good. Do not show up unexpected!

60. *On average, how many dates are required before you consider yourself to be in a relationship?* If I choose the person, it only requires one date.

61. *Is the dating game a mystery or are the rules clear? If clear, what are the rules?* It is not a mystery, but there are different rules for different people. Once you know whom the player is, then you know how to play the game.

62. *Do you consider yourself to be a game-player in the dating arena?* Yes, especially when I am out with an ass or egotistical, self-absorbed dick.

63. *Is spirituality important to you?* Yes, very much so. I want to be surrounded by good energy, good people, good everything. I am not particular about affiliation, as I don't follow any organized religion. But I have a deep faith in the greater being.

143

Below the belt questions:

1. *Is sex an important factor in deciding whether you will continue to date someone?* Absolutely. If the sex isn't good, don't kid yourself -- you'll be shopping around soon.

2. *Do you enjoy wearing lingerie?* I always wear a thong and a pretty bra. I like to feel pretty underneath my clothing. Other than that, I don't care much for lingerie. However, I love to wear my man's collared dress shirt over my naked body once he takes it off.

3. *Have you ever experienced ménage à trois?* Yes. Always with two men and me. My first job out of college was working at a law firm. There was a late night meeting of staff and they brought in dinner as we were helping to prepare a document for the printer. It was 10:30ish at night and everyone was wired and exhausted. We finished and there were three of us who stayed back to wrap up -- two gentlemen and myself. I sat on the very long, thick, beautiful and glossy mahogany conference table to remove my high heels. I was rubbing my foot when one of the men came over and jokingly began to massage my foot. It was so good that I unintentionally moaned. The other man came over to see what was going on. He said, "Let me in on that and grabbed a hold of my other foot. It was so good I just let go and lay back on the table, never mind that I was wearing a skirt. The next thing I knew, I heard the door shut. I playfully rubbed one guy's crotch with my foot and he was hard and firm. The other guy came over and put his hands under my skirt and pulled my underwear down. The next thing I knew, I felt his warm, steamy breath between my legs. It was a wild and crazy night on the conference room table. I'll never forget it!

4. *What is sexy to you in a guy?* Confidence and a genuine sense of humor about himself. A little bad boy in him never hurts, but he really must be a good person. I like tall men with beautiful eyes and arms, long legs, big hands, and who are strong and intelligent. A man who knows how to dress is hot!

5. *Does the size of a penis matter?* Yes, of course. Anyone who says it doesn't is lying. It can certainly be too big and then all bets are off. If it is too small, they better be good in other areas.

6. *Do you prefer circumcised or not?* Definitely circumcised. If not, have them get it done.

7. *Do you prefer more or less hair on a man?* Less hair. Laser therapy is good. Waxing is second best.

8. *Do you prefer tanned or natural skin?* Not "Casper white," but not melanoma tan.

9. *Will you kiss and tell your friends or do you keep it private?* Of course, why not? That is the fun part. Especially if he is really good. You normally don't tell if he wasn't good.

10. *What do you think of athletic clubs as a place to meet someone?* Not really a good place as it makes future workouts uncomfortable if it doesn't work out. Also, because there are a finite number of possibilities, you can wear it out quickly.

11. *What do you think of the work environment as a place to meet someone?* Maybe, if you're planning to leave or get fired. Otherwise, this just isn't a good idea; it leads to potential legal difficulties.

12. *What is your opinion about surgically enhancing your body?* Whatever is right for the individual. I think people should do whatever they want to make themselves feel good. If new boobs are in order, then go for it. But don't complain later that everyone looks at your boobs.

13. *How many sexual partners have you had in your life?* Many.

A DIVA JUGGLES HER MEN

When I was younger, I could not decide exactly what I wanted in a man so I went out with many at the same time. They all knew about one another and there was no exclusivity. While honesty was the name of the game, play was the nature of my game.

The funny thing is that when a girl goes out with a bunch of guys and they all know about the situation, they normally call her a slut. In my case, they felt privileged and did not refer to me derogatorily because I made them feel like they were one of the lucky chosen few to be with me. I went out with them one at a time, had a great time, and made sure they had a great time.

They tried very hard to meet my needs, sexually, personally and mentally. I never liked to make appointments or set schedules ahead of time. They made accommodations for me; I called them on the spur of the moment to go to a concert or out to dinner. The more accommodating they were to me, the more I went out with them.

Sexually, it was always all about me. That was fantastic. I needed a lot of excitement and newness in my sexual life without getting too perverted. I needed them to take charge and make me happy. I wanted them to make my time worthwhile because I could have gone with any of the others.

I showed up at this one guy's house unannounced. I knocked on his door. He opened the door and pulled me into his strong arms. He gave me a passionate long kiss. He put on some romantic Latin music. The lights were dimmed. Without a word, he took me to the bedroom, removed my clothing one piece at a time, kissed me all over, and then made mad passionate love to me. The next time, he would do something completely different. We would meet on his boat. We would water ski and then have a lovely time having sex on the deck of the boat.

The guys were hoping that I would commit to one of them; they would compete for my attention. Although they had their other relations as well, each guy wanted me to commit to him. However, the more I had them, the more I needed all of them in my life. One relationship was not complete by itself. They each had different things to offer me. One would provide unbelievable sex. One made me laugh like crazy and I enjoyed every second with him. One was adventurous and we did crazy, outdoor, exhilarating stuff. Another was more of a quiet intellect and was perfect when I needed to calm myself and reflect. Another was a crazy dancer and allowed me to express myself that way. We would go to discotheques and dance all night long. Those nights ended in a fun car ride with sex in the front seat, the back seat, or on the hood. The cars were fabulous; it was so restrictive and we had to work hard to move around, forcing us to be creative in our passion. Although we had somewhere to go, we enjoyed our time in the car the most.

One time, I was with the adventurous one and we got lost in the woods. We had been at a social outing and lost our way back to the car. It was 5 p.m. We decided to take our clothes off and run around in the woods, playing hide-and-seek. I chased him after finding him behind a tree. I caught him. We fell onto the ground, laughing and rolling in each other's arms. We then had mad passionate sex right there on the pine needles. We enjoyed our moment in nature.

HOW TO MASTER THE BREAK-UP
WITHOUT GUTTING THE GUY

How you break off a relationship depends on where you are in the relationship. If you are in a committed relationship, but not married, and you are not feeling it anymore, you better get out. That is the best thing for both parties. Usually, when they feel that it is time to move on, the guy gets clingier and needier. That makes it more evident that time is of the essence. The best thing to do is to cut it cleanly; don't take prisoners. You also want to make sure that you don't crush his ego while breaking it off.

You start by removing yourself from the situation more and more; you are physically present but emotionally detached and distanced. He will start feeling the change; and he will notice that you are not present even though you are physically next to him. This change is short-lived. Your next move is a nice home-cooked dinner away from other people. After dinner and some kind of alcohol, spring it on him as follows:

> Listen, I have really enjoyed our time together. I have learned a lot, laughed a lot, and cherished our time together. I feel that I am going through a different stage in my life and I really need to get to know myself. I need my time for me right now. It is unfair to drag you along with me at a time when I don't know what I want. I know what I do want and that is your friendship. You add value to my life. I respect and admire you too much to not be honest with you. I therefore need to leave this relationship. I hope we can stay friends forever.

After hearing this, his mouth drops open, his head is shaking back and forth, and he is gesturing in disbelief. He's pissed and tongue-tied because you have left no room for discussion. This behavior is expected so don't be surprised. Just sit quietly and look at him with big understanding and empathetic puppy eyes. You walk over and offer a hug, but he will shirk you and leave.

The next couple of days are crucial. He will call you, text you, and email you. Pick up every time he calls. Return every text and email. Don't ignore him; even if you are making love to another guy. Pick up the phone. Hear what he has to say; just listen. Stick to your story and don't be swayed or pulled back in. Cut it off.

147

If you are not committed, but only dating, it is simpler. Start with "It's not you, it's me." Then say, "I am at a stage in my life where I'm emotionally unavailable and need to find myself. I enjoyed our time together and I'm sure we'll see more of each other as time goes on. But right now, you deserve better."

Always blame it on yourself. Always respect the other person. Truly understand that it is not he; it is you who is looking for a change. Empower him to be the one to break up with you if at all possible. Whatever you do, do not tear him down – do not point out his faults; do not put it on him. Respect relationships on all levels.

VI. An Interlude with the 20's –
A Breath of Fresh Air

In the early twenties, young adults are just beginning to feel themselves out. They have not discovered whom they are or who they are looking for in the dating world. They may have preconceived notions based upon the experiences of family, friends, television, movies, books, and magazines. However, they haven't had enough personal experience to develop an in-depth dating relationship with others, let alone themselves. At this age, theories on relationships are just forming and litmus tests are a fantastical ideal. The early litmus tests and list of ideals is often based upon physical and superficial factors.

A. Interview with a Female Collegiate

1. *Contributor age*: 20's
2. *Gender:* Female
3. *Education Level:* College
4. *Profession*: Student
5. *Personal Status:* Single
6. *Are you looking for a long-term relationship or a meaningful one-night stand?* Long-term relationship.
7. *Interests/hobbies:* I like playing softball, cheerleading, partying, dancing, bumping music, laughing, napping, clubbing, beaching it, watching stars, shopping, photography, and relaxing.
8. *What kind of style do you like?* Urban.
9. *What initially attracts you to the opposite sex?* At first, looks, but past the initial attraction, personality, a good sense of humor, connection, similar interests, and the ability to keep up a conversation. He should share similar values and have the ability to compromise.
10. *What do you find appealing in a date?* It really depends on each and every guy, but what I find most appealing is politeness and courtesy, as well as a sense of humor. Their thoughtfulness and honesty are also two major factors. They should keep a bit of mystery about themselves while, at the same time, making a genuine connection with me.
11. *What do you find to be a turn-off in a date?* Turn-offs include an extreme unattractiveness (since it has to be pleasant to look at them) and a guy that fits the stereotype (only wants sex, know-it-all, boring, con-

trol freak). Another turn-off is when I get the vibe that a guy is simply using me to get something he wants. Turn-offs can be outweighed by turn-ons, but they definitely impact the overall view of the person.

12. *Where do you meet people?* I meet people through my activities: going to the gym, at a party, at the club, through my friends, or at friends' gatherings (a birthday dinner). I also meet some people in my classes here at UCSD, but most of them are antisocial and think I'm weird for being friendly.

13. *When you are out with your friends and you see someone who catches your eye, what do you do?* I say, "Ooh, that guy is cute!" But I won't do anything about it unless he expresses interest first, otherwise I would seem too eager.

14. *Where do you hang out?* I hang out around Los Angeles and here in San Diego. I'm usually at the beach, around my residence hall, with friends, or busy with sorority events.

15. *What are your thoughts about online dating?* From personal experience, I hate online dating. I found my father cheating on my mother on an online dating site. It was disturbing and simply shameful. Breaking the news to my mom was the worst part, knowing that it would hurt her twice as much. Online dating is sneaky, and you can build a profile of yourself to make an image that is not you. It is overrated.

16. *Have you ever had trouble moving on from a past relationship?* My ex-boyfriend of eight months cheated on me and it took me a while to get over it. To get over it, I needed time and self-discovery. I considered becoming bisexual for the summer because I lost all faith in men and the way that they went about hurting women, including me. Other things that helped me were all girls' nights out and shopping, and doing anything else to get my mind off of it.

17. *What do you think of one-night stands?* Personally, I don't believe in one-night stands because, when you participate in them, you are giving them a part of your heart. As cheesy as this may sound, one-night stands are not within my value system because I am not willing to sacrifice that part of myself to a total stranger with whom I may not have a connection. I think people who do participate in them are not necessarily prostitutes, but everybody makes mistakes.

18. *How do you break off a one-night stand or short relationship without being hurtful?* I feel like being honest and blunt is the best way to break off a short relationship without being hurtful. It would hurt more if you did not tell them and you let them linger.

19. *What are your rituals for preparing for a date?* I usually try to make myself look presentable, but other than that, I will be myself. If my date likes me, he should like me for who I am, and not for the clothes I wear or anything like that.

20. *Type of lingerie you would wear on a first date?* Whatever I'm comfortable in for the first date, and it depends for the following dates.

21. *Where do you go/what do you do on a date?* Dinner and a movie, getting ready for a party together and then going to the party, or going out to lunch with mutual friends.

22. *If you don't know your date well, do you meet at the designated place or does your date pick you up?* I start off with a group date if I do not know my date well, so usually we just meet at the designated place.

23. *Would you be interested in going for coffee and a walk instead of a dinner date for the first date?* I would be interested in that because it does not really matter what we're doing, as long as we're connecting and I'm not bored.

24. *If you were a candy, what kind would you be and why?* I would be a Blow-Pop because it takes time to get to my sweet core, meaning it takes a while to really get to know me.

25. *How often do you have a girls' night out? Where do you go with your girlfriends?* I have a girls' night out usually once a month, and we usually go out to dinner, Karaoke, the beach, clubbing, a party, or anything with other people.

26. *What do you hope to happen when out with the girls?* I hope to just have a good time and, if a cute guy passes by, we can laugh about how dumb they all are.

27. *What frustrates you in the dating scene?* What frustrates me in the dating scene is the amount of shallow guys who do not understand a woman's worth. We are more than just a pretty face; we have values and dreams. Another thing that frustrates me is the number of girls who just throw themselves at guys when they are clearly worth more.

28. *What are you looking for in a relationship?* I am looking for an honest, hardworking, genuine, cute, funny, entertaining, and interesting guy who shares some of the same values. He has to get along with my family and friends and hold respect very high in his value system.

29. *Would you date someone who had a child from another relationship?* I would probably not.

30. *If you were to live with someone, how long would you be willing to live with him without a permanent commitment?* I would probably be willing to live with him up to one year without a permanent commitment.

31. *Are you hoping to find a man who is financially secure? Is financial security more important than love?* I do hope to find a man who is financially secure, but it will not be the main reason why I share my life with him. Financial security is not more important than love, even though, in my culture, it is.

32. *Would you consider financially supporting a man with whom you happen to fall in love?* If it has to come down to it, I would consider financially supporting a man with whom I was in love and had a permanent commitment. Otherwise, I would not.

33. *How does it make you feel if your date flaunts his assets?* It is okay, but not if it defines who he is.

34. *What type of clothing do you prefer your date to wear?* Urban clothing, casual and classy yet laid back and not super fancy (unless it's part of his job).

35. *What is your preferred body type and shape for a man?* My preferred body type is in shape, but not extremely skinny.

36. *How do you feel about tattoos and piercings?* Tattoos are fine as long as it means something to him, and piercings are okay for me except in any unusual places like nipples, nose, eyebrows, or bellybutton.

37. *How do you feel about perfumes and colognes?* I love colognes, especially if it is a good scent. Other smells such as garlic, onion, and body odor are turn-offs.

38. *How important is the first kiss?* The first kiss is important because the feeling that you get inside will define how much of your heart is in the kiss.

39. *Do you expect your date to pay on the first date?* I do not expect my date to pay for the first date, but he does earn points when he does. I do not mind paying for my share, but it seems to be a courtesy nowadays for him to take me out and treat me like a princess.

40. *What is your preference and philosophy on who should pay the bill on dates with you?* My preference is that the man should pay the bill on dates.

41. *Will you have sex on the first date?* I will not have sex on the first date. It can take a lot of dates until I feel comfortable having sex.

42. *Would you have sex with your date if he were drunk?* If I were comfortable, probably.

43. *How do you make sure a new sexual partner is free of STD's?* I will ask my new sexual partner if he is free of STD's. It always matters because it is my health.

44. *Once you have decided to have sex with your date for the first time, are you free and uninhibited in the act or more conservative and reserved than normal?* I will probably be free and uninhibited in the act since I am this comfortable with him and on this level.

45. *Where would you feel comfortable having sex with your date?* I would probably feel comfortable anywhere that he does.

46. *Where is your favorite place to have sex?* A bed.

47. *Do you use protection and if so who provides it?* He should use protection and he should provide it.

48. *What do you do if protection is not immediately available?* Get protection.

49. *What if you liked your date and he did not call you the next day or week? What would you think and do?* If I really liked him, I would text him and ask him, "What is up?" Otherwise, I would just drop him.

50. *What if your date called you a month later? What would you say and do?* I would tell him that he lost his chance and only keep him as a friend.

51. *What age range do you date?* I date guys who are 19 – 21 years old.

52. *What was your parents' status when you were growing up?* It was married, then divorced, and then both of them remarried.

53. *How do you characterize yourself?*
    Positive attributes: Cute, funny, nice, polite, good at conversation, funny, honest, genuine, loving, caring, loyal.
    Negative attributes: Too busy, lazy, tired, not trustful, and scared.

54. *Please include a detailed description of your ideal date.* Dinner and a movie, going sightseeing at a place to watch the stars, and a good-night kiss, including good conversations and learning a lot about him.

55. *When you meet someone new, how long does it take you to know if the person is "the one" or has the potential to be "the one"?* It takes a couple of dates to know if they are "the one."

56. *Do you believe in "love at first sight"?* I do not believe in love at first sight; I feel like that is really shallow.

57. *Do you believe there is a game people play when dating? If so, describe the game.* I feel that it is a chase of one another and, once they

ultimately realize they like each other, the game is over. Some parts of the game include not contacting someone because they don't contact you, or you setting up tests in the way you bring up a topic or situation in order for them to react.

58. *If interested in a further date, would you wait for him to call you or would you initiate further communication?* I would wait for him to call me unless I really liked him.

59. *If you were not interested in another date, would you let him know?* I would let him know by telling him we should just be friends.

60. *Would you mind if your date contacted you immediately after your date?* No, I would not.

61. *How much attention is too much or too little after the first date?* Too much attention would be hanging out an hour after we left. Too little attention would be not having contact within a week of the date.

62. *On average, how many dates are required before you consider yourself to be in a relationship?* Probably twenty dates before I considered myself to be in a relationship. A date includes anything that is one-on-one and with a mutual understanding that there is an interest between the two.

63. *Is the dating game a mystery or are the rules clear? If clear, what are the rules?* The dating game is a mystery based on the different guys you meet and their challenges to you. The game is to win over each other's hearts.

64. *Do you consider yourself to be a game-player in the dating arena?* No.

65. *Is spirituality important to you?* As long as my date has a good heart and intentions, then his beliefs do not interfere with my own.

Below the belt questions:

1. *Is sex an important factor in deciding whether you will continue to date someone?* No.

2. *Do you enjoy wearing lingerie?* Sure.

3. *Have you ever experienced ménage à trois?* I would probably not consider it, but if I did, it would be male female female.

4. *What is sexy to you in a guy?* Intelligence, sense of humor, smell, dress, and charm.

5. *Do you prefer more or less hair on a man?* I prefer a good amount of hair on a man, but not too much. If a man is too hairy, he should fix it by wax or something.

6. *Will you kiss and tell your friends or do you keep it private?* I will probably tell my friends because they know everything about my life.

7. *What do you think of athletic clubs as a place to meet someone?* It's a great way to meet them because they obviously share the same interest of staying in shape.

8. *What do you think of coffee houses as a place to meet someone?* It's great.

9. *What do you think of the work environment as a place to meet some-one?* This is bad, work and love should be kept separate.

10. *What is your opinion about surgically enhancing your body?* No en-hancements, I was born with grace.

11. *How many sexual partners have you had in your life?* 1.

B. Interview with a Male Collegiate

1. *Contributor age:* 20's

2. *Gender:* Male

3. *Education Level:* College

4. *Profession:* Student

5. *Personal Status*: Single

6. *Interests/hobbies:* Working out, talking at coffee shops, kickboxing, playing bass guitar.

7. *What initially attracts you to the opposite sex?* Something unique. A body, too, but more of a distinct look. She stands out above the crowd.

8. *What do you find appealing in a date?* Witty, intelligent, not necessar-ily a supermodel, but like coffee shop cute.

9. *What do you find to be a turn-off in a date?* No sense of humor. Being stuck-up.

10. *Where do you meet people?* At parties.

11. *When you are out with your friends and you see someone who catches your eye, what do you do?* If I'm at a party, I will go up and talk to her. Otherwise, I might "eye fuck" her, but probably not go up and talk to her.

12. *Where do you hang out?* At the fraternity house. I go to a lot of par-ties.

13. *What are your thoughts about online dating?* Maybe I'll do it when I'm like 35.

14. *Have you ever had trouble moving on from a past relationship?* Yes. Senior year of high school, I went out with a girl for eight months; she ended up cheating on me. She broke it off and she went with that guy. It was a really fucked-up situation. I liked her a lot (more of a physical thing). I was not expecting the break-up and she moved on right away. I found out right before I went to college, so I didn't really have time to put closure on it. I couldn't think of girls for a while.

15. *What are your rituals for preparing for your date?* Shower, clean myself up. I don't really go out on dates, though, more of just a party hook-up person.

16. *If you did go on a date, where do you go/what do you do?* Might take them to lunch at a deli or perhaps for a coffee.

17. *If you don't know your date well, do you meet at the designated place or do you pick your date up?* Pick her up.

18. *Would you be interested in going for coffee and a walk instead of a dinner date for the first date?* Yes, I would prefer that.

19. *How often do you have a boys' night out? Where do you go with your friends?* All the time. Get drunk, we hang out; we go out and play pool.

20. *What frustrates you in the dating scene?* At UCSD, there is no dating scene – there are no hot girls. I really don't prefer dating – I prefer not being emotionally into the girl. Not at my age.

21. *What are you looking for in a relationship?* Not looking for a relationship. But if I were, it would be a sex-filled relationship.

22. *Would you go out with a married woman?* Say that I wouldn't, but I might.

23. *Would you date someone who had a child from another relationship?* Maybe a MILF [Mother I'd Like to Fuck]. If she was ridiculously hot.

24. *If you were to live with someone, how long would you be willing to live with her without a permanent commitment?* A few months.

25. *Do you smoke?* I smoke weed; not cigs. I do mind if she smokes cigs; I wouldn't like it, but it's okay if she smokes weed.

26. *Would you consider financially supporting your partner?* Absolutely.

27. *What makes an impression on you regarding your date?* Appearance is the most important. Intelligence.

28. *What type of clothing do you prefer your date to wear when you go out on a date?* In fashion, more creative than just Abercrombie. Unique.

29. *What is your preferred body type and shape for a woman?* 5'7" (few inches shorter than me), fit, and kinda petite.

30. *How do you feel about tattoos and piercings?* Kinda hot. The more tattoos and piercings, the more I want to hook up with her than actually have a relationship.

31. *How do you feel about perfumes and colognes?* A girl's perfume and scent is very important and sometimes underrated. It has a huge importance.

32. *How important is the first kiss?* Pretty important, but it takes a few before you know with what you are dealing. But your first hook-up is still important (you can tell how experienced or not she is and what kind of future you want with her). I like a girl that is experienced.

33. *Do you want to pay on the first date?* I like to split it.

34. *Any other behaviors that bother you when on a date?* Talking about her ex's.

35. *Will you have sex on the first date? If so, would you talk to your date about your preferences freely?* Yes, I would be down for sure. I wouldn't be up front about it.

36. *Would you have sex with your date if she were drunk?* Sticky situation. It really depends on the situation, and I would definitely not take advantage of her.

37. *Do you wear boxers or briefs?* I like to switch it up.

38. *How do you make sure a new sexual partner is free of STD's?* I use a condom and hope to god she doesn't have anything.

39. *Once you have decided to have sex with your date for the first time, are you free and uninhibited in the act or more conservative and reserved than normal?* I test my limits, but not excessively crazy.

40. *When on a date, where would you be willing to have sex with your date if you're hot and horny?* My house or her house.

41. *Where is your favorite place to have sex if you had a choice?* I like her bed.

42. *Do you use protection and, if so, who provides it?* Yes, always.

43. *What do you do if protection is not immediately available?* I would probably just pursue oral sex.

44. *What if you liked your date and she did not return your call the next day or week? What would you think and do?* I wouldn't be clingy, but it would definitely hurt. I would make sure to approach her differently.

45. *What if your date called you a month later? What would you say and do?* I would probably talk to her, but I would be condescending and not so excited.

46. *What age range do you date?* 17 and up.

47. *What do you think of one-night stands?* I'm perfectly fine with them and say most of my sexual activity is based off this.

48. *How do you break off a one-night stand or short relationship without being hurtful?* Just stop talking to them.

49. *How do you characterize yourself?*

    Positive attributes: Cultured (wannabe), attractive, witty, intelligent, great guy, sensitive, hilarious, easy-going, happy go lucky, conversation flows like water.

    Negative attributes: Extremely disorganized and forgetful, a little bit cocky, not the most reliable.

50. *Please include a detailed description of your ideal date.* A 5'7" stunningly beautiful French foreign exchange student named Jasmine -- she would have black hair and blue eyes -- we would go to a beautiful restaurant on the beach, walk on the beach, watch the sun go down, and walk on a little trail. Then we're gunna get attacked by a bunch of robbers and I would save the day.

51. *When you meet someone new, how long does it take you to know if the person is "the one" or has the potential to be "the one"?* I would say pretty quickly.

52. *Do you believe in "love at first sight"?* I believe in extreme sexual attraction.

53. *What is your personal philosophy on monogamy and monogamous relationships?* It's okay to be open. I think it is bound for failure because people screw up.

54. *What are some of the common terms in today's dating arena?* How's the bush or the bush needs trimming (the girl's pubes).

55. *Do you believe there is a game people play when dating? If so, describe the game.* Yes, absolutely, and I think it is completely psychological. I think the concept that girls have of true love is stupid and it is completely a game that guys play to try and get some. If you're a guy that knows what he is doing, you could almost manipulate the situation and get what you want by making the girl believe something that is not true. Getting girls is about manipulation (hate to say it, but I think this is true).

56. *Is the dating game a mystery or are the rules clear? If clear, what are the rules?* It's a mystery to a lot of people, but the rules are there and you can know what you are doing. It's like boxing. If you don't know what you're doing, you can still box, but you'll get your ass kicked. But if you know the rules and how to box, you can succeed.

57. *On average, how many dates are required before you consider yourself to be in a relationship?* Like 5 or 6.

58. *Have you ever been on a date with a girl who turned out to be a bitch?* Yes. It ended really badly (my ex- girlfriend). Ended awkwardly with negative emotions on both sides. Actually, I end up getting a lot of bitches.

59. *What source of communication would you like to use after the first date?* A lot of texts, texting is very useful – it's low key and it's easy to respond and easy to say exactly what you mean.

60. *If interested in your date, how long do you wait to communicate with her?* I will probably text her the next day and call her that night as well.

61. *If you were not interested in dating her again, would you let her know? If so, how do you let her know?* Stop talking to her; don't respond to her texts or calls.

62. Would you mind if your date contacted you immediately after the date? No, but that would make me believe that she was too clingy.

63. *Is spirituality important to you?* No, but culture is.

Below the belt questions:

1. *Is sex an important factor in deciding whether you will continue to date someone?* Very.

2. *Do you enjoy it when your date wears lingerie?* Yes, black and lacy.

3. *Have you ever experienced ménage à trois?* No.

4. *What is sexy to you in a woman?* I like that foreign or exotic feel to a woman. I like unique and different things. Girls with accents are hot.

5. *Does the size of her breasts matter?* Yes. But it's more important about how perky and nice they are and how nice the quality is.

6. *Do you mind surgical enhancement of breasts, lips, teeth, etc? How much body enhancement is too much?* Actually, it's a turn-off. I like natural, but not massive. I don't like artificial and huge.

7. *How much make up is too much?* When you can tell, but I like a good amount of make up.

8. *Are skimpy, body-fitting outfits a turn-on or a turn-off?* Definitely a turn-on, but it's going to make me pursue sex instead of a real relationship. It makes me think with my wee-wee instead of my brain.
9. *What do you think of athletic clubs as a place to meet someone?* Actually, it's a great way to meet people.
10. *What do you think of coffee houses as a place to meet someone?* I think it's the best.
11. *What do you think of the work environment as a place to meet someone?* Working with someone, you get to know them really well, but it's awkward if it doesn't work out.
12. *Do you prefer tanned or natural skin?* Natural.
13. *Do you prefer a particular pubic hair design?* Triangle shape.
14. *How many sexual partners have you had in your life?* 4.

VII. It's a Give & Take

Some characters straddle the line between givers and takers. These characters offer something to their partners while taking something in return. The characters that fall into this category can be both selfish and considerate.

A. The Apple & Forbidden Fruit: Give plenty of ecstasy and pleasure, but take a part of your soul.

The Apple or Forbidden Fruit is naughty by nature. She is one of a kind. She is sexy, seductive, enticing, captivating, alluring, intelligent, witty, and very dangerous to those men who fall under her spell. She feeds off of their energy, taking a bit of their soul with each encounter. She finds that the energy brings her youth. With each encounter, she looks and feels younger and more vivacious. Each sexual relationship rejuvenates her. She will be with single and married men, alike. She is all about sex, sex, and more sex. She is humorous and fun. She makes men feel like gods while they are with her until she casts them away. Once with her, men cannot get her out of their heads. She is illusive; no other woman can compete with her once a man has had her. From that point on, he will think of her even when he is with others. She will ruin him.

There is never a second time with the Apple. Every time is a new time, a first time. You never know what is going to be offered while you are in her presence. She adds value to your life; she gives you confidence in yourself. She makes you feel alive. She awakens you. She puts a forever spell on you. She is a master manipulator.

Her lovers appreciate that Apple is never emotionally available. That is part of who she is. If she were available emotionally, her lovers understand that they never would have stood a chance to be with her. It is the power of knowing that she owns them and they have no ownership over her that keeps her motivated. It the temporary rush of adrenaline that inspires her.

The key difference between men and women is that women become emotionally invested and involved through sex. Men typically don't. Apple is unique because she turns the normal paradigm on its head. The female Apple is similar to a man in that she does not become emotionally invested. Furthermore, she knows how to please her lovers and will stop at nothing until they have become emotionally invested in her. She keeps her emotions completely separate from the sexual act while capturing the emotions of her lover. She simply enjoys sex and all of the games that result from emotion-free sex. Where most men use power for sex, Apple uses sex for power.

The Forbidden Fruit may be male as well. Some men also use sex for power. Like the Apple, the male Forbidden Fruit offers pleasure with no strings attached. He gets a mental orgasm knowing that he is fulfilling a void and offering pleasure to a character who has suppressed her own needs and desires.

For stories about the Forbidden Fruit, refer to the chapters on the Forever Bachelor, the Fantasizer, and the Responsible Adult.

AN APPLE TELLS IT LIKE IT IS

1. *Gender:* Female
2. *Age:* 40's in years only; I feel like I'm in my 20's.
3. *Occupation:* Independently employed.
4. *What is your personal status?* I'm in a committed relationship. Our relationship goes beyond sex and is on a spiritual level. One man simply cannot appease me; he would die trying.
5. *How do you choose your lovers?* There has to be chemistry between us. But I always choose someone whom I can help to get to the next level. They are almost there, but they just need me to give them the final push to get them there.
6. *How do you know who needs you?* The pheromones guide me. I just know.
7. *Have you ever been sorry about your choice?* Never. I have learned something from each and every one. The only kind of man who would be wrong for me would be a self-centered, egotistical, self-absorbed man who was mean and hurtful. That would bring out the worst in me. I would want to crush his ego.
8. *Have you ever been caught in a situation where you couldn't get out?* No, never. They are always grateful to get anything from me. They want to keep the relationship going for as long as they can. They know it will come to an end at some point and on my terms. They will never do anything to jeopardize the relationship.
9. *How long do you keep your relationships going with these men?* As long as they need me and as long as I enjoy them.
10. *How long have you been casting your spell on men?* I don't cast a spell. Men have a strange way of thinking with their penises. I become one of the boys in bed. That's what men love. I become the aggressor while being the sensual buddy who sits and watches sports with them. We joke around. I make them so comfortable. I am both feminine and masculine; they don't know what to do with me. That's my secret. Humor is the most important thing when you are having

sex. It makes people feel good when they laugh and have unexpected moments when having hot passionate sex. Where some people enjoy fighting and then making up with "make-up sex," I enjoy interrupting sex for silly things like getting a glass of water. I get energy from knowing that they are always thinking about me when they are with other people and knowing that they can't have me. That empowers me.

11. *Where do you get your sexual confidence? Where did you learn your skills?* I was born with it. I have always been very comfortable with my body. You either have it or you don't. You cannot learn it. There are people, for instance, who have perfect bodies, but are not comfortable with themselves. I make the other person feel comfortable with his body. They become confident through my confidence. The men with whom I have been end up looking better, feeling better, and becoming better people in life. They become more confident with themselves. They start to take life less seriously. They enjoy each moment more. Their guilt and hang-ups disappear, realizing that society has imposed them from the time they were little boys. They end up loving themselves and becoming good people. They end up loving life and appreciating all the little moments. They appreciate having had the best thing and realize that they will never have anything better. They know they have touched the best. It is called a taste of heavens. Once you have had the taste, you relax. You become enlightened. Giving enlightenment energizes me. I am a total giver. I feel great about myself.

12. *Do you believe that you have a higher sex drive than most people?* I am certain of it. I enjoy sex thoroughly. I like to experiment with new things. I love new experiences. I first realized that I was a sexual person when I lost my virginity in my later teens. The first time was fabulous and it unleashed the beast in me. I think God created men as toys for women. Sex toys to be exact. I love giving head; I love beautiful penises. It is the size and proportion of the stalk and head that makes a penis perfect; I like the shaft to be the same size from the bottom to the head rather than graduated. A perfect size for me is about eight inches long and two to two and one half inches in diameter. My favorite thing is to go down on the guy. The secret is to use lots of tongue and lots of touch. The most sensitive area tends to be between the testicles and the anus. Give the entire stem, front and back, loving attention with your mouth and lips. French kiss around the dome. To

give him maximum pleasure, when he is ready to cum, put your index finger inside his anus.

Most people have sex just to have sex. They don't put much thought into it. Married people have sex because it is convenient and available. It is a duty to some. To others, it is a quick stress release. Some make love and their sex is very emotional. In that case, there is no expectation to perform. Once they fall out of love, they realize that sex is no longer because the emotions are gone. The best kind of sex is purely physical. When you find a man or a woman who is physically compatible with you and they have the right tools and know how, the sex can be amazing. When you are having physical sex all senses are at work -- smell, touch, taste, feel, sight, and hearing. Since there are no emotions involved, you are in for pure ecstasy. You are not thinking; your brain is asleep at this time and your senses take over. Your bodies become intertwined into one another and your sense of touch is at its highest level. The reason that this kind of sex is so good is that you are not thinking about the kids, picking up the laundry, or emotional baggage. You are not thinking at all; you are feeling and sensing, period.

13. *Do you want anything in return from your lovers?* I don't accept any gifts. I want nothing material. I simply want to know that the experience has been two-sided and fantastic for both. I want to feel that their life has improved because they have been with me.

14. *How do you feel about the married ones?* They are more delicious because it is more challenging to bring them over without guilt. The guilt always creeps in. I enjoy watching the emotional oscillations that guilt causes.

15. *What happens when you first see a man who is interested in you?* All the men are interested in me. All I have to do is turn on the heat. Let me tell you about the heat: All I have to do is look into their eyes. I am not subtle. I wet my lips. I wear a seductive outfit to attract him. It could be sweats worn in a seductive way. It is the energy. I am very selective, but once I have selected him, I go all out. I flirt and make him understand that I am there for the taking. He sees my confidence and must have a taste. He cannot resist.

16. *How does a guy let you know that he is ready for you?* They start drooling and they don't want to leave my side. They become like puppy dogs. If I say jump, they jump. The men I select have characters that are above others. To begin with, they are always good peo-

ple. Good means decent individuals who deserve me. They deserve to have a taste of heaven. They have never hurt others; they are considerate; they are in need of ecstasy; and I know I can give it to them.

17. *How do you bring the men to the next level?* First, I find the sexual hook. I find what they like and then I make them crave it. I need to be firm and sometimes I have to give them tough love. For example, I can only handle a man's guilt for so long. You can't be both enjoying and repenting simultaneously. So, I show them what ecstasy is. After they have experienced it, they desire it so badly, but I leave them hanging for a while to determine which way they want to go. Will guilt win over ecstasy? It is always ecstasy that ultimately wins. That makes them a better person -- they become completely aware of what they are doing. Once you are completely aware, you enjoy what you are doing.

18. *Has there ever been any man who took your breath away?* No. I am still waiting. I'm sure he's out there. I am ready to be taken to a higher level by the one. I think I would die if there were a man like that. I wouldn't know what to do. I would probably feel like the guys feel when they are with me.

19. *Describe your fantasy:* Of course, tall and handsome. Of course, confident beyond belief. Great body – not bodybuilder muscular, but toned and shaped. Smells like a peach. Great smile. Highly sexual and into my sexual needs. Always ready to go. Big hands and well endowed. Completely gifted with a beautiful penis. Fabulous sense of humor. Relaxed and able to take it easy. Financially secure on his own; someone who has lots of free time. Spontaneous. Let's just get up and go somewhere. Respectful to other people. Athletic. Funny. Playful. Considerate of others. Compassionate. Loves to learn new things; loves to read; loves to socialize; of course, non-judgmental and non-critical. Strong. Above all, someone who lives in the moment!

20. *Do you think this guy exists?* I'm sure, but I haven't found him yet.

21. *Have you always been looking for this particular guy?* No, I don't waste my time looking for anything. Things find me. People find me. They always have.

22. *If you found him, what would you do with your fantasy man?* I'll be with him. I'll enjoy his company for whatever moment and time is available.

B. The Desperate Dater: Gives a headache and takes your energy.

There are a million ways to end up in the inauspicious category of the Desperate Dater. The Desperate Dater may have been too choosy to commit, holding out for the next best date that never arrived. They may be unattractive to others because they have a challenging and unattractive personality or because they are intimidating in their looks or confidence. They may simply have never met the "one" and their fertility gong is ringing loudly. There are many lonely engineers out there in the dating scene who have been stuck in a pathway with limited opportunities. There are female black widows who have treated past relationships badly and now their reputation repels men. However they have reached their point of desperation, these characters are willing to lower their standards and settle for someone who will not make them happy in the long run.

This group keeps friendships with their past relationships and has a very difficult time letting go. Without fully letting go of the past, they are not free to find their future mate. They are imprisoned by their own fear of being alone. Rather than being themselves, they attempt to be something that others will want. Smelling desperation, those in the marketplace will either steer clear of Desperate Daters or take advantage of them.

BEWARE: This character settles and will always be wondering about what could have been. Later in life, Desperate Daters in their 40's and 50's will leave looking for their true love, soul mates, and happiness.

DESPERATELY OKAY WITH BEING DESPERATE

I don't believe in love at first sight. I want thoughtfulness, generosity, independence and communication in my relationships. Relationships should be easy. This is my first boyfriend in ten years. I have gone out with different people, but I have a full life with my family and friends. I want someone to add value to my life rather than give me a headache. Although I would like to have a husband and kids someday, I am beginning to think that I will be okay with my family and friends if it doesn't happen.

I met him at a bar. My friend was promoting her stripper pole at the bar. I had a lot of alcohol in me and I wasn't really looking for anything. He was open, sincere and uninhibited. He was up front and knew what he

167

was looking for. He was attractive. It was rare to meet someone like him. People are a lot more guarded these days. There was no game playing. We were making out by the door. I punched my phone number into his phone and sent it to myself. After I got home, I was practicing on the stripper pole and I texted him, telling him that I had fun.

When I woke up, I couldn't remember kissing him. My friend told me we were making out. It was the tequila shots. T hat morning he texted me and said he enjoyed it. He again texted me, asking if I wanted to talk that night. I had a date with a co-worker that I was not looking forward to be- cause I wanted to keep business and fun separate. My co-worker was hav- ing personal issues with his mom and I didn't want to let him down. I wanted to be there as a friend for him. I went on the date with him and he tried to kiss me; he viewed it as our second date. But I declined. He was disappointed, but I explained that I wasn't comfortable dating someone from work. The same night, I talked to the guy from the bar on the phone for three hours. We seemed to just click.

I met the guy from the bar for a second date. I enjoy good food, wine and cooking. So we decided to get together at his house and cook dinner. I love talking; talking gets me closer to them and getting to know about their beliefs and values and who they are. This was a perfect occasion for us to get to know each other. We talked about dating history and medical conditions. I told him I am very cautious and that I would only have sex when there is a condom available. Our night went well; we had safe sex and enjoyed each other.

After a couple of dates, he said he wanted me to be exclusive. Al- though I was hesitant, I found myself agreeing to it. I wasn't comfortable being exclusive yet, but I believe in marriage and want kids. He is not in a professional field and I never thought I would be dating someone without a college degree. He wanted to be my boyfriend -- he tried to give me a key to his house after only ten days. My mouth dropped open and I did not react well. He did not give me enough room to breathe; he told me he was falling in love with me. I was hesitant. I was feeling suffocated. He told me he could tell that I loved him as well by the way I treated him. I could not say it back. I did not say it back. He came across very confident, but I still rejected the key. I said I was not ready for that.

He took it as a rejection of him and avoided my calls for the next cou- ple of days, even though we had arranged for me to come to his place the next night. I showed up at his house because I thought we were going to get together, but he didn't answer the door. Against my better judgment, I kept calling. Finally, he answered and indicated that, if I had a key, I would have been able to get in that night. He told me that he had fallen asleep waiting for me.

Rather than running from this relationship, I justified the relationship and I found myself settling. Clothes and cars can change, can't they? He can go to school and get a degree later, right? I can make enough money to keep myself happy, can't I? It is okay if he doesn't make enough right now, isn't it? He is a good guy; he picks me up when I'm down like my friends. I knew I was seriously settling. My family was pushing me to have a family. They were looking at me like there was something wrong because I was over thirty and not married yet. My friends were all getting married around me. I was always the maiden of honor in their weddings. They were starting to have families. I was feeling left behind and my biological clock was ticking.

I was remembering my trip last year to Eastern Europe. I went by myself and realized how much I missed having a companion on the trip. It was an eye-opener to see that lonely is not good. I wanted someone with whom to share my life and have children. I read the book Secret to pep myself up. When I came back, I was ready for a relationship. Everything I was afraid to face, I faced. I had a few men in my life that I had to clean up. I said goodbye to all the men who were afraid of commitment and started new. But it seemed that I was following the same pattern again. I was justifying and settling. I was feeling pressure to commit to this guy because he wanted to commit to me. I refused to succumb to the pressure and broke it off. I am still looking for Mr. Right.

DESPERATE ONLINE

We met on an online site for wealthy people. After a few weeks of texting and email messaging, I finally asked him to have a face to face. I suggested we meet half way since he was in Laguna and I was in San Francisco. He said he had a meeting coming up in San Jose and asked where we could meet. I gave him few options for hotel accommodations. He texted me fourteen hours before our meeting, reminding me that there were only fourteen hours left until our meeting. He texted me every hour until I picked him up at the airport. I thought it was cute.

On his profile description, he said that he was tall, fit and good-looking. So, at the airport, I was looking for someone who fit that description. Suddenly, a short chubby man appeared in front of me and said,

"Hello." At that moment, I was thinking to myself, "Oh Lord, please don't let it be him." But, I guess the Lord was busy laughing at me. This man was dressed as if he had just stopped by the Salvation Army Thrift Store and had picked up the last pieces of over sized clothing with huge snags and moth holes covering the pants and the jacket.

I was dumfounded; I didn't know what to say or do. Like any respectable lady, I decided to just go along with it and not hurt his feelings. We proceeded to go to a bar in the area and sit at the farthest table away from the view of others. We ordered drinks and the terrible night was underway. He kept staring at me and saying how beautiful and hot I looked. He pushed his chair closer to me and started kissing my arm, which I found repulsive. I gently pulled away and asked him to remain a gentleman. He asked me why I was ruining the moment. I told him there was no moment and that I didn't even know him.

After a few back and forth attempts on his part to find a moment between us, I finally asked him to stop and sit still. He wasn't very happy with my move. He asked me to put my hand on the table, which I did. He asked me to tap on the table three times. I did as he asked. He said, "If any one of us during this date taps their hand three times on the table, it means the date is over." I thought he was bizarre.

Not only was he a liar, but he was demented as well. I just wanted to get out as soon as possible and never look back. He suggested we get a start on dinner. I thought maybe this guy's blood sugar was low and dinner would be a good thing. I suggested we go to a fancy restaurant and he was fine with that. He picked a very nice wine and suggested we split a meal. At that time, I wasn't arguing. I was fine with eating half an entrée and just wanted the night to end.

At dinner, he started with more of his disgusting touching and kissing of my arm. I again had to push him back. Again, he said, "Why are you ruining the moment?" And we started all over where we left off. He tapped on the table twice and looked at me. At that point, I didn't know if I should laugh or cry for allowing the date to continue this long. We finished dinner, he paid, and he abruptly got up, indicating that we were leaving. I was thrilled. "Sure, let's go," I said. I dropped him off back at his hotel thinking to myself, "I am not getting out of my car."

I thanked him and said it was nice to meet him. He got out of the car and walked over to my window. I rolled down the window to say goodbye. He asked me to text him when I got home so he would know that I got home safely. When I started the car, he asked me to roll up the window. I couldn't understand why he cared whether my window was up or down. I shrugged and asked, "What?" He said, "Roll up the window." I did. He then tapped on the window three times and left.

My jaw dropped and I hit the gas, getting away from such a psycho man as fast as I could. But, then again, here is the problem: I got home and texted him to say I got home safely. Don't ask me why I did. I just did. He responded, "Okay," and he has never stopped texting me since. He texts things like, "You are the woman of my dreams," " I want us to be lovers," and "I saw you and you were all that I ever wanted." I think the man needs help. I need help for going along with the guy for this long.

The moral of the story is: Don't believe anything you read online. People pad their resumes to the hilt, thinking once you see each other you're going to forget the profile description. I have news for you: NOT. Tall means short. Handsome means a lot to be desired. Rich means, "I am looking for a one-night stand online that I don't have to pay for so I can stay rich."

HOW TO AVOID FEELING DESPERATE
IN THE DESPERATE TIMES

We received the following correspondence from a woman in her 40's who wanted to share her thoughts about the down times with other women.

I think it is great to get women to talk about their thinking processes when it comes to dating and relationships. I think when we are forced to say our thoughts out loud we are better able to sort through and come to conclusions.

I have been married twice and started dating when I was 15. I am pretty sure that I have tried every theory out there on how to meet the right guy: blind dates, taking classes, on line, joining a church, join a gym, class reunions, mom fixing me up, clubs, work, team sports. You name it; I have tried it. What I have found is that you will eventually be in a relationship. The hard part is managing the in-between times.

During the in-between times, you are convinced that the whole world has become Noah's Arc and everyone is divided into twos except you. You do a mental head count of all your friends that are married. You wonder what the official age for "spinster" is. You begin to resent your cat. You wonder if all the money that you spent on Victoria Secret lingerie would have been better spent as a down payment on a condo?!

171

Oh, yes.

I think that, if we learn how to navigate through the in-between times, it helps find healthier relationships in the end. One in-between time in my twenties was very nicely spent and I actually had fun. I had moved to Hawaii by myself and I didn't know a soul except for the people with whom I worked. I spent the first month going from work to home thinking that I couldn't go out by myself. I worried what people would think about me if I did go out by myself? I finally came to the conclusion that if I were going to enjoy living in Hawaii, I needed to get out a bit. I got dressed up, got directions and headed out to Waikiki. I was scared and wondered what people would think of me, but soon found that by being by myself, it opened up the possibility for people (women, too) to talk to me. I made friends fast and didn't have to worry about what time I wanted to go home. It was just me. I was free and unencumbered.

Now, Hawaii is different from the Bay Area. It is not uncommon for people to move to Hawaii by themselves or go out by themselves, but here, it is a little different. I would watch how my girlfriends would refuse to do something fun because no one would go with them. I saw how they would stay home on weekend nights by themselves. This is a crying shame and not the life for me! I have a closet filled with pretty dresses. I work hard all week and am not going to be young forever!

One Saturday while lying around watching Lifetime, I came to the conclusion that I would really like a nice night out – a nice dinner, wear something sexy, curl my hair. So, after the heroine on the program killed her second husband, I jumped into the shower. I decided that I would go to an upscale place in Los Altos. It has low lighting, music, a center bar, and great food. It was busy when I got there, so I had to wait for a seat at the bar. Once sitting, I realized that I might like some company. What to do?

Now, what some women don't know is that men will go out to eat by themselves. They don't care about the company; they really just like to enjoy the food while people watching. I looked around the bar and noticed a reasonably handsome guy with a nice face who was by himself sans ring. I calmly walked over to him and asked if his name was Robert. I had never seen him before, but decided to pretend that I was waiting for an online blind date. He said "No." He then asked me if I was on an online date. I said that I was and that my "date" was late, but that I never saw a picture and the description matched him. We *joked and talked about it for a minute and then I resumed my seat. He came over two minutes later and asked me to join him. We had a really nice dinner and great conversation and even went out one more time. I had a ball!*

It is empowering to know that we as women can enjoy ourselves. We can educate ourselves, work in high paying careers, excel in sports, take ourselves out for dinner, and decide later that we might enjoy some company. Maybe it isn't always a firecracker romance, but if we can romance ourselves during the in-between times, it can certainly set the stage for the right relationship.

INTERVIEW WITH A BLACK WIDOW

1. *Contributor age:* 20's
2. *Gender:* Female
3. *Education Level:* College
4. *Are you financially secure?* Yes
5. *Profession:* Market research analyst
6. *Personal Status:* Single
7. *Are you looking for a long-term relationship or a meaningful one-night stand?* I am looking for a long-term relationship. I am kind of out there.
8. *Interests/hobbies:* I like working out and staying fit. To be the whole package, I like to keep myself looking eligible. Going to the beach and partying. Sporting events – I am a big hockey and basketball fan.
9. *What initially attracts you to the opposite sex? Past the initial attraction, what keeps you attracted?* Height. Smile, kind of the way they carry themselves. Past the initial attraction, I like a sense of humor. I love to be funny. Humor makes me feel comfortable.
10. *What do you find appealing in a date?* Relaxed environment. Not intense. It gives me anxiety. Bring me flowers, restaurant by the beach. I like someone who is carefree and not trying to overload me with complements. Sexual attraction is the most important thing. I am sexually attracted to a man who makes me feel like a woman. I am also looking for financial security.
11. *What do you find to be a turn-off in a date?* A cheese ball is the epitome of dorkyness and is a huge turn-off. They have that dorky laugh.

12. *Where do you meet men?* I try not to meet them at bars. In the wintertime, I am forced to go to bars. In the summertime, I meet them at concerts, sporting events, and festivals.

13. *When you are out with your friends and you see someone who catches your eye, what do you do?* I usually make myself noticeable. I stand in an area where I know they will be looking. I smile, but I never go up to them. If they have balls, they will come up to me. One guy came up to me, pretended to bump into his friend who then bumped into me and he stepped in to see if I was okay. But he turned out to be a huge cheese ball.

14. *What are your thoughts about online dating?* I have thought about it, but I don't think I'll ever do it. I feel that the kind of guy I would be attracted to would not do it. Unless it was a millionaire matchmaker site. I wouldn't take the millionaire match seriously, but why not?

15. *Have you ever had trouble moving on from a past relationship?* Never. I always break the guy's heart. I am the black widow. I chew them up and spit them out. I play more of a guy role. I need to be free.

16. *What do you think of one-night stands?* They happen. I am not opposed to them. I don't judge anyone. Certain people who are high and mighty judge you.

17. *How do you break off a one-night stand or short relationship without being hurtful?* I met this guy in San Francisco and he was a soccer player. I thought he had everything going for him and I couldn't figure out why he was still available. I wondered whether he had a vagina. We had one beer; he was very sexual. We exchanged numbers and talked every day for a week. He took me out to dinner and then said, "I need to tell you something." He told me that he was divorced, but immediately followed that news with a story about his nephew who had cancer and he started crying at the dinner table. Of course, I forgot all about the divorce. All my girl friends saw him crying. Later, we went back to my house. I thought, "I'm horny, let's do this." We were making out and in the middle of getting it on, he stopped and said, "I take sex very seriously." I didn't want to look like a slut, so I said, "Sure me, too." He then said, "I have really bad gas. I don't think we should do this." We started watching television. I totally forgot about the gas and the farting. I was so horny for him that I got all over him. I was on top of him and, all of the sudden, he said, "Whatever you're doing, don't stop." He then said in a deflated voice, "I have performance anxiety." I was so annoyed. We went to sleep. The next morning he

blew mud in my bathroom. He woke me up with it. I wanted him to get out of my house. I got dressed and he was naked. He said, "You know...what we should do today is to stay in bed naked and listen to music all day." I told him I needed to go to class and he needed to go. I am direct with them and nine out of ten appreciate directness.

18. *What are your rituals for preparing for a date?* Fully waxed, I love to pop open a bottle of champagne and drink while I put on my makeup.

19. *Type of lingerie you would wear on a first date? And the following dates?* I read somewhere that red is the color for men. When I wear red lingerie, I get a lot more attention and action.

20. *Where do you go/what do you do on a date?* Eat them alive. Dinner, movie, cocktails, I like to make things social. I like to meet a new guy where I know other people. It is safer.

21. *How often do you have a girls' night out? Where do you go with your girlfriends?* Often. Wednesday is dinner and a movie. Thursday is a fun night -- Karaoke in a total dive bar.

22. *What frustrates you in the dating scene?* Most guys have the majority of the whole package, but they are missing one important thing like height, job or good teeth. I date men from 25 to 40 years.

23. *What are you looking for in a relationship?* Someone to whom I am attracted and who makes me feel sexy and womanly; someone with whom I really feel comfortable; I love to laugh. I love a guy who is confident. He could be wearing a florescent pink shirt and feeling confident, confidence is such a turn-on.

24. *Would you go out with someone who was married?* No. I can't seem to get a hold of my own life, let alone getting involved with someone else who is unavailable.

25. *Would you date someone who had a child from another relationship?* It would take a lot of information. I want my own kids sometime.

26. *If you were to live with someone, how long would you be willing to live with him without a permanent commitment?* I don't know. It has never been a factor in my relationships. I consult my family a lot. I often wish that I had listened to my parents sooner in my relationships so I hadn't wasted my time. They always give me their opinion; it sits in the back of my mind for the rest of the time that I date the guy.

27. *Do you smoke?* Occasionally.

28. *Are you hoping to find a man who is financially secure? Is financial security more important than love?* Yes to both.

175

29. *How does it make you feel if your date flaunts his assets?* It is not very attractive.
30. *What type of clothing do you prefer your date to wear?* Nice jeans, long-sleeved colored shirt.
31. *What is your preferred body type and shape for a man?* Tall, thick, and I don't mind a little pooch; I want a real man. A meaty body. Football body. As long as he makes me feel small.
32. *How do you feel about tattoos and piercings?* I love tattoos. Secretly, I love them. It is just sexy. Inside their arm or on the back of their calves. Lip rings are okay. They are so sexy.
33. *How do you feel about perfumes and colognes?* I don't pay attention. As long as they have no body odor.
34. *How important is the first kiss?* It is very important. It sets the sexual mood, a good kisser is good and a bad kisser is not good. Not too much tongue and no porno tongue like a dog.
35. *Do you expect your date to pay on the first date?* 110% yes.
36. *What is your preference and philosophy on who should pay the bill on dates with you?* He should. Doesn't mean I won't offer. If I offer and he accepts, it is bad.
37. *Will you have sex on the first date? If so, would you talk to your date about your preferences freely?* Yes. Yes.
38. *Lights on, off or dimmed?* OFF!
39. *Do you prefer your date to wear boxers or briefs?* Boxers.
40. *How do you make sure a new sexual partner is free of STD's?* If a one-night stand, it is hard. You either know him from a friend of a friend, or you just get a good vibe. It is not a great way to find out. I get checked and I get sick all the time. My immune system isn't great. I should be careful.
41. *Once you have decided to have sex with your date for the first time, are you free and uninhibited in the act or more conservative and reserved than normal?* I have had guys put it in my ass the first time we had sex. I enjoy anal sex. I feel that you get a completely different orgasm. Not very many girls like it because it hurts. The girl needs to be in charge and direct the guy. If I feel comfortable with the guy, I am totally uninhibited. I like being adventurous and dirty. I like to watch anal sex. I like to watch pornography.
42. *Where would you feel comfortable having sex with your date?* Car.

43. *Where is your favorite place to have sex?* I am imagining having sex on the cloud. The washer and dryer are fantastic. I want the guy to pick me up and throw me on there.

44. *Do you use protection and, if so, who provides it?* I do. I ask them if they have something with them.

45. *What if you liked your date and he did not call you the next day or week?* I might text the next day saying, "Thanks, it was good."

46. *In your opinion, at what age does a man know himself, his body, and his needs?* At age 42 -- could be comfortable, but doesn't necessarily know what he is doing. They should watch porn and see how things are being done.

47. *In your opinion, at what age does a woman know herself, her body, and her needs?* Depends on experience and how comfortable they are with masturbating. The more experimental they are, the more comfortable they are. Can't be closed- minded.

48. *What age range do you date?* 28-40 years.

49. *How do you characterize yourself?*

> **Positive attributes:** Very honest, and straightforward. If a guy asked how he was doing when going down on me, I would say, "Not good cause you are talking." I will make a fool out of myself. I love to have fun. I am nurturing. I love taking care of people. Great in bed and confident.
> **Negative attributes:** I am a pleaser and can't say, "No." I tend to double book. I can be impatient.

50. *Please include a detailed description of your ideal date.* Something clever, the guy picks me up and takes me to a basketball game, cocktails after, and a fairy ride. Something that is not so structured. I like him to fly by the seat of his pants. I like guys who can take control. I like guys who are confident and take charge.

51. *When you meet someone new, how long does it take you to know if the person is "the one" or has the potential to be "the one"?* Couple of dates.

52. *Do you believe in "love at first sight"?* Totally.

53. *What is your personal philosophy on monogamy and monogamous relationships?* I think you should be faithful to your partner. It is not a fair belief. I think if a woman wants to test the waters, she should be able to do it. I want to be desired by everyone. I don't mind telling him and having a threesome. I like it when guys look at me. My man has to be able to handle it.

54. *Do you believe there is a game people play when dating? If so, de-scribe the game.* Yes. Like the "I am not into you part." "I am not go-ing to put myself out there to get hurt." Unless you put yourself out there, nothing can come of it. I am guilty as charged; I act as if I am not interested. The guys should pursue me and not be so sensitive.
55. *Would you mind if your date contacted you immediately after your date?* I wouldn't mind.
56. *Is the dating game a mystery or are the rules clear? If clear, what are the rules?* It is not a mystery. When you are a teenager, it is a mystery. Feel each other out. Mutual respect. See if you want to have a hot sexy session or go grocery shopping.
57. *Do you consider yourself to be a game-player in the dating arena?* I am a player only when they are playing. I invented the game.
58. *What books on dating have you read? Out of those books, which ones do you recommend?* I Hope They Serve Beer in Hell. The best book hands down. By Tucker Max. This guy has done things to girls that I can only imagine.

Below the belt questions:

1. *Is sex an important factor in deciding whether you will continue to date someone?* Yes, but not the most.
2. *Do you enjoy wearing lingerie?* Yes.
3. *What is sexy to you in a guy?* Confidence; the way he carries himself.
4. *Does the size of a penis matter?* No. As long as the guy is hot and sexy. We can use vibrators and watch porn.
5. *Do you prefer circumcised or not?* Circumcised. I don't like it other-wise.
6. *Do you prefer more or less hair on a man?* I like a little hair.
7. *Do you prefer tanned or natural skin?* Tanned.
8. *Will you kiss and tell your friends or do you keep it private?* Close friends, I tell.
9. *What do you think of coffee houses as a place to meet someone?* Cof-fee guys are a bit feminine with their laptops.
10. *How many partners have you had?* More than 28 and every one of them has a pet name.

HE CANNOT TREAT ME THAT WAY!

A Desperate Dater may put herself into a position where another can and will treat her badly. She will stay because she simply cannot believe the other person is treating her so poorly. She is often in shock.

While on a tour in the city, she met a guy who looked as good as the famous soccer player David Beckham. He was actually a medical student. They agreed to have a date, but he had no car. She agreed to pick him up. She showed up at his house and he was already drunk, falling off the stool at the counter. They were going to a party where they were supposed to bring wine. On the way to the party, they stopped at a store to pick up the wine. Her drunken date had forgotten his wallet. She rolled her eyes and bought the wine. They continued on to the party. He was not talking in the car. She asked him why. He said, "I don't want this to sound rude, but I don't have tolerance for mindless chatter." So she thought she should not say anything else for fear of giving him mindless chatter. It was a long, silent drive to the party.

When they got to the door, they rang the doorbell. Her date handed the bottle of wine to the host, who then thanked him profusely for bringing such a nice bottle. He took the credit for choosing such a wonderful bottle, while she just stood there with her mouth open. He was the life of the party. At the party, someone was selling tickets for a hockey game that night. He suggested that she buy the tickets so they could go to the game after the party. She did.

While at the game, he became thirsty and hungry. She put out again. She thought that he was becoming her "bitch." After the game, she took him home, expecting him to perform in bed as good as he looked. To her amazement, he passed out on the bed and crashed. She could not wake him. She went to bed horny and disappointed.

The next morning, he was expecting breakfast. She could not believe her ears. They went out for breakfast on her dime again. After breakfast, she drove him back home to the City. She stopped by the gas station and he remained in the car while she got out to pump the gas. He called out the window, "Hey sweetie, could you get me a Red Bull?" She didn't acknowledge him. She paid for the gas and bought one Red Bull . . . for herself. She chugged it in the car in front of him.

She dropped him off at home and was expecting some sort of thank you or apology, but there was nothing. He tried to kiss her good-bye and she turned her face. He texted her that afternoon, requesting a second date. He said, "I bet you are missing me and would like to see me again tonight." She texted him back, "You bitch! Not."

C. The Trapped: Gives commitment and needs nurturing.

The Trapped is in a committed relationship that has gone wrong for one reason or another. It may have been a relationship where commitment was initially forced by one of the parties for either cultural reasons or social convention or the parties may have simply drifted apart over time. For the Trapped, the relationship becomes unbearable. The Trapped tries to do the right thing, but the home environment gradually sickens him or her. They take a lot for a long time, but ultimately become interested in getting relief and validation from outside.

The Trapped seeks nurturing from outside through co-workers, acquaintances, neighbors and anyone else who may be aware of their circumstances. This character exudes sadness and depression. His or her energy picks up once he or she becomes involved with a nurturing figure.

The Trapped might use the nurturing figure as a temporary band-aid because he or she does not want to leave his or her family. However, the Trapped can be lured away from his or her family by a nurturer with an agenda. A Gold-digger or a Home Wrecker may not be looking out for the best interests of the Trapped; they may have a selfish motive behind their gentle touches. If the Trapped is in a high socioeconomic status, he or she should beware of such manipulative nurturers. If the Trapped finds nurturing from a Gold-digger, the nurturing will be temporary; it is all an act. On the other hand, if the Trapped is lucky enough to find a true Nurturer, he or she may be happier with the new partner. However, the Trapped will rarely initiate the first step out the door. Leaving blatant signs of his or her infidelity, the Trapped hopes to be caught by the spouse. Once the spouse discovers the infidelity and demands that the Trapped make a choice, the Trapped may take the opportunity to run out the door.

If the spouse does not want to open that door, he or she should step back to see why his or her mate is unhappy and focus on repairing the damaged relationship.

BEWARE: Unless your relationship is unbearable and beyond saving, you can always try to work it out. If your relationship and family are worth saving, do your best to work on it. Relationships are work on both sides; perhaps you have not been putting in enough effort on your end.

THE TRAP OF NEW MONEY

They married young and were in love. Even though they had dated for five years, he would have much rather waited to get married. She insisted and persisted until he gave in to her desires. He was an upcoming, young, wealthy executive and she was a beautiful young woman with her two-year degree, working at a department store.

The first five years of marriage went along smoothly. They played and enjoyed themselves. They traveled the world, partied, spent time with crazy wacky friends and surrounded themselves with adoring fans. The more successful he became, the more showy and obnoxious she became. They had three kids; hundreds became millions; and houses were replaced with mansions and penthouses with full staffs at each.

The more debonair he became, the more flashy and spoiled like a starlet she became. The money went to her head and she no longer had consideration for anyone other than herself and her own needs. Her behavior toward her children, her husband, and family members became unbearable.

From the outside looking in, their life appeared to be a fairy tale. But, from the inside, the life had become a nightmare for the husband. She was unbearable and unstoppable, her vulgarity and rudeness had no end. She became verbally abusive to her partner in front of friends and family. He was a gentleman and a diplomat. When she berated him, he would only smile and drop his head down in shame and sorrow. He tried for years to communicate with her about her attitude, behavior and social standing. She was a girl from the wrong side of the tracks who had come into incredible wealth. The money exacerbated her true self, her insecurities, and her attention-seeking, selfish personality.

She didn't see any problem with her behavior. Most people around her kissed up to her and praised her for her foulness. Her husband, on the other hand, wanted to make their marriage work and tried everything in his power to do so. But she was who she was. She had come from a dysfunctional, abrasive, rude, classless family. Although she had a good heart, she was abrasive and had no social etiquette. Her husband tried for many years to help her to evolve into a more pleasant individual, but to no avail.

After many years of marriage, feeling trapped and physically ill, he turned his attention elsewhere. He found a true nurturer who was content with herself and wasn't looking to get hitched. She happened to be a co-worker. They became great friends and eventually enjoyed a torrid affair. He gradually came out of his funk, becoming himself again. He was looking better, feeling better and he became stronger.

He confronted his wife about her negativities. She noticed the positive change in him and his outlook. She became suspicious. She hired a private investigator to find out why he was so happy. He made no effort to hide his affair and the investigator easily discovered the secret to his happiness. It was an intelligent, caring, nurturing, self-made, naturally beautiful wholesome woman. Upon this discovery, the wife went off the deep end and reported the affair to the board of directors at his company. There was a very strict anti-nepotism policy at the company.

While happy and in love with his nurturer, he would never have left his family had his wife not opened the door. She paved the way for him to move forward with divorce proceedings by exposing and embarrassing him to the public. She had not contemplated the repercussions of her vengeance. She made it possible for him to ask for divorce. She was dumbfounded when he initiated divorce proceedings. She begged for him to stay. It was too late. She tried to make the divorce nasty. He did not play into her agenda. He is a free and happy man. He is still dating his wholesome beauty, but is in no rush to settle down.

INTERVIEW WITH A MAN IN A LIFELESS MARRIAGE

1. *Contributor age:* 50's
2. *Gender:* Male
3. *Education Level:* Graduate Degree
4. *Profession:* Engineering Design
5. *Relationship Status:* Divorced
6. *What happened with your marriage(s)?* I have been married once for 27 years. I recently initiated divorce proceedings. We had three kids. Somewhere in the midst of it all, I was lost in the shuffle. We had a turbulent life together. We had a child with severe health issues and another with severe learning disabilities. We struggled through those issues together. Then, my wife's parents both became ill at the same time. She was the only child and was charged with their care. She refused to get help for the longest time. I had to take over the care of our kids while she took care of her parents for over ten years. Our relationship died during those years. There was nothing left for me. I

didn't want to leave the family; I was the glue that held the family together. I felt like I couldn't leave, even if I wanted to. What an asshole I'd look like. My wife was barely holding it together and the kids were a mess. I would be the pariah of the town. So, I stayed. After my wife's parents passed, things did not improve. The relationship was dead. I wanted to go out and do things; she wanted to stay home and watch television. I wanted to travel; she wanted to stay home and watch television. I saw my life passing before my eyes and my life was stagnating; I was like a piece of petrified rock. I was not looking to leave. I would never have left.

I went on a bike ride one day and ran into a neighbor. We rode together and we talked and laughed like I hadn't done in fifteen years. I felt light. I felt excited. We met three mornings a week for a ride up in the hills. It seemed as if she enjoyed my company as much as I enjoyed her company. We began texting throughout the day. She texted me one evening. My wife grabbed the phone and assumed that we were having an affair. She hit me on the head with a skillet. She told me that I couldn't have them both and that I would have to choose. I moved out the next morning. I continued biking with my neighbor; we became very good friends. It never developed any further; she was dedicated to her family and was not ready to leave her husband. She provided me with everything that I had been lacking though. She cared how I was feeling and about what I was doing. She was interested. My wife and I have been living separately now for about a year. I know that she has tried dating and that she would take me back in a minute. She wants an apology for something that I never did. I don't feel that I did anything wrong. I feel a huge sense of relief that it is over. I am ready to live again.

7. *Interests/hobbies:* Cycling, bike racing, golf, and traveling.
8. *What initially attracts you to the opposite sex?* A healthy look and a sparkle in her eyes.
9. *What do you find appealing in a woman?* I want a woman who wants to live life and who can keep up with me. I have a lot of energy and want to lead an active lifestyle. I want a woman who wants to do the same.
10. *What do you find to be a turn-off in a woman?* A television junkie. Someone who wants to spend her free time reading rather than doing. I don't like a loud, obnoxious woman. I don't want a drunk.

11. *What do you want from a woman and how do you want to be treated by a woman?* I want a woman to treat me like a man. I want her to want me and I want her to want me to want her. Equal desire and effort.

12. *How have your desires changed over your life?* When I was younger, I wanted a sexual and physical relationship. Then, I wanted a good mother for my children. I never wanted to play second fiddle, but I was willing to do it for the good of my family. Now, I want a sexual, physical, and emotional relationship all wrapped up in one.

13. *When you are out with your friends and you see someone who catches your eye, what do you do?* We discuss it amongst ourselves and then I let my friend call her over to our table and make an ass out of himself. I will break into the conversation at the right time. I will invite her to sit with us and she will usually sit with me.

14. *Where do you hang out?* I hang out with my friends; we watch games and shoot pool at a couple of the guys' houses. We go to a couple of hot spots in town where we have made a group of single friends. I have started to go on a weekly ride with about twelve other men and women who cycle. We are all in training for one goal or another. We hang out at a coffee place after our rides.

15. *What are your thoughts about online dating?* I am not sure about it. I won't do it now. I feel like I am meeting a lot of fun and eligible people out there without the crutch. It might be for people who are shy or who don't have a big support group of single friends.

16. *Have you ever had trouble moving on from a past relationship?* Of course, haven't we all? My wife was my high school sweet heart. I have known her for most of my life. It was very hard to leave our relationship. I had to leave to save my life. I think it will save her life in the long run. She will be forced to get out and meet people. Maybe she can find her old self again. I want the best for her.

17. *Where do you go/what do you do on a date?* We go out to dinner or we go out to a dance club. If she is into bicycling, we can go for a ride and then go for a picnic. An active date is preferred for me, but I also love to go out at night.

18. *How often do you have a boys' night out? Where do you go with your friends?* I've been going out with the boys on Thursday through Sunday evenings. Monday morning has turned out to be a real bitch. It is worth it though. As long as my performance at work is not being adversely affected, I can continue with the Sundays.

19. *What frustrates you in the dating scene?* The gamesmanship from the girls. Many of the women have been on the circuit for a long time and they have known most of the guys intimately. It is a bit incestuous in our small little town. The real gamers end up with a bad reputation; they are looking for loot and I've put my gold in the safe.

20. *What are you looking for in a relationship?* I am looking for a happy, energetic, caring person who looks good.

21. *Would you go out with a married woman?* To tell you the truth, if I stay in my age bracket, most women have been married at least once. If not, there is probably something wrong with them. Oh. I see . . . I would go out with someone who was married, but I wouldn't sleep with her. If she were separated, it would be a different story. Separated is as good as divorced from my perspective.

22. *Would you date someone who had a child from another relationship?* Absolutely. Children make people caring human beings.

23. *If you were to live with someone, how long would you be willing to live with her without a permanent commitment?* I am not looking to get married again. I was married for a very long time. I am not going to jump right into marriage again. I would be happy to live with someone for a long time, maybe for the rest of my life, without marrying. After divorce and, at this point in my life, finances play a larger role in deciding whether to marry. Things get very complicated. It's easier to keep everything separate.

24. *Would you consider financially supporting your partner?* Probably not. I will be supporting my ex for the rest of her life or for the rest of mine. I wasn't looking to leave her stranded; I want her to have a comfortable life. I don't want to support two women.

25. *What type of clothing do you prefer your date to wear when you go out on a date?* Casual.

26. *What is your preferred body type and shape for a woman?* Athletic and firm.

27. *How do you feel about tattoos and piercings?* I'm not into them at all. My son and daughter both have them and I think it is a huge mistake. One of my son's earlobes is about ready to rip off because his plugs are so large. I don't think plastic surgery could fix it; I think he'll end up lopping off his ear lobe when he looks for a job that isn't in a coffee shop.

28. *How do you feel about perfumes and colognes?* They are okay if used sparingly.

29. *How important is the first kiss?* It shows a connection with the other person.
30. *Do you want to pay on the first date? And after the first date?* Sure, I'll pay.
31. *Will you have sex on the first date? If so, would you talk to your date about your preferences freely?* Now we're getting to the crux of the matter. I don't know that I want to jump right into bed with a woman. I know that women attach emotions to sex. I want to be careful before I get emotionally involved again. I want to know that the woman is a happy, carefree person before I let myself become emotionally attached. I want someone who is going to make me feel good emotionally as well as physically.
32. *Would you have sex with your date if she were drunk?* If I were drunk, it would be more likely to happen.
33. *How do you make sure a new sexual partner is free of STD's?* Boy, dating is different today than it was when I was dating my ex. I haven't figured this one out other than to make sure I wear a condom until I really know the person.
34. *Where is the most interesting place you have had sex?* When my ex and I were young and foolish, we climbed a water tower and had a dangerous rendezvous.
35. *Do you use protection and, if so, who provides it? If you don't use protection, how do you stay safe or is it an issue?* I always use a condom these days.
36. *What do you do if protection is not immediately available?* I'll go to the 24-hour drug store and buy a pack of condoms.
37. *What age range do you date?* I am planning on sticking to women in the age range of 37 to 50.
38. *What do you think of one-night stands?* If both parties can handle it, more power to them. I am still navigating through this area. I have never been a one-night stand kind of guy. I guess if I was confident that the girl was disease-free, wasn't a stalker, and wouldn't be hurt by it, I might consider it.
39. *How do you break off a one-night stand or short relationship without being hurtful?* Let her know before it occurs and give her the choice up front.
40. *What was your parents' status when you were growing up?* Happily married for 60 years. It broke my heart when my marriage had to end in divorce.

41. *How do you characterize yourself?*
    Positive attributes: Loyal, honest, nurturing, active, good-provider.
    Negative attributes: Letting others dictate my life for too long.

42. *How do you think others see you?* I think others see me as a nice guy and a loyal friend. I think they see me as still in my shell; I have a few friends who are trying to get me to come out of my shell.

43. *Please describe what you would do and where would you go on a date if you could do anything?* I would go on a bike ride along the coast. We would stop in at a lovely hotel on the beach where we would clean up and then we would go to a nice dinner and talk and get to know one another. If things went well, we would return to the hotel for a passion-filled night.

44. *When you meet someone new, how long does it take you to know if the person is "the one" or has the potential to be "the one"?* I know right away.

45. *Do you believe in "love at first sight"?* I fell in love with my ex right away. Yes, I say it does happen for sure. She always told me that she loved me at first sight as well. I am waiting to see if it happens twice in a lifetime.

46. *What is your personal philosophy on monogamy and monogamous relationships?* A definite requirement for me to be in a relationship. Once the trust is gone, so is the relationship. When my wife accused me of cheating with my neighbor and she wouldn't believe me that I had never cheated on her, I knew that she didn't trust me and would never trust me again.

47. *Do you believe there is a game people play when dating? If so, describe the game.* The game is one of first impression. Make the best first impression you can make because you might not get a second chance. But, what I am trying to remember is that first impressions are often wrong impressions.

48. *If interested in your date, how long do you wait to communicate with her?* I would tell her before the end of the date and see if she was feeling the same way.

49. *If you were not interested in dating her again, would you let her know?* I would tell her that I enjoyed meeting her and that I'm exploring the dating world right now.

50. *Would you mind if your date contacted you immediately after the date?*
    I wouldn't mind at all. People should do what they feel like doing; if
    the person is right for them, they will appreciate what you have done.
    If the person is not right, then it is better to know early so you can
    move on.
51. *Is spirituality important to you?* I'm not a big believer in religion.

Below the belt questions:

1. *Is sex an important factor in deciding whether you will continue to
    date someone?* Yes. The connection is important.
2. *Do you enjoy it when your date wears lingerie?* It doesn't do anything
    for me.
3. *Have you ever experienced ménage à trois?* No. I don't think I would
    be up for that.
4. *What is sexy to you in a woman?* A happy, confident, energetic, ath-
    letic woman with sparkling eyes.
5. *Does the size of her breasts matter?* No, smaller is fine with me. They
    get saggy if they are large and real. I'm not into plastic surgery.
6. *Do you mind surgical enhancement of breasts, lips, teeth, etc?* I don't
    think it is a healthy thing.
7. *How much make up is too much?* If you need to make a comment that
    her make up looks nice, it is too much.
8. *Are skimpy, body-fitting outfits a turn-on or a turn-off?* They are a
    turn-on as long as they are not showing too much skin. If it is body
    fitting and the body is good, then it is great.
9. *What do you think of athletic clubs as a place to meet someone?* I'm
    not comfortable with this. This one place has been my salvation for
    the last fifteen years. I don't want to complicate it with unsuccessful
    relationships.
10. *What do you think of the work environment as a place to meet some-
    one?* It's always a possibility, but I feel the same way as I feel about
    the athletic club.
11. *Do you prefer tanned or natural skin?* Tanned in spite of sunscreen.
12. *Long hair or short hair?* It doesn't matter as long as it's blonde.
13. *Do you prefer a particular pubic hair design?* I don't care. Boy,
    things have changed. I'm not going to be shaving and cutting on mine
    so I don't expect the girl to do it either. If she wants to, more power to
    her.

14. *How many sexual partners have you had in your life?* 2.

D. The Socially Awkward: Fill space.

The Socially Awkward are insecure people who have had a hard time in the dating world, either because they are passive and shy or because they are aggressively overcompensating for their insecurities. These aggressive characters put themselves out in the marketplace as loud mouth jerks, abrasive attention-seekers, and obnoxious pranksters. The passive characters are simply so shy and introverted that they have a hard time getting themselves out in the market and making a good first impression once there. These passive characters are observers, learners, and they are interested in bettering themselves.

NOTE: All is not lost. The Passively Awkward are capable of learning how to date and may become very successful in the marketplace. If the Aggressively Awkward can learn to relax, they too may find success in the dating scene. For those who do not learn or evolve, they remain awkward and may become Desperate Daters.

1. AGGRESSIVELY AWKWARD: THEY GIVE YOU THE HEEBIE JEEBIES AND TAKE YOUR TIME AND ENERGY.

In some circles, they are known as jerks. The Aggressively Awkwards have no consideration for anyone else and are mainly concerned with their own immediate pleasure. They can be offensive, loud, rude, obnoxious, and go too far when giving into their impulses. Their clothing can be tasteless. They lack discretion and will gossip freely. They do not want others delving into their private lives, but will not miss a beat when it comes to exposing others for fun. The Aggressively Awkward character is a heavy drinker and partier. The more they drink, the more obnoxious they become. They are extremely opinionated and judgmental, but they do not see themselves that way. They can be completely inappropriate in their usage of language, gestures and behavior.

They often find themselves gravitating toward the good old boys so that they can be part of the group and the "in-crowd." They are the class-clown. They will do almost anything for a laugh. The in-crowd likes to have them around because they are entertaining and will do the dirty work for the group. They provide the needed out-of-the-box outrageous entertainment. They will moon people for a laugh. However, they take it too far and don't know when to stop. Interestingly, they can both dish it and take it. It doesn't bother them a bit to be the butt of a joke. They are used to being the butt.

They care what people think about them because they want to stay in the "in-circle." They are name-droppers. They are suck-ups. They'll deny any wrongdoing. They spin losses and failures as someone else's fault. They cannot accept responsibility. When things get tough, they get tougher, gruffer, and obnoxious.

It takes a strong, tough mate to weather the storm with an Aggressively Awkward. The mate may find herself or himself constantly smoothing the ruffled feathers of those who have been offended by inappropriate pranks, jokes, and gossip. To his or her credit, this character is family-oriented. While he or she will flirt like there is no tomorrow, he or she will rarely cheat. Listening is not his or her strong suit. They do have a great sense of humor and can be great fun. It is very difficult to stay angry at this character because he or she has a childish charisma about him or her. They can be the life of the party if the alcohol is limited. If the alcohol is not limited, they become a sloppy drunk.

BEWARE: Do not tell your secrets to this character. Be discreet in front of them. Otherwise, the whole town will know your intimate details.

THE LEACH

I met this guy at a friend's wedding and I made the mistake of talking to him when I was waiting at the bar for my drink. He was one of the guests and mistook my friendly approach for genuine interest in him. Once I received my drink, I walked to my table and he followed me. He actually moved the woman's purse from the chair next to me and sat down.

I was confused and wondered what he was doing. He said, "I guess this is the best seat in the house and I have it." I told him that my girlfriend was sitting there and he would have to move. He said, pointing across the table, "I guess your girlfriend can sit on the other chair." I was appalled and annoyed. I got up and went to find my friend. He followed me and touched my lower back with his hand as I walked. He was very forward and I guess he was trying to let me know that he was walking with me, as if I didn't know.

I cringed and asked him to please not do that. I asked him why was he following me. He told me that he enjoyed being around me and that he would like to chat further. I was shocked at his behavior. I didn't want to be rude at the wedding, but I didn't want to be stuck with him for the rest of the night.

I politely told him that I wanted to spend some alone time with my girlfriend because I hardly ever got to see her. He said, "Oh, okay. Then maybe we can dance later." I said, "Maybe (thinking NOT)." I found my friend and told her about him. We had a good laugh and we were still laughing when we got back to the table. We stopped laughing when we saw him sitting there waiting for us.

We both immediately turned and walked back to the bar. He followed us to the bar and approached me saying, "Why are you avoiding me? Don't you want to talk to me?" I told him that he was being obnoxious and was making me feel uncomfortable. I told him that he needed to learn social etiquette. He said, "I don't understand. Help me. People have told me that before."

I took pity on him and asked him to sit with us. During dinner, I enlightened him. I told him the following:

1. When someone says, "Hello," it does not mean, "Follow me, hover and come fuck me."
2. After the first "Hello," you can try to initiate a more in depth conversation, but if it doesn't go anywhere, leave it and move on.
3. Learn to take a hint. Never go sit next to someone without being invited or without asking first. Do not be rude and presumptuous.
4. In social gatherings, be on your best behavior. Do not take advantage of the fact that you are not in a bar with strangers, but that you are amongst friends who will feel required to be more tolerant of bad behavior. If you do take advantage of the situation, you will not be invited again.
5. Trust me, if someone wants to be with you, they will find you and let you know. Don't force yourself upon them like a leach.
6. The less you talk and do, the more appealing you become. Make the first move, sit back, and let the chips fall where they may.

After he ate his entrée, he excused himself from the table and moved to the kids' table – the only table with an open seat.

AN INTERVIEW WITH A PRACTICAL JOKER

1. *Contributor age:* 50's
2. *Gender:* Male
3. *Education Level:* College
4. *Profession:* Marketing
5. *Relationship Status:* Divorced
6. *How many times have you been married?* I have been married twice and divorced twice. The first woman I married was my girlfriend from college. We first met at a pledge party for my fraternity. She hated me because of all the pranks my roommate and I played on her sorority sisters and her. A semester later, we ran into each other at another fraternity party and hooked up. We started dating from that point on. We dated throughout college, but we were not completely exclusive. We broke up several times over the six years that we dated; pretty much any time I wanted to see another girl, I broke up with her. She kept taking me back when I came whining with my tale between my legs. After college, she started pushing me to marry her and I finally relented. I would have been happy to live as we were forever. She wanted kids. That turned out all right; we have three fabulous kids. She became hateful as the years passed and resented my practical jokes more and more. She grew into a bitter person who was judgmental and mean to others. I never cheated on her, but I fantasized about many women in our social circle. She accused me of having an affair with another woman from our group and wouldn't believe it wasn't so. She left me. I kept the house and fought for as much custody as I could get so that I could lower my child support payments.

After the divorce, I joined a Bible study group where I met a neighbor. We had quite a chemistry together and her husband traveled a great deal. We ultimately got "biblical" and she ended up leaving her husband for me. We married. It was a mistake. She didn't like me playing mixed doubles at the tennis club; she became more and more controlling. She wanted me to stop playing tennis. She wanted me to only do things with her. She wanted me to drop my friends. I convinced her to take up tennis so that we could play together. We played on a mixed combo team, but quickly found that we could not play on the same side of the net. She would chastise me no matter what I did and how I played. She got me so frustrated that I ended up beaming a ball at her. She made a big deal about it and I was kicked out of the tennis club. I divorced her within a year.

7. *Interests/hobbies:* I like to rebuild old cars; I always have one going in the garage. I did this with my boys; it was a great father-son activity. Then we would sell the revamped car and buy a better shell and start all over. I love tennis; I have since joined another tennis club. I have a lovely Asian partner who doesn't make a peep, no matter what I do on the court. We have begun dating now. I know she doesn't like my prank jokes. One time, I cut the pleat in her tennis skirt so that, when she bent over to pick the ball up, I had a clear shot of her beautiful ass. She didn't speak to me for a week. The other women are still rumbling about it; I don't know why they can't take a joke. The guys loved it!

8. *What initially attracts you to the opposite sex?* The first thing in a woman that attracts me is her looks, then her body, and then her brain. She then needs to be nice, friendly, and respectful of the elders.

9. *What do you find appealing in a woman?* The woman's walk and body. I imagine being with appealing women I see on the street all the time. It always puts a smile on my face. Sense of humor is key. They must be okay with my jokes.

10. *What do you find to be a turn-off in a woman?* I can't stand a clown, a woman who wears a lot of make-up. I like a naturally beautiful woman who is happy with herself and who doesn't feel that she needs to slather on a bunch of putty all over her face. I don't like lip stick either. It often tastes disgusting. I cannot stand an emotional woman who complains about her period, acts like a victim or is an attention-seeking drama queen. I do not like girls who talk about themselves, look at their phones when they are out with me, or who are rude to the waiter or who tip badly (that is, if they are paying for dinner).

11. *What do you want from a woman and how do you want to be treated by a woman?* I want to be treated like I am the only man for her. I want her to appreciate all the little things that I do for her. I want her to show me gratitude. I want her to do little things for me that show me how much she cares for me. I want her to respect me. I will adore her.

12. *How have your desires changed over your life?* My desires really haven't changed too much over my life. The priority on sex has de-

creased a little bit, but, other than that, I am looking for the same kind of woman as I always have. I want someone who will sit quietly and not complain; who will laugh at my jokes; and who will keep my house neat and clean without complaining about it. I love a good meal so I hope to find a woman who knows how to cook. I like to grill, so I have that part covered.

13. *When you are out with your friends and you see someone who catches your eye, what do you do?* I will send her an oddball drink and then go up to her to see if she likes it. If she doesn't, I tell her she can choose a weird one for me and I'll drink it down in front of her. It is an easy way to break the ice.

14. *Where do you hang out?* I hang out with my guy pals. We go to lots of sporting events and sports bars. There are more and more single friends now that the kids are all leaving for college. It is nice having the guys around without any whining wives.

15. *What are your thoughts about online dating?* It's not for me. I rely on friends, family, and tennis to get me introductions to women. The on-line dating thing seems really very desperate to me. You could say anything about yourself and get an introduction to a woman. The same is true the other way around. You could be "Jack the Ripper" masking yourself as "Johnny Next Door." Similarly, "Heidi Hooker" could be disguised as "Mother Theresa." You just don't know whom you are really meeting.

16. *Have you ever had trouble moving on from a past relationship?* Nah. There are a million fish in the sea.

17. *Where do you go/what do you do on a date?* I usually take them to an X-rated movie to get them hot and horny. Ha. Ha. I'm only kidding. You know, the standard. Dinner and a movie or a hockey game or a ball game. Maybe a concert.

18. *How often do you have a boys' night out? Where do you go with your friends?* I go out with the guys at least twice a week during the work-week and hang out with them on the weekends. We have a softball team on Saturday afternoons and I play basketball when I'm not play-ing tennis. I like to get sweaty with the guys.

19. *What frustrates you in the dating scene?* Things are much more diffi-cult than they used to be. People seem to be so much more uptight and stressed out than they were thirty years ago. Life is faster-paced than it ever was. You have to move on to the next stage in a relationship much quicker than ever before. Everything is faster. Everyone is on

information overload and there is a total lack of privacy. People can Google you and find out everything about you, including your credit rating and your mortgage payment. Also, AIDS and venereal diseases seem to be out there much more than they were before; at least people seem to be more concerned about it. A lot of people are getting tested frequently. Women are demanding condoms; I just won't wear a condom. It doesn't feel good. If you are going to be with me, you need to trust me.

20. *What are you looking for in a relationship?* What I am looking for now may be a little different from what I was looking for thirty years ago. Previously, I looked for attractiveness, a good potential mom for my kids, a woman who wanted to have kids, a solid family background, hard-working (I think it is important for a woman to pull her weight and bring home a good living so that she can contribute to the family budget), having an appreciation for sport, and finally, respectful of me and older people. I am not looking for another family, so the qualities about motherhood and wanting kids are no longer relevant. However, I would like to find a woman who is good with kids so that she will be good with my grandchildren when my kids have children.

21. *Would you go out with a married woman?* I did go out with someone who was married and I married her. However, I did not go out looking for a married woman. I don't think I would do it again; it was a lot of angst to go through and then you feel responsible if you break up the marriage; it's a big burden to carry. Then, they are looking at you to be the new provider.

22. *Would you date someone who had a child from another relationship?* I prefer it; then I know they won't be disappointed if I don't want any more kids. I am too old to be having my sleep disturbed by an infant at this point. A woman who has had children is usually more nurturing than a woman who hasn't had them. I like to be nurtured and taken care of by my woman.

23. *If you were to live with someone, how long would you be willing to live with her without a permanent commitment?* At this point, I would live with a woman forever. I don't know that I will ever get married again. There is something glorious about knowing that you can just get up, pack your bags, and walk out the door.

24. *Would you consider financially supporting your partner?* I have done it and it leads to a situation where you have a dependent; there is no parity in the relationship. I would rather have a self-sufficient woman

who has her own things going on. I want her to have her own money, especially now. I am already supporting two ex-wives and several kids in college.

25. *What type of clothing do you prefer your date to wear when you go out on a date?* I want her to dress in a classy and sexy way, but leave things for me alone to see. Don't share everything with the world.

26. *What is your preferred body type and shape for a woman?* I like an athletic woman who has kept in shape. I don't want saggy Kegel muscles. If she is going to put the Ben Wah Balls in, then I would prefer them to stay up there as opposed to clanking down on the sidewalk as we walk through town. Muscle tone is very important as we all age.

27. *How do you feel about tattoos and piercings?* I am not into them at all.

28. *How do you feel about perfumes and colognes?* I like a subtle scent on a woman. If I enjoy a scent on a woman who walks by, I won't hesitate to let her know how great she smells. I think it is important to let them know. Likewise, I wouldn't hesitate to point out to a woman with a fabulous ass that the panty lines are getting in the way of the view.

    Back when I was dating my first wife, I dated another woman at the same time. She had really funky breath. I couldn't figure it out until I realized that she was an alcoholic. The sour rotten smell was actually coming out of her pores.

29. *How important is the first kiss?* The first kiss is very important; if she can't get me hard with a kiss, I'm not interested in going further.

30. *Do you want to pay on the first date? And after the first date?* I do pay on the first date; I usually end up paying. I would love it if the woman would offer once in a while. It gets really tiring being the sugar daddy. I don't know where all this women's lib stuff has gone; when you go out on a date, it seems to have evaporated. The women only use it to their advantage; they don't really want equality. They only want equality when it gives them an advantage.

31. *Will you have sex on the first date? If so, would you talk to your date about your preferences freely?* Of course, I'll have sex on the first date if the opportunity presents itself. Usually, there isn't much talking; it is a lot of doing instead. I love a woman who will take charge in the bedroom. I love a woman who will ask me what my fantasies are. I love to have a woman dress up in little costumes and act out my fantasies.

32. *How do you make sure a new sexual partner is free of STD's?* Well, I look at her and see how her hygiene looks. If she has nicely pedicured feet and manicured nails, I'm guessing that she has taken care of her box [vagina] as well. I'm not saying that only ugly girls get VD, but girls who are not particular with their bodies are probably more likely to get it.

33. *Once you have decided to have sex with your date for the first time, are you free and uninhibited in the act or more conservative and reserved than normal?* I am always myself in the bed. I am game for whatever she dishes out. I will try anything.

34. *Where is the most interesting place you have had sex?* I had this girl who thought it would be a great idea to climb up into a referee's chair on the tennis court and have sex up high. The problem was that the chair was not very sturdy when it started rocking back and forth. The chair fell over and she hit her head. We ended up in emergency and she had a concussion and broken ribs because I landed on top of her. That was the most interesting place, but not the most orgasmic place.

35. *Do you use protection and, if so, who provides it? If you don't use protection, how do you stay safe or is it an issue?* I don't like condoms. I would prefer to go bare.

36. *What do you do if protection is not immediately available?* If I feel like she is clean, that wouldn't stop the show as far as I was concerned.

37. *What age range do you date?* Ranging from 32 to 45. I love women around 40. They are horny and ready to experiment.

38. *What do you think of one-night stands?* I have never had a one-night stand; they have always lasted at least a week. I'm not saying that I saw them more than once, but I at least talk to them or text them over the course of the next week.

39. *How do you break off a one-night stand or short relationship without being hurtful?* You let them down easy and then just fade away.

40. *What was your parents' status when you were growing up?* Married; that's why I always look for someone from a stable family life. It hasn't worked out so well for me and I guess my kids won't pass my own test.

41. *How do you characterize yourself?*

> **Positive attributes:** Honest, caring about others, generous, contributor to the community, appreciative of what the older generation has contributed to our society, I try to do unto others as I would want done unto me, when the going gets tough, I get going and pride myself on coming out strong and staying on top.
>
> **Negative attributes:** My mouth gets me into trouble even though I just say it like I see it; a lot of people cannot appreciate honesty

42. *How do you think others see you?* I think they see me as a fun guy who likes to play practical jokes.

43. *Please describe your fantasy date.* I would go camping; there is nothing like a night in nature to see how much a woman will complain. That would be a great way to weed the complainers out. Oh, and I might forget the bug spray so she didn't want to leave the tent. Yeh, I would forget her sleeping bag as well, but I would offer her a spot with me in mine!

44. *When you meet someone new, how long does it take you to know if the person is "the one" or has the potential to be "the one"?* I don't think there is "one" for everyone; there are many who can potentially fit the bill.

45. *Do you believe in "love at first sight"?* No, but definitely lust at first sight.

46. *What is your personal philosophy on monogamy and monogamous relationships?* I think it is very important for the trust in a relationship. If the trust is gone, you might as well walk out that door. I have never cheated on my spouse. I believe in the sanctity of marriage and the vows you take. Funny that it didn't carry over to my neighbor, but they weren't my vows being violated; they were hers.

47. *Do you believe there is a game people play when dating? If so, describe the game.* Of course. I believe there are many games in life. There is a dating game, a bar game, a friends' game. All the games are based upon one premise: everyone is trying to package themselves to sell to others. You sell yourself to get a job; you sell yourself to get a date or a spouse; you sell yourself to make and keep your friends. Life is a sales job. That's why I studied marketing.

48. *Have you ever been on a date with a girl who turned out to be a bitch?* Sure, I dated several sorority girls back in college who ended up thinking they were much better than they were. They were the ones who would talk about their own friends behind their backs in order to get an upper hand with the guys. Someone like that cannot be trusted in any capacity – they are in it only for themselves.

49. *If interested in your date, how long do you wait to communicate with her?* I usually play the game; I'll wait three days. I love it when the woman caves in and calls me first.

50. *If you were not interested in dating her again, would you let her know?* If I slept with her, I'd play the fade away game. If it were only dinner or a movie, I would probably not say anything.

51. *Would you mind if your date contacted you immediately after the date?* I like an aggressive woman and can appreciate the effort. Even if I wasn't going to go out with her again before she contacted me, I might give her a second chance for the effort – unless I am getting that stalker vibe. Usually, you can just tell if they are desperately seeking a mate for life.

52. *Is spirituality important to you?* Yes, I am a man of the church. I have a very strong faith and I try to live by the cardinal principles. I believe in forgiveness and that I will be forgiven if I falter. I want a woman who has a moral background and who has a strong value system.

53. *What books on dating or any other would you recommend as a good read?* Playboy.

Below the belt questions:

1. *Is sex an important factor in deciding whether you will continue to date someone?* Yes.

2. *Do you enjoy it when your date wears lingerie?* I don't care much for lingerie. I do like costumes and fantasy outfits. Bondage is a huge turn-on for the look, but I don't want to be hurt. I won't kick a girl out for wearing fancy panties, though.

3. *Have you ever experienced a ménage a trois?* Yes. I loved it. I did two girls and me. If I had an opportunity at this stage in my life, it would be a stretch, but I might give it a whirl.

4. *What is sexy to you in a woman?* Confidence and respect.

5. *Does the size of her breasts matter?* No, I don't care about the boobs. I am more of a butt man.

6. *Do you mind surgical enhancement of breasts, lips, teeth, etc?* I like a natural woman.

7. *How much make up is too much?* Almost any is too much for me.

8. *Are skimpy, body-fitting outfits a turn-on or a turn-off?* Depends on what is being revealed. If the dress goes down to the coccyx, I am not loving having her on my arm – it looks trampy. If she cannot sit down without having her underwear show, it is a turn-off. If there is the perfect amount of beautiful leg showing and her ass is cupped just right, it is a turn-on.

9. *Are the women whom you meet in a bar a potential long-term relationship or are they a one-night stand?* I don't look at things like that. I live in the moment. If I enjoy her company, she is a potential person with whom I can have a relationship beyond the current conversation.

10. *What do you think of athletic clubs as a place to meet someone?* Lots of gossip; I love learning about other people's torrid affairs at the clubs. It is always a fun topic of conversation. However, I am a private person and it is hard to refrain from making yourself part of the gossip when dating someone at the club. However, that is probably the best place to find someone who is into keeping herself in shape.

11. *What do you think of coffee houses as a place to meet someone?* Sure. You can meet a quality woman almost anywhere.

12. *What do you think of the work environment as a place to meet someone?* This hasn't worked out so much for me. I had a few complaints filed against me at my last company and was forced out when I asked a witch out for a date. She said I made her uncomfortable. All she had to do was tell me she wasn't interested. She had been flirting with me for months. It's not like I am a stalker or anything. If you tell me, I'll get the hint. But you have to tell me!

13. *Do you prefer tanned or natural skin?* Tanned from being outdoors is good.

14. *Long hair or short hair?* Definitely shoulder length or longer. I like light brown.

15. *Do you prefer a particular pubic hair design?* It doesn't matter, but I've noticed that a lot of women are shaving, plucking, tweezing and lasering down there lately. I'm not really into going down there, so it really is irrelevant as long as they keep everything clean and odor-free.

16. *How many sexual partners have you had in your life?* Around 20.

2. PASSIVELY AWKWARD: THEY TAKE INSTRUCTIONS AND GIVE EFFORT.

The passive, shy and awkward introvert is often intelligent, choosing a career in fields that don't require social skills or sales skills. There are many Passively Awkward engineers and scientists. After watching others work the social scene to their advantage, an older and more confident Passively Awkward will analyze the scene and try to figure an analytical step-by-step approach to success in socialization. They think too much. They want it to be like a computer program, not understanding that emotions and people don't run in 1's and 0's. This character is often referred to as a nerd or geek.

In high school, this character often builds up a fantasy mate in his or her head, feeling that he or she is worthy of finding such a mate. However, this unrealistic ideal leads to disappointment in the real world because beauty is not often attracted to persons without charisma and natural sexual appeal. While others practice their social skills by dating and going to dances with the opposite sex, this character sits at home with his or her passive companions, drooling and fantasizing about persons in magazines and on posters pinned to the walls.

As they mature, the Passively Awkward characters put their intellect to use and study dating. They read books and articles on the subject and sometimes take incorrect advice. While it is possible for a Passively Awkward man to evolve into a Player, most want to settle down and have a family. Usually successful in their careers, these characters should be careful of the daters who are looking for an easy meal ticket.

Sometimes the people in the most prestigious and powerful positions in our economy are the most passively awkward. They marry later when wiser and wealthier. With maturity, they understand that the physical fantasy created in their youth is unattainable and that a companion of a similar intellect will be more fulfilling. This character is loyal and content, once he or she settles down. They are fully committed and make wonderful spouses and parents.

The Passively Awkwards are honest and full of integrity. They are active in politics and philanthropy because they want to help others and find it important to improve the world. They work to improve the environment and the health and well being of others in our society and throughout the globe.

INTERVIEW WITH A SOCIALLY AWKWARD WOMAN

1. *Contributor age:* 30's
2. *Gender:* Female
3. *Education Level:* PHD
4. *Are you financially secure?* Yes
5. *Profession:* Marketing/PR
6. *Personal Status:* Single
7. *Are you looking for a long-term relationship or a meaningful one-night stand?* Long-term relationship.
8. *Interests/hobbies:* Skier, golf, garden, paint, photography, and travel. Last minute travel is great.
9. *What initially attracts you to the opposite sex?* Clean cut, some sort of drive. I don't want him to look at me as if I'm an easy meal-ticket. They should have some kind of a drive.
10. *What do you find to be a turn-off in a date?* Too possessive, I can't deal with it. I need my space. Limiting me and not hearing what I want. I must have children before the age of 35 due to my ovarian condition. I started my business when I was 16 so I would be able to stay home with my kids when I had them. However, I wouldn't want a man who thinks a woman must stay home with the kids.

    I wouldn't like a man who was inappropriate. I asked the last guy I went out with what he thought of his other women. He made terrible comments about them and I didn't like that. I wouldn't like a man with less education than I have. I have dated people with two PhD's. I am not a citizen; I don't lie to men. I have seen other women who would lie to the man to get him. I wouldn't want the man I go out with to leave me for another who lies. I think guys think it is a turn-off if a woman doesn't order a drink on the first date.
11. *Where do you meet people?* I don't date in my social circle. I use on-line. I refuse to do Match.com. It is a place to get laid. It's hitting mainstream now. I may start an on-line dating site myself.
12. *When you are out with your friends and you see someone who catches your eye, what do you do?* I used to go up to them. When I was skinnier I would go up to the men, but now I don't. I exercise like crazy to remain average in size due to my medical condition. My advice is to get married when you are in your 20's, otherwise you'll be single for a long time.

13. *Where do you hang out?* I throw big events and house parties.

14. *What are your thoughts about online dating?* They used to be excellent. My friend is a multi-millionaire and can't find a mate. Certain people don't want their pictures out there. There are sites where you pay a $1500 flat fee to be set up on twenty dates. I used it and we all became friends, but it never worked out for more than that. I might set up my own agency for the right reason. I have set up eight people and it worked out every time.

15. *Have you ever had trouble moving on from a past relationship? If so, what did you do to finally get over it?* I move on, but sometimes things linger. I get along so well with men, but all of a sudden they snap and are scared to go further in the relationship. I expect people to stand behind their words.

16. *What do you think of one-night stands?* I don't see a problem with them. When I was younger, it was fine. Now, when I go to weddings, I take my girlfriend, and, if the opportunity presents itself, I go for it for the fun of it. We both know in reality, it won't work for the long-term, but we figure, "Let's self-medicate." People in the United States have a very different view on sex and sexuality; people from other countries are typically more realistic and freer with their sexuality. It isn't such a big deal.

17. *How do you break off a one-night stand or short relationship without being hurtful?* I have been accused of being like a guy. I haven't spent a night at the guy's house. I would hate for someone to get hurt.

18. *What are your rituals for preparing for a date?* I need time to myself. To get ready and get a breather. I need my personal time. Men turn me down because of my weight. The men I befriend love skinny women. They seem to have this fairy tale of a woman in mind. Don't they realize that they might marry a skinny woman who gains permanent weight after being pregnant? Nobody knows how a body will react to pregnancy. Then what are the men going to do? Leave the family for a few extra pounds?

19. *Type of lingerie you would wear on a first date?* Because my clothes are not coming off on the first date, I would wear something that makes my clothes look good.

20. *Where do you go/what do you do on a date?* I go for a walk and take my dog. Sometimes, I even take my friends on the dates with me. I have had so many dates that turned out badly that I at least try to get

some exercise by walking my dog or have a friend there so that we can have a good time even if the guy is a dreadful bore.

21. *If you don't know your date well, do you meet at the designated place or does your date pick you up?* I will do either; I will meet at a place or, I figure that if I let a guy pick me up at my place and I die while having fun, it is okay. They can pick me up. Live it up. I feel I have done what I can in life, if someone wants to pick me up, fine.

22. *How often do you have a girls' night out? Where do you go with your girlfriends?* Often. There is a big group of us that have dating issues so we all go out together.

23. *What do you hope to happen when out with the girls?* I have a friend who is 38 and horny as can be. She is looking for at least a one-nighter whenever we go out. I'll take it as it goes.

24. *What frustrates you in the dating scene?* Being an immigrant, the guys often think I am looking for a Green Card. I also get extremely frustrated when I see women who are not as good morally as I and they are able to get married and have kids. I have had this great life and there are certain things that I have not done out of respect to my future husband. Some women who lie and cheat get more. The unfairness of bad people getting it and the good not. Many of my single male friends have married these cheating, conniving women. Now, they are sorry.

25. *What are you looking for in a relationship?* Someone who wants to get married and have kids.

26. *Would you go out with a married man?* I would not. I did date one guy who was married and, when I told my father, I felt like an ass. There was one who said he was separated, but I found out later that he was married. He used a different name when we were out.

27. *Would you date someone who had a child from another relationship?* I had once and it doesn't bother me. I need to have my own kids though.

28. *If you were to live with someone, how long would you be willing to live with him without a permanent commitment?* I wouldn't do it again. I lived with a person who was controlling and cheating.

29. *Do you mind if your date smokes?* It does bother me, but it is not exactly a deal breaker.

30. *Are you hoping to find a man who is financially secure?* Depends. If he had money and then lost all his money in the world, would you still love him? It wouldn't bother me.

31. *Is financial security more important than love?* I could have married many in my life and not loved them. I have to love him to get married.

32. *How does it make you feel if your date flaunts his assets?* Men who flaunt their possessions turn me off.

33. *What type of clothing do you prefer your date to wear?* Clean-cut, business casual, khaki pants, no earrings or tattoos, nice watch, a simple polo golf shirt or a pressed shirt. Glasses. I love glasses.

34. *What is your preferred body type and shape for a man?* If he has the same goals as I do, I don't mind shape and size.

35. *How do you feel about tattoos and piercings?* Not for me. Depending on their attitude. If they are good persons and clean-cut. I presume most of the tattoo people won't like me; they seem to do drugs.

36. *How do you feel about perfumes and colognes?* I have no opinion unless it is too much. I don't mind the man having bad body odor during sex, but, other than that, it is not okay.

37. *How important is the first kiss?* I have been running into a group of men who are not making any moves at all. I wouldn't know how the first kiss is with them.

38. *Do you expect your date to pay on the first date?* I always offer to pay. But I would like to see someone who can give. I would like someone who can force me not to give.

39. *What is your preference and philosophy on who should pay the bill on dates with you?* They should pay since I cook for them.

40. *Will you have sex on the first date? If so, would you talk to your date about your preferences freely?* Yes. I think so. I would be conservative.

41. *Would you have sex with your date if he were drunk?* Yes.

42. *Do you prefer your date to wear boxers or briefs?* This mechanic and I went to a romantic place; he got mostly naked and was ready to have sex. He was wearing a silver thong bikini. He ruined the romantic moment with that damned bikini. We had sex that night because I felt badly for him, but it was a real turn-off. That was a pity fuck. Anything but thongs or "Playboy" underwear.

43. *How do you make sure a new sexual partner is free of STD's?* I won't date someone who dates a lot. It is more about looking at the person's history.

44. *Where would you feel comfortable having sex with your date?* All but the restrooms.

45. *Where is your favorite place to have sex?* Bedrooms, living rooms, high-class boardroom table. I lost my virginity when I was fourteen.

46. *Do you use protection and, if so, who provides it? If you don't use protection, how do you stay safe or is it an issue?* I don't like to use protection. Condoms if any. I would like to get pregnant and would like to do it with the person who would not get mad at me.

47. *What if you liked your date and he did not call you the next day or week?* I would be upset. I wouldn't call him. I would send him a thank you with email or text. When I throw a party, I would send an invitation to him.

48. *What age range do you date?* I never dated younger than I. I dated an older guy who had two PhD's. But that didn't work out. We got along great, but he didn't want to get married. I date men up to 60 years old. They are still fertile.

49. *What was your parents' status when you were growing up?* Happy married life. They looked out for each other. Here I am afraid people are looking out for themselves.

50. *How do you characterize yourself?*

    Positive attributes: Overall a good person, giver, taking care of people, successful, athletic, great with gardening, due to my condition I have to have organic food.

    Negative attributes: I think not being from this country, I am very honest. Sometimes, I am too honest. I am curvy.

51. *Please include a detailed description of your ideal date.* He would make the plans. I don't care. Anything but shopping – I don't like to go shopping.

52. *When you meet someone new, how long does it take you to know if the person is "the one" or has the potential to be "the one"?* Women are very quick on that. I give it two dates.

53. *Do you believe in "love at first sight"?* Connection on first sight.

54. *What is your personal philosophy on monogamy and monogamous relationships?* I am fine with it. It is interesting that some of my married friends say marriage should be a three-year contract and, after the kids, the contract expires. I would like to find a person who can be monogamous to me.

55. *Do you believe there is a game people play when dating? If so, describe the game.* Yes. I don't play it. I like to date shy guys who don't play it. Women play the game in that they put their best foot forward, not caring about who they hurt in the middle. I keep thinking the guy

will recognize that I am honest, but that hasn't happened. To get attention, you can use a nice ring tone and have your girlfriends call you.

56. *Have you ever been on a date with a guy who turned out to be an ass?* I went out with a doctor recently. He wouldn't say much about himself. Instead, he said he wanted to hear things about me that I didn't want to tell anyone else. He said, "I am going to grant you one wish, tell me what it would be." He was hoping that I would ask him to kiss me. I was wishing to get as far away from him as possible. He was an arrogant ass.

57. *If interested in a further date, would you wait for him to call you or would you initiate further communication?* I would wait for him to call.

58. *If you were not interested in another date, would you let him know?* I would say, "I am not interested, but I know someone else that would like to go out with you."

59. *Would you mind if your date contacted you immediately after your date?* I find that sexy. I don't like the game.

60. *How much attention is too much or too little after the first date?* At least contact me by the third day. Waiting two weeks not good.

61. *On average, how many dates are required before you consider yourself to be in a relationship? What qualifies as a date?* I learned that, when living in the U.S., you need to have the talk. Sex is different outside this country. Having sex does not mean you are in the relationship. I met this professor in the movie theater that was from my country. He asked what something meant in the movie. When I turned to tell him, my lips touched his and we ended up dating, watching TV together, and having sex. He ultimately told me that he just wanted to have sex; I was hurt, but it was fine. Here, women who have sex are considered sluts. This Protestant culture has been imbedded in the Americans and how they view others in their dating practices. It is all very hypocritical. Sex is a natural thing.

62. *Is the dating game a mystery or are the rules clear? If clear, what are the rules?* I wonder if I am a bitch. It is a mystery why the mean people can get married and have kids and the good ones don't.

63. *Do you consider yourself to be a game-player in the dating arena?* People consider me to be the game player, but I am not. They think I am a woman who can get easy sex, but just because I want to have sex doesn't mean anything. I like to be in a monogamous relationship. I learned to be in a relationship with two or three guys at the same time

so you are not left sitting home alone. My friends think I play the game because I am always dating more than one person at a time.

64. *Is spirituality important to you?* Overly religious people freak me out.

65. *What books on dating have you read? Out of those books, which ones do you recommend?* Women, We Don't See the Small Things; Men Do Relationships Like Fools Do Brain Surgery; I love David DeAngelo.

Below the belt questions:

1. *Is sex an important factor in deciding whether you will continue to date someone?* It can get better as times goes on.

2. *Do you enjoy wearing lingerie?* Not really.

3. *Have you ever experienced ménage à trios? If not, would you consider it?* No. No.

4. *What is sexy to you in a guy?* Glasses. I love them when they are on the bed stand and belong to someone who is clean cut. Someone who made himself from nothing.

5. *Does the size of a penis matter?* Yes, I have been with gorgeous men with small penises. That doesn't work so well; especially since I don't much like men going down on me. I have also had men who were too big and it took half an hour just to get it in and the whole experience was not comfortable.

6. *Do you prefer circumcised or not?* As long as it is clean looking. I don't mind giving head, but if it is something that I don't want to give head to, then forget it!

7. *Do you prefer more or less hair on a man? If a man is too hairy, what should he do about it?* If a guy trims, it means they are playing around. They are trying to make it look bigger. I don't mind the hair down there, completely shaved is not good.

8. *Will you kiss and tell your friends or do you keep it private?* I do kiss and tell.

9. *What is your opinion about surgically enhancing your body? How much enhancement is too much?* The people who have plastic surgery actually look worse as they age. The mathematics of clothing changes. The scarring is bad and ugly.

10. *Do you treat dates with long-term potential differently than fun quickies?* I like the fun quickies; I don't dress up.

11. *How many sexual partners have you had in your life?* I have had quite a few. I would love to have one partner in my life, but when you date a married person they expect you to have only them and maybe one more partner.

EMAIL COMMUNICATIONS FROM THE FUNNIEST SHY GUY

During our research, we met a very shy man who was really very fun underneath it all. He had a wealth of worldly experiences under his belt, but he was feeling that he had missed his opportunity in the relationship realm. He was interested in very attractive women who would find him boring on the surface and wouldn't give him a chance. If they did give him a chance, they would find a charming, energetic, quick-witted character beneath it all. It is too bad most people only get one chance at a first impression.

We decided to help him figure out how to make a better first impression. We helped him augment his drab work out clothes for colorful fun outfits that would get his nice body noticed. We gave him some hints about where nice women hang out. We tried to steer him away from the women who would crush him like a bug.

He is still working on himself, inside and out. He has been an outstanding student. Here are some of his funny emails along the way.

1. The place to meet lots of women is near the theaters when the next "Sex And The City" movie comes out. Hundreds of women will go to see it at any given weekend showing. The last movie brought out many, many groups of women who flooded the local scene, both after AND before the movie. So, check the show times, and go hang at the clubs, bars, and restaurants within walking distance of the theater. A BIG tip off is any group of 4 nicely dressed women drinking "cosmos" at a bar, but any number of such women on such an evening will do. It helps if you've seen the TV show or movie, and know something about Carrie's favorite shoes.

2. For the guy who is not so good at "opening lines" in the supermarket, become skilled at the "dropped

rolling can technique" when in the supermarket - making sure your can of food bumps into the feet or shopping cart of that hot babe, to be followed by a pleasant introduction, "thank you"...

3. Subject: RE: Hi, I missed the class...
    Hi,
    Though I've always thought, "aerobic exercise is a great spectator sport," I'm going to broaden my view and check out the classes that are easy on the feet (I've a bad right foot, and am waiting for my new foot orthotics to arrive).
    At the moment I have mostly lots and lots of black clothes and a couple boring colors (gray, burgundy, navy), BUT, I have a couple new shirts on order, one primarily red, the other a royal blue, each with contrasting dark color like the one you showed me in the boutique.
    The "extreme make-over" of SG has started! ...Thanks to you!
    Ciao,
    SG

4. Subject: Zumba
    I am really enjoying the Zumba classes! Great exercise and a new world of lovely women, wow!
    Merci beaucoup!
    BTW, I prefer meeting someone in person like at Zumba, the gym, tonight's party, cafe, etc. over websites.
    a bientot, (see you soon)
    SG

5. Subject: Boxers or Briefs?
    About 15 years ago, after a life-altering experience prompted me to explore other things to do in life besides work all day on a computer, I tried to tap into, and grow my "emotional self." I thought this might help me meet and interact

better with people, and perhaps improve my dating prospects. It has been said, "Fame is an aphrodisiac." Well, if I became even just a little famous that would be fine, along with a more fun persona.

So, I decided to take acting classes in Palo Alto, San Jose, and San Francisco. This led to me getting TWO agents, and a "beeper" - those things many of us had long before cell phones became ubiquitous. Now I still had a day job with a large computer company, but I also had a wonderful manager who would allow me to take a 2.5 hour "lunch" when the beeper summoned me to an audition for a possible acting/modeling job in the city.

On one "cattle call" audition up in the city, I landed a job modeling casual business wear for Levi's! Yes, Levi's at one time liked the way I looked!!! And so, my job was to go to a modeling shoot up in the city with 6 - 7 other models. Little did I know about some of the things that go on during a modeling shoot. The first thing is that you spend a lot of time waiting around and standing in your UNDERWEAR. I wish someone had told me that. But at least the pure white BRIEFS I wore that day were clean. The second thing someone should have told me is that the waiting and dressing area was co-ed, with little privacy. So, I spent most of the day in the back area in my white briefs among slim, tall, high-cheek-boned women in their bras and bikini briefs. At the end of the shoot one of the models said to me, "It was fun spending all day with you in your underwear." Well, men's white briefs are very brief and can be sheer, revealing more information than intended. It was quite embarrassing at times.

So, after that shoot I immediately invested in the "boxer-briefs" that I saw the male models wearing — these look more like swim trunks. I've been a "boxer-brief" man ever since! And I've not

been doing any modeling lately.
Cheers,
SG

6. Subject: Hello, house party underground...

For those of us who experienced the 70's, the house party may be remembered fondly. For the singles out there today, the house party scene has survived, in a hidden, almost underground form, available for those "in the know."

There truly IS something always going on, but the events are more controlled than they were in the 70's so as not to invite a visit from the neighborhood police. The parties are a bit more selective than the wide-open kegger scene of the 70's. Those who become sloppy drunk, break the host's china and chairs, or fail to treat the other guests with the respect you would at least give your co-workers are encouraged to quickly shape-up or leave the scene. So, the modern version of the 70's house party has been updated "sans" sloppy drunk, but going strong with a fun loving and slightly more sophisticated crowd. Sure, there are the women who'll lose their tops before jumping into the swimming pool; there are the occasional fashion models, and burly men from the weight training gym. Add to these the soon to be successful techies, your young real estate and mortgage brokers, double EE's (electrical engineers - not bust size!), the "got rich in the dot.com boomers," construction workers, health care specialists and so on.

And so you may ask, how does one find out about where the next big bash is going to be? Well, there is a communication underground of sorts. It makes use of the Internet. And a hand-full of people manages or controls the dissemination of information. If you are fortunate enough to make the acquaintance with one of these people, your social

life will have a huge chance to improve. (But it's
still up to you to say, "Hi," if you want to get to
know that model from Milan, Italy!) Various email
lists are used to share the party info. Rumor is
that there is a party list for San Francisco, one
for Marin, another for San Jose, a list for Penin-
sula partiers, and one for Santa Cruz. Rumor also
is that someone known to most mainly as "The Mayor"
will let you know about parties in the South Bay.
If you can find him (or her - as I've not met The
Mayor yet) and persuade him or her to add you to
the list, you too can be "in the know" and finally
have a chance to experience house parties in the
new millennium.

E. The Perpetual Kid: Spoiled adult who does whatever feels right at the moment.

The Perpetual Kid straddles the line between a taker and a giver.
Really all this character wants to do is play, play, play. However, innocent
he or she may be, others may view this character as taking life and dating
as a game.

The Perpetual Kid is sometimes unreliable, much like a kid. They
start out with good intentions and then get lost along the way. A child will
beg for a puppy, promising the world. After getting the puppy, they will
no longer be interested in walking it, feeding it, and picking up its poop.
The Perpetual Kids are typically not organized or detail-oriented. They
often leave projects on the table, having started many projects at the same
time. They only finish the few projects that have captured their true passion. Once the project becomes a chore or a bore, the Perpetual Kid will
move on.

They are impetuous. They need instant gratification and can be easily
distracted by a more immediate excitement. True to their nature, they are
playful, fun to be around, love change, and become bored easily. They are
loyal friends and pleasers.

They are easy going and go with the flow. They are always invited to
parties and social gatherings. They are high energy and often have a high
sexual drive. There is no hidden agenda. They cannot read minds; they
are simple-minded, but intelligent. The Perpetual Kid does not hold a

grudge; it is too much burden. They do not keep clutter in their brains. They love to laugh, have fun, live life, and feel as if life is a candy store and they are the kid in the store.

They become overwhelmed by life's required monotony and stagnation. Domestic chores and routines are the worst possible punishment for them. They love to jump into exciting and unknown territories and situations to see what will happen. They have no fear and love the adrenaline rush.

When people confront them, they step back and look bewildered. They do not respond well to confrontation as they often grew up with authority figures that enabled them, trying to keep them happy and giving them few restrictions on their freedom. Their freedom is their song. If someone tries to limit their freedom, they will run the other way and do exactly as they please.

The Perpetual Kid tends to settle down with a person who offers organization and who will take care of the mundane. The Perpetual Kid is not the one to do the bills and maintain the credit of the household. They are free with their money and very generous. They find it almost impossible to keep track of a checking account; they need a responsible partner to do so. The Perpetual Kid is not good at keeping track of time either. They are often late as they become immersed in whatever they are doing at the moment.

The Perpetual Kid does not like to hurt others. He or she finds it very difficult to break off relationships and usually allows the other to do the breaking off. They tend to remain friends with past relationships. They do not like to disappoint, but will find a way to keep the other happy while still keeping themselves happy.

The Perpetual Kids do not have ambition; they are focused on the ride and enjoying the moment as opposed to the destination and pre-set goals. It is important for those around them to remind them of future consequences and keep them focused on achievable goals. They often take a long time to finish college. A pass-no pass grading system is right up their alley, as they do not have to worry about grades. They are the true procrastinators. While they will work hard when they have to, they do not do so willingly and will do as little as necessary to get by. They can get by on little effort because they are intelligent and adept at efficiently working the system when they put their mind to it. Others around them want the Perpetual Kid to succeed because they like him or her.

The Perpetual Kid likes to be in control of his or her freedom and domain. In order to have another join them, the other must be willing to go with their flow. They like to have the last word. They will allow others to voice their opinions, but the Perpetual Kid will do exactly as he or she wants. Monogamy is a very difficult requirement for a Perpetual Kid to uphold, but he or she will try his or her best.

They have tons of acquaintances, but only a select few can penetrate the inner circle. They trust everyone to be true and can sometimes be naïve about others and gullible about their agendas. The Perpetual Kids will give others around them enough rope so that they can either climb to the top or hang themselves. The ones who hang regret it later as they will never have the standing with the Perpetual Kid again.

INTERVIEW OF A PERPETUAL KID

1. *Contributor age:* 40's
2. *Gender:* Female
3. *Education Level:* College
4. *Are you financially secure?* For the most part. I get some help from my friends and family when I need it. They are always there to back me up.
5. *Profession:* Entrepreneur
6. *Personal Status:* Committed & Divorced -- I was married for a long time and divorced about three years ago. I have been dating someone for the last two years. I am committed to our relationship, but am still dating others.
7. *Interests/hobbies:* Laughing, writing, playing, having fun, social gatherings, talking, laughing again.
8. *What initially attracts you to the opposite sex?* Before I got married, I seemed to be attracted to the "bad boy" look. But variety is the spice of life and there really wasn't one type that worked best for me. For marriage purposes, I like the clean-cut, intelligent, tall and handsome look. I looked at my husband and saw my children in him. He had a great gene pool, which was of the utmost importance for the future father of my children.
9. *What do you find appealing in a date?* Someone who is easy to relate to, who is funny with a great sense of humor. Someone who is confident and relaxed to be around. I can't handle uptight individuals. I

married an uptight man and it was a source of friction for twenty years.

10. *What do you find to be a turn-off in a date?* I don't like to work hard being around people. If I have to wonder what they are thinking or worry about hurting their feelings or even wonder why I am out with them, it's a big turn-off. If a guy tries too hard to please me, it could also be a turn-off. However, I appreciate it when they try very hard to please me in bed. That is a turn-on.

11. *Where do you meet people?* Anywhere and everywhere. I enjoy talking to people. I meet a lot of people through my friends and acquaintances. People are always excited to be involved in my projects and to go out with me so they like to bring their friends along. My circle of acquaintances is ever expanding.

12. *When you are out with your friends and you see someone who catches your eye, what do you do?* I go over and introduce myself.

13. *What are your thoughts about online dating?* It is for people who lack social skills and confidence or for those who are desperate, older, or are afraid of rejection.

14. *Have you ever had trouble moving on from a past relationship?* Yes. I take life easy and I like life to be easy around me. Confusion bothers me. If I don't understand a person and their behavior, it eats at me and I need to get to the bottom of it. At that point, I am no longer interested in the person, but I need to understand the action and the reasoning behind it. I like to have the last say; I won't let them have it.

15. *What do you think of one-night stands?* It is a great change of pace for temporary sexual satisfaction. It is not an affair; an affair requires emotional attachment. Less headache and hassle. I am usually emotionally involved with only one person at a time. I cannot handle more. If I engage in a one-night sexual encounter with an acquaintance, I expect to have the same relationship with the person as I had before. Disrespectful and unpredictable behavior is confusing and makes me uncomfortable. In my opinion, when guys act weird after a one-night stand, it is their attempt to get my emotions involved. I need to learn not to get sucked in by guys who do that.

16. *How do you break off a one-night stand or short relationship without being hurtful?* Respectfully through use of communication. Merely let the person know that it was great, but it was only that one time. I am upfront about my intentions from the beginning and am always surprised when they don't understand that I meant what I said.

17. *Type of lingerie you would wear on a first date?* I am not much of a lingerie person. I like nothing underneath. I like to be free. I find restraining undergarments to be very uncomfortable. I like to be comfortable.

18. *Where do you go/what do you do on a date?* If the purpose is a one-night stand, I would like to go to the guy's house, have him cook for me, and then jump in bed. If it is for a longer-term relationship, I would like to start with a dinner out in a quiet place so we can talk and get to know one another. I live an active life-style and would enjoy sharing active time with a potential long-term relationship.

19. *If you don't know your date well, do you meet at the designated place or does your date pick you up?* I like to drive my own car at all times in case I don't like the date. I don't like to allow myself to be under the control of another. If I want to go somewhere else, then I want to be free to get myself there.

20. *Would you be interested in going for coffee and a walk instead of a dinner date for the first date?* Only if it is not a one-night stand deal. If it is a one-nighter, there is no need to get to know the person.

21. *If you were a candy, what kind would you be and why?* A bag of Jelly Bellies. I never know what type of Jelly Belly I am going to be when I wake up in the morning. I might be a hot cinnamon Jelly Belly when I wake up and then a tart blueberry Jelly Belly a few hours later. Maybe I'm a coconut Jelly Belly when I go to bed. Every day, and for that matter, every minute, is new and fresh. I am whatever I feel like at the moment.

22. *How often do you have a girls' night out? Where do you go with your girlfriends?* Here and there. Wherever we can go and have a good time.

23. *What do you hope to happen when out with the girls?* Make fun of guys, find a one-night stand, and talk about it the next day.

24. *What frustrates you in the dating scene?* The clinginess after a one-night stand.

25. *What are you looking for in a relationship?* Before I got married, I was looking for a future father for my children and a great supporting, confident husband. Now, I am looking for someone who can understand that I am a free spirit and that he will never be able to change that. If I am not free, I might as well not be living. I am loyal to my family, but need to be free to enjoy myself in all ways. One-night encounters are meaningless ways to fulfill my sexual being. I am fine

with him doing the same thing. Sex is natural. I don't expect that I'll ever marry again.

26. *Would you go out with someone who was married ?* No, I would not become emotionally tied to a married man. However, I would be willing to sleep with one for the fun of it so long as I knew that he wouldn't become emotionally involved with me. I don't like sticky, emotion-riddled situations.

27. *Would you date someone who had a child from another relationship?* It depends if he is worth that much trouble. He'd have to be awfully wonderful.

28. *If you were to live with someone, how long would you be willing to live with him without a permanent commitment?* A long time. I am not much of a committed person. So I don't care. I like change. Once I commit, I take it seriously so this would allow me more freedom. This is actually the best of both worlds.

29. *Do you mind if your date smokes?* Hate it.

30. *Are you hoping to find a man who is financially secure? Is financial security more important than love?* I would like the man to be able to make a living, but if I make more money, I don't mind sharing. Love and a great family are more important than money.

31. *Would you consider financially supporting a man with whom you happen to fall in love?* Of course.

32. *How does it make you feel if your date flaunts his assets?* If it is one-night stand, go for it. If not, he doesn't belong with me.

33. *What type of clothing do you prefer your date to wear?* White collared shirt with jeans if we are going casual. Nice suit with black T-shirt underneath if we are going to a fancy place.

34. *What is your preferred body type and shape for a man?* Fit and tight.

35. *How do you feel about tattoos and piercings?* Don't like them at all.

36. *How do you feel about perfumes and colognes?* I prefer very little smell, if any.

37. *How important is the first kiss?* It's not a deal breaker, as I will teach them to do it my way.

38. *Do you expect your date to pay on the first date ?* It doesn't bother me. If I feel like it, I just pay.

39. *What is your preference and philosophy on who should pay the bill on dates with you?* Whoever feels like it and can afford it should pay. It just isn't a big deal.

40. *Will you have sex on the first date?* Absolutely. I would be totally free and let him know what I like. This might be the only night we are together so why waste time?

41. *Would you have sex with your date if he were drunk?* As long as he can perform.

42. *How do you make sure a new sexual partner is free of STD's?* This is a tricky question. I should be more careful, but sometimes, in the heat of the moment, I just do it. However, I can almost be sure that the people I choose for sexual partners are okay. I hope to God and cross my fingers. I usually just go with life and try not to worry too much. I trust people to be good.

43. *Once you have decided to have sex with your date for the first time, are you free and uninhibited in the act or more conservative and reserved than normal?* So uninhibited that I scare myself.

44. *Where would you feel comfortable having sex with your date?* Depends on the moment, the person, and how much I have had to drink.

45. *Where is your favorite place to have sex?* In the bed. You can move around easier. The beach is too sandy. Sand gets in all crevices and can cause a huge problem.

46. *Do you use protection and if so who provides it? If you don't use protection, how do you stay safe or is it an issue?* I should, but I don't always insist upon condoms. They interfere with sensation. My tubes are tied so I don't worry about pregnancy.

47. *What do you do if protection is not immediately available?* I should be more careful. But I want everything now. Instant gratification. I don't like to let the moment go.

48. *What if you liked your date and he did not call you the next day or week?* I would consider him a bad communicator, a person with low self-esteem, not confident, and an all-together loser. However, I usually don't wait for them to call me. Regardless of the outcome and what I want from them thereafter, I call and let them know. I like to have the last word.

49. *What age range do you date?* Over 25 to under 55.

50. *What was your parents' status when you were growing up?* Very married.

51. *How do you characterize yourself?*

   Positive attributes: Fun, exciting, honest, confident, happy, humorous, easy going, strong mental attitude, loving, childish, energetic, fantastic to be with, inspiring, non-judgmental, one of a kind, love change.

Negative attributes: I need instant gratification, unreliable, need constant change, non-compassionate, zero tolerance for stupid people, zero tolerance for whiney people, zero tolerance for lazy and no good people.

52. *Please include a detailed description of your ideal date.* I drive to my date's beach house. He is preparing food, has light jazz music on with the windows open and a light breeze is blowing in. As he is cooking, I am caressing him all over. A nice bottle of Chardonnay accompanies us into the bedroom while we make hot passionate sex, take a shower, and come back to the kitchen in our underwear to continue cooking. After dinner, we take a short walk on the beach and then relax on the deck for another two hours of hot passionate sex. I leave around 2 a.m. to go to my place. I thank him the next day for the wonderful night and move on.

53. *When you meet someone new, how long does it take you to know if the person is "the one" or has the potential to be "the one"?* Right away.

54. *Do you believe in "love at first sight"?* No. But I do believe in attraction at first sight.

55. *What is your personal philosophy on monogamy and monogamous relationships?* Once in a relationship, one should consider staying monogamous. I have been unable to remain sexually monogamous, but I have successfully remained emotionally monogamous. My ex-husband couldn't appreciate the difference. Everyone has a meaningless onesy-twosy now and then.

56. *Do you believe there is a game people play when dating? If so, describe the game.* Of course. Like anything else, dating is not different. Everyone is a sales person, selling themselves in different situations. At work, school, home, in the dating scene and so forth. The game is to try to figure me out. The rules change depending on one's objective and what's at stake. For a one-night stand, it is all about looks and magnetism. For this game, one should only look good, smell good and be charming and one should keep his or her mouth shut till the deed is done. For a long-term serious relationship, the rule is natural attraction; one being himself or herself and hoping the other is doing the same. However, if the objective is other than a one-night or long-term real relationship, and it is more about money, then spe-

cial skills are required. This is a high-stakes game of strategy, patience, trickery, allusion and capture at the end. Professional gold-diggers play this game very tactfully. One should not attempt to get into this circle if not fully skilled. It can be embarrassing, as you will very quickly be found out and ousted on your ass.

57. *Have you ever been on a date with a guy who turned out to be an ass?* Most of my one-night stands are asses. That is why they stay one-night stands and it is easy to get rid of them afterward. I think I actually choose asses for this purpose so that I don't have to worry about it later.

58. *What source of communication would you like to use after the first date and thereafter?* I like texting. It is fast, quick and to the point. It is also okay to make spelling mistakes.

59. *If interested in a further date, would you wait for him to call you or would you initiate further communication?* I would call right away, as I don't have patience to wait. Time is precious.

60. *If you were not interested in another date, would you let him know?* I would communicate right away. I would say, "I had a great time last night, thank you. I'll be in touch."

61. *Would you mind if your date contacted you immediately after your date?* No.

62. *How much attention is too much or too little after the first date?* I love attention. Go for it. As long as they don't make a fool out of themselves or me.

63. *On average, how many dates are required before you consider yourself to be in a relationship?* One.

64. *Is the dating game a mystery or are the rules clear? If clear, what are the rules?* It is not a mystery if you know the objective. Know what you want and behave accordingly.

65. *Do you consider yourself to be a game-player in the dating arena?* Absolutely. I love playing games. That is what I do. Why not, as long as I don't hurt anyone? This can be fun for all, if played nicely.

66. *Is spirituality important to you? If so, what if your date has different beliefs than you do?* Sure. I like to believe in something greater than myself.

Below the belt questions:

1. *Is sex an important factor in deciding whether you will continue to date someone?* It is all about sex.
2. *Do you enjoy wearing lingerie?* Sometimes.
3. *Have you ever experienced ménage à trois?* Yes.
4. *What is sexy to you in a guy?* His body, eyes, height and they way he carries himself.
5. *Does the size of a penis matter?* Yes, of course. Must be at least average length and a bit thicker than normal.
6. *Do you prefer circumcised or not?* Definitely circumcised.
7. *Do you prefer more or less hair on a man? If a man is too hairy, what should he do about it?* Less hair. Shave it or wax it.
8. *Will you kiss and tell your friends or do you keep it private?* Only if he was really good.
9. *Are the men whom you meet in a bar a potential long-term relationship or are they a one-night stand?* Only a one-night stand.
10. *What is your opinion about surgically enhancing your body? How much enhancement is too much?* If it makes the person happy, I have no problem with it.
11. *How many sexual partners have you had in your life?* Many.

A KID IN A CANDY STORE

I was a difficult child to tame. Although I was always polite and well mannered, I always had my own agenda in mind. I enjoyed spending time with people, as long as it was enjoyable and pleasing to me. This particular characteristic marked me as being spoiled, selfish, and self-centered. So be it. I liked taking my own car and paying my own way everywhere I went. This way, I had more flexibility and control.

When I was younger, I loved playing around with young men. I loved to juggle four or five guys at one time because I would get bored easily. I didn't want a long-term relationship with one; I wanted long-term relationships with all. At the same time, I didn't want to be categorized as a one-night stand dater. I did not want to be thought of as a slut. I wanted to be free to change my men as I pleased.

I was like a free bird. I wanted to be free to experience life to the fullest without answering to anyone and without being responsible for anything or anyone. I just wanted to have fun in everything I did and I didn't want to do anything that I didn't like to do.

The guys loved me. I didn't play games; I was straightforward; I was exciting; I was loving when required; I was fun; and I was totally sexy and sexual. I was low maintenance. My one expectation was that the guys would oblige me when I asked them to meet a specific need or request. If they failed to do so, they were dropped immediately. I didn't waste my time. The name of my game was play, play, play and fun, fun, fun!

I went to college when I was sixteen. I was accepted to the local university with an undeclared major. I was given a special faculty-parking pass. My family bought it from a faculty member who had a bicycle. Being 16 and entering a university of 60,000 with special parking privileges was not a good thing as it did not teach me responsibility; it made things easier and I was not forced to grow up or face any kind of hardship.

I partied all day and all night; only studying enough to get passing grades. I had no interest in school whatsoever. I tested my car's performance level by putting it through rigorous obstacle courses. By the year's end, I had become very good friends with the sheriff and the local highway patrol. They knew me on a first name basis. Each time they pulled me over for a speeding violation, they called my name over the loudspeaker as they followed me with their lights on. My reckless driving escalated and I had a few accidents. I wound up doing crazy stunts with the car. My last stunt resulted in breaking the axel, blowing up the turbo engine, and completely totaling the car.

By then, my parents had become frustrated with me. They had decided it was time to set down the rules. Hallelujah, someone was finally going to set down some guidelines and boundaries and give me some sense of direction. I had wondered since I was five, "Why doesn't anyone offer me guidance, set down rules and boundaries, and tell me, 'No'?" I had never heard the word "No" in my entire upbringing.

It all started when I drove the car home with a broken axel. I have to say it wasn't easy to drive home because I could only make left turns. My mother, being the queen and the matriarch of the family, was a firm decision maker. She allowed things to run their course and then she would intercede and dictate how things needed to progress from there in order to achieve her expected results. Seeing that I was wasting my life and that I took nothing seriously, my mother decided to take my broken car away and enroll me in a trade school as punishment.

A tow truck towed my car back to the dealership where we had bought the car eleven months earlier. We followed the tow truck in my mother's car. My mother told the dealer to take the car back at whatever price the car was worth. The manager took the car and gave us a small amount of money back. My mom agreed and the deal was done. I was left with no car and silently wondering what was next.

As we drove away in my mom's car, she gave me a lecture and said that I needed to see the difference between a trade school and a university in order to appreciate my position in life. While driving and lecturing, she suddenly hit the brakes and pointed at a trade school on the corner. We pulled into the parking lot and she said, "This will be a good lesson for you."

The sign in front said, "Cosmetology School: County Welfare to Work Trade School." We entered the building. As we entered, we saw immediately on the left a large built in office counter with one attendant. Behind that desk was an office with large plate glass windows, overlooking the floor comprised of rows of beauty stations. A student in a white uniform occupied each station. Some of the students were wearing thick black leather ankle bracelets. My mom told the attendant that she wanted to register me to attend the school. The attendant asked my mother if she was a social worker. She said, "No." The attendant asked for my paperwork and county number. We obviously did not know what she was talking about. She suggested that we look into a privately run trade school down the street.

Before she had a chance to finish, my mom stopped her and said, "My daughter is attending this school. How much do I need to pay?" The attendant asked for the director who was sitting in the glass office overlooking the floor. The large woman came out from behind the glass and listened to my mother's story. My mother explained why she wanted me to attend the school and the director explained that the county school was intended to rehabilitate persons in the criminal justice system so that they could have a trade when released from jail. She explained that the county subsidized the tuition of $2200 a year and that we would not qualify for the subsidy. I saw a devilish grin on my mother's face. I knew she was thinking this school would be perfect to make me appreciate the university experience. She figured I would stick around for a few days and then I would be begging her to go back to college.

She had no idea whom she was dealing with; I was a kid in a candy store. I knew this would be a great experience for me and it would provide me with great entertainment. I saw this as a challenge and I actually looked forward to being there. My mom paid the $2200 and I would start the next day.

I showed up the next day and they gave me my white uniform and a small blue case with the tools of the trade for my own use. I asked if I could have an ankle bracelet and they denied me saying they were reserved for very special individuals who needed 24-hour supervision.

As usual, I made friends quickly; learned the trade fast; and learned everything there was to learn about street drugs and pills, such as speckled eggs, black beauties, uppers, downers, as well as the ins and outs of drug dealing and other interesting things. I met a lot of interesting individuals whom I would never have met in my own circles. I also learned that my new friends' dating practices were not unlike my own. Commitment was not their strong suit and they enjoyed lots of sex. The difference was that they did not know how to avoid diseases and pregnancies. I taught them every thing I knew.

After three months of attending the school, it was my mom who was begging me to quit the trade school and return back to college. I was enjoying learning life's lessons from the people who lived life to the fullest. I believe my new friends were enjoying learning lessons from my life as well. My mother gave up asking me to quit and I graduated from the program. After graduation, I went back to college.

After returning to college, I met this guy who was drop-dead gorgeous, drove a Porsche, and had any girl he wanted. He was arrogant, egotistical, and charismatic. He was also from a privileged family. We met at a party. Girls surrounded him and guys surrounded me. Our eyes met and I went over to introduce myself as I have no fear and am quite secure with myself socially. At that time, all I wanted was to get into his pants. My intentions were purely that. I cut through all the girls and got to him to say, "Hello." I invited him to come talk to me when he had a minute.

Later that night, he came over to talk to me. There was nothing of substance that I can recall; I wasn't listening to him. I heard, "Blah, blah, blah." All I could think about was ripping his clothes off. He kissed me right there and I reciprocated. He asked me to go over to his place that night, thinking that I wouldn't. He didn't realize that all I wanted was his beautiful body.

He looked like candy and I wanted to lick him all over. We had a fabulous night. He was well endowed and had stamina like you wouldn't believe. After we finished our fun, I thanked him and went home. I didn't give him my phone number. I didn't have his either. Later, I heard from a friend that he was looking for me. We met up at the school through mutual friends; he was with another girl. I said, "Hello," and I believe that he was expecting me to get jealous, urging me to look at the other girl who was Miss Runner Up America. I didn't notice and he noticed that I didn't notice. He introduced her as his girlfriend and I said, "Nice to meet you," as I introduced myself. I continued to eat my food. He got up and left with the girl.

A few minutes later, he came back and he put a piece of paper in my hand, leaving again. It was his phone number, with a note to call him. I thought, "Why not?" So, I called him and we had great one-nighters here and there for about a year -- sometimes, twice in a day. But then, he became clingy to me even though he had girls all over him. My intentions with him never changed. It was always meaningless, fun, great sex.

When he started getting clingy and proposed to me, I took my out and ended the relationship. I was sorry to see the candy walk out the door; he was the best sex play toy I had ever had. I treated all my guys like sex toys and that is all they were to me. I have always been genuine in my feelings and what I say. People cannot understand and always look for the hidden agenda and games. I don't play games; I just play.

VIII. An Interlude with the Middle Ages – A Breath of Fresh Air.

By the time people get into their thirties and forties, they are bringing baggage with them to every new relationship, sometimes unwittingly. We are shaped by our experiences. By this time in a person's life, he or she has usually had several relationships and some dating experience. They have learned more about themselves through these relationships; they have a more defined view of whom they are and what they hope to get out of a dating relationship. Below, we have a man who divorced his best friend because they wanted different things out of life. We show another man who is in a committed live-in relationship, but who hasn't taken the next step yet as far as proposals go. Then, we have two women who have various opinions and attitudes about marriage and dating. All of these interviewees have clear preferences and opinions about the dating world based upon their growing life experiences.

A. Divorced Guy

1. *Contributor age:* 40's
2. *Gender:* Male
3. *Education Level:* Graduate Degree
4. *Profession:* Investment Banker
5. *Personal Status:*   Divorced
    How many times have you been married and for how long? Once for over 18 years. I would want to get re-married.
6. *Interests/hobbies:* Education, politics, sports, kids (my own), movies, public speaking, Japan and Japanese translations. My sport is tennis.
7. *What initially attracts you to the opposite sex?* Depends on the individual. Physical beauty.
8. *Past the initial attraction, what keeps you attracted?* Personality. Thought process -- the way they think. The person who makes you feel comfortable, warm and fuzzy. Interactive.
9. *What do you find to be a turn-off in a date?* Talking a lot about themselves without being prompted. I hate panty lines. If I see a woman walking down the street with panty lines, I want to tap her on the shoulder and tell her about thongs. There is no reason that anyone should have panty lines!

227

10. *Where do you usually meet people?* Anywhere. Library, coffee shop. Seminars. Company. Work. The antenna is always up. Usually, when you are looking, it is not going to happen.

11. *When you are out with your friends and you see someone who catches your eye, what do you do?* Talk about her. If I have good co-pilots, I will send them out to snoop around. But I have really bad co-pilots. I go out with a bunch of married guys. A friend can be used as a crutch.

12. *What are your thoughts about online dating?* Many people have been rejected by online sites; one rejected me because I was not picky enough. I got too many hits. You have to be too picky and describe exactly what you want. This can be the best thing or the worst thing. I would have never met my former wife if I had only looked for a list of specific qualities. Do people really know what they want? It is good to experience life with someone who different from yourself. You learn more about yourself that way and you grow more.

13. *Have you ever had trouble moving on from a past relationship? If so, what did you do to finally get over it?* Oh yes. Getting over everything is a hard thing. It was hard to get over the first relationship after my divorce. It was unfortunate timing for her, as I was technically still married. I had been separated and living apart from my wife, but the divorce was not final. I never introduced her as my girlfriend. I broke it off. Later, when I wanted to get back together, she had already moved on.

14. *Where do you go with your date?* Dinner. Rather not go to a fancy place.

15. *If you don't know your date well, do you meet at the designated place or do you pick up your date?* Either way. It depends on her comfort level.

16. *Would you be interested in going for coffee and a walk instead of a dinner date for the first date?* Sure.

17. *How often do you have a boys' night out? Where do you go with your friends?* I really don't have time for boys' nights out; my married friends don't really get to do that as they all have young kids. I have a child also. My free time is spent with her and taking her to her various activities.

18. *What frustrates you in the dating scene?* The game. Calling too much, not calling enough. Knowing restaurants, not knowing the restaurants. You can't be yourself. This is like business; you have to sell yourself. You have to get in. Too anal, not anal enough. As soon as I get inter-

ested in one person, I get another date to make sure I have dates all the time. You are more attractive when you have others who are interested in you. Sometimes, you want what you can't have. Make yourself a little inaccessible.

19. *What are you looking for in a relationship?* Best friend. Partner. My ex-wife was my best friend. I lost my best friend when we divorced. It was really difficult.

20. *Would you go out with a married woman?* I would. I wouldn't call it a date. It would only be for physical reasons. Too many complications for anything more than the physical. Depends if they have children or not. If they were technically married and not happy and simply sharing space with their husband, I would do it. I would call this "getting together."

21. *Would you date someone who had a child from another relationship?* Yes.

22. *If you were to live with someone, how long would you be willing to live with her without a permanent commitment?* I am not a big living with someone person. I am a commitment person.

23. *Are you hoping to find a woman who is financially secure?* No. It's not a deal breaker. At the end, it is about feelings.

24. *Is financial security more important than love?* Of course not.

25. *Would you consider financially supporting a woman with whom you happen to fall in love?* Yes.

26. *How does it make you feel if your date flaunts her financial assets?* It is only good if it is when the check comes. Otherwise, it is a negative.

27. *What type of clothing do you prefer your date to wear?* Conservative style. Sexy and flashy is not good, as people will start staring at you. I like classy and sexy.

28. *What is your preferred body type and shape for a woman?* Thin and shapely. Not too big of a bust. Not too big of a rear. Athletic is the best and I am a huge legs person. I also love skin; smooth skin. Soft hands. Dry skin is almost a deal breaker.

29. *How do you feel about tattoos and piercings?* Wouldn't be my first choice. Piercings would be interesting from a physical point of view. A small little tattoo is not bad.

30. *How do you feel about perfumes and colognes?* Perfume is great.

31. *How important is the first kiss?* Not. It can add more than it can subtract. Mind set is more important because, if you are open to it, good sex can become great sex.

32. *Do you want to pay on the first date?* No. I always assume I am. I have trouble accepting it when they want to pay.

33. *What is your preference and philosophy on who should pay the bill on dates with you?* I don't mind a few times, but I like to split after a few dates. I over think things a lot.

34. *Will you have sex on the first date?* Sure. Not a good idea. Anyone can have a bad night.

35. *How do you make sure a new sexual partner is free of STD's?* I protect myself. Condoms. I don't talk about it. Buyers beware.

36. *Once you have decided to have sex with your date for the first time, are you free and uninhibited in the act or more conservative and reserved than normal?* I would like to be uninhibited, but it depends on the woman and the situation.

37. *Where do you go to have sex?* Everywhere and anywhere.

38. *Where do you feel comfortable having sex with your date?* Anywhere. Depends on the situation.

39. *What do you do if protection is not immediately available?* I still do it.

40. *What if you liked your date and she did not return your call the next day or week? What would you think and do?* Find another date. That is the game.

41. *What age range do you date?* Young twenties would be a physical thing. Late 20's to early 50's are what I date for a relationship.

42. *What do you think of one-night stands?* I don't think about them. They serve as an outlet for release. Everyone participates. Married and not married.

43. *How do you break off a one-night stand or short relationship without being hurtful?* Say good-bye.

44. *What was your parents' status when you were growing up?* Married and best friends.

45. *How do you characterize yourself?*

    Positive attributes: Optimistic, thoughtful, overly thinking, interested in others, trustworthy, fun, reflective.

    Negative attributes: I wish I could sometimes be happy for others without immediate jealousy. I would like to be less judgmental.

46. *What is your ideal date?* Someone who was attractive, dressed well with the thong and soft hands, full of life, and excited about life. Someone who is focused on me. One who has passion. Dinner at her

place or my place, where we cook together. Sit down with candle light, wine, dinner and then just the same till the morning breakfast.

47. *When you meet someone new, how long does it take you to know if the person is "the one" or has the potential to be "the one"?* A few days. I tend to have a few dates before I make up my mind.

48. *Do you believe in "love at first sight"?* Yes. Some sort of connection and understanding to be able to read each other well. It is the natural ability to anticipate one another's moves.

49. *What is your personal philosophy on monogamy and monogamous relationships?* Wonderful if possible. If someone deviates, it is because they are not getting what they need from their partner. If you are content, you don't need anything more. Good sex doesn't mean good relationship, but a good relationship requires good sex.

50. *Do you believe there is a game people play when dating? If so, what is the game and what are the rules?* Yes. It is just like business.

51. *On average, how many dates are required before you consider yourself to be in a relationship? What qualifies as a date?* It is more physical. Once we start sleeping together, it is a relationship.

52. *If interested in your date, how long do you wait to communicate with her?* It depends on the person. Going back to the game.

53. *If you were not interested in dating her again, would you let her know? If so, how do you let her know?* Yes. Indirectly. I will say, "Sure, let's get together sometime and I will give you a call in couple of weeks." But I will not call.

54. *Would you mind if your date contacted you immediately after the date?* I would jump for joy even if I weren't particularly interested. Game over.

55. *What form of communication, if any, would you prefer from her?* Phone. Talking. Everything makes more sense when talking. Cute little texts are good. Stupid texts are great.

56. *What books on dating have you read? Out of those books, which ones do you recommend?* Blink.

Below the belt questions:

1. *Is sex an important factor in deciding whether you will continue to date someone?* Not really; you can learn to be compatible if you care enough.

2. *Do you enjoy it when your date wears lingerie?* Thongs are important. Other lingerie is an added bonus.

3. *Have you ever experienced a ménage a trois? If not, would you consider it? If so, what combination of male/female?* No. Yes. Two women and me.

4. *What is sexy to you in a woman?* Skin, legs, arms, eyes, and walk.

5. *Does the size of her breasts matter?* Not too big. Smaller is better than bigger.

6. *Do you mind surgical enhancement of breasts, lips, teeth, etc? How much body enhancement is too much?* Big negative. Having a lot of surgeries means the woman is not happy with herself; she will have more and more of them and still not be happy.

7. *How much make up is too much?* If I am afraid to see them in the morning without their make up, it is too much.

8. *Are skimpy, body-fitting outfits a turn-on or a turn-off?* Depends on the situation. Wearing that kind of outfit on a first date is a negative.

9. *Do you prefer a particular pubic hair design?* I am not a huge fan of completely shaved. I like it trimmed.

10. *Do you treat dates with long-term potential differently than fun quickies?* I treat fun quickies differently in that I never say the truth. I have a clear goal to get into their pants and it is a different game. I only say silly things.

11. *How many sexual partners have you had in your life?* 40

B. On the Verge of Proposal

1. *Contributor age:* 30's
2. *Gender:* Male
3. *Education Level:* Graduate Degree, working on PHD
4. *Profession:* Professor
5. *Personal Status:* Single
    If single, are you looking for a long-term relationship or a meaningful one-night stand? I'm in a relationship. Over a year in the relationship.
6. *Interests/hobbies:* Action games, listening to rock music.
7. *What initially attracts you to the opposite sex?* Being able to have a conversation with someone with whom I can communicate and talk about things in which we are both interested.

232

8. *What do you find appealing in a date?* Some sort of activity that we can share and have a good time doing. Joint fun. I like to talk and think. Something that is neither too passive nor overactive. I enjoy going out to dinner and having a couple of drinks.

9. *What do you find to be a turn-off in a date?* Being in some crowded and unfun place. I can't stand someone who is getting sloppy drunk. Party animal.

10. *Where do you meet people?* Through friends and colleagues. I met my current girlfriend at the university. My girlfriend was my former student. I waited until she was no longer in my class.

11. *When you are out with your friends and you see someone who catches your eye, what do you do?* I am not one of those, "Look, damn she is hot" kind of guys. I am unlikely to do anything.

12. *What are your thoughts about online dating?* It is the way of the new dating world. It is more and more becoming part of our time and reality. It is not weird. But I never tried it. There are risks; especially when people misrepresent themselves.

13. *Have you ever had trouble moving on from a past relationship?* Not any more than anyone else has had. The blues that go along with that are pretty typical and general to all who go through it. Spend time with friends and family, know and understand that time heals. There is no reason to fall into deep down misery; no girl is worth that.

14. *What are your rituals for preparing for your date?* Get myself cleaned up and ready to go.

15. *Where do you go/what do you do on a date?* Coffee houses. Lounges where we can talk. Movies. Mini golf. Evening things.

16. *If you don't know your date well, do you meet at the designated place or do you pick up your date?* Have done both. Typically meet at a place. It is easier to do so.

17. *Would you be interested in going for coffee and a walk instead of a dinner date for the first date?* Yes. That is my type of thing.

18. *How often do you have a boys' night out? Where do you go with your friends?* Not often. But we get together and watch football games at a sports bar every weekend during football season.

19. *What frustrates you in the dating scene?* The hectic nature of it all. Presenting yourself the way they want to see you and vice versa. It gets tiring. I just want all that to stop and move on with my relationship. We knew each other and didn't have to go through that – the process of show was not part of our deal.

20. *What are you looking for in a relationship?* Someone with whom I am comfortable and who makes me happy. I want someone who understands that the world is bigger than just one's own world of trouble.

21. *Would you go out with a married woman?* No.

22. *Would you date someone who had a child from another relationship?* Yes.

23. *If you were to live with someone, how long would you be willing to live with her without a permanent commitment?* Two or three years. I wouldn't want to be spinning my wheels. I do want kids. But it is great to be able to kick the tires.

24. *Do you mind if your date smokes?* I prefer not.

25. *Would you consider financially supporting your partner?* Yes.

26. *What type of clothing do you prefer your date to wear when you go out on a date?* Casual. Jeans and a t-shirt.

27. *What is your preferred body type and shape for a woman?* I don't have a preferred body type. Someone that is healthy. Not morbidly obese or anorexic skinny.

28. *How do you feel about tattoos and piercings?* Fine.

29. *How do you feel about perfumes and colognes?* I don't mind them.

30. *How important is the first kiss?* Not as important as the second kiss. The first one is the nervous kiss and the second is the real.

31. *Do you want to pay on the first date? And after the first date?* No one ever wants to pay, but I pay. Alternating is good. It depends on who is making the money.

32. *Will you have sex on the first date? If so, would you talk to your date about your preferences freely?* Yehhhh. Sure. Yes.

33. *Do you wear boxers or briefs?* Boxers.

34. *How do you make sure a new sexual partner is free of STD's?* I ask. In the most easy way. Prior activity. "Do you have a history of any STD's that we need to be aware of?" The idea of trust is the big element of things. I have not tested myself or needed to unless I suspected something. In the last ten years to now, the dating world has become a completely different world. I don't remember this sort of randomly hooking up being as prevalent as it is now. Sure, people in school have always done it, but it wasn't the norm. The norm wasn't hooking up. Now, hooking up is the normative behavior. Of course, alcohol has always been a part of early college life and guys going out and looking to get laid has been normal. However, this random partners thing has just evolved. Today, there seems to be a more open

view of sexuality. Shows like "Sex in the City" urge this openness along. The media has a lot to do with it as well. This behavior gets carried into the work place. The entire nature of "relationship" has changed. We are too busy at all levels of society for courtship. Now the kids say, "I am going to drink and hook up with someone." That is their agenda on Thursday through Sunday nights. In the last five to seven years, this behavior took off. As I sort of got into grad school in the last five years, I started seeing more and more kids in the early 2000's with this goal of hanging together and hooking up with one another.

I think the change has come about because of the way kids are raised today. Kids are extremely sheltered before college. The kids now care about nothing. They have no responsibilities. Families have become too busy to pay attention to the kids. There is no time to chill and be a family. Everything is scheduled. Even the talks about "the birds and the bees" take place in the school rather than at home. The early exploration of sexuality is now happening in the early teens rather than the late teens.

35. *Once you have decided to have sex with your date for the first time, are you free and uninhibited in the act or more conservative and reserved than normal?* First time is more reserved.

36. *When on a date, where would you be willing to have sex with your date if you were hot and horny?* Parking lot. Home.

37. *Where is your favorite place to have sex if you had a choice?* Beach.

38. *Do you use protection and, if so, who provides it? If you don't use protection, how do you stay safe or is it an issue?* Yes. I provide a condom.

39. *What do you do if protection is not immediately available?* Wait.

40. *What if you liked your date and she did not return your call the next day or week? What would you think and do?* Take it as a sign that it was not meant to be. I will call once and that is it.

41. *What if your date called you a month later? What would you say and do?* "What happened? Your mom died?"

42. *What age range do you date?* Five years younger and older than I.

43. *What do you think of one-night stands?* Just about everybody participates in them. They aren't for me.

44. *What was your parents' status when you were growing up?* Divorced in elementary school.

45. *How do you characterize yourself?*
> **Positive attributes:** I am funny, relaxed, good conversationalist, and intelligent. I like to think that I have a fair amount of knowledge about what I talk about.
>
> **Negative attributes:** Shy in one-on-one instances, but I have no issue lecturing to an auditorium. Not very aggressive. I tend to put other peoples' wants ahead myself.

46. *How do you think others see you?* Relaxed and fun.

47. *Please include a detailed description of your ideal date.* Going out to some sort of a coffee house or a park where we can talk about something interesting, watching a football game. Not too over dramatic.

48. *When you meet someone new, how long does it take you to know if the person is "the one" or has the potential to be "the one"?* Couple of weeks. Few times. I tend to read people very quickly. Everyone is putting on the show for the first few times.

49. *Do you believe in "love at first sight"?* I believe it can happen. We are looking for it and looking for a soul mate. Sometimes it happens; sometimes it does not.

50. *What is your personal philosophy on monogamy and monogamous relationships?* I think it is good thing.

51. *Do you believe there is a game people play when dating? If so, describe the game.* Yes. Put on a show. This is not limited to dating; it is part of life. You put on a show for family, friends and everyone. You perform a routine.

52. *Is the dating game a mystery or are the rules clear? If clear, what are the rules?* The problem is that the rules are not clear and times have changed from the idea of dating where (1) the boy asks a girl for a date to (2) "I ask, I pay" to (3) the reality of no dating where boys and girls meet at parties and randomly hook up. Dating doesn't occur till the third or fourth time of hooking up. After a sequence of parties, the dating of one individual might occur, but it is rare. If it does occur, then we go back to the old rules.

   I don't believe anyone should play games. In a perfect world, people should not present an image based upon what they think a person wants to date. Just be yourself. Most people want to be desirable and what people are looking for, they want to be what a suitable partner should be: well dressed, well mannered with a good car, the cliché thing. They should really be more comfortable about themselves. If you build up the beginning of the relationship on a modified truth, you have to start the game again from the beginning; this time being yourself. It becomes extremely tiring when you are trying to maintain the acting game.

53. *On average, how many dates are required before you consider yourself to be in a relationship? What qualifies as a date?* Dating has changed so much. Dating is hanging out. You almost have to ask, "Are we a couple now?" I guess you have to ask the question. It is much more casual today.

54. *Have you ever been on a date with a girl who turned out to be a bitch?* Yes, she was rude to people around us and she became worked up over minor things. Someone cut in front of us in a movie line and she started shouting at the person. The best part of the evening was when it was over. She didn't care that she made me extremely uncomfortable; I don't even think she realized that I was uncomfortable by her scenes.

55. *Once you meet a person whom you would like to continue to date, what source of communication would you like to use?* I prefer email. The younger kids prefer texts.

56. *If interested in your date, how long do you wait to communicate with her?* I wait a couple of days, maybe the next day. Not five minutes later cause that would be a stalkerish thing. You run the risk of being too intense. I would probably do something the next day. Give it a day.

57. *If you were not interested in dating her again, would you let her know?* Yes. I would let her know right away. "Hey, it was nice and all, but I don't think this will work for me."

58. *Would you mind if your date contacted you immediately after the date?* It would depend on the date. If I had a good time, I wouldn't mind it.

Below the belt questions:

1. *Is sex an important factor in deciding whether you will continue to date someone?* Yes, of course. Sex is important when in a relationship.

2. *Do you enjoy it when your date wears lingerie?* It is not a turn-on for me; I think it is overrated. Maybe okay as a Valentine's thing once a year.

3. *Have you ever experienced ménage à trois? If not, would you consider it?* No. Call me old fashioned.

4. *What is sexy to you in a woman?* Intelligence and social intellect. Physically, her eyes and smile.

5. *Do you mind surgical enhancement of breasts, lips, teeth, etc? How much body enhancement is too much?* Not something I am into. If someone is trying to define themselves, that would not be a good thing. That chain never stops.

6. *How much make up is too much?* A little is fine. If it involves hardware, tools, or electrical appliances to apply, it is too much!

7. *Are skimpy, body-fitting outfits a turn-on or a turn-off?* Depends on the body in the outfit.

8. *What do you think of coffee houses as a place to meet someone?* A great place to meet people; everyone is there in a social context. If the place was busy, I might say, "Mind if I sit here?" I would comment on the fact that she was reading a book that interested me.

9. *What do you think of the work environment as a place to meet someone?* It is the way of the world. It is where we spend our time. I think the rules have to be there for certain reasons. Sexual harassment is largely a problematic rule. The rule has its heart in the right place, but it does not really work. Academia is not a real work place. There is not a middle management at the university. The rules are understood, but they are not written: "Remove yourself from the harassment situation and don't date students." However, there are no repercussions at the academic place of work if you violate the unwritten rules.

10. *Do you prefer tanned or natural skin?* Natural.

11. *Long hair or short hair?* Long hair, any color.

12. *Do you prefer a particular pubic hair design?* Not seventies' bush. Maintained.

13. *How many sexual partners have you had in your life?* 2.

C. Girls Looking for Fun

2 GIRLS IN THEIR THIRTIES: Some interviews were done with individuals; others were done with more than one. These very good girl-friends had a great time with the interview and provided many moments of fun and laughter. Where their answers were separate, we numbered them. Otherwise, they answered our questions together.

1. *Education Level:* College

2. *Are you financially secure?* Yes

3. *Profession:* (1) nurse; (2) marketing

4. *Personal Status:* (1) Divorced (2) Single, but committed

   (1) *What happened with your first marriage?* I married someone who came from an abusive background; he came across as confident and intelligent. He kept bad feelings inside. He left because he fell out of love with me.

   (2) I dated a drunk who ordered one or two bottles of wine whenever we went out. He had commitment problems. He couldn't commit because he thought there was always something better out there.

5. *Are you looking for a long-term relationship or a meaningful one-night stand?* Both are looking for long-term relationships.

6. *Interests/hobbies:* (1) Running, softball, skiing, girls' night out, outdoors; (2) Golfing, sleeping and napping.

7. *What initially attracts you to the opposite sex?* (1) Physical, eye contact, and their face, height, and good hair; (2) I like bald, intelligent, good conversationalist, sensitivity, witty, fun, open to experiencing new things, well-traveled, cultured, and into arts.

8. *What do you find appealing in a date?* (1&2) Classy and put together, someone who can make you feel comfortable right away and someone to whom you can talk, a shy person who doesn't or can't make you comfortable is hard to date initially. However, the shy person can be worked on in a couple of dates. Confidence is key.

9. *What do you find to be a turn-off in a date?* (1) Immature and unintelligent, someone who is closed-minded, who doesn't understand that everyone has an opinion, and it's okay to accept others for who they are, black and white thinking. Values are very important. (2) Drunk, loud and vulgar.

10. *Where do you meet people?* (1) Sometimes at the bars, not anymore -- that was last year. On Valentine's Day, I met this guy at a local bar. We were talking the whole evening. He left at the end, but his friend was there and I wrote down my number and gave it to his friend. The guy I had been talking to the whole night called me six weeks later and we ended up dating. The reason he waited so long to call was because he had a girlfriend – he called me after he dumped his girlfriend. But, he ended up being a lush. He was a flake and wanted to party with his friends all the time. He was in his mid-twenties; I was over that stage of my life. I tried to drop him, but he continued to text message me. We continued talking and having booty calls. He would give me mixed messages and he would continually tell me that he loved me. I

felt like a kid in the candy store because I had gotten out of the four-year dead-end marriage. I went along with him because he was younger, fun and entertaining. I saw it as a time to have fun. If you don't feel like the biological clock is ticking, you can be out there to have fun. Life is too short to not enjoy yourself.

(2) Online is where I meet people. I meet people at my company in their late 30's. Really, I meet them in a combination of places. I dated this hot guy and the sex was good. On the third date, we had sex. I became irritated by how he treated his kids. He flaked on his daughter in order to see me and I didn't like that.

(1) I dated a Latin lawyer who was building his house. One night on a date, we had sex on his architectural plans. I liked that he was married before; the dates were going great. I still see him. I like the traditional date of going out ice skating, bowling, or to sporting events.

11. *When you are out with your friends and you see someone who catches your eye, what do you do?* (1&2) Nothing. We all stand there and nominate one of us to go and talk to the group of guys. We talked to one person who was from Atlanta and he turned out to be stupid. We wait for the guys. (1) Depends on the alcohol content. When in Vegas, no rules apply. We went to dinner in Vegas with six of us; we went to a burlesque show with topless dancers. We met a bunch of guys there. One of our friends knows how to approach the guys. We sat at the bottle service table[7] full of Canadian businessmen. Some had rings on; some didn't. That is where I met the Latin lawyer – he was one of the single ones and I made out with him. I made out half way cause I knew it was wrong to make out all the way, but not half way, when I was dating someone. Kissing is kissing. Is it cheating? How do you define cheating? Three of us got in a limo with the six guys. We went to a dance club. We went to another strip club. They paid for everything. The Latin guy wanted to take me in the back with the stripper. I thought he wanted me to watch him with the stripper. He kept insisting and I said, "I am not doing anything," but then I thought, "What the heck?" We got in line. The stripper was beautiful and she kept telling me, "It is not what you think it is; we can set limits." She did a whole dance and was touching me while he was watching right next to me. We had not even kissed at that point. I was nervous. The stripper made

---

[7] In a crowded hip spot in Vegas, a table may be purchased by a group of men. Women then angle for an invitation to sit at the table.

me more comfortable. It was a "G-rated" ménage a trios and it was expensed as $500 on the guy's business account. We all left after that and I still see the Latin guy.

12. *What are your thoughts about online dating?* (2) Works for me, I don't go out to bars, I am working and have no time. There seems to be a lot of quality people using online dating. I don't prefer it; I like to meet people organically. I found my current boyfriend online; I also met a lot of duds, people lying about themselves. You should have a really open mind. You can meet someone good or someone really scary. I can weed people out really quickly. I can read it very well. I deleted 900 people. I can delete very fast. Lots of guys say that sex is important; I delete them right away. They put down in order of importance: food, water, sex. There are lots of agnostic people.

13. *Have you ever had trouble moving on from a past relationship?*
(1) Yes. Marriage. My husband just got up and left one day without warning. It was shocking to me. It was a sudden move. I didn't see it coming. I jumped in bed with someone right away in order to get over it. It didn't work; I needed time to process and got a therapist to help me with questions that were not answered.

(2) I was dating someone who was eight years younger than I. He was still in school. He wanted to party and have fun. What was supposed to be a fling turned into a ten-month relationship. I got really sick and he left me. It was not a healthy relationship. I took time off to focus on my health and myself. I was forcing myself to go on dates so I would not be too depressed. It took a few months to get over him. You can meet people so much faster through the Internet. The best way to get over a break up is to get back in the saddle right away. The on-line world has brought dating to the forefront of experience because now you have more options. I wish I had learned that in my 20's. I would meet someone right away and find the cutest guy, younger, model-like and hot.

14. *What do you think of one-night stands?*
(1) My girlfriend is 43, single, financially secure, and in a high-powered position. It was her birthday and she had no prospects. We encouraged her and egged her on to pick up the waiter. She did. She took him to her beach house and they spent the night together. He didn't want to leave the next day; she had to kick him out. It was funny. She put him in her Facebook so her friends could see her birthday fling.

241

(2) I don't believe in them. Hope to never have one. In school, a one-night stand is when you are drunk.

15. *How do you break off a one-night stand or short relationship without being hurtful?*

    (1&2) A guy would send you a text message saying, "Sorry, but I am busy." Most, however, don't send anything. I have done the direct route of asking where things stand, but that has not worked too well lately. Once I had sex with someone and got up and left in the morning because he sucked at sex. Some guys are classless. Some suck at sex. I had to tell him, "I think you are a selfish lover and I think you will be selfish in a relationship." Sex is important and it is the heartbeat of marriage.

16. *What are your rituals for preparing for a date?*

    (1) Shower, shave, wax, bleach my teeth. (2) Choose clothes.

17. *Type of lingerie you would wear on a first date? And the following dates?*

    (1) I don't wear cute under-wire bras because I don't want to be tempted to have sex. (2) I wear thongs and try to match my bra.

18. *Where do you go/what do you do on a date?*

    (1&2) I love to be wined and dined. Music. I don't want the guy to cook me dinner the second night. It is a turn-off. Good dates are sailing, hiking, and tennis.   I like different things that are creative.

19. *If you don't know your date well, do you meet at the designated place or does your date pick you up?* (1&2) We meet at a neutral place. We don't want someone to pick us up at our home until we know them.

20. *Would you be interested in going for coffee and a walk instead of a dinner date for the first date?* (1&2) Yes, definitely.

21. *Do you treat dates differently when set up by a friend or relative?* (1&2) No.

22. *How often do you have a girls' night out? Where do you go with your girlfriends?* (1&2) Two to three times a week. Dinner out. San Francisco, Palo Alto, Los Gatos.

23. *What do you hope to happen when out with the girls?* (1&2)   Just spend quality time with them.

24. *What frustrates you in the dating scene?* (1&2) Lying. The more technology there is, the less personal interaction there seems to be. What is really irritating is when someone asks you out through a text. I told him to call me rather than texting. Guys not paying for or planning the dates; there are lots of last minute arrangements being made.

There are a lot of people who are non-committal. Wishy-washy, they don't say what they mean and they don't know what they want; I have had to tell them what they want. People are not honest and are liars. They represent themselves in a certain way, but that is not who they are. A lot of them are non-committal because they think there is always someone better. As soon as you hit a rough patch, they leave.

25. *What are you looking for in a relationship?*
(1&2) Longevity and someone who stands by your side. Supportive. Someone who can add value to my life and make me a better person. Committed. Encouraging. Good listener. Sensitive makes a better partner. Motivated. Trustworthy at the end of the day.

26. *Would you go out with a married man?* (1&2) No. I was married and it is just not right.

27. *What about someone who is separated, but not divorced or has a girlfriend?* (1) Yes, it takes six months to go through a divorce and they are available at that point. (2) No.

28. *Would you date someone who had a child from another relationship?*
(1) Undecided. I kind of like it because you are no longer under pressure to have kids.
(2) Yes.

29. *If you were to live with someone, how long would you be willing to live with him without a permanent commitment?*
(1) Two years in my 20's; in my 30's, I don't know.
(2) It is a better idea to be engaged before you move in with the guy; otherwise the guy has it too easy.

30. *Are you hoping to find a man who is financially secure? Is financial security more important than love?* (1) Both important. (2) Yes. I don't want to be a sugar mommy.

31. *How does it make you feel if your date flaunts his assets?* (1&2) Cheesy and tacky. Shows insecurity in other areas. (2) He has a little weenie.

32. *What type of clothing do you prefer your date to wear?*
(1) I like hip, take risk with fashion, leather pants, have imagination.
(2) Nice, casual. No suit and tie. Clean cut.

33. *What is your preferred body type and shape for a man?* (1) Six foot, two inches, 190 pounds, and fit. (2) Tall, fit, and muscular.

34. *How do you feel about tattoos and piercings?* (1) Don't like it. Hate it.
(2) I can deal with it.

35. *How do you feel about perfumes and colognes?*
    (1) No garlic or body odor; a little cologne is nice.
    (2) I prefer natural pheromones. Natural animal scent. I want to jump the guy when I smell that.
36. *How important is the first kiss?*
    (1) Very, it is a pre-curser to what happens next. Some bad kissers could be really good in bed. Passionate, not too overwhelming. Sensual, no tongue right away.
    (2) Something soft and sensual; not too overwhelming; empowering. Good breath is essential.
37. *Do you expect your date to pay on the first date?* (1&2) Yes. Absolutely. If they ask me out, they should pay. If the girl asks, then split the bill. In the beginning, it is very nice for the guy to pay; more traditional.
38. *What is your preference and philosophy on who should pay the bill on dates with you?* (1&2) The guy should pay for every date at the beginning. Then it can go to 80/20. As you progress, it is nice to offer to split.
39. *Will you have sex on the first date?*
    (1) Four dates after.
    (2) No.
40. *Do you prefer your date to wear boxers or briefs?*
    (1&2) Boxer briefs.
41. *How do you make sure a new sexual partner is free of STD's?* (1&2) We have the discussion before. I always use condoms. I ask them, "When was the last time you were tested and what was the result." I want them tested for Syphilis, HIV, and HPV. I make them go. Then I insist on using condoms anyway.
42. *Where would you feel comfortable having sex with your date?*
    (1) Their home and you can be like the guy and ditch them. My story is that I have to let my dog out.
    (2) Home.
43. *Where is your favorite place to have sex?*
    (1) Outdoors. Ski resort.
    (2) Woods. Beach.
44. *What do you do if protection is not immediately available?*
    (1) Make out and just don't have sex.
    (2) I don't have sex.

45. *What if you liked your date and he did not call you the next day or week? What would you think and do?*

(1) Send a text asking how he is doing and telling him that I am checking in. If nothing happens, drop it.

(2) Just wait.

46. *What if your date called you a month later? What would you say and do?*

(1) I will not respond. Unless he was really good.

(2) Depends who it is.

47. *How do you characterize yourself?*

Positive attributes: (1) Positive, easy-going, conservative at times, educated, fun, wild.

(2) Positive, intelligent, balanced, in tune with who I am and what I want, spiritual, goofy.

Negative attributes: (1) Sometimes judgmental, I give people too much of a chance, too caring.

(2) Negative attributes: Rigid, judgmental, think too much, over-analyze.

48. *Please include a detailed description of your ideal date.*

(1) Go somewhere tropical, beach, dinner, simple.

(2) I thought nobody would ever ask me this question! Guy picks me up in his private jet and takes me to Paris, we go shopping all day long, in the evening we go to the museum and dinner.

49. *When you meet someone new, how long does it take you to know if the person is "the one" or has the potential to be "the one"?*

(1) You'll know the connection right away. Two or three dates.

(2) Several dates and months.

50. *Do you believe in "love at first sight"?* (1&2) No.

51. *What is your personal philosophy on monogamy and monogamous relationships?* (1&2) It is a good thing. When you are not, it doesn't work out very well.

52. *Do you believe there is a game people play when dating? If so, describe the game.*

(1) Chase to get the girls emotionally; then ditch them.

(2) They act as if they are interested, but they are not. They are not true. They leave me dumbfounded.

53. *Have you ever been on a date with a guy who turned out to be an ass?*

(1) Yes. He would be talking to other women and flirting while I was

sitting with him. I confronted him and he couldn't understand why it was not okay with me.

54. *If interested in a further date, would you wait for him to call you or would you initiate further communication?* (1&2) Wait to get their call.

55. *If you were not interested in another date, would you let him know?* (1) I would tell him that I was not interested in an email.

56. *Would you mind if your date contacted you immediately after your date?*
(1&2) I love it. It is nice. Text right away. Simple and sweet.

57. *How much attention is too much or too little after the first date?*
(1&2) If someone calls me on the phone right away, it is bad, but an immediate text is good. Wait a day or two to call.

58. *On average, how many dates are required before you consider yourself to be in a relationship? What qualifies as a date?*
(1&2) Have "The talk" to know where you stand.

59. *Is the dating game a mystery or are the rules clear? If clear, what are the rules?*
(1&2) The rules are clear if they are stable people. This is not rocket science. Give enough space. Don't talk about marriage and kids on the first date. No ex-relationship talk. No medical conditions mentioned on the first date.

60. *Do you consider yourself to be a game-player in the dating arena?*
(1) I am a little bit. I won't let people know how I feel. I keep myself closed up. Leave a mystery.
(2) No.

61. *What books on dating have you read? Out of those books, which ones do you recommend?* (1&2) <u>Secret</u>. <u>If the Buddha Dated</u>.

Below the belt questions:

1. *Is sex an important factor in deciding whether you will continue to date someone?* (1&2) Yes.

2. *Do you enjoy wearing lingerie?* (1&2) Sometimes.

3. *Have you ever experienced ménage à trois?*
(1) No. I would with two guys.
(2) No and I wouldn't.

4. *What is sexy to you in a guy?*
(1) Tall. Sexual knowledge. If they are retarded forget it.

(2) Confidence, good looking, intelligence.
5. *Does the size of a penis matter?*
   (1&2) Yes. (1) Seven inches and above. (2) Average to above.
6. *Do you prefer circumcised or not?*
   (1) Circumcised.
   (2) If not, have him take a shower and cover it up with a condom.
7. *Do you prefer more or less hair on a man?*
   (1) Hairy chest is good.
   (2) Less.
8. *Do you prefer tanned or natural skin?* (1&2) Natural.
9. *Will you kiss and tell your friends or do you keep it private?* (1&2) Of course I tell!
10. *Are the men whom you meet in a bar a potential long-term relationship or are they a one-night stand?* (1&2) Depends on the person.
11. *How many sexual partners have you had in your life?* (1) 10 (2) 7

IX. The Givers

Compared to the Takers and the characters in the Give & Take section, the Givers are more considerate of others and are more in tune with other people's feelings. They have empathy for others. They don't have game, but are often stuck in someone else's game. They are upfront and communicative. Dating for these characters is typically about the process, learning, and loving another person.

A. The Fantasizer: Pleases everyone else, but is guilt-ridden when pleasing self.

Typically in a committed relationship and fantasizing about naughty play, the Fantasizers are conservative in their dress, rarely wearing the latest fashions. They are not risk-takers in any aspect of their lives. They are socially correct, concerned about what people say about them. They are extremely judgmental about others' transgressions. They are creatures of routine and they are extremely meticulous. For example, when disrobing for a sexual encounter, the clothing is neatly folded and put away. If married, the Fantasizer will remove his or her wedding ring when meeting with the Forbidden Fruit. This can be out of respect for the spouse or simple fear of losing their ring and then having to explain the loss to their spouse.

They are not out looking for an affair, but if a Forbidden Fruit falls into their lap, they have a hard time resisting. Their indiscretions usually start with a friend or co-worker whom they trust. However, once the relationship evolves beyond a sexual fantasy, it is easy for the Fantasizer to become emotionally attached. If a Fantasizer becomes involved with a manipulative lover, he or she can be lured away from his or her prior commitments. If, however, the other party is not available, the relationship may serve as temporary pleasure for both.

At the beginning, guilt and fear of hurting their loved ones keep the affairs short-lived. The initial oscillation between ecstasy and emotional pain can be draining on the Fantasizer's lover. But, the guilt is also exciting. Once having tasted the Forbidden Fruit, the Fantasizers become highly addicted and desire frequent bursts of pleasure and ecstasy until their guilt and fear gets the better of them. At that point, they repent, feeling remorse, fearful and caught between pleasurable fantasy and mundane reality.

Once having had an affair, it becomes easier for the Fantasizer to act upon his or her fantasies. As the Fantasizer becomes accustomed to acting upon his or her desires, starting with a nibble of the "apple (forbidden fruit)" and gradually building up to a bite, the Fantasizer will find himself or herself moving on to the whole orchard as his or her self-confidence improves.

THE FINGER OF SEDUCTION

I wasn't looking for anyone in particular as I was happily married, had my children, and most everything was provided for me. It was just another casual night out with the girls. We went to our usual neighborhood hangout where everyone knows everyone else.

We ordered drinks, talked about our husbands and how wonderful they are, our kids and plans for summer vacations. We also talked about sex and more sex. A few of us girls had been very naughty in our early 20's and 30's. A few of us continued being naughty after marriage. That night, none of us showed up with naughty thoughts.

After 40, being happily or unhappily married with children, some women want more than one man to satisfy their sexual needs. It was no different for my friends and me who were all in our mid-40's and looking hotter and wilder than ever. Around 10:00 p.m. that night, we were on our second and third round of drinks.

A group of four guys whom we knew from the neighborhood and community walked in for their boys' night out. They came over to our table and asked if they could join us since there wasn't any other table available. We had enough chairs to accommodate them. One guy in particular grabbed my attention. I had seen him before at our girls' volleyball games, but I never had a chance to speak with him at length during the games.

We hit it off that night. We talked about our girls, our spouses, and moved on to our careers. I seriously had no intention of being naughty that night. It was supposed to be a quiet fun girls' night out where we would plan our next naughty get away weekend.

I turned to my friend who was sitting right next to me and said, "Too bad this guy is a sweetheart. Otherwise, I'd be in his pants in a second." Of course, I was just joking. My friend, who had one too many, replied, "Why not? Maybe he'll turn out to be dick." That's all I needed to hear. It gave me a green light to go for it.

My claws came out, my horns popped out of my red hair, my eyes became sultry, my hair fluffed up, my breasts became perky and my voice deepened by at least one octave. I felt myself turning into a vampire. I transformed in a matter of seconds into a sultry, hot, seducer. The poor guy had no idea what hit him. I turned to him and whispered into his ear, "What if I said I wanted you?"

He was looking down as I was whispering into his ear. After I whispered, he did not move or breathe for a good 10 to 20 seconds. I wanted to make sure he was okay. I reached over to his chin, gently turning his face up toward me with my middle and index fingers. I said, "It's okay. I was just playing with you."

To my surprise, he said, "Don't stop." I had every intention of stopping. But, my claws were already out, my lips were wet and plump, and he was there ready for the taking. I couldn't resist. As I left the bar that evening, he texted: "Are you as excited as I am?" I replied, "I like your enthusiasm." He asked, "Will my enthusiasm get me to you?" I said, "Yes." This is where the trouble really began.

Sweethearts are usually well spoken, animated, and emotional. They are pleasers. I arranged for our first meeting to take place at a nearby hotel on an early afternoon. I was overly seductive and horny. He was quite receptive and a well put together package. I could have and should have stopped right after that day, but he was too good and too delicious. I was too selfish to stop.

Our encounters went on for a few weeks; we met two to three times a week. In one of our encounters, he mentioned that he could easily get used to our weekly meetings and he would like to have a weekend getaway with me. I had no intention or desire to have a relationship and I knew that was where he was headed. I told him that I would let him know and gradually lessened our encounters to once every two weeks. I was just waiting for his guilt and emotional upheavals to catch up to him so that he would want to stop himself. I tried to help him out by staying away as much as possible and coming up with excuses not to see him. I ultimately attempted to end the relationship by playing into his emotional need. I sent him an email and told him that it would be best for us to start all over as if nothing had ever happened and for him to look at this experience as a once in a life time adventure. He was grateful that I initiated the break. He was relieved, as he had been miserable in his inner turmoil, not knowing what to do with himself, his wife, his life, and me.

Our e-mail communications toward the end went as follows:

My dear Fantasizer,
Here is a note to let you know how much I have been enjoying our encounters together and what a wonderful man you are.

251

You possess qualities and attributes that raise your
charm to a higher level. Women desire you because of your
natural animal charm. However, at this time, because of
you, I would like to keep our relationship as strictly
friends without the benefits. This will be good for you
and I will feel much better knowing your mind is at
peace.
Your friend,
Forbidden Fruit

Email from the Fantasizer:

Dear Forbidden Fruit,
Thank you for the wonderful note. I could not have said
it better. You have read my mind and used the words that
I have been struggling with for the last two weeks. You
are a beautiful, intelligent, vivacious, and incredibly
horny woman. It has been a pleasure knowing you and being
with you. I will look back at this time with you with a
smile. It is best for us to remain friends.
Fantasizer

A few weeks went by and the Fantasizer couldn't get Forbidden Fruit
out of his mind. Forbidden Fruit was also fueling the fire by initiating in-
nocuous emails. Forbidden Fruit and the Fantasizer continued to meet despite the previous conversation. The Fantasizer put his guilt on the shelf
and sought out more pleasure from Forbidden Fruit. They met, had passionate, amazing toe-sucking sex in weekly intervals of two hours. Again,
the pattern continued. The Fantasizer's guilt crept back in and he sent the
following email:

Good Morning Forbidden Fruit,
A few weeks ago, you sent me a note describing why we
should only remain friends (without the benefits). You
were absolutely right and that is the way we need to go
from here. Deep down, I have never been fully comfortable
and I think you know that. I do consider myself to be a
good person and I don't want my actions to hurt anyone I
love. It is time to start thinking with my heart and not
my dick!! You are a beautiful woman who meets my every
desire. And I enjoy our friendship. I want to keep it
that way. I will look forward to seeing you at our social
gatherings.

This is the right decision for me and I hope you understand.
Fantasizer

In response Forbidden Fruit wrote:

Good morning to you,
You have taken a trip to fantasyland and now you are
ready to return rejuvenated to your life. Deep down, this
trip for you was overdue. As a good person, you deserved
it and you needed it. Now, you are thinking with your
other head. Our encounter was for you and always about
you. I was simply there to bring you joy and I enjoyed
it.
See you,
Forbidden Fruit

Two months passed and Forbidden Fruit sent an email to the Fantasizer because she wanted to reconnect with him. She sent an email saying, "How are things?" She received an automatic out of office reply. Another week went by and there was no answer.

She sent another email: "No answer from you. :("

He replied right away: "Hi. I've been incredibly busy with work. Sorry I couldn't get to you earlier. Maybe I can make it up to you some other way."

Forbidden Fruit's eyes brightened and she wrote: "I'm open to suggestions. What do you have in mind?"

The Fantasizer responded: "I have something big and hard that you might like! Fits well in your mouth and other places."

She was salivating as she read his email. He wrote, "Interested? If so, tell me when and where."

She replied within seconds, "Keep talking. I am intrigued. You are wetting my . . . appetite and maybe sometime next week we should get together. Our usual spot, usual time?"

He wrote, "See you then."

The next day, he responded, "My wife scheduled an appointment for me at our designated time; we'll have to reschedule."

Forbidden Fruit knew that it would be a couple more months because the Fantasizer's guilt would creep back in. But, she wanted to empower him to act upon his desires. She noticed that he was feeling better about himself and that he was more secure with himself. He had been working on himself physically, emotionally, and mentally.

Forbidden Fruit knew that her Fantasizer was coming over to the dark side. Her mission all along had been to bring him over. A few weeks later, she initiated contact with a text: "?" They no longer emailed. They would communicate by text from then on.

Fantasizer responded right away: "Hi. On vacation – on my way back home. This week is busy. Let's talk later."

Forbidden Fruit: "Look forward to it. Keep it hard."

Fantasizer: "Always for you!"

Forbidden Fruit: "☺"

Fantasizer: "What are you going to do with it?"

Forbidden Fruit: "Oh Babe. I'm going to suck it hard and then put it inside me to keep it warm."

A few days passed and Forbidden Fruit and Fantasizer ran into each other at the drug store. After their chance meeting, Fantasizer texted: "How did I look? Good enough to eat? I want your lips and tongue on me."

Forbidden Fruit: "You are HOT. You looked delicious. I wanted to rip your clothes off right there and lick you all over from your head to your toe and stay in the middle for a while. The girls are going to have a hard time keeping their hands off of you."

Fantasizer: "I am HARD. I need a quickie. How do we do it?"

Forbidden Fruit: "Do you need instructions or just ME?"

Fantasizer: "You on me!! A nice slam, bam, thank you ma'am!"

This was the first time he spoke to her like that. She knew he had crossed over to the dark side.

Forbidden Fruit grinned: "Where? When?"

Fantasizer: "Usual time; usual place."

They met for two hours and had incredible sex. Their pattern would continue to go on every two months or so. Forbidden Fruit would initiate;

she was calling the shots. Forbidden Fruit made it clear to him that she was seeing others as well. She encouraged him to expand his encounters beyond her. She knew that he was ready for others.

Finally, during one of their meetings, she did the unthinkable while sucking and licking his penis; she stuck her index finger into his rectum. He looked down at her surprised and let out an involuntary sigh. She moved her finger in such a way that he came immediately and intensely. He saw fireworks. He felt violated, but loved it at the same time. She owned him after that.

Only a few days after the finger encounter, he texted her as follows: "I am yours. I will be there whenever and wherever you desire. You own me now." She knew that she had broken him and that he was forever emotionally hers. The Forbidden Fruit knew that all she had to do was find the sexual hook and her lovers would be under her spell forever. She never initiated another contact after that.

THE IMPORTANCE OF A GOOD BOOK

Three weeks ago, I had a chance meeting with a woman on my morning ferry. She had a habit of reading the Bible during her morning commute on the ferry. For four mornings in a row, we sat next to each other. We talked and walked together to the subway station. I saw that she was wearing a wedding ring, but we had an incredible chemistry. Sometimes, I view a ring as an invitation to get to know someone. It is a challenge. One Friday, she suggested that we get together for lunch "sometime." I agreed, and said we'd do so when I returned from my vacation/business trip two weeks hence.

A few days into my trip, I couldn't get her out of my mind and I emailed her, suggesting that we put a date on the calendar. She agreed and seemed to be quite excited about going out with me. She sent me a number of cutesy emails while I finished my trip in Arizona. We both were looking forward to drinks and dinner the following Thursday.

After I returned home, we saw each other on the ferry a couple of days before our date – it was our first face-to-face interaction in two weeks. It was clear to me that something had changed. The excitement in her was gone and she was evasive when I asked her, "Are we still on for Thursday?" When we exited the ferry, she said, "I'll send you an email today once I look at my schedule." I was quite skeptical about our date at this point. Not surprisingly, I did not receive an email from her.

Done, over, time to move on, right? In my sad little life, nothing is quite so simple, however. On Wednesday evening, we happened to ride the same ferry together. When she saw me, she called out my name and motioned for me to sit next to her. After a half hour of talking and laughing together, her excitement reappeared and it was clear that the dinner was back on. We had great chemistry. We touched as we talked; she made my heart race.

Now comes the fun part. Here's our email exchange on Thursday, the day of our date. Note that her email was sent at 4:38 p.m., a half an hour before I was ready to leave work to go meet her.

She emailed on Thursday at 4:38 p.m.:
"Hi!
I'm sorry I haven't e-mailed sooner. Beyond busy!!!!! I will not be able to meet with you tonight. I am married. I enjoy talking with you on the ferry, etc., but I am uncomfortable with having dinner. I hope you understand and that we can still talk and laugh. Thanks for asking and encouraging!!!
With warm regards."

I responded with any angry email back to her:
"Well, you did mention "husband" during our initial conversation, so this does not come as a complete surprise. And, you were wearing a ring all along. I would, however, have appreciated a "heads up" a bit earlier in the process, especially in light of the rearranging of schedules that was necessary to make tonight's meeting possible."

She shot off another email immediately: "I do deeply apologize. I was reminding myself all day. Again, I am sorry.
With warm regards."

I sent another response:
"Subject: RE: Dinner
Not cool, not cool at all. Ironic to see you reading the Bible every morning . . ."

She replied:

"I make mistakes, but I am a good person and I am still saved! I still have my faith in Jesus Christ, my savior and Lord! I am still saved and loved by God!!! Praise the Lord for his tender mercies and unconditional love! Praise God that He is NOT a man.
With warm regards."

I realized that I had pushed her beyond her comfort level and that, had I played my cards right, giving her time to deal with her guilt, we would have enjoyed the chemical romance for some time. I could have kept her fantasy going. It was my mistake to push it. That was five years ago. I have never seen her again.

B. The Responsible Adult: Provides stability.

Contrary to the Perpetual Kids who become adults without growing up, the Responsible Adults grow up, never enjoying a childhood. They did not play; they never learned to play. They did not relate well with other children. As children, they liked to hang around adults, even when the adults tried to shoo them away. They always felt the need and pressure to be perfect in every way – the perfect student, the perfect son or daughter, the perfect friend, the perfect parent, the perfect mate or spouse. The Responsible Adult wants to be the best at everything – everything turns into a competition. It is a lot of pressure. This self-imposed expectation of perfection, however, may result in a more powerful suppression of wants, needs and desires than that caused by morality and guilt instilled from religion or society.

Responsible Adults welcome with open arms the responsibilities that come with adulthood and deal with the incumbent challenges without complaint. They run the books in the household and are afraid to let their mates touch the books. They are good with money, but won't become wealthy overnight. They are conservative with their money, avoiding "get rich quick" schemes and risky investments. They are control-freaks in almost all aspects of life. They do not like surprises. They would much rather receive a check or cash for a gift so they can buy what they want. They do not like to leave things up to chance and will do all the research necessary to feel that they know all possible outcomes of an event. They are worriers. They are rule followers. They are very private people. They are goal-oriented. They do not like germs. They are planners.

The Responsible Adults often have road maps of where they want to be in life from a very early age. They have planned when they will be married, when they will have children, how many children they will have, what color their eyes will be, etc. Obviously, they set themselves up for disappointment because all things cannot be controlled and planned. The Responsible Adult becomes insecure when he or she learns that life cannot be controlled and that random occurrence is part of life.

INTERVIEW OF A RESPONSIBLE WOMAN

1. *Contributor age:* 30's
2. *Gender:* Female
3. *Education Level:* Graduate Degree
4. *Are you financially secure?* Yes, working for a living.
5. *Profession:* Attorney
6. *Personal Status:* Divorced
7. *If married, how many times have you been married and for how long?* Once, for ten years.
8. *Interests/hobbies:* Reading, tennis, golf, shopping, good food and wine, and movies.
9. What initially attracts you to the opposite sex? Initially, I am attracted to a tall, fair-skinned man with a full head of blonde hair. His eyes must be alive and sparkly. After that, he must have a sense of humor and be both mentally and socially intelligent.
10. *What do you find appealing in a date?* I love a polite man who comes to my door with flowers and who has planned a romantic evening for us. There is nothing like a nice suit and tie on a man and a good smelling cologne. He should be fit, confident, honest, and thoughtful. I will not date a man whose parents have been divorced; I believe that a man needs to have both parents as role models to grow into a self-assured and normal man. A great smile melts my heart! Great conversation about things we have in common and an electric chemistry always helps to get things off to a great start.
11. *What do you find to be a turn-off in a date?* I cannot stand a dumb and dull man. Attractiveness is in the eye of the beholder; model gay good looks are not really a turn-on for me – more of a turn-off due to the attitude that normally accompanies such looks. An egotistical man is a

no-go. Someone with a huge ego cannot support another person and encourage them to reach their own potential. A tightwad is not going to happen either. I like to shop and expect to find someone who will not resent it when I buy a new outfit or a new pair of shoes. I only buy what I can afford and never rack up the credit cards, so my man should respect me enough to know that I am responsible with my money.

12. *Where do you meet people?* I meet them playing golf and tennis or through family and friends.

13. *When you are out with your friends and you see someone who catches your eye, what do you do?* I will look at him and give him a quick smile; maybe raise my glass at him. The rest is up to him. I do think you have to be careful out there and I would never initiate contact unless I was with at least one friend who had my back.

14. *Where do you hang out?* I hang out at home and at my friends' houses. I hang out at my club where I workout and play tennis; most of my socializing is at the club and at work.

15. *What are your thoughts about online dating?* I would be deeply concerned about engaging in online dating. I have friends who have done it and they have told me that there is a lot of false information out there. It seems easy to portray yourself as someone who you are not in order to get people to agree to meet you. I know people are really busy today and once you are out of school, it gets much harder to meet decent and intelligent guys. The co-pilot doesn't really work with online dating and I would be really nervous to meet someone that way. In fact, one of the sites suggests that you bring your "slum car" to the initial meeting so that you don't intimidate your date by the car you drive. That plays into the whole thing about not being who you are. I don't think it is possible to have a long-term relationship or get married to someone if it is started on a faulty foundation. If my Maserati intimidates you on the first date, then so be it!

16. *Have you ever had trouble moving on from a past relationship?* Yes, when I look back to my younger days, I had a difficult time moving on from relationships. I did not like to hurt someone else and when I knew I had to break it off, it was very difficult. I have rarely remained friends with the guys after breaking up with them. Sometimes, it was too painful at first. Other times, they were mad about it. I did not date a whole lot; I was pretty much a monogamous dater. That makes it much harder when it doesn't work out. When guys broke up with me, they were usually moving on to someone else, which is sometimes

hard to accept. I always felt better when I bought a new pair of shoes or when I became interested in another guy and started a new pursuit.

17. *What do you think of one-night stands?* I don't like one-night stands; it makes you look cheap and as if you have no self-respect. I actually have never participated in one. I don't jump right into bed; I have to feel that there is some long-term potential before I will go there. I think there are people with high libidos and people with low libidos. I have had horny friends who constantly participated in one-night stands and they enjoyed their youth very much. They, of course, were the ones who ended up with warts and other STD's because they were not as responsible with the protection as they should have been. I have always been a very cautious person and was afraid of getting pregnant. I had things I needed to do and I didn't want any unexpected surprises.

18. *What are your rituals for preparing for a date?* I always get a new outfit if it is a new guy. I take extra care with my make up and look forward to it with excitement. I listen to great, fun music as I get ready. I love U2.

19. *Type of lingerie you would wear on a first date?* I am not into lingerie at all. Clean underwear and bra is all.

20. *Where do you go/what do you do on a date?* Typical dates are dinner and a movie. I've had great dates in Fisherman's Wharf in San Francisco, Carmel, and at Disneyland. It is also fun to go to the Boardwalk in Santa Cruz.

21. *If you don't know your date well, do you meet at the designated place or does your date pick you up?* If I don't know my date well, I will meet him and I will insist that it is in a spot where my friends are. They watch out for me.

22. *Would you be interested in going for coffee and a walk instead of a dinner date for the first date?* I'd meet a guy at Starbucks or Peet's Coffee, but I would not be much into a walk. If we get along, I want a real date. Also, why would you go to walk in some isolated place with a perfect stranger? I guess we could go for coffee and a walk in the mall.

23. *If you were a candy, what kind would you be and why?* I would be a Hershey Bar because I love chocolate and the endorphins that go along with it! Additionally, it is a classic.

24. *How often do you have a girls' night out? Where do you go with your girlfriends?* I go out with the girls a couple times a month. It is hard to go out during the week when you are busy at work.

25. *What do you hope to happen when out with the girls?* I hope to have a good time with my friends.

26. *What frustrates you in the dating scene?* It frustrates me when people don't know themselves and it really frustrates me when they do know who they are and they pretend to be someone else. If everyone would just be themselves, it would be a lot less stressful and people could actually enjoy the process. It also frustrates me when girls are getting desperate and they start acting desperately. When you are confident in yourself and you are not looking, it will come to you. It also frustrates me when my friends settle for someone who is not right for them because they are afraid to be alone.

27. *What are you looking for in a relationship?* I am looking for a life-long companion who wants to share passion, adventure, family, and friends.

28. *Would you go out with a married man?* Absolutely not. I would not want someone to go out with my husband and I am a big believer in Karma. If you are willing to steal someone else's man, then someone will be out there licking her lips at your man.

29. *What about someone who is separated, but not divorced or has a girl-friend?* No, I want my man to be completely available and free. There is too much baggage with a separation; in fact, the guy may not know what he wants and go back to his wife. When I invest, I want the return to be pretty certain.

30. *Would you date someone who had a child from another relationship?* It depends on the circumstances. If it was a divorce, I would not. If the spouse had died, I might. The children rarely accept the stepparent and I am not looking for that kind of a battle. I am not certain that I even want my own children let alone someone else's. If you marry someone with kids, you have to accept them as your own. I don't know whether I would be able to do that.

31. *If you were to live with someone, how long would you be willing to live with him without a permanent commitment?* I would not live with someone until there was a permanent commitment. Even then, the span of time until the marriage could not be long. It is too easy to get comfortable and not move forward. Once combining households, it is very difficult to divide them if it doesn't work out. Inertia and convenience have a way of taking over.

32. *Do you mind if your date smokes?* Yes -- I don't like it when people smoke in front of me. I can't stand it when I go into a shop and I am

forced to hold my breath because people are smoking near the door. Try walking out of a Starbucks without getting a lungful of smoke. Even though the law says that people are supposed to smoke no closer than 25 feet to the door of a public establishment, the law is never enforced. It drives me crazy that people suck on their cancer-sticks and pollute my air.

33. *Are you hoping to find a man who is financially secure? Is financial security more important than love?* Love is certainly the most important thing when deciding with whom you are going to spend the rest of your life. I hope my man will have enough ambition and education that we can live a comfortable life without worrying about money. I would like to be able to stay home if I have kids, but if I can't stay home, we just won't have them. I would not bring kids into the world unless I felt that we were financially set.

34. *Would you consider financially supporting a man with whom you happen to fall in love?* That is not out of the question, but I would not fall in love with a man that wanted to sit home and eat Bon-Bons all day. I have always supported myself in my adult life and it would be hard to be totally dependent on another individual. I would probably want to keep some control of the financial portion of the relationship. I think it is very dangerous for a woman to give up total knowledge and control of the finances. It is also very important for a woman to have her own separate credit. If a husband leaves or dies, a woman can be financially stranded for a long period of time if she has no credit and does not know how the finances worked in the household or where the accounts are located.

35. *How does it make you feel if your date flaunts his assets?* I don't like people who show off in any way. Humble is nice. That is not to say that you should not toot your own horn when the occasion calls for it. For example, at work, you need to let the powers that be know that you are worthy.

36. *What type of clothing do you prefer your date to wear?* Whatever is appropriate for the occasion. California is pretty casual and jeans go almost anywhere; I don't like a t-shirt on a man. I like a collared golf shirt for casual over a t-shirt.

37. *What is your preferred body type and shape for a man?* I like an athletic and fit person, not a runner's body. I like cut and shapely arms, but not so big that they are stretching the seems of a shirt. Please no

wife-beater shirts or sleeveless work out shirts – gross! Let me feel the arms before I see them.

38. *How do you feel about tattoos and piercings?* I don't like them at all. Fifty and sixty year old men with flabby earlobes look ridiculous with earrings or holes in the lobes.

39. *How do you feel about perfumes and colognes?* A nice, subtle scent on a man is wonderful. Cologne is too strong; I prefer an after-shave. Body odor is an immediate turn-off as is flatulence.

40. *How important is the first kiss?* The first kiss is very important as it indicates tenderness and passion or lack thereof. I love to kiss and, yes, the tongue is an important part of it!

41. *Do you expect your date to pay on the first date?* Absolutely. This shows their manners. If they don't pay, they likely won't be opening the door for you or lending you their coat when it is cold outside. Chivalry is not dead; at least, I hope it isn't.

42. *What is your preference and philosophy on who should pay the bill on dates with you?* If we are both working, we can take turns; I would prefer the man to pay at all times.

43. *Will you have sex on the first date? If so, would you talk to your date about your preferences freely?* No. I need to get to know the person before having sex. I will kiss a lot on the first date, but that is about it. I will hold out for as long as practical. Once we are ready, I will talk about it freely.

44. *Would you have sex with your date if he were drunk?* Depends on how drunk he is and whether I am tipsy as well. He has to be able to put on the condom correctly!

45. *Do you prefer your date to wear boxers or briefs?* Boxers or boxer briefs. No regular briefs; they are for little boys.

46. *How do you make sure a new sexual partner is free of STD's?* I ask and try to get a detailed history. I insist upon a condom. I would have him use a condom until we were married.

47. *Once you have decided to have sex with your date for the first time, are you free and uninhibited in the act or more conservative and re-served than normal?* By then, I am so horny and turned on by the guy that I am an animal in bed.

48. *Where would you feel comfortable having sex with your date?* I would be okay having sex anywhere that we wouldn't get arrested.

49. *Where is your favorite place to have sex?* I love to have sex in water. The problem with it is the condom issue. I haven't figured that one out yet.

50. *Do you use protection and if so who provides it? If you don't use protection, how do you stay safe or is it an issue?* I insist on condoms. I keep a supply of them, but the guy usually provides them. Frankly, if a guy refuses to wear a condom because "it doesn't feel as good," then the guy doesn't care about you. My retort is always, "It feels better than nothing!"

51. *What do you do if protection is not immediately available?* I won't do it. We'll go to the store and get some, right then. We might have to do it in the car at that point.

52. *What if you liked your date and he did not call you the next day or week? What would you think and do?* I would be bummed, but figure that it wasn't meant to be.

53. *In your opinion, at what age does a woman know herself, her body, and her needs?* From what I hear, a woman's needs change over time. She knows herself by the time she is 30, but her body keeps changing with age. Women get very interested in sex by the time they are 40; it may be a physiological thing because their fertility is ending. It is a cruel irony that men peak so much earlier than women because a lot of men are not there to satisfy their women during the women's sexual peaks.

54. *What age range do you date?* Always four to eight years older. Men are less mature than women at all ages.

55. *How do you characterize yourself?*

    Positive attributes: Loyal and caring friend, honest, strong, intelligent, and practical.

    Negative attributes: Cautious, control-freak, skeptical, and don't like germs.

56. *Please include a detailed description of your ideal date.* My date would pick me up, arriving at my door with a beautiful bouquet of flowers. We would have a drink at my house and share a kiss. We would then go to Carmel and shop around, have a picnic on the beach while we sit on soft cashmere blankets, and enjoy a gorgeous sunset. My date would then take us to the Lodge at Pebble Beach where we would have a room overlooking the water. We would drink fine wine, have room service, and make mad passionate love all night long. He would propose to me in the morning.

57. *When you meet someone new, how long does it take you to know if the person is "the one" or has the potential to be "the one"?* I know right away if there is potential.

58. *Do you believe in "love at first sight"?* Yes. All I can say is that you just know. You will spend the rest of your courting process verifying or allowing your mate to figure it out for himself, but when you know, you know. It is not: "Maybe this is the one." It is: "I just met my husband!"

59. *What is your personal philosophy on monogamy and monogamous relationships?* I think monogamy is the only way. Trust is an important part of a long-term relationship. Once monogamy is gone, so is the trust and commitment.

60. *Do you believe there is a game people play when dating? If so, describe the game.* Yes, the game is be someone better than you are or be someone for whom you think the other person is looking. That will never work. Be yourself!

61. *Have you ever been on a date with a guy who turned out to be an ass?* Yes, I dated a guy who did turn out to be an ass. I went to a party with him and he ended up in a room doing coke with a friend's boyfriend. He had lots of problems. He almost killed us one time driving on a winding road after he had too much to drink. He lost control of the car, it was sliding toward the edge of the cliff, and somehow the adrenaline kicked in and the tires gripped the road. I am fanatical about not driving if I've had a drop of alcohol. He ended up cheating on me and knocking up the girl. Better her than me!

There was another time when I was on a date with a guy who started making out with another girl in the group. He came back to me later and wanted some from me. I told him to forget about it. He didn't understand why I was mad.

62. *What source of communication would you like to use after the first date?* I really would like a phone call; I enjoy talking on the phone and getting to know someone. I view texting and email as practical, but not personal.

63. *If interested in a further date, would you wait for him to call you or would you initiate further communication?* At the end of the date, I would let him know that I really enjoyed the date and that I looked forward to a call from him.

64. *If you were not interested in another date, would you let him know? If so, how would you let him know?* I would probably say that I had to

run in to use the restroom and thank him for the date. I would let him know if he called me again, but I would be hoping that he felt the same vibe and simply didn't call.

65. *Would you mind if your date contacted you immediately after your date?* I would love a quick text to tell me how much he enjoyed the date or, if I had met him at the place, to make sure that I got home safely. Other than that, call me the next day. Don't wait too long though. I hate waiting by the phone for a call. Two days is way too long. If they make you wait too long because they've read all those ridiculous rulebooks from sorry people, they may have control issues – they know you are waiting by the phone and they are enjoying it!

66. *How much attention is too much or too little after the first date?* Give me a call or send me a nice note. Don't expect me to go away with you for the weekend right away. Please don't show up at my place of work unless I have invited you.

67. *On average, how many dates are required before you consider yourself to be in a relationship? What qualifies as a date?* It depends on the first date. It could be as few as three or as many as two months' worth. It really requires communication and "the talk" to figure that one out.

68. *Do you consider yourself to be a game-player in the dating arena?* No, I try to be true to myself.

69. *Is spirituality important to you? If so, what if your date has different beliefs than you do?* Yes. I have a very strong faith in God. I do not believe in organized religion because I feel that when large groups of people get together behind a dogma, they can become dangerous and hypocritical. Religions of all kind have been abused throughout history and still continue to be. People need to be independent thinkers, but I do believe that there must be a higher being. I could not date someone who was a blind hook, line and sinker believer in any religion.

Below the belt questions:

1. *Is sex an important factor in deciding whether you will continue to date someone?* Sure. It would be good to be sexually pleased and satisfied for the rest of your relationship.

2. *Do you enjoy wearing lingerie?* Not really. If the guy likes it, I'll wear it for him once in a while, but I am not going to be a slave to Vic-

toria Secret. It would be pretty annoying if all of my gifts from my guy came from there because they would really be gifts for him.

3. *Have you ever experienced ménage à trois?* Yes, but it was very awkward. One of the guys was very jealous and they ended up getting into a big fight before we finished.

4. *What is sexy to you in a guy?* Masculine confidence with sensuality.

5. *Does the size of a penis matter?* A nubbin just won't do, but it is possible for a penis to be too large. If you are 6'8" and your penis goes with your body, you better be able to control yourself so you don't shove your penis through her abdomen.

6. *Do you prefer circumcised or not?* Definitely circumcised; there are cleanliness issues. I think it is also ugly if it is not.

7. *Do you prefer more or less hair on a man? If a man is too hairy, what should he do about it?* I prefer less hair on a man. If the back is too hairy, maybe he should get it waxed or lasered. I don't know; I think there is a link between testosterone and hair and if a man is a hairy ape, maybe he is awesome in the sack!

8. *Do you prefer tanned or natural skin?* In between. Naturally tan from sports or being active, not from being lazy by the pool.

9. *Will you kiss and tell your friends or do you keep it private?* I always tell my close friends. What are friends for if you can't share your experiences?

10. *Are the men whom you meet in a bar a potential long-term relationship or are they a one-night stand?* They are most likely losers. Meat markets are just that and a lot of the meat is old and smelly. In some cases, it has already turned bad and will make you sick the next day.

11. *When you go to a bar, do you hope to find someone?* A cute waiter with a drink.

12. *What do you think of athletic clubs as a place to meet someone?* I think it is not a good place to meet people. That is the time to focus on yourself and you should be free to do so without having people prowling around sniffing out their next lay.

13. *What do you think of coffee houses as a place to meet someone?* It is a varied clientele at the coffee houses; I can't see myself with a guy who has time to sit there and drink coffee all day.

14. *What do you think of the work environment as a place to meet someone?* It is not a good place if you want to stay with your job. If you are not married to your job, it can work out okay. It depends on the office policy on inter-office dating. Let's be real though. After you

get out of school, where do most people spend most of their time? At work. And where are you most likely going to find people with common interests? At work. This is really a tough one. It should be okay, but it just isn't.

15. *What is your opinion about surgically enhancing your body? How much enhancement is too much?* Whatever makes you feel good about yourself. You have to be careful not to get addicted to plastic surgery and body improvement. It can lead to, "Just one more thing and then I'll be perfect." Love yourself for who you are. By all means, remove the mole or wart, but leave the cheekbones and butt alone.

16. *Do you treat dates with long-term potential differently than fun quickies?* I don't like to go on set-ups because, while friends can mean well, it can be very awkward trying to explain to your friend that the guy was a poor-mannered slob who farted all evening. Maybe that is the test of whether your friend is a true friend.

17. *How many sexual partners have you had in your life?* 5.

AN IMPRUDENT MOMENT

I was 27 and engaged to be married within a year. I was working as an executive at a television station; I was in charge of programming. I wasn't a typical 27-year old; I had always been wise beyond my years and always too responsible for my own good. I was never a child. My parents expected perfection and when they didn't, I did. I was fanatically neat from the time I was a child and I have always tried to avoid germs. I have cringed about shaking hands with the public, especially after witnessing how many people do not wash their hands upon leaving the restroom.

Being who I was and knowing that I needed to let go a little bit in order to allow myself to have fun, I tried to date in high school. My relationships lasted a week at most and ended up in respectful great friendships. The boys all wanted me as a friend because I brought a different aspect of life to the typical irresponsible teen-agers. They related to me as they did not relate to adults; I provided the voice of reason when necessary. I became the sounding board for them. This was the story of my life. Did they not think that I needed some excitement of my own? I became reckless and crazy in my head, looking for a relationship. All I wanted was a casual, calculated, clean, fun, spur of the moment, quick fuck without all of the incumbent strings. It never happened. I did go out on dates and I always had a date for the prom or the upcoming dance. However, I was afraid I would graduate as a virgin because they all seemed to be afraid to touch me; they respected me too much. I, in fact, did graduate as a virgin.

The college years were a little bit different. As I became more forceful and demanded that my needs be met by my dates, I unleashed the beast inside of me on some poor frat boys. They didn't know what hit them. I was no longer going to allow my responsible side to rule my sexual side. I had a lot of fun in college. There were a few scares here and there, but not enough to put a damper on my new found freedom.

I graduated with high honors and found a job easily. I took a job at the television station where I met an older executive with whom I fell in love. I was always attracted to the older and wiser guys. We set the date for our wedding and we were off to see the wizard.

Low and behold, while on a work trip in the Bahamas, I worked on a shoot with a famous actor from Los Angeles, California. He was hot, hot, hot. We hit it off immediately. There were sparks and fire all over. My heart was pounding out of my chest; my juices were flowing. My palms were sweating and I was salivating to the point where I would choke on drool when I talked to the guy.

After the first shoot, we were all exhausted and tired. Somehow his hut was flooded and he needed a place to get cleaned up for dinner. I told him he could use my hut. He gathered his stuff and brought it over to my hut. I invited him in and asked if he wanted me to leave so he could get ready in private. He undressed and got into the shower right in front of me. I grinned as he stepped into the shower with a come-hither look. Before I thought about what I was doing, I was naked and stepping into the shower with him.

Something was smacking me in the back of the head, "What are you doing, what are you doing? You are about to marry the man of your dreams. Don't blow it!" This bat was interfering with my moment. He reached over and grabbed my neck and gently pulled me toward him. He began kissing me and I could feel his hard erect penis rubbing on me. The water from the rain head was soothing and heavenly. I melted into his arms and thought no more. Our bodies took over and we had a passionate encounter in the shower.

Hours later, I realized what I had done. I was no longer in college and it was not an experimental time. I felt a huge responsibility and guilt for what I had just done. I had cheated on the love of my life and I could not believe that I had not controlled myself. He could see the guilt in my face and the stress that was enveloping my whole body. He wanted to reassure me that things like this happen all the time. He told me this wasn't a one-time deal for him and that he wanted a relationship with me. That made it even worse; I wasn't in a position to give him what he wanted. Now I was disappointing three people in my life, my fiancé, myself, and the actor.

I could no longer fight my inner core and the responsibility that I had felt my entire life. I told him that this was a mistake and it should have never happened. I apologized for my selfish actions and he was offended that I was apologizing for having sex with him. He grabbed his stuff and said, "I feel sad for you; you will never allow yourself to enjoy the finer things in life." I knew exactly what he was talking about and this is something that I have struggled with throughout my life. I have always been committed and responsible; I have never been free to just be. I have always chosen security over frivolity.

The workweek ended and I flew home to the States. I resumed my life as it was and tried not to think about the encounter. Although, I will never forget it, I will never let it happen again. I married my fiancé and we are happy. However, I cannot seem to get the memory of the forbidden encounter out of my head. I have avoided tropical work trips to this day. I want to trust myself again.

BEWARE: If the Responsible Adult slips, he or she will live with regret and remorse. The foundation of his or her being will be shaken, resulting in one of two possible outcomes. He or she may realize that "Perfection is attained by slow degrees; it requires the hand of time."[8] In this case, the Responsible Adult will suppress his or her fantasies for responsibility, loyalty and love and he or she will spend the rest of his or her life trying to be a perfect mate or spouse. Or, the Responsible Adult may discover that perfection is beyond attainment and he or she may fall into a spiral of risky and careless behavior. In this case, the Responsible Adult becomes a Fantasizer who ultimately gives into temptation and lets go of his or her self-imposed expectations and inhibitions. Now a Fantasizer, the internal fight will be with guilt and morality imposed from the outside.

---

[8] http://www.brainyquote.com/quotes/v/voltaire_133391.html

C. The Nurturer: Provides compassion.

Genuinely nice, the Nurturers define themselves by taking care of others. They are generous and selfless. They are the caregivers in any relationship. They are good with children; they are family-oriented people. They often usurp all of the nurturing roles in a relationship, but then find themselves overwhelmed and overextended. They enjoy making others happy; they enjoy helping others to feel good about themselves. Cooking often enables the Nurturer to share his or her love through food, earning this character immediate gratification and praise. The Nurturer is the parent who sits with a sick child. The Nurturer puts his or her own desires behind that of his or her mate. The Nurturer will not have it any other way. They do, however, want and need to be appreciated. They need to be needed.

WARNING: Do not take advantage of the Nurturer, as he or she will give until he or she can give no more. If they do not feel appreciated, the joy of giving will evaporate over time and they will become resentful.

THE GOOD SON

I grew up in a very large family. I was the youngest child out of five. My mother always told me that she had me so that I would take care of her when she was old and infirm. In fact, she very much dissuaded me from dating when I was young.

I recall an instance where there was a very mean girl in junior high school who made me crawl into my shell. We were at a seventh grade dance. I gathered up the courage to walk across the great divide in the middle of the gym to ask her to dance with me. I approached her smiling and asked if she would dance with me at the next dance. She looked around, turning her head left and then right. Then, she looked right into my eyes and said that she didn't care to dance with me. I walked away with my tail between my legs, only to see her dancing with several other fellows later that night. I came home and told my mother my sad tale. She told me that women are mean and scornful and that it would only get worse as I got older. She told me that she was glad that I had discovered the truth about women at the young age of twelve.

I spent the rest of my youth making very good friends with my female classmates. I would always be there to hear their stories of triumph and defeat in the dating world. I would be there to offer a shoulder to cry on. I loved one girl, but I could never work up the nerve to ask her out. I had always wished that she would give me the green light or some signal, but she never did and I was afraid to risk the rejection and the friendship.

I went to college and didn't date much there, either. When I graduated, my mother became sick. I went home to be with her and to take care of her. She was ill for three years. While my other siblings were living their lives and having families of their own, I was stuck at home with my mother, nursing her until her death. I did what I needed to do. I did what I knew how to do. Thirty years later, I am feeling a bit resentful.

After my mother died, I went back to school and earned a graduate degree in engineering and business management. I found a fabulous job that allowed me to travel the world. When I came back to the United States, I really thought it was time to settle down and have a family of my own. I met a woman. We dated and ultimately moved in together. I like things neat and would do most of the housework. One day, she came unglued because I had folded her laundry incorrectly. She was screaming at me. I put up my hand and told her that she was welcome to do her own laundry; if not, she could show me how she liked it to be done and I would try to do it as she liked. At that point, I knew that we were not meant to be together forever.

A year later, we moved out and she quickly found another man who asked her to marry him. We remained friends. In the mean time, she became blind and could no longer drive. Her fiancé worked all over the country and was gone a lot. She called on me to take her shopping and drive her places. We became the best shopping friends. Her fiancé does not seem to mind that I take her where she wants or needs to go. I take her to the doctor. I take her grocery shopping. I take her to the mall to buy clothing. I spend so much time taking care of her that I have very little time to spend dating other women. The few women that I have dated over the last couple of years have not appreciated my friendship with my ex-live-in girlfriend. I just can't leave her though; she needs me.

INTERVIEW WITH A NURTURER WHO WOULD LIKE TO BE NURTURED

1. *Contributor age:* 50's
2. *Gender:* Male
3. *Education Level:* College
4. *Profession:* Retired IT
5. *Personal Status:* Single
   > *If single, are you looking for a long-term relationship or a meaningful one-night stand?* Long-term.
6. *Interests/hobbies:* International travel, movies (action, comedy, romance), beach, restaurants, going out to eat, shopping, clothes, museums, watching team sports like basketball, baseball and such, concerts (Eagles), gym and working out, snow skiing.
7. *What initially attracts you to the opposite sex?* Her appearance, smile and conversation. Positive welcoming feedback. Good chemistry would encourage me to continue. I see myself as shy and I am reluctant to approach women because I might get rejected.
8. *What do you find appealing in a date?* Behavioral things. Friendly, conversational and not closed down. Measure of reciprocity; not seeing me as the entertainer and waiting for me to make her laugh. Sense of humor. Open to sharing stories about her and myself.
9. *What do you find to be a turn-off in a date?* Inquisition questioning. Wanting to dig into me as to why I have never been married. Some girls think that means there is something wrong with me.
10. *Where do you meet people?* Gym, coffee shop, fun European style outside dining spots. Bars are not my thing. In the bars, people are not themselves. Or they are and I don't want them. I tried the speed-dating thing. Nothing happened.
11. *When you are out with your friends and you see someone who catches your eye, what do you do?* Usually stare till she is terrified that I am going to attack her. I usually don't go beyond looking. I fumble. I feel more comfortable going out with friends; they give you more confidence. Usually one of the guys makes a comment regarding the woman as to how hot she is. None of us makes a move.
12. *What are your thoughts about online dating?* I have not tried it yet. I have set-up my profile and only contacted one person. I feel uncomfortable and odd about it. People in their 50's tell me to try it just to meet people. I think the online dating thing is not natural.

13. *Have you ever had trouble moving on from a past relationship?* Yes.
    It took me a couple of months. I had the feeling of betrayal; I was an-
    gry. I thought she misjudged me and I would have gone back to her. It
    was when I was living in Paris. I was dating a woman, everything was
    going great and she just cut me off without any notice. I saw her do
    this to other people in her life, even girlfriends. When they were of no
    more use to her, she cut them out of her life, leaving them befuddled.
    She discarded me like the others. She initially came across as an out-
    going, delightful person. She was the life of the party. She was very
    happy when I would spend money on her, buying her expensive
    scarves. At the end, I was happy to get rid of her. I met someone else
    fairly quickly and moved on.
14. *What are your rituals for preparing for your date?* Shower, shave,
    and iron clothes.
15. *Where do you go/what do you do on a date?* Out to dinner and drinks.
    I pretty much stay local.
16. *If you don't know your date well, do you meet at the designated place
    or do you pick up your date?* Meet at the designated place.
17. *Would you be interested in going for coffee and a walk instead of a
    dinner date for the first date?* Yes.
18. *Do you treat dates differently when set up by a friend or relative?*
    Probably. I would not want to make a bad impression.
19. *How often do you have a boys' night out? Where do you go with your
    friends?* Once a week. Same boys, two to four of us on any one eve-
    ning. We go to bars.
20. *What do you hope to happen when out with the guys?* To meet some-
    one interesting.
21. *What frustrates you in the dating scene?* My own level of social
    skills. I have made a few attempts to get out of my shell. I took acting
    classes. I played roles from the county sheriff to a wild man in a res-
    taurant. I liked the psychopath role. I have tried to be a much more
    spontaneous conversationalist, learning to move the conversation
    along. I have learned to go with the flow as well. It is always good to
    be clever, witty, and funny.
22. *What are you looking for in a relationship?* I like a girl that is awe-
    some, gorgeous, fun, positive, happy, and delightful to be around. It
    would be good if she had some college education, and was smart,
    spontaneous, and a planner. I would love to have a genuine partner.
    Someone who is not high-maintenance. I give back – I would like loy-

alty, commitment, a woman who is thoughtful and supportive, who does things that need to be done, and who comes up with suggestions and ideas; I could use support.

23. *Would you go out with a married woman?* I try to stay away from that.

24. *What about someone who is separated, but not divorced or has a boyfriend?* I started to do that once and I was uncomfortable with it.

25. *Would you date someone who had a child from another relationship?* Yes.

26. *If you were to live with someone, how long would you be willing to live with her without a permanent commitment?* A long time.

27. *Are you hoping to find a woman who is financially secure?* It doesn't bother me one way or the other.

28. *Would you consider financially supporting a woman with whom you happen to fall in love?* I wouldn't mind.

29. *How does it make you feel if your date flaunts her assets?* It is a red flag. She is looking for someone to provide things for her.

30. *What type of clothing do you prefer your date to wear?* Modest.

31. *What is your preferred body type and shape for a woman?* Fit.

32. *How do you feel about tattoos and piercings?* Not too crazy about them.

33. *How do you feel about perfumes and colognes?* Perfumes can be nice, but not the flowery kind. Body odor kills!

34. *How important is the first kiss?* Can be negative if they don't kiss passionately. I went out with a bad kisser and I stopped seeing her. It indicates how passionate they are. A great first kiss should just be there.

35. *Will you have sex on the first date?* Very unlikely. Being afraid of STD's, it would suggest that the person who wants sex right away is not afraid of STD's. It could happen on a second date.

36. *Would you have sex with your date if she were drunk?* No. I feel it would be meaningless.

37. *Lights on, off or dimmed?* Dimmed because you want to appreciate her beauty.

38. *Do you wear boxers or briefs?* Boxer briefs.

39. *How do you make sure a new sexual partner is free of STD's?* I always use protection. Talk about it. I start talking about her history first. I am very nervous talking about it. You don't know if they are

telling you the truth or not. Use protection to be safe no matter what they say.

40. *Once you have decided to have sex with your date for the first time, are you free and uninhibited in the act or more conservative and reserved than normal?* Conservative and inhibited.

41. *Where would you feel comfortable having sex with your date?* Home, car.

42. *Where is your favorite place to have sex?* In bed.

43. *What do you do if protection is not immediately available?* I did it once, but might not want to do it again. I was very nervous afterward. She assured me that she was on the pill and that she could not get pregnant. There is more to worry about than pregnancy these days.

44. *What if you liked your date and she did not return your call the next day or week?* I would call her again within two weeks.

45. *What age range do you date?* Late 30's to 55ish.

46. *What do you think of one-night stands?* I don't do them myself and I think they are risky and shallow. They are disrespectful of the other person. Younger people frequently engage in them. They are people who don't know what they want and can't figure it out. People who are not interested in a long-term relationship participate in them.

47. *How do you break off a one-night stand or short relationship without being hurtful?* I don't break them off. I withdraw.

48. *How do you characterize yourself?*
>   **Positive attributes:** Nice, polite, try to behave like a gentleman, intelligent, smart, academic, stable, good provider, nurturer.
>   **Negative attributes:** Momma's boy, goody two shoes, and rule follower.

49. *Please include a detailed description of your ideal date.* Pick her up and take her to her favorite restaurant, happy and talkative, nice music, service would be attentive, long conversation type dinner, go some place for more talking, I would ask what she would like to do: go back to her place or mine?

50. *When you meet someone new, how long does it take you to know if the person is "the one" or has the potential to be "the one"?* I know by the second date.

51. *Do you believe in "love at first sight"?* I would like to, but it seems to be only comprised of infatuations. It results in disappointments.

52. *What is your personal philosophy on monogamy and monogamous relationships?* Yes. I am in favor of it.

53. *Do you believe there is a game people play when dating? If so, describe the game.* Yes. Women are looking for a provider and a protector. Guys flaunt their dates. I am not experienced in much dating, so I am not that aware of the game. The women I see turn out to be different from who I thought they were initially.

54. *Is the dating game a mystery or are the rules clear?* It is a mystery.

55. *Do you believe emotions interfere with the dating process?* They can produce an incorrect judgment. Too many assumptions.

56. *On average, how many dates are required before you consider yourself to be in a relationship? What qualifies as a date?* Third date. A date is spending more than one hour with a woman.

57. *If interested in your date, how long do you wait to communicate with her?* Right at the end of the date.

58. *Would you mind if your date contacted you immediately after the date?* No.

59. *Is spirituality important to you? If so, how important is it that your date shares your belief system?* Only some things are okay.

60. *What books on dating have you read? Out of those books, which ones do you recommend?*
      Women are from Venus and Men are from Mars
      Neil Clark, Finding the Love of Your life on E-harmony
      Finding your Strengths 2.0
      Options as a Strategic Investment

Below the belt questions:

1. *Is sex an important factor in deciding whether you will continue to date someone?* Yes.

2. *Do you enjoy it when your date wears lingerie?* At home, yes. It's great; I enjoy it.

3. *Have you ever experienced ménage à trois? If not, would you consider it?* No/yes.

4. *What is sexy to you in a woman?* The way she smiles, looks at you, walks, dresses, sound of her voice, and the way she talks about things. Women are sexy.

5. *Does the size of her breasts matter?* To some degree yes. B cup or larger.

6. *Do you mind surgical enhancement of breasts, lips, teeth, etc? How much body enhancement is too much?* No. When it is too noticeable it is not okay.

7. *How much make up is too much?* You know it when you see it.

8. *Are skimpy, body-fitting outfits a turn-on or a turn-off?* Turn-on, but it depends on what's underneath.

9. *Are the women whom you meet in a bar a potential long-term relationship or are they a one-night stand?* I hope for long-term, but the bar is probably not the place to find it.

10. *What do you think of athletic clubs as a place to meet someone?* This is my primary place to pick up on women.

11. *What type of a person do you look for in a club?* Someone who is attractive, takes care of herself, and seems to like herself. I don't like a woman who is closed off and is only into herself and her workout.

12. *What do you think of coffee houses as a place to meet someone?* I like them.

13. *What do you think of the work environment as a place to meet someone?* Less and less.

14. *Do you prefer a particular pubic hair design?* I don't care; by the time I get down there, I am thrilled no matter what the styling!

15. *How many sexual partners have you had in your life?* I don't know.

D. The Intellectual: Gives loyalty.

The Intellectual is confident, but tends to be rigid and pessimistic. He or she is overly cautious, a doubter, and a naysayer. The Intellectuals are overly analytical criticizers who analyze everything and everyone. While generally nice and well-meaning people, they are not socially politic; they don't understand the difference between honesty, diplomacy, and courtesy. They are non-communicative. They believe what they say is the last word on any subject and they do not like to be challenged. They look down on others who are not on the same intellectual level. They have no sense of humor about themselves. They are controlling. They are know-it-alls.

Intellectuals are not big spenders, socializers, or chit-chatters. They are usually introverts. They are frugal savers, except when it comes to themselves – they feel entitled to splurge once in a while given the burden of responsibility that they have imposed upon themselves. However, they highly resent the splurges of their mates. Unlike Responsible Adults who welcome responsibility with open arms, Intellectuals resent it. They cannot delegate. Every activity becomes a chore and every chore becomes stressful. They become overwhelmed and lash out at their loved ones because the burden they have taken upon themselves is too great.

The Intellectual is typically good at everything he or she puts his or her mind to. They prefer to learn from instructions and manuals rather than from lessons. A little bit of information turns this character into an expert on any subject matter. Intellectuals cannot take criticism; they are perfectionists. They can be highly judgmental at home because they see themselves as perfect in whatever they do. Unlike the Responsible Adult who strives for inner perfection, the Intellectual is confident in his or her perfection and expects perfection of others. Where the Responsible Adults are hard on themselves, the Intellectuals are hard on those around them. It is very hard to meet their expectations. The Intellectuals will not hire someone to do work that they can do themselves because they are sure the work will not be done to their specifications – in fact, the work probably won't be done "properly" because the bar is set so high.

They are consumed by education, self-betterment, and a social conscience. They are not materially driven; however, they do want to keep their mates materially happy. They possess an extremely high self-esteem and consider themselves worthy of the most beautiful and select of mates. They often find beautiful, vivacious, and equally intelligent mates for life, leaving those outside wondering how they were able to capture the hearts of the unlikely pairing.

They are focused, genuinely nice, unpretentious, responsible, and highly dependable – the perfect mate from the outside looking in. The Intellectual is not a sexual being, but is loyal and monogamous. He or she is looking for a best friend and life-long partner. This character has qualities that make him or her a fabulous spouse: they are responsible, caring, nurturing, and good parents. At the same time, this character has qualities that make him or her a bear to live with over the long-haul: they are not exciting; they are critical and controlling; they expect perfection from those around them; and they have zero tolerance for mistakes. However, it is very hard to leave this character because he or she is a responsible, trustworthy, good person who will always offer stable support to his or her mate in the end.

Intellectuals secretly yearn to be free and to go with the flow, but they are afraid of the consequences of doing so. They don't know how to let go and have fun. They are uptight and out-of-sight. In order to let go, they need an extraverted mate who will take the fault if things don't work out.

This is why the Intellectual may find a perfect partner in a free-spirited Perpetual Kid. Intellectuals do not do well with others who like control. For example, a Diva may spice up the Intellectual's life, but she will refuse to live under his thumb. Similarly, a Responsible Adult would not be a good fit for this character, given that both like to take control. Whoever the mate is, he or she must be able to live under the Intellectual's thumb.

This type usually marries someone younger. They enjoy sharing their knowledge with their younger mate and they enjoy the control that comes with an advantage of age over their partner. They are often engineers, attorneys and doctors. The older they get, the more introspective and introverted they become. As they age, they become less willing to put effort into social companionship.

BEWARE: The Intellectual has few friends outside of his or her marriage; his or her spouse may be his or her only friend. This tendency can lead to a very lonely existence and puts a lot of pressure on the other spouse who might need an outside social network. The Intellectual grows to resent such outside diversions. While the Intellectual does not accept criticism well, when their controlling behavior becomes unbearable, careful and well-timed communication that points out the character's lack of perfection and shortcomings in their spousal role may shock them and threaten the foundation of the relationship, resulting in a positive change in behavior. Fear of losing his or her mate who is the Intellectual's everything is one way to motivate the Intellectual into loosening the leash.

THE PONTIFICATOR

I am in my early fifties. I am Swiss with a little Italian. I like to say that I got the best of both genetic dispositions. I am punctual, precise, and a fine working machine, but at the same time, I think I am a fun guy. I am an engineer with a degree from one of the finest universities in the world. I have been with many companies from the start up stage. My mother raised me with European sensibilities; my father died when I was eleven. I enjoy fine wine; I have studied wine over the last decade. I wear colors that bring the color out in my face; I look especially good in salmon. I am secure in my masculinity; salmon is one of my best colors and I wear it frequently.

1. *How many times have you been married?* I have been married once
    and engaged twice. I have one daughter by my first wife. We were
    married for three years. When my daughter was one, my wife went
    back to work. She worked the swing shift at a manufacturing job so
    that we could handle the childcare arrangements. She worked from
    3:00 p.m. to midnight. She started coming home at 4:00 in the morn-
    ing. I told her that the bars closed at 2 a.m. She didn't have a good
    explanation for her whereabouts. I asked her when she was moving
    out. She said, "Next week." We shared custody of our daughter and
    she was a wonderful mother. I have a wonderful daughter.
2. *How do you find the dating market to be for men over 45?* Men marry
    the most attractive women their money can buy. Women marry the
    richest men their looks can attract. Men over the age of 45 must either
    have a Ferrari or a Ferrari house to attract women.

    It all goes back to the dawn of time. A woman is programmed to
    be with a man who can provide the basic needs for her. She wants and
    needs a provider. Men need and want a woman who can produce
    strong offspring. It is genetically programmed. Men are designed to
    pollinate multiple flowers. Women are designed to be with one man.
3. *How have you formed your ideas and opinions on dating and male and
    female relationships?* I read a lot, but nothing on dating and relation-
    ships. I used to read books, the thicker the better. But now, I hate to
    say it, but I mostly read magazines like *Fortune, Forbes, Tennis,* and
    Men's Health. I don't read as many books as I used to read. Many of
    my theories came from my mother. For instance, she always told me
    that women marry the man with whom they fall in love; men marry the
    woman that they are with when it is the right time to marry.
4. *How do people see you?* I am practical to a fault. I think I am. I come
    from a background of Swiss descent where people are described as
    bankers, rigid, and cold cactus personalities (prickly). We are thought
    of as thorny and hard outside and soft and mushy inside. Fortunately
    for me, I am half Italian. I have the passion of the Italian and the disci-
    pline of the German. My Swiss handicap in relationships is that I have
    trouble expressing myself.

    I used to play a lot of tennis. I never knew how people viewed me
    till one day a girl at the tennis club, who I ultimately ended up dating,
    told me that I was viewed as a snob. She said, everyone thought I was
    arrogant because I walked into the club, did my business and left. I
    didn't stay and socialize. I didn't play with people of a lower skill set.

Tennis is a very egotistical sport; it is not a team sport. I had little time and I would much rather use my available tennis hours to play with the experts than to socialize around with novices.

Some of my friends have complained that I am a cheap skate. I don't want to be the first one to grab the bill; that sets precedent. I like to save my good wine for worthy occasions; I don't like to waste expensive wine on people who won't appreciate it. It is always a fine line between being tight and not allowing yourself to be taken advantage of.

Some women complain that I am a chauvinist. I am the furthest thing from it. I have a daughter and I want good things for her. However, I don't believe in fighting nature. We are animals with set genetic patterns.

5. *How do you see yourself?* I consider myself to be of European etiquette and cultural upbringing. My pet peeve is when you are toasting with wine and people don't look you in the eye. In Europe, they always look you in the eye. Most Americans look at the glasses instead.

6. *Do you believe in love at first sight?* No, I believe that you can know right away if a person fits what you are looking for and your predetermined criteria. My parents were 20 years apart in age. My mother had traveled extensively in Europe; she was from Europe. In her mid 20's she was working as an accountant in a hotel in Switzerland. My father was traveling and he worked in the radio station. He lived in Hollywood at that time. My mother tells me that the moment she saw my father in the hotel where she was working, she said to herself, "That is the guy I am going to marry." She said, "He is going to take me to Hollywood."

7. *How long does it take you to know whether someone is good for a long-term relationship?* You'll always know when the person is not the right person for you, but you don't know if it is the right person. It takes me six months to get to know someone. There must first be infatuation. But many young people confuse infatuation and love. Attraction is not love.

Love has many definitions. Love is very easy, love is when you care about someone else's being as much as your own. If you feel that way, then you are in love. And if you enjoy being with them and making their life better, then you are in love with the person.

I have only been in love two and a half times. In my thirties I fell in love. The timing was not right and I let her go. I look back and wonder what could have been with that one. I have learned that love is more important than timing, but trust is more important than love.

Two points I have to make. I fall in love slowly and fall out of love very slowly. Love is when you care about someone as much as you care for yourself. Infatuation is the newness and it is when everyone is on their best behavior, they are always clean, shaved, showered and looking their best. Everyone falls in love for different reasons. With my fiancée, I kept telling myself, "It will happen." I was trying to look for all the good qualities. On the eve of the wedding, it hadn't happened and I had to pull out.

8. *What are you looking for in a woman?* The number one quality in a woman is her independence, both financially and emotionally. I do not want a woman who is hovering or smothering. I am not a settler. I don't think anyone should settle. Women settle because they want children and security. Men settle for sex. Men have trouble in life when they continuously chase women for sex. Men like to think they can fix any woman who is not good in bed. That is not true. If a woman is not good in bed, she will never be a good fit. All women in the world think they are good in bed. What women don't realize is that a man always climaxes, it has nothing to do with the skills of a woman. A man always gets the nut. However, a woman believes that, if she has made a guy climax, she has done something amazing.

The last woman that I dated for a lengthy period was thirteen years younger than I. We both wanted kids. She was confident and she was making it in the man's world. She made big money and spent big money. She could go toe to toe with the guys in business and hold her own. I liked that. I want a woman who can hang with the guys. I want a woman who can just hang with me. A woman needs to be hang-worthy. If I don't want to be with the girl all day and if I don't want to just sit on the couch and watch television with her, it will never work.

All men want women who are a sex kitten by night and a mother by day. I want a woman with whom I am proud to be and a woman who makes other men jealous. I want someone whom I can respect, who is somewhat my equal, physically compatible, and modest. These are the criterion that I think about when I meet a woman.

9. *Are there any rules amongst the guy friends in dating?* One rule I live by is "Dicks over Chicks" or "Buds over Babes." That means that you don't go out with a girl that your friend is clearly interested in. Well, I

usually live by that rule. I ended up engaged to a girl that my friend was hot after. I had not seen him in years and I ran into him at a party. He introduced me to this athletic, hot, blonde woman. He needed an excuse to get together with her again and convinced me to go on a double date with him and one of her friends who had also been at the party. I reluctantly agreed to help him out even though I wasn't interested in the other girl. We played volleyball. He was strutting around without his shirt. For some reason, my machismo came out and I had to show her my fit and trim body as well. So, I took off my shirt. I saw her watching me as I walked over to serve the ball. My friend and I went to clean up in the locker room and my buddy was just drooling over the girl. He convinced me to continue the date and we went out for drinks. I was pretty cool to the other woman; she was probably pissed at me. I just wasn't into her at all. While at dinner, I heard my guy friend telling the girl, "Let's go to New York; let's do this; let's do that." He was pulling out all the stops to impress her.

A day later, I got an email from the girl. I called my buddy to see why he gave her my number. He told me that she wanted it for business purposes; she was in sales in my industry. I called her and she said, "I heard you mountain bike and I want to know more about your company. Let's do lunch on Wednesday." On Wednesday, I received an email from her that said, "I can't make lunch Wed., let's do Friday at my house."

It took me over an hour and a half in traffic to get to her house on Friday. When I arrived, she greeted me warmly and said, "I have an open bottle of wine." I needed a drink after that drive and I drank most of the bottle. Then, we went out. Around midnight, we got back to her house and I knew that I had a tennis game the next morning with my buddy. I never do more than a little petting on the first date. I was standing at the front door debating with myself whether I should kiss her. I kissed her cheek. She asked if I wanted more drinks, but I was worried about my tennis game. She was leaning in, giving me clear signals. I thought, "Maybe, why not a little light petting?" From that point on, she took over and provided the protection. We did it four times. By the end, I was dying; I was hung over; and I knew that, in a few short hours, I had to play tennis with the guy who wanted her. I was a mess. I was a physical wreck.

The next morning, I played tennis with my buddy. When we were showering after our game, he noticed that I had scratches all over my ass and on my back. He asked what happened to me. I told him that I had wild sex the day before. He high-fived me. The girl turned out to be hyper-interested in me. She wanted to show that she wasn't a bad girl because she had slept with me on the first date. For the next two months, we dated and she held back sex. A few weeks into our relationship, I ran into my buddy. I told him that I was going out with the girl. He said, "I had a feeling." So, as long as the woman leaves the buddy and moves in on the friend, it is socially acceptable to break the unwritten rule about "Dicks over Chicks."

We got together and she was on a mission to marry me and have kids. We dated for two years and then it was time to take the next step. I was telling myself to compromise even though I wasn't in love with her. I thought maybe it would happen if I gave it more time. She asked me to buy a house with her. I gave her a challenge that I thought she couldn't meet; I told her to find a three million dollar house that was on the market for two million. She ultimately did and she sold her house for her share of the down payment. We bought the house and moved in together. Her mother came for a long visit and helped her doll up the house.

Immediately after moving in, she changed. Her whole life revolved around the house. Everything was about the house. I thought she didn't care about me any more; it was all about her and the house. I had leveraged myself to buy this house; I was feeling pressure immediately. I was not in love with her. We lived together for two years with increasing tension. She ended up being a flake. I thought maybe I was being too critical, but she really was a flake. She wouldn't follow through with what she promised; she was always late. She forgot to bring things home. She would forget to do something and then blame me because I didn't remind her. Most women never say it is their fault; they will never say, "I am sorry." At the beginning of the relationship, I had only met her representative; her true self did not appear until we moved in together. Her representative had the best qualities.

She gave me an ultimatum and said it was time to get a ring for her and move on to the next step. My mother always told me that women marry the man with whom they fall in love, but men marry the women they are dating when they think it is time to get married. I was thinking it must be time to get married. It would be good to have another child. I enjoyed having my first daughter. I kept telling myself to settle and be more realistic. I finally broke down and bought her a

285

ring. We made plans for the wedding. We were trying to work it out and, right before the wedding that was going to be in the back yard at the house, I got cold feet. I called it off and sent out an email to friends and family saying that we couldn't get our plans together and we were delaying the date.

While we were living together after the break up and trying to figure out what to do with the house, she traveled to San Francisco and drank like a drunken slob. We lived in separate bedrooms in the same house. We were friendly together, but I finally decided to buy her out. She "bent me over," but I just wanted to get out of it. I wrote her a check and helped her move to the city. She got married and had a baby and now we are friends. I give her a lot of credit for staying friends throughout all that.

10. *When you are out with the guys and you see someone who interests you, what do you do?* Girls generally don't approach guys and introduce themselves. They need to give out signals to show they are interested. Once the man approaches the woman, then the woman has all the power. Women use sex to get intimacy and men use intimacy to get sex. When a man approaches a woman, it is usually for sex.

11. *What kind of woman are you looking for?* My equal. To me, relationships are about partnerships. I want parity. I want a girl who is on the same plane intellectually, financially, and educationally. I don't want a dependent. I don't want to be responsible for bringing her happiness. I am not saying that she must be a Stanford graduate; I believe experiences can be a substitution for education. However, I would not date a forty-year-old waitress. I don't think that I could have anything in common with a woman like that. There is a certain life style that a woman becomes used to. Her ambitions would not equate with my expectations.

12. *What is your definition of success?* Meeting your own expectations. Achieving what you are set out to do. I believe lower level jobs are gap strategies for people who are between jobs. If you are permanently in a gap-level job, either you have no ambition or you have no intelligence. You are not suitable to be my friend or my girlfriend.

13. *What do you think about women whom you meet in the bar?* On my birthday, I went out with my friends. I saw a girl that I had dated for a while. She was so annoying that the sex just wasn't worth it. I stopped calling her. She turned out to be my buddy's brother's ex-wife. He told me that I had dodged a bullet because, "She was pure evil."

Another time, we were at a bar and we had a few drinks. We noticed that the posse of pussies showed up with their leader. I was a little buzzed. The leader sat next to me and we started talking about alcohol and any other nothing topic. She was aggressive. She kissed me all night. We parked in front of her place. We were half nude in the car and I looked up to realize that she was the roommate of the pure evil girl. I told her that she had to get out of the car and I drove away as fast as I could.

14. *What is sexy in a woman?* Good mother by day, sex kitten by night. She keeps in shape and wears a teddy. It is about being sexy. She understands that understated elegance is more attractive than the alternative. The hair and makeup are done right, her shoes are sexy, the way she walks and carries herself. I get good wood on that. If a woman looks like a hooker, the minute you are done, you want nothing more to do with her.

WHY DON'T YOU?

Why don't you spend more time with me? Where are you going? Why do you need to go out? Why do you spend so much money? Why don't you do humanity work instead of your commercial projects? Why do you need to sleep in past 7 a.m.? Etcetera, Etcetera . . .

Being married to an Intellectual for many years has had many ups and downs. I wouldn't have done it differently as I have learned a lot and gained a lot. I am proud of my children who have become who they are partially by having their wonderful father and an amazing decent role model.

It was worth turning the other cheek for all these years because I have learned tremendously how to handle stressful interpersonal relations. What I have learned is that the good comes with the bad. Until you complete your mission (i.e. children out of the house), you are willing to swallow the bad. However, after the mission is complete, you come to the realization that life is too short to put up with your partner's continual criticism, negativity, nit-picking, whining, pouting, emotional drain and over-controlling of your life and decisions.

Now that I'm in my 40's, my tolerance level has decreased and I am thinking more about myself, my well-being, and what I want to do with the rest of my life – both professionally and personally. I realize many women my age feel these same feelings, especially when their husbands have not been the most exciting, supportive or interesting companions.

People go through different stages in their lives and their needs and interests change. After the years of selfless nurturing of kids and family nears the end, there is an overwhelming need and desire for the woman to take care of, nurture, and pamper herself if she hasn't been taken care of by her partner. Neglect and being taken for granted breeds the need to escape. Escape can be found in professional pursuits, new friendships and relationships, and self-improvement.

Once I confronted my husband with the truth about his shortcomings, he was hit by shock and awe because everyone had always tuned him out and turned the other cheek. We were all afraid to confront him because there was no winning with him. It has and always will be his way or the highway.

My husband viewed marriage as ownership and he maintained a traditional view of the relationship, wanting me to serve his emotional needs. Because he was not a social person, he expected me to be his only friend and his everything. He took my mental freedom away by refusing to say what he meant, always expecting me to read his mind – he never learned to communicate. He believed that, as his wife, I should want to meet his whims and that I should succumb to his every rule. He wanted to spend every minute with me and he ultimately suffocated me. He is insatiable because I am his only companion, friend, and outlet. He has no hobbies.

So now, I am faced with a decision. What is important in my life? My kids come first and I come second. But the kids are gone. Now what? I want to spend the next forty years of my life with peace of mind without being brow-beaten, having someone continually on my case, or having to answer to someone else's unrealistic expectations of me. I want freedom of mind.

I would love to make our relationship work for me. All I want is for him to accept me for who I am. I don't want or expect him to change. I just want him to not expect me to change. I want him to realize that I am not perfect.

SERENDIPITY

I was finishing my graduate degree and one of my female teachers came onto me. She was pretty good-looking and very smart. She was five or six years older than I. She asked me out and we ended up going out a couple of times. I'm not a dater; I like to be in a relationship and to know that it is going somewhere. I don't like to waste my time; I'm busy with my studies. On the third date, she kissed me. She invited me in and we made love. I went home for the night. I thought she was pretty special.

A week later, I found out that she was going out with another graduate student. I didn't know whether that meant that we were done or that she was going out with more than one person at one time. I wanted to know where our relationship stood. I approached her in her office. I sat down and she smiled. I told her: "I understand that you are also going out with one of my classmates. I really like you and I don't mind that you are seeing other people. But I am looking for an exclusive relationship, so I would appreciate it if you would think about it and decide if you want to be with me or continue dating others." She told me that she appreciated my candor and honesty and that she would think about it and let me know that month.

As luck would have it, I met someone that afternoon. She turned out to be the love of my life. We were engaged and married within the month. It just happened. Later that month, my professor asked to see me after class. She was excited to talk to me. She began by telling me that she had made a decision. Before I could let her know that things had changed in my life, she told me that she had decided that she wanted to be my girlfriend and could commit to me. I didn't know what to say to her at the moment. I just stood there with my mouth hanging open. I didn't have a wedding ring on; it was being inscribed and resized at the jewelers.

I told her I was married. She laughed and grabbed my left hand and said, "You're so funny!" I looked at her and said; "I am serious. I really did marry an undergraduate woman. She took my breath away." My professor cleared her throat and said, "Well, I guess congratulations are in order. Please give my best to your bride. You sure don't waste any time."

I grinned and rubbed my ring finger. I told her that I hoped she would find someone to make her as happy as I was.

This was the only spontaneous thing I have ever done in my life. I have always prepared and planned my actions. Thirty years later, I look back at the power of serendipity and I am thankful that I was able to let go for that one moment in time.

E. The Addict: Gives complete attention to your needs.

Many of our characters are addicts in one form or another. For example, Forbidden Fruits are addicted to the power of sex; Diplomats, Magnets, and Sportsmen may be considered by some to have sex addictions as well. The Forever Bachelor and the Fantasizer become addicted to the Forbidden Fruit. Psycho Dramas and Has-beens are hooked on drama. Gold-diggers are addicted to money; Smotherers are addicted to relationships; and the Diva is addicted to freedom. Perpetual Kids are addicted to fun and games while Responsible Adults and Intellectuals like control and perfection. You might say that most characters are "addicted" to something or someone; that is what defines them and makes them different from the rest.

However, the Addict in the dating scene is a fundamentally empty character with a very low self-esteem who becomes addicted to whatever seems to fulfill him or her at the particular moment in time. He or she is addicted to being addicted. They may become addicted to dating married people, sex and porn, drugs, gambling, or even a church. They are pleasers by nature. Addicts rarely go for a sexual relationship without becoming friends first; they need to become addicted to the person in order to establish an intimate relationship; he or she needs to be comfortable. The Addict becomes an expert in whatever he or she is addicted to at the moment. For example, if addicted to sex, he or she will be a phenomenal sexual partner. If this character finds a grounded person who has patience, the Addict may find permanent happiness and fulfillment.

The Addict may become a jealous, partially due to an overly imaginative mind that can make him or her overly suspicious. They may become stalkers when they cannot let their addiction go. He or she will hover until the partner becomes sick of the suffocating attention.

BEWARE: If seeking a healthy relationship, just don't. However, if you are a Nurturer, the Addict may be just whom you are looking for because he or she needs a great deal of tender loving care.

ADDICTED TO AN OLDER MARRIED WOMAN

It started as an affair. She was 45 and unhappily married; he was a 32-year-old golf professional, working at a local country club. She took lessons from him over the course of a year and they became friends. They began to see each other away from the club for an occasional movie, dinner or drink. In time, they discovered a common interest: perverted sex. She had a high desire to experience new sexual avenues, including, but not limited to, the newest sex toys, sex clubs, sex groups, and pornography. He had a high desire to please and satisfy the needs of an older woman. He eagerly joined her in her adventures.

The sexual adventures went undetected by anyone for over a year. Knowing that she was growing tired and bored with him worshipping her, he introduced drugs into the relationship to spice it up. For a short while, it added zest and excitement. However, she noticed that he was becoming addicted to the drugs just as he had become addicted to her and their perverse sexual activities. He did more and more drugs, while she attempted to distance herself from him.

She began to see other men. He became paranoid and delusional. He started to stalk her by showing up at her place of work and her home, where her husband and children lived. She became scared and told her husband about the affair. Her husband divorced her. Her children disowned her. But the Addict could not move on. He was certain that she would fall back into his arms now that she was divorced and available. He couldn't have been more wrong. She hated him for what he had done to her family. She had no interest in him. She suggested that he get help for his drug addiction.

He checked himself into a drug rehabilitation facility, sought expensive counseling, and began dating another drug addict. This trend went on for years, moving from one addiction to another. While the therapist could not help him, he charged the Addict more than he could afford. The Addict lost his condo.

The Addict found God as part of the Narcotics Anonymous program. He went to church every Sunday. He began reading The Bible and attending church events and social gatherings. He threw himself into the church. While attending church, he began dating another older married woman. She was beautiful and in an abusive relationship. She needed someone like him to lift her up and build her self-esteem. The match was made in

Heaven. The sex was simple, missionary and toys only. There was no porn. There were no drugs. There was no voyeurism. There were no additional partners. And, he was fine with it all. He loved her. He worshipped her.

INTERVIEW WITH AN ADDICTIVE PERSONALITY

1. *Contributor age:* 20's
2. *Gender:* Male
3. *Education Level:* College
4. *Profession:* Sports pro
5. *Personal Status:* Single

   If single, are you looking for a long-term relationship or a meaningful one-night stand? Yes, I am looking for a long-term relationship. I love to be in a relationship.
6. *What initially attracts you to the opposite sex? Past the initial attraction, what keeps you attracted?* Smile and confidence, persona, friend-zone person.
7. *What do you find appealing in a date?* I am a romantic, going on a hike and a picnic is what I like. I would try a lot harder than my date. Outdoorsy. I like to talk to my date and look at her.
8. *What do you find to be a turn-off in a date?* Texting and any distractions such as phone calls, or simply paying no attention to me. I can't take the uncomfortable silence.
9. *Where do you meet people?* In church, at the club. I went out with a married woman for a while. I meet lots of nannies, but I like older women.
10. *When you are out with your friends and you see someone who catches your eye, what do you do?* Depends on the setting. I need to feel comfortable.
11. *What are your thoughts about online dating?* I signed up for an online dating service, but no one ever responded. I don't like computers that much. You have to be committed to it and it just isn't my thing. I like the singles' group at church.
12. *Have you ever had trouble moving on from a past relationship?* Yes. I spent three years with a married woman. Her son found out about us and started acting out. The woman went into mom mode and she spent less and less time with me. She met another guy and I became crazy over that. Looking back, I pushed her to him. We had broken up many

times over the three years. My emotional status was a wreck; I had to keep a secret at my work because she worked there as well. She was bubbly, confident, and warm-hearted – a woman that anyone would be attracted to. I started therapy to find out why I stopped caring about myself. I am a pleaser and put everyone else's feelings before mine. I was sacrificing myself. Toward the last months of the relationship, I felt as though I didn't love myself. If I did, I would have left her earlier. She taught me that sex toys are important and most guys are intimidated by that fact.

In college, I slept with the cleaning lady. The maid showed me the anatomy of a female's body. It was all about sex, but I realized that I don't like sex without a connection. I need a connection in my life.

I have never broken up with a girl. They have always broken up with me.

13. *What do you think about one-night stands?* I am not into one-night stands. I taught the married woman stuff that I wouldn't necessarily do now. We went to swinger clubs. We had to be interviewed as a couple at one swinger club. The interview questions were looking to see if we were a legitimate couple, we had to provide a picture/head shot. There were lots of hot girls there; many of the girls were on Ecstasy. When we went back one night for a try-out, she was approached by a couple of guys, but didn't do anything. There were women who were servicing three guys at one time. There was a room with ropes and chains where two girls were making out with each other. They invited us to join them, but we were chickens. I felt badly because I had been the one to suggest that we go there and my lover was uncomfortable. I went to Amsterdam when I was 18 and watched a sex show. That got me really into voyeurism. I like to read Erotica. I have also been to a place in San Francisco where you pay $30 bucks to get in and you can watch or participate in anything you want or can imagine.

I want sex to be sacred. Toys are great. I like porn. I like to use vibrators. I like to bring pleasure to women. I love wild crazy sex. I like Missionary with a toy. I love hearing women cum. I also went to drug rehab. I have an addictive personality.

I had to go back to God. I like hanging out with older people. When things weren't working out with the married woman, I became very lonely and I was definitely not loving myself. I couldn't sleep so I started doing black tar heroin. My dad had an affair on my mom while I was going through my shit. I was very upset by that. It threw me over the edge. During that time, I had a close call when I was pulled over by the police after work. I got lucky. Someone had called the cops on me the previous night when I was smoking dope while driving. The cops waited for me to pull out of work the next night. I lucked out that they didn't see me grab my pipe and my dope when I grabbed my wallet. I was carrying cocaine and heroin in the glove box and, as I grabbed the wallet, I grabbed it. As soon as they let me go, I started smoking in the car. I was asking for help. I didn't care. For me, drugs and sex became intertwined. It was all an effort to escape.

I got out of rehab and had a couple of one-night stands. When you are on drugs, you become desperate. While in rehab, I met a lesbian. We were both so desperate for companionship and a connection that we tried to have sex. I just couldn't get hard because of the methadone. I finally got to the point where I realized that I just didn't know myself. I found myself again when I went back to church.

14. *What are your rituals for preparing for your date?* I use my hands a lot and I love hand lotion. I use hemp-scented lotion.

15. *Where do you go/what do you do on a date?* I love the comedy shows, jazz, and going to plays. I am fake gay, which means cultured. I love women.

16. *If you don't know your date well, do you meet at the designated place or do you pick up your date?* I meet at the place. I'd rather do an afternoon date than an evening date. I am more comfortable with casual dates. I have a good mother. I believe you should be a gentleman on the outside and a sexy man in bed. The same with the woman. She should be a lady on the outside and an animal in bed.

17. *What frustrates you in the dating scene?* I hate awkward silence. I don't want to over work the situation to fill it. I am a monogamous dater and I want them to be exclusive. People play games and don't show who they are. I want people to know who I am and I never know when to start telling her about myself.

18. *What are you looking for in a relationship?* I want to have a shiver every time I see her. I am dating such a woman now. When we first had sex, I told her that I couldn't have sex unless I was getting into the relationship. Connection is important. The age thing doesn't bother me. I am looking for a best friend and 100% honesty. Mutual respect, not being afraid to show who you are. We should have almost the

same goals in life for the future. Be able to flirt and not feel all weird. Enjoy each other's company. I love to go to Costco or shopping with her. Cuddling is huge. I love physical contact. When I love the person, I love her scent. We both cried having sex during our orgasms. I am very sensitive and I cried because she cried.

19. *Would you go out with a married woman?* Yes.
20. *Would you date someone who had a child from another relationship?* Yes.
21. *Would you consider financially supporting your partner?* Yes, but I don't make much.
22. *What type of clothing do you prefer your date to wear when you go out on a date?* Whatever she is comfortable wearing. Jeans and T-shirt.
23. *What is your preferred body type and shape for a woman?* I like 5'6" or 7" with a little bit of a curve.
24. *How do you feel about tattoos and piercings?* Tattoos are fine; I have three. The ones that are colored in really hurt when you get them. Not much into piercings.
25. *How do you feel about perfumes and colognes?* Every once in a blue moon I will wear it. A little bit is fine. I am a lotion person. You can get scented lotion instead.
26. *How important is the first kiss?* Huge. I am the world's best kisser. Enough to tell her that you're not the cousin and or the sick pervert that sticks his tongue down her throat. I am the best kisser that I have ever known.
27. *Will you have sex on the first date? If so, would you talk to your date about your preferences freely?* Yes. I went to a sports bar with an older woman. She grabbed me and kissed me. I am a lightweight and a glass of wine was just enough for me to be loose. She had picked me up and then I drove her car. After the bar, I drove us to a public parking lot where we fucked in the car. It was raining outside; it was very cozy. We were in the back of the SUV totally naked. The car was on so we could have the heater going. All of a sudden, we heard a knock on the window. I was naked. The police asked for our licenses. They came back laughing and saying, "Have a nice evening, Mrs. Robinson (from <u>The Graduate</u>)," and they told us to wrap up and go home.
28. *Do you wear boxers or briefs?* Boxer briefs.
29. *How do you make sure a new sexual partner is free of STD's?* I always wear a rubber. My penis is sleeping twenty some hours a day and once it is awake, it needs to go. The mind goes out and the penis

comes out. I love a beautiful pussy. There are ugly ones and pretty ones. The ugly pussy looks like a roast beef sandwich where it hangs like a turkey. It has an odor and it is dark. A pretty pussy is small, pink, not a taco. The Kegel muscles are in good shape. It has a good landing strip. I always do a scent test before I go down on them, go in with the finger and then decide. Once in a while I will wear a cock ring. There is no nice word to describe a pussy. Clit is the better way of saying it. I am a total feminist.

30. *Where is your favorite place to have sex if you had a choice?* Bed. Public bathroom. I love Missionary style.

31. *What age range do you date?* 35-45 years.

32. *What do you think of one-night stands?* I don't like them. I was messed up and it was fine then. Ecstasy makes them fun though. I prefer to wake up next to the woman.

33. *What was your parents' status when you were growing up?* Fucked up and married. My dad had an affair.

34. *How do you characterize yourself?*

> **Positive attributes:** I am loyal, caring, attentive, a good listener, good in bed, pleaser, lover, sweet and best friend.
>
> **Negative attributes:** I have an addictive personality, I treat others better than I treat myself, my loyalty is my worst thing, I can't get over things. I am in the moment, and I do not often use my logic.

35. *How do you think others see you?* I wish I could look into the mirror and see what people say about me and see it in myself. I eventually would like to be a person who doesn't have to hide anything. I want 100% total honesty. I am amazing at multi-tasking, but can't finish things. I am not a good goal setter. I live one day at a time.

36. *Please include a detailed description of your ideal date.* A walk in a scenic place. A real connection. Knowing that I am not in friend zone. Get to know her. I am cheesy. I play a twenty questions game to learn about her.

37. *When you meet someone new, how long does it take you to know if the person is "the one" or has the potential to be "the one"?* I have never broken up with anyone. I was obsessed; never in love.

38. *Do you believe in "love at first sight"?* No.

39. *What are some of the common terms in today's dating arena?* Drunken dialer is someone who you would call after midnight for a booty call. Brown paper sack special, beer goggles on.

40. *Do you believe there is a game people play when dating? If so, describe the game.* Yes, I hate that stuff. There are a million games. I think it is ludicrous. I think people play the game to prove who is stronger. I think it is stupid as hell. They do this to protect themselves. If you don't want to go out, then don't. One reason I don't date girls in my own age group is because they are looking for a challenge. People in other countries don't make such big deals of sex. We do.

41. *Is spirituality important to you?* Yes.

Below the belt questions:

1. *Is sex an important factor in deciding whether you will continue to date someone?* Yes.
2. *Do you enjoy it when your date wears lingerie?* Not really.
3. *Have you ever experienced ménage à trois?* Yes. Two guys and a girl. His thing was massive.
4. *What is sexy to you in a woman?* Confidence, sense of style, smile, I like people who have lots of different groups of friends. I like women who do charity. A woman who can be naked and cool about herself. I'm not saying she needs to vacuum the house naked. She should just be comfortable with herself.
5. *Does the size of her breasts matter?* I like the nipples. Size doesn't really matter.
6. *Do you mind surgical enhancement of breasts, lips, teeth, etc?* Whatever makes them happy.
7. *Long hair or short hair?* Long and blonde now, but I usually go for brunette and the girl next-door look.
8. *Do you prefer a particular pubic hair design?* I like a landing strip. Smell is important – do a finger test first.
9. *How many sexual partners have you had in your life?* 7.

F. THE TWINS: Give support, service, and peace.

There are some relationships in which one partner tolerates repeated disrespect from his or her mate. Sometimes classified as "doormats" by outsiders, these characters can be divided into two groups: Put Upon Somebodies, those whose stay is negotiated, and Stepped Upon Nobodies, those who are subservient and afraid of being alone.

1. THE PUT UPON SOMEBODY OR PUS

The Put Upon Somebody [PUS] can be male or female, but is more often thought of as being female. PUS ends up taking a back seat to his or her mate. They are often political spouses who have given up their own careers to advance that of their mates. They are strong people who are strong supporters of others. PUS is a great friend. This character is highly intelligent and put together. He or she is friendly, attractive, and knows how to keep the façade; if upset, no one can tell from his or her outward appearance.

PUS has formed a united partnership with his or her mate from the beginning, building an empire together. It is not a one-sided relationship. PUS manages everything from the household to the business affairs and always appears to be in charge. They make themselves important by taking a lot of responsibility. They do all of the dirty work, the menial jobs, and the necessary work. They take control, leaving their mates free to focus on their own careers.

People wonder why PUS stays with an unfaithful mate. The answer is simple. It is worth it to stay for some reason. They stay for the kids' sake, or for the power that they enjoy, or for the money involved in the relationship, or because their own identity is inextricably wrapped up in the mate and the mate's career. This character remains in control of his or her destiny. PUS's continued love and support is conditional on money or status; there is something in it for them. They are Mrs. or Mr. Somebody as part of the team, even if they are put upon. PUS fears the demotion to a Mr. or Ms. Nobody as an ex-Put Upon Somebody.

However, their stay is a negotiated one, at least in their own minds, allowing them to live with themselves and survive the pity party that surrounds them. While they are free to leave, they understand that, if they do leave, they will lose their spouse, career, and identity in one fell swoop. For them, it is all about the team and they are a team player. They are martyrs. They have worked hard to build the fortune and empire. Why should they give it up? Some think that Hillary Clinton stayed for political power and status while Elizabeth Edwards stayed for her children. The list of political wives who have remained in political marriages despite the public infidelities of their mates is long.

While in public, PUS will stand by his or her spouse, but in private, he or she will stand up for himself or herself. No one wants to experience the wrath of this individual, once wronged. The mate's life will be hell for years to come. The mate rarely leaves PUS because he or she needs PUS as badly as PUS needs him or her. They are inextricably intertwined. PUS enjoys seeing his or her mate suffer at home, while everyone on the outside thinks it is he or she who is suffering.

While he or she does have a lot of self-esteem, PUS will barter or sell his or her self-respect for success. However, when the time is right, PUS may leave the poison relationship, but it will be on his or her terms. If and when they decide to leave the relationship, they will have gotten what they need from their mates prior to leaving. This character can stand on his or her own two feet.

I AM NOT A DOORMAT!

I met him in college. We were both driven, had fantastic grades, and were looking forward to successful careers. We challenged each other intellectually. We would debate social and political issues with each other and our small circle of friends. We were very casual in college; we wore jeans, t-shirts, and flip-flops. We spent our money on books and coffee. We hung out in bookstores and the student union.

We were married right out of college. I went on to law school and my husband immediately began his career. During the early years of our marriage we worked hard and established ourselves in the community. We worked on social issues together in our spare time. We did not have children immediately; I was not sure how I could navigate a legal career while having a young child.

I made partner in my law firm when I was first eligible. I worked hard and long hours. My husband also worked long hours. We had agreed that I would have a child after making partner. We had a daughter. I was only willing to have one child.

At that time, my husband's career was soaring and he was given the opportunity to become the CEO of a company that was about to take off. However, we were asked to move across the country. This was the most difficult decision I have ever had to make. I left the partnership after working so hard to get there and we moved. I set up our new home, spent time with my daughter, and worked in our new community so that I could reestablish myself.

My job became promoting my husband and supporting him in his career. I did not resent it; it was a team operation and I was a key player on the team. My husband appreciated my suggestions and effort and always made me feel worthwhile to his success.

Low and behold, the company made it big and we became millionaires many times over. It seemed to be too good to be true. I was busy with my daughter, managing the household, running the social calendar, and making sure my husband had as little stress at home as possible.

He was a celebrity in our community. He looked good, worked out, took care of himself, and loved to socialize. He was dynamic and the talk of the town. When we walked into a gathering, all eyes were on us. It became apparent that he was a magnet for women who were interested in our money and the power that he possessed. Women flocked all over him. It became a little annoying.

He gradually became carried away with his own success, forgetting the team. I would remind him that it was the two of us who built our empire, but that it would only take one of us to destroy it. He went a little too far in his social endeavors and betrayed my trust in him. Although I know that men have sexual appetites and desires, they should have more control over themselves than he was displaying.

One afternoon, a woman with whom my husband worked ran into me at a local restaurant where I was having lunch with a friend. She inquired about my welfare and asked how I was coping with my husband's relationship with a woman at his office. Everyone seemed to know about this infidelity. I looked at her with stone cold eyes and said, "Don't you have anything better to do than to mind other peoples' business. The information you have is incorrect. Have a wonderful day." I watched her face turn different colors of purple, and, while I knew she meant well, she had crossed a line that no one should cross. Indiscretions happen all the time; messengers get shot.

Nobody ever again brought to my attention the flirtations of my husband. My husband became insatiable with his sexual dalliances and I simply did not care about him anymore, but I did care about my family and the appearance of my family. We put on a united front in public while living separate lives at home. We had an understanding. It was a business relationship. I also wanted my daughter to have a two-parent household. I did my thing; he did his thing. He learned to be discreet. I became even more discreet.

I filled my time and kept busy. I set up a foundation where I spent my time and energy and he continued to run his company. I became more involved in house expansion and decorating projects. I surrounded myself with a loyal team of people who worked to make me happy. I also focused on my daughter's activities.

I understand that other wives thought I was a doormat and in denial about my husband's affairs. They simply did not understand the investment I had made in time and money and that I could not separate business from my marriage. Don't judge me until you are in my position. I gave up my career to support my husband; he became my career. I enjoy being married to him and will not give it up. I don't have to. It is my choice.

INTERVIEW WITH A PUT UPON WIFE

1. *Age:* 50's
2. *Education Level:* Graduate Degree
3. *Are you financially secure?* Yes
4. *Relationship Status:* Married
5. *Interests/hobbies:* Reading, world affairs, politics, and family.
6. *What attracts you to the opposite sex?* Intelligence, charisma, swagger, ambition and a sense of entitlement.
7. *What do you find appealing in a man?* Romance, good stimulating conversation, good food and good company.
8. *What do you find to be a turn-off in a man?* Bad conversationalist, low IQ, milk toast, or boring.
9. *When you are out with your friends and you see someone who catches your eye, what do you do?* We giggle.
10. *Where do you hang out?* Friends' homes.
11. *Have you ever had trouble moving on from a past relationship?* I never had trouble moving on from a relationship per se, but I have had trouble moving through stages within a relationship. In my marriage, it was very difficult to transition from the fun loving youthful student relationship to the responsibility laden adult and parent relationship.
12. *What do you think of one-night stands? Who do you think participates in them?* I know it happens, and it must serve a purpose because a lot of people do it.
13. *How do you break off a one-night stand or short relationship without being hurtful?* Don't do it and you don't have to worry about it.
14. *Type of lingerie you would wear on a first date? And the following dates?* I'm not much into lingerie.
15. *Where do you go/what do you do on a date?* Out to dinner, theater or symphony.

301

16. *How often do you have a girls' night out? Where do you go with your girlfriends?* I enjoy going out with my girlfriends -- we go to chick flicks.

17. *What do you hope to happen when out with the girls?* Nothing. Good and fun conversation.

18. *What frustrates you in the dating scene?* Back in the day, it was difficult to find a man who was the crème de la crème. Most men were looking for frivolous one-night stands. Few men were worthy and intelligent. I would say that the pool of men who fit my criteria has become even smaller today.

19. *What are you looking for in a relationship?* I looked for someone with whom to grow professionally and who would be supportive of my career as well as his own. I wanted someone with ambition and who would work hard to build a good life. I wanted someone who would be equally committed to the team. Today, I would look for someone different. I would look for a free-loving, exciting, loyal, and adventurous guy.

20. *What do you want from a man and how do you want him to treat you?* I want a man who is confident and not intimidated by an intelligent woman. I want a man who doesn't expect me to stay home and make cookies.

21. *Would you go out with someone who was married?* No. I would not disrespect another woman that way.

22. *Would you date someone who had a child from another relationship?* No, unless the children were grown. It is too difficult for a young child to accept another adult authority figure.

23. *If you were to live with someone, how long would you be willing to live with him without a permanent commitment?* I would not live with someone unless we were married.

24. *Are you hoping to find a man who is financially secure? Is financial security more important than love?* Absolutely. I want a man who has the potential to have a successful career. Money is not the end all be all. It is the power they posses. It is the power and the influence they can exert. Power is sexy.

25. *Would you consider financially supporting a man with whom you happen to fall in love?* No.

26. *What type of clothing do you prefer your date to wear?* Clean and pressed.

27. *What is your preferred body type and shape for a man?* Healthy.

28. *How do you feel about tattoos and piercings?* Not.
29. *How do you feel about perfumes and colognes?* A masculine musk.
30. *How important is the first kiss?* Always nice.
31. *Do you expect your date to pay on the first date?* It is a proper thing to do if he asks me out.
32. *Will you have sex on the first date?* No. I will have sex when the time is right and when I know there is a long-term potential. Let's say hypothetically that I had the opportunity today. I would need to know the person and make sure that he was able to deal with my situation. I will never leave my husband. I need to make sure he can be discreet.
33. *How do you make sure a new sexual partner is free of STD's?* That is scary. That is why I wait until I know the person very well.
34. *Once you have decided to have sex with your date for the first time, are you free and uninhibited in the act or more conservative and reserved than normal?* Pretty conservative.
35. *Where is the most interesting place that you have had sex?* On the floor.
36. *Do you use protection and if so who provides it? If you don't use protection, how do you stay safe or is it an issue?* Of course. I have always been on the pill.
37. *What do you do if protection is not immediately available?* Nothing will happen.
38. *What if you liked your date and he did not call you the next day or week? What would you think and do?* Call him to find out where we stand. I don't believe in wasting time or "pussy-farting" around.
39. *What age range do you date?* Within five years of my own age.
40. *How do you characterize yourself?*

    Positive attributes: Intelligent, driven, ambitious, good mother, supportive wife, career woman, good and loyal friend, team player, good manager, diplomatic and understand people well.

    Negative attributes: Zero tolerance for ignorance and mistakes.
41. *Please include a detailed description of your ideal date.* Dinner, theater, and good conversation.
42. *When you meet someone new, how long does it take you to know if the person is "the one" or has the potential to be "the one"?* A while.
43. *Do you believe in "love at first sight"?* No. I believe you can quickly recognize someone who meets your criteria. I believe another can

make you feel great immediately. It may or may not be love. It takes time to figure that out.

44. *What is your personal philosophy on monogamy and monogamous relationships?* It is important to a successful and respectful relationship.

45. *Do you believe there is a game people play when dating? If so, describe the game.* There shouldn't be a game for intelligent people who know what they want and who are secure enough to be themselves.

46. *Have you ever been on a date with a guy who turned out to be an ass?* No. I have always been very particular about my associations. I always knew the person before I went out with him. I had done my homework up front. However, that's not to say that the guy doesn't act like an ass at one time or another.

47. *If interested in a further date, would you wait for him to call you or would you initiate further communication?* I would prefer a call first from him, but I wouldn't hesitate to call him.

48. *If you were not interested in another date, would you let him know?* I would let him know. It's only fair.

49. *Would you mind if your date contacted you immediately after your date?* I would find it refreshing.

50. *How much attention is too much or too little after the first date?* If it is authentic and from the heart, it is fantastic.

51. *On average, how many dates are required before you consider yourself to be in a relationship? What qualifies as a date?* That is a negotiated subject between the two.

52. *Is the dating game a mystery or are the rules clear? If clear, what are the rules?* There shouldn't be a game. I don't like games.

53. *Do you consider yourself to be a game-player in the dating arena?* No.

54. *Is spirituality important to you?* Yes, I want my partner to be a good person and to answer to a higher power.

55. *What books on dating do you recommend?* I read many books, but I haven't read any on dating. I did read <u>I Am Charlotte Simmons</u> when my daughter was getting ready to go to college. It was a fabulous read. It was eye-opening.

Below the belt questions:

1. *Is sex an important factor in deciding whether you will continue to date someone?* Not particularly.

2. *Do you enjoy wearing lingerie?* No.
3. *Have you ever experienced a ménage a trios? If not, would you consider it?* No, no.
4. *What is sexy to you in a guy?* Quiet confidence.
5. *Do you prefer circumcised or not?* Circumcised and clean.
6. *Do you prefer more or less hair on a man?* I don't like too much hair.
7. *Do you prefer tanned or natural skin?* Natural.
8. *Will you kiss and tell your friends or do you keep it private?* No. I keep my personal life to myself.
9. *What do you think of the work environment as a place to meet someone?* It is a place where you can meet others with things in common. But it can be a minefield and you have to be very careful.
10. *What is your opinion about surgically enhancing your body? How much enhancement is too much?* When necessary, it is perfectly appropriate.
11. *How many sexual partners have you had in your life?* 3.

2. THE STEPPED UPON NOBODY OR SUN

The Stepped Upon Nobody [SUN] can be male or female and can be rich or poor. This character is often thought of as a doormat or lap dog. Unlike PUS, this character is not an integral part of a team; he or she is simply there to serve his or her mate. They are subservient. They have no self. This character is indecisive and will wait for direction and affection from his or her mate. SUN takes a lot of abuse without condition, as he or she is afraid to be alone. They focus their time and energy on making life more comfortable for their mates. You can count on SUN to do your mundane everyday chores without complaint.

Contrary to PUS, SUN is a weak character that leaves the mate in complete control of his or her life and happiness. SUN is unable to leave on his or her own volition. SUN must be kicked to the door. They are completely dependent upon their mates for their emotional fulfillment. They need someone else to make them whole. They are completely empty. SUN's biggest fear in life is to be alone. They would rather stay in an abusive and unhealthy situation than be alone. SUN will not push back or stand up for himself or herself. They are non-assertive. SUN will put more and more effort into the relationship as the mate pulls back and puts in less and less effort. When SUN is finally putting in 100% of the effort, the mate will put an end to it. However, the mate will have to push hard to get rid of SUN.

Where PUS slips into his or her role due to life's circumstance, SUN is born into his or her character. Whether genetically predisposed to subservience or brought up culturally to serve the mate, they will not change. They are peaceful creatures and shy away from confrontation. They bring peace to their mates and aggravation to those outside the relationship who simply cannot understand why anyone would put up with the abuse. Their love is unconditional. They are followers. They are passive and easily manipulated by others. While they will not share their opinions with others, they are highly judgmental and inwardly socially correct. They are not noticed; they are invisible. They simply take up space.

SUN is exceptionally self-conscious about his or her appearance as he or she finds validation in his or her beauty. SUN can be the stereotypical "trophy" who will make a great companion and will keep his or her mouth shut. You can dress a SUN up and take him or her out to functions; SUN will always make you proud. SUN will never make a scene, even at home. They will suffer in silence, knowing their place. As long as you can support their spending habits, they will bury their suffering in their materialistic spending. Shopping therapy is always a quick pick-me-up for SUN. Because of SUN's focus on retail therapy, this character might come across as pretentious. Others might find SUN to be aloof and distant. However, they are simply insecure within themselves.

Outsiders pity SUN and can easily take advantage of him or her. SUN will be overly generous in social circumstances, always picking up the bill. SUN will support his or her friends until the time comes to take a stand on behalf of the friends. They won't stand up for their friends; they don't want to make waves. This is not surprising, though. How can you expect someone to stand up for you if they cannot stand up for themselves?

SUN is a great caretaker, nurturer, mother, or father. They may become wonderful, nurturing parents, focusing their attention on the children. However, they can be overbearing and hovering parents; they can be clingy, needy, and pathetic with their children. Sometimes, the children might wonder who the parent is.

NOTE: SUN often dates Players, Gold-diggers, Smotherers, or Opportunists. These characters will take advantage of SUN without compunction. They may even emotionally abuse SUN.

A SUCKER

Like Pavlov's dog, the doormat is trainable. Once conditioned, they will be the same from relationship to relationship. It is a stimulus response. When their basic needs are fulfilled and they feel needed, they will take whatever abuse is dished out.

We met at a party through friends. She looked beautiful. She seemed to carry herself well. I spent quite a long time talking with her about her life, her career, her likes and dislikes, her frustrations, and her relationship status. I was thrilled to find out that she was single and that she was looking for a long-term relationship. She came across as very shy and reserved and, when she wasn't sure about something, she put her little finger in her mouth and nibbled on her nail. That turned me on. She seemed to have all the right moves.

I consider myself to be an eligible bachelor; I hold a good position in a good company; I make great money; and I am a good-looking man. I have a beautiful home and drive fabulous cars. I had everything, but love. I had so much love to give, but had been very unlucky in that department. She came along out of nowhere and blind-sided me.

Before I knew it, she had moved in with me and was redecorating my house. She moved her kids in as well. I had an instant family and was very excited and happy about the new situation. I cared for the two teenagers as if they were my own kids. I loved and cherished her. I provided for her wardrobe, her food, her hair, and her every need and desire. I loved to do it for her; I loved to see her happy.

She began to make plans as to our financial future. However, I noticed she was planning with my money. For instance, she paid for a five-year membership to the local country club in her name. She said it had to be in her name so the kids could use it. She bought two years worth of spa treatments for her upkeep, claiming she was doing it to make herself look good for me. She surprised me on my birthday with a Porsche, which I had no intention of driving; I don't think much of men who drive Porsches. The funny thing was that the title to the car was in her name only and she had not taken a loan; she paid cash out of my checking account. Her sixteen-year old son ended up driving the car because I was happy with my Cadillac SUV.

I began to question her judgment with the finances. I didn't want to ruffle any feathers or to make her uncomfortable, but I wanted to make sure we had enough to live on in the future. She was spending the cash like it was growing on trees. I worked hard for the money and it wasn't coming in as fast as it used to or as fast as it was being spent.

She did not like me questioning her and seemed to distance herself from me. She thought I had insulted her. I bent over backwards to please her and to show her that I had no problems with her having what she needed, but that we had to be a little more careful. She did not like it; she did not want any limits on her freedom.

She began to go on girls' nights out and left me at home with her kids while they did their homework. Her attitude towards me had changed. She was no longer cuddly in bed; nor did she seem to be interested in sex with me. I heard from people on the scene that she was flirting heavily with other guys and she may even be fooling around with a few of them. My feelings were hurt and I didn't believe it. I tried to make it up to her. I contacted her best girlfriend to see what I could do to get her out of her funk. The girlfriend mentioned that she wanted a summerhouse for her birthday. Although I would have rather waited to make such an investment, I too had always wanted a summer place. So, I bought her a summer place with her name only on the deed.

Her birthday came and her friend and I planned a huge surprise party for her at the new beach house. She arrived and was ecstatic and cried when she found out the house was hers. I was so happy to see her back to her old self. That night was the greatest night that I can remember. She was an animal in the sack.

The next day, I had breakfast ready for her out on the veranda overlooking the ocean. She surprised me when she said she was moving out of our other home in town and would be living at the beach house. I was happy that she liked it as much as she did. Enjoying the ocean fog on my face, I told her it would be difficult for me to commute to work that far every day, but that I would make it work. She said I didn't have to worry because I wasn't going to be moving into the beach house with her. My jaw dropped and I could not believe what I was hearing. She wanted out; she had met someone else and hadn't gotten around to telling me before her birthday.

She thanked me for the house and the car and said that we could be friends and that she would always have a place in her heart for me. I contacted her best friend to find out what I had done wrong. I found out that they also had a falling out when she found out about my wife's plans; she had been duped into suggesting the house as a gift. She apologized like there was no tomorrow. I knew that we had both been fooled, but I still loved her and would take her back in a flash if she would only come back. I miss the kids. I loved them, too.

NO PROMISES

She met him when he came to her check out line at the grocery store. They had been flirting around in her line for a couple of years. He was a very successful developer and was always looking for the next project. She had been a grocery clerk since graduating from high school five years ago. He came in to buy his food twice a week and would stand in her line even if other lines were shorter. He finally asked her out and they have been together for twelve years now.

He does not believe in marriage and does not feel that it is natural for a man to commit to one woman for the rest of his life. He told her that from the start; she fell madly in love with him anyway and ended up pregnant after they were living together for six months. He stuck to his guns and continued to live with her, but never offered to put a ring on her finger. Over the past twelve years, they have had two more children together. Her parents appreciate the life he provides for their daughter and grandkids, but they want more for their daughter and the kids.

He has been an outstanding father. She is subservient and meets his every need. She keeps the house nicely. She keeps up her appearance and is a wonderful mother to his children. He is happy to support her and to pay for her expenses as long as she takes care of their children and his needs without interfering with his business.

He openly cheats on her, but never admits to anything. If she gives him too much trouble, he shows her the door. She will never walk out the door; rather she stays put with the humiliation of knowing of his infidelities. She suffers in silence and serves his every whim. She stays with him because she loves him and hopes that he will one day commit himself to her. He stays with her because she offers him peace and tranquility at home. Why wouldn't he stay? He has his cake and eats it, too.

INTERVIEW WITH A COLLEGIATE STEPPED UPON NOBODY

1. *Contributor age:* 20's
2. *Gender:* Female
3. *Education Level:* College
4. *Are you financially secure?* My parents are.
5. *Profession:* Student
6. *Personal Status:* Single
7. *Are you looking for a long-term relationship or a meaningful one-night stand?* Long-term.
8. *Interests/hobbies:* Music, dancing, partying, socializing, playing the flute, watching movies, going to concerts, and raging.
9. *What initially attracts you to the opposite sex?* I like calves and ankles, hair, sense of humor, and someone who has the patience to put up with me.
10. *What do you find appealing in a date?* Being able to be comfortable with the person, really comfortable; dinner and a movie is the ideal date. Or pizza and a movie.
11. *What do you find to be a turn-off in a date?* High-expectations, when they expect me to be super cute all the time or have super good manners. Don't like condescending people. Don't like downers.
12. *Where do you meet people?* Through friends or at parties.
13. *When you are out with your friends and you see someone who catches your eye, what do you do?* I look at him and make sure that I am in his general area of view. I stand there and look cute.
14. *Where do you hang out?* Peoples' homes.
15. *What are your thoughts about on-line dating?* Not necessary.
16. *Have you ever had trouble moving on from a past relationship? If so, what did you do to finally get over it?* Yes. I'm clingy, and I know it's bad. When it didn't work out, it was really hard to move on by myself. My biggest fear in life is being alone; I hate being alone. I love having fun, but I need to have fun with someone. I try to make other people happy and try to make them laugh. I am always with friends.
17. *What do you think of one-night stands? Who do you think participates in them?* I never do one intentionally. I would hope it would have meaning. I end up having them when I black out at a party. If I hook up with someone, I think it should be exclusive. I date down by seeking unattractive guys with great personalities because I am insecure. I

310

don't know why I do that; I think I am a really cute and petite girl and I generally don't have a hard time attracting guys, but the cute guys make me nervous and uncomfortable.

18. *What are your rituals for preparing for a date?* Shower, dry hair, straighten hair, do makeup, pick out clothes, shoes, jewelry, deodorant, lotion, perfume, brush teeth, mouthwash.

19. *Type of lingerie you would wear on a first date? And the following dates?* Depends on what I am wearing. Black thong.

20. *Where do you go/what do you do on a date?* Let the guy decide. Don't really care.

21. *If you don't know your date well, do you meet at the designated place or does your date pick you up?* Don't really go out with strangers, so he would pick me up.

22. *Would you be interested in going for coffee and a walk instead of a dinner date for the first date?* Yes, you get to talk and get to know the person.

23. *If you were a candy, what kind would you be and why?* Gooey taffy because I'm sweet and good, but clingy; clingy could be good cuz you have some for later.

24. *How often do you have a girls' night out? Where do you go with your girlfriends?* Once a week. My place and we drink wine. Get to talk. Gossip. Love talking.

25. *What do you hope to happen when out with the girls?* Just to be with the girls and girl bonding.

26. *What frustrates you in the dating scene?* Guys that are douche-bags and don't communicate their issues. I feel like everything could get solved, but when people bottle their feelings, shit happens. Changing someone doesn't necessarily mean a bad thing, but compromise could be nice. In a good way changing could be good.

27. *What are you looking for in a relationship?* I have been looking for that one person since high school to have a family with; I am looking for a guy that would be a good father. He doesn't need to be attractive. Afraid that if he is attractive, then I will have to be attractive . . . so that is insecurity.

28. *Would you go out with someone who was married?* Nope.

29. *What about someone who is separated, but not divorced or has a girl-friend?* Yes, that's okay.

30. *Would you date someone who had a child from another relationship?* Yes, because I want a family. It would be okay if the child were ugly.

31. *If you were to live with someone, how long would you be willing to live with him without a permanent commitment?* I could live with someone for a long time without knowing what his intentions were.

32. *Do you smoke?* I smoke a lot. It might be better if he did smoke.

33. *Are you hoping to find a man who is financially secure?* Yes, but not more important than love.

34. *Would you consider financially supporting a man with whom you happen to fall in love?* Yes. I wouldn't mind, but I don't really want to.

35. *How does it make you feel if your date flaunts his assets?* Makes me feel kind of special.

36. *What is your preferred body type and shape for a man?* Nice calves and ankles, slender and toned.

37. *How do you feel about tattoos and piercings?* Love them.

38. *How do you feel about perfumes and colognes?* I like them, but they are not necessary. If they smell neutral, it's okay. Sometimes, it's better that they just don't wear any (if they have a distinct smell).

39. *How important is the first kiss?* 70% important.

40. *Do you expect your date to pay on the first date?* Yes. After that, I don't mind paying.

41. *What is your preference and philosophy on who should pay the bill on dates with you?* Don't really care. I don't want to do it all the time, but it's not fair the other way around.

42. *Any other behaviors that bother you when on a date?* Talking about ex's.

43. *Will you have sex on the first date?* If no drinks are involved, then probably not.

44. *How do you make sure a new sexual partner is free of STD's?* I usually ask how many girls they have been with and, if it is a high number, then I ask.

45. *Once you have decided to have sex with your date for the first time, are you free and uninhibited in the act or more conservative and reserved than normal?* Conservative, insecure.

46. *Where is your favorite place to have sex?* In the bedroom.

47. *Do you use protection and if so who provides it? If you don't use protection, how do you stay safe or is it an issue?* I'm on birth control so I don't care if he wears anything.

48. *What if you liked your date and he did not call you the next day or week? What would you think and do?* I would be devastated. I would

312

call him or text him. I would call or text him three times within two days.

49. *What if your date called you a month later? What would you say and do?* I would be confused, but I would go out again if I weren't with someone else.

50. *What age range do you date?* 18-25 years.

51. *How do you characterize yourself?*

   Positive attributes: Funny, happy (happiest with other people), carefree, jokester, laugher (maybe too much), short (love it), bubbly, and spunky.

   Negative attributes: Clingy, maybe too carefree.

52. *Please include a detailed description of your ideal date.* Pizza and a movie, preferably on a rainy night or during a lightening storm.

53. *When you meet someone new, how long does it take you to know if the person is "the one" or has the potential to be "the one"?* A week.

54. *Do you believe in "love at first sight"?* No, maybe love at first talk.

55. *What is your personal philosophy on monogamy and monogamous relationships?* I believe in them.

56. *Do you believe there is a game people play when dating? If so, describe the game.* Yes, constantly trying to prove yourself to the other person; always trying to show that you're good enough for them, trying to convince them that you're something they want. So the game is being something that you're not.

57. *Have you ever been on a date with a guy who turned out to be an ass?* Yes, we did date, but we ended up breaking up -- we are still friends. He is an asshole, but he's nice to me because he says I'm special.

58. *If you were not interested in another date, would you let him know?* Nope, I would keep going out, but subtly try and stop.

59. *Would you mind if your date contacted you immediately after your date?* No, I would love that.

60. *How much attention is too much or too little after the first date?* Never too much.

61. *On average, how many dates are required before you consider yourself to be in a relationship?* It's not a relationship until he says, "Do you want be my girlfriend?"

62. *Do you consider yourself to be a game-player in the dating arena?* Nope.

Below the belt questions:

1. *Is sex an important factor in deciding whether you will continue to date someone?* Nope.
2. *Do you enjoy wearing lingerie?* If I am comfortable in it.
3. *Have you ever experience ménage à trios?* Yes, with another girl and it was awkward. It was not really fun. I wouldn't do it again unless it was with two guys.
4. *What is sexy to you in a guy?* Having a sense of humor.
5. *Does the size of penis matter?* Nope.
6. *Will you kiss and tell your friends or do you keep it private?* Yup.
7. *What is your opinion about surgically enhancing your body?* You can do it, but I won't.
8. *Do you treat dates with long-term potential differently than fun quickies?* I don't have fun quickies.
9. *How many sexual partners have you had in your life?* 13 -- half of them were virgins. I once had sex on a school bus and, while doing it, I was talking with my friend who was also having sex on another seat. Good times in the marching band!

X. The Lost Surfer: Idealistically looking for love.

There are many Lost Surfers out there. In fact, most of us start out in this category of dater. Lost Surfers ride one wave into the next without knowing who they are. Accordingly, they don't understand themselves well enough to know who they should be looking for in a mate. They have not had or taken enough time for self-discovery. People evolve and grow over time – it takes a long time to become the real you. In her graduation speech at Stanford University, Oprah talked about the evolving nature of people over time:

> It's being able to walk through life eager and open to self-improvement and that which is going to best help you evolve, 'cause that's really why we're here, to evolve as human beings. To grow into more of ourselves, always moving to the next level of understanding, the next level of compassion and growth. .... I think about one of the greatest compliments I've ever received: I interviewed with a reporter when I was first starting out in Chicago. And then many years later, I saw the same reporter. And she said to me, "You know what? You really haven't changed. You've just become more of yourself." And that is really what we're all trying to do, become more of ourselves. And I believe that there's a lesson in almost everything that you do and every experience, and getting the lesson is how you move forward. It's how you enrich your spirit. And, trust me, I know that inner wisdom is more precious than wealth. The more you spend it, the more you gain.[9]

Prior to 21, the majority of us are surfers, learning who we are through our experiences. We are learning who we are, partially by whom we date and our experiences in the dating world. We learn what we like and what we don't like. Every dating experience is a learning experience. We learn about our sexuality. If one marries without much dating experience and ends up divorced or widowed, he or she becomes a surfer once again, searching to learn about himself or herself through different partners until he or she learns what makes him or her happy. The key surfing times

---

[9] http://news-service.stanford.edu/news/2008/june18/como-061808.html

seem to be in the teens and twenties and then, again, in the forties. While surfing, you never know what characters you are going to meet and what you are going to learn from them. However, you have to be careful when surfing so that you don't hit the rocks and a shark doesn't eat you!

The modern day dating phenomenon of not dating – only going out with packs of other kids in high school and then "hooking up" for continuous strings of one-night stands at this party or that in college -- appears to be creating a situation where people are not learning enough about themselves and the opposite sex in the teens and early twenties. Without learning how to relate to the opposite sex early on through dating when still in the safety of their parents' homes, kids are being thrust into a new world in college where there are few adult role models, if any, and few guidelines to follow. The mixture of hormones, new freedom from parental control, alcohol, and drugs leads to the culture of "hooking up" that leaves many empty in the long-run. The long-standing rituals of dates and dating are gone and have been replaced with a no holds barred free sexuality where young men and women do not take the time to get to know one another or themselves before serially hopping from one sack to another. Accordingly, the surfing years are being pushed off until the mid- to late-twenties when people used to be looking to settle down.

One problem with surfing after college is that it becomes much more difficult to find potential mates as the pool of possibilities shrinks by the mere fact that the available people your own age become much more spread out throughout society. When you spend most of your time working and many people now work from home, there is very little time to meet other eligible people. Even if you work in the traditional confines of an office, the workplace has become a very muddled place to date due to the increasing rules against inter-office dating. Fishing off the company pier is frowned upon in many industries. This, in turn, leads to many falling into the Desperate Dater category and many who are settling in order to have a family. This again, post-pones the surfing years until after the divorce once the children have left the nest and may even lead to surfing through affairs during the marriage.

INTERVIEW OF A FEMALE LOST SURFER

1. *Contributor age:* 20's
2. *Gender:* Female
3. *Education Level:* Graduate Degree
4. *Are you financially secure?* Yes
5. *Profession:* Student
6. *Personal Status:* Single
7. *Interests/hobbies:* Working out, going to nice restaurants, reading and taking hikes.
8. *What initially attracts you to the opposite sex?* Obviously, looks are first. Now, past looks, a sense of humor is very big. If you can make me laugh, you can win me over. The ugliest guy can win me over if he has a great sense of humor.
9. *What do you find appealing in a date?* Someone who is interesting and with whom I can be engaged in the conversation. Someone who cares, pays for the first date, does not talk about himself all the time, and doesn't talk about ex-girl friends. This one guy was playing this game where he was telling me about all the hot girls he was with. I am super insecure when a man talks about pretty girls and how hot they are. He never asked questions about me, he always talked about himself. That bugged the heck out of me. He was making it uncomfortable for me.
10. *What do you find to be a turn-off in a date?* Drinking too much, checking his phone, or wearing a t-shirt.
11. *Where do you meet people?* I have more recently been meeting people at my athletic club. I also meet them through my friends. I met my current boyfriend at a bar. This year has been a hard year for me. All my friends are either engaged or married. My support system is not as big as it was. When you don't have a boyfriend, it is good to have good friends around. As I get older, my group of friends seems to be shrinking and it is a little scary.
12. *When you are out with your friends and you see someone who catches your eye, what do you do?* I don't do anything. Maybe a smile.
13. *Where do you hang out?* School, library, at the club, and in town.
14. *What are your thoughts about on-line dating?* It scares me.
15. *Have you ever had trouble moving on from a past relationship?* Yes. He was older than I. I was so dependent on him. The break up came

out of nowhere. He broke up with me. He was rude to me all weekend; I knew something was happening. He said he needed to be single. We continued to hang out months after that. I was a crazy woman and couldn't get over it. I was in love with him. He was amazing. I was not myself. After the break-up, I moved in with six girls. It was great to be distracted by that. I went out a lot and surrounded myself with a lot of people. I cried and was depressed. I started dating a lot of other people. Time healed. But never isolate yourself when you are in that situation. A year later, I went to visit him again and I did not have the same feelings for him. I was over him.

16. *What do you think of one-night stands? Who do you think participates in them?* It disgusts me. I feel different about sex now. It is so special now. I love being comfortable around a guy who loves me. In college I didn't cared as much. I wasn't aware as much. Then, a one-night stand was a funny thing. You would have the walk of shame when going home in your clothes from the night before. Everyone who saw you knew what you had been up to and you knew they knew.

17. *How do you break off a one-night stand or short relationship without being hurtful?* The girl expects a relationship with sex more than the guy. I think the girl finds more meaning in sex than the guy. While girls might say they don't care, I don't believe them. They are hoping for more, but they know the reality. They are protecting themselves by pretending to be okay with it all.

18. *What are your rituals for preparing for a date?* I get ready like I normally do. I have a habit of leaving tags on me. I make sure I have all my tags off. Make sure I have no eyebrow fuzz or mustache. If I do, I shave it off.

19. *Type of lingerie you would wear on a first date? And the following dates?* I'm not so good with lingerie.

20. *Where do you go/what do you do on a date?* Dinner or drinks.

21. *If you don't know your date well, do you meet at the designated place or does your date pick you up?* Meet.

22. *Would you be interested in going for coffee and a walk instead of a dinner date for the first date?* I would be interested going to the gym and working out together. I like a no alcohol setting.

23. *If you were a candy, what kind would you be and why?* Something with an intense flavor. I would be a Fireball!

24. *How often do you have a girls' night out? Where do you go with your girlfriends?* We have a supper club once a month. One person hosts

dinner at their house and everyone brings wine. Then we rotate houses the next month. It is really fun to be with the girls in a relaxed setting. We really get to talk.

25. *What frustrates you in the dating scene?* First impression is a big thing. If you say something stupid, people might read too much into it and might not call you the next day. If someone didn't call me, I would question myself as to what I said. I don't like it when I can't read a person and I can't tell what they are thinking. If they make me nervous, then I can't be myself.

26. *What are you looking for in a relationship?* Family background - coming from a solid family and not a broken home. No abandonment issues. Boys who grow up with mothers seem to need to go from one relationship to the next and they don't know how to treat a woman.

27. *Would you go out with someone who was married?* No.

28. *Would you date someone who had a child from another relationship?* Yes.

29. *If you were to live with someone, how long would you be willing to live with him without a permanent commitment?* I would move in with someone if I knew we were going to be engaged.

30. *Are you hoping to find a man who is financially secure? Is financial security more important than love?* Love is the most important thing.

31. *Would you consider financially supporting a man with whom you happen to fall in love?* I want the whole package. I want someone who is motivated.

32. *How does it make you feel if your date flaunts his assets?* Flaunting your material possessions is very unattractive.

33. *What type of clothing do you prefer your date to wear?* Nice collared shirt. Nice shoes.

34. *What is your preferred body type and shape for a man?* Muscular, but not a meathead.

35. *How do you feel about tattoos and piercings?* I am okay with tattoos, but not piercings.

36. *How do you feel about perfumes and colognes?* I like colognes. I like the one from Channel. Bad breath sucks.

37. *How important is the first kiss?* Pretty important. No tongue.

38. *Do you expect your date to pay on the first date?* Yes.

39. *What is your preference and philosophy on who should pay the bill on dates with you?* When I was working and had a job, I would pick up

the tab. I feel the one who is more financially secure should pay. And also whoever asks should pay.

40. *Will you have sex on the first date? If so, would you talk to your date about your preferences freely?* No. It is a situational question. More than three dates probably.

41. *How do you make sure a new sexual partner is free of STD's?* I ask him. I want him to get tested. I always get tested. If I had a new boy friend, I would get tested.

42. *Once you have decided to have sex with your date for the first time, are you free and uninhibited in the act or more conservative and reserved than normal?* I am inhibited, but would like to get to a point where I feel more free and uninhibited. I would love to feel comfortable with it all.

43. *Where would you feel comfortable having sex with your date?* Home and the hotel, not the car or restroom.

44. *Where is your favorite place to have sex?* Bed.

45. *Do you use protection and if so who provides it? If you don't use protection, how do you stay safe or is it an issue?* Usually guys have condoms. I don't care much about sex because I get bladder infections. So, if they don't have it, we won't do it.

46. *What if you liked your date and he did not call you the next day or week? What would you think and do?* I would be disappointed and I would want to know what happened.

47. *What if your date called you a month later? What would you say and do?* I would probably not take it very seriously. I would laugh and say, "Are you kidding me?"

48. *What age range do you date?* 28 to 37 years.

49. *How do you characterize yourself?*

> **Positive attributes:** I am caring, healthy, hard-working, I am a people pleaser.
>
> **Negative attributes:** I care too much for others, I see things as black and white, I jump to conclusions very fast, and I over analyze things.

50. *Please include a detailed description of your ideal date.* A clean-shaven, well-dressed man with his hair done whisks me away to Mexico or Hawaii for a two day vacation where we stay in a nice hotel, go to the spa for massages, and eat nice dinners. We are in La La land for the entire time.

51. *When you meet someone new, how long does it take you to know if the person is "the one" or has the potential to be "the one"?* I know within moments.
52. *Do you believe in "love at first sight"?* Not really.
53. *What is your personal philosophy on monogamy and monogamous relationships?* It is the only way to go without causing yourself stress/heart attack/unnecessary drama. It is the smartest decision. If you fool around, it always ends up badly.
54. *Do you believe there is a game people play when dating? If so, describe the game.* Not 100% representing who you are. We talked for 6 hours and he didn't ask for my number. He just started showing up where he knew I'd be. He asked for my email to show me pictures of his trip and then sent me his phone number. He was acting not interested to make me more interested.
55. *Have you ever been on a date with a guy who turned out to be an ass?* I was working as a hotel concierge and a guest would come in to party. I got his number and our first date was a work out. When he started drinking it became obvious that he had a drinking problem; he became an ass and was ruthless with his mouth. He was hung-over for breakfast and ordered a Mimosa. We sat next to a dad with his two daughters; he asked the guy sneeringly how he could sit there with two kids. The dad replied that he loved it.
56. *If interested in a further date, would you wait for him to call you or would you initiate further communication?* I wait, especially after reading He's Not That Into You.
57. *If you were not interested in another date, would you let him know?* Yes, I would tell him it was me and that something was going on in my life and I needed to work it out on my own. It is always good to sit on your thoughts before you text something that you can't take back. I love to make journal entries instead of texting what I feel at the moment! It's safer.
58. *Would you mind if your date contacted you immediately after your date?* No, I would like that.
59. *How much attention is too much or too little after the first date?*
    Too little – no call for 2 days
    Too much – calling the morning after. Wait for the evening, people have to work.
60. *On average, how many dates are required before you consider yourself to be in a relationship?* You have to have the talk; at least three

dates. I reconnected with a guy on My Space and that was our main form of communicating. He changed his status to "In a Relationship" instead of the talk. I thought it was really sweet and cute.

61. *Is the dating game a mystery or are the rules clear? If clear, what are the rules?* The rules are clear. Call if you are interested. Plan events in advance; no last minute get-togethers. Lonely people tend to lead others on and let them think they are interested. As for dating in college: sex is too casual. Girls hang out in groups and boys hang out in groups. The groups mix it up. There is power in the group. I have noticed a lot of 40-year old women who met their husbands in college are now divorcing. I am glad I did not marry someone from college.

62. *Do you consider yourself to be a game-player in the dating arena?* No.

63. *Is spirituality important to you? If so, what if your date has different beliefs than you do?* Yes. The most "moral" people are hypocritical and are really not nice people. I want someone to really share my moral values and not to pretend to share them.

64. *What books on dating do you recommend?* He's Not That Into You and The Ten Stupidest Things Women Do by Laura Schlessinger and Why Men Marry Bitches.

Below the belt questions:

1. *Is sex an important factor in deciding whether you will continue to date someone?* Yes, passion saved my current relationship when he was being a jerk.

2. *Do you enjoy wearing lingerie?* Not really.

3. *Have you ever experienced a ménage a trios?* No, not interested.

4. *What is sexy to you in a guy?* Body, clothes, smile and sense of humor.

5. *Does the size of a penis matter?* A one-incher just cannot do the trick. Tiny is bad.

6. *Do you prefer more or less hair on a man? If a man is too hairy, what should he do about it?* Less hair to no hair; no hairy back or butt. He should shave it.

7. *Do you prefer tanned or natural skin?* Tan.

8. *Will you kiss and tell your friends or do you keep it private?* Yes, I will tell my girlfriends.

9. *Are the men whom you meet in a bar a potential long-term relationship or are they a one-night stand?* They are a potential long-term relationship.
10. *When you go to a bar, do you hope to find someone?* Yes.
11. *What do you think of athletic clubs as a place to meet someone?* Good/Best.
12. *What do you think of coffee houses as a place to meet someone?* No, weird crowd.
13. *What do you think of the work environment as a place to meet someone?* Good.
14. *What is your opinion about surgically enhancing your body? How much enhancement is too much?* All for it. Whatever makes you feel good about yourself.
15. *Do you treat dates with long-term potential differently than fun quickies?* I am way more myself when it is a fun quickie and it doesn't matter – I would like to be that way with everyone, but I am usually more reserved. I am free when it doesn't matter.
16. *How many sexual partners have you had in your life?* 18.

LESSONS LEARNED SO FAR: Don't isolate yourself when you are depressed over a break up. Keep a journal to keep track of your thoughts. Write a journal entry instead of texting when you are emotional! Think about it first!!

THE EYES

While in college, she dated a guy for about a year before he left for a semester abroad. Neither she nor he was sexually experienced when they met. They were both still in the process of getting to know themselves. He did not know about foreplay and was actually so large that he would hurt her when having sex. When they were making love, she would lie there hoping his penis wouldn't come out of her throat.

He lied throughout their relationship. He lied about doing drugs. When she caught him doing cocaine with some buddies at a party, she believed him when he said he would never do it again. She had to pay for many of their dates because he was frequently out of money even though he worked 30 hours a week and he lived at home. When he went abroad, she visited him. The phone rang while they sat on the bed in his little apartment. Instead of answering the phone, he pulled the phone out of the wall. He told her he was getting crank calls. When his semester abroad was over, he came over a week or so after he had gotten home. He didn't want to go out to dinner or really to talk. He wanted to get busy in the sack. She agreed.

She noticed that he was trying things he had never tried before. He went down on her; something he had never done before. He made her uncomfortable when he kept looking up at her with his big brown eyes to see how she was enjoying his new skill. All she could think about was that someone had obviously taught him a thing or two while he was away. She asked him why he was down there and he looked up and asked, "Don't you like it?" She asked, "Who taught you to do that?" He denied having learned from anyone and said he was simply trying something new. He stopped and they began having sex, but she was worried because he wasn't using any protection. She didn't see him again, but heard from her friends a few weeks later that he was getting married to a pregnant French girl.

LESSON LEARNED: She learned that one way to spot a cheating mate was when there is an unexplained effort to try something new in the bedroom.

A GIRL AT THE BOOKSTORE

She was sitting on the big chair at the bookstore, reading self-help books and looking very depressed. I was waiting for my coffee when she looked up at me and said "Hi." I said, "Hi" back and asked if she was going to read all five books on "letting go." She smiled and said that she needed to read a lot more than five books to get out of her mood. I asked her about her mood. She said that it was a long story. I told her that I had all day to listen. I offered to get her a cup of coffee and she agreed. We went to an outside deck to talk.

I needed a friend who could understand what I was going through at that moment as well. She was a perfect stranger, but we were at a similar place in life. She asked why I was interested and I told her that I was also trying to get over someone and had come to the bookstore to look in the self-help aisle. I told her that her story might help me. She was thrilled to hear that and she proceeded to tell me her story.

She was a 34-year-old Stanford graduate who worked at a successful company in New York City and made good money. She had been briefly married. She met her husband through mutual friends, dated him for six months and then they married. She wanted to have children as she was getting close to 30. After being married for a few years, they divorced once they realized that they weren't a good match for one another. Her husband was a very successful engineer at her company, but was lacking life. He spent hours on the computer and loved his work more than anything. She tried very hard to make their marriage fun and exciting, but it was becoming more of a job than a fun relationship. Luckily, they did not have children together. They are still friends.

After the divorce, she was looking for someone with whom she could spend time talking, walking, going to the movies, or enjoying a picnic by the beach. She wanted someone who was relaxed and spontaneous at the same time. She saw herself as easy going; she viewed herself as someone who loves life and enjoys the beauty in everything. She was honest, forthright, self sufficient, caring, compassionate, and respectful to others' feelings and needs. She was always the best in her class, great at her job and excelled in everything she put her mind into. She was ready to settle down. But she did not want to die in a relationship.

She decided to change her dating habits and get out more with her friends. Always hanging out with work friends did not allow her to expand her dating field beyond work. She had already tried that avenue. One night she went out with her friends to a high-end bar. There, she met this very handsome, charming man. He seemed to be very friendly. He and his group of friends had come from a basketball game.

Her group of girlfriends soon mixed in with his group of male friends. She and the charming man hit it off and they agreed to meet for a later date. She was elated to find out that he was not married, was financially secure, and had a delightful personality. They decided to meet at a restaurant in downtown Manhattan.

When she arrived at the restaurant, he was there with the same group of friends who had been with him the previous night. He asked her to join them. She was a little confused as she thought this was going to be just the two of them, but she went along with it. It turned out that she ended up having a lot of fun. At the end of the night, he asked her to go to his car and talk a little. She agreed and they proceeded to walk to his car, which was parked right in front of the restaurant.

They sat in the car, talked for a while, and started kissing. She didn't want this to go any further so she called it a night and told him that she had a very nice time and would like to go out again. He called her a cab and kissed her good night.

The next day she received a text from him, saying how much he enjoyed his time with her and that he would like to see her again. She was excited to have found such a man. The next date was to be at a bar at a hotel where he was conducting business. They were meeting for drinks after 10:00 p.m.; he had a business engagement that he had to attend earlier that evening.

She met him at the bar in the beautiful hotel. Again, he was there with a group of friends and she joined them. She was beginning to think this guy was afraid to be alone with her. Around 12:00 midnight, he asked if she wanted to spend few hours alone with him in a room upstairs. She knew what he was talking about and honestly didn't mind it. He got them a room and they spent a good couple of hours having fun passionate sex.

After he took a shower, he told her that he had to go home. She was confused. "Home?" she asked. He replied: "Yes. I can't stay out all night. I am married." Her jaw almost dropped to the ground. She couldn't breathe for a few minutes and she suddenly felt like shit. How stupid was she, she thought to herself. Why didn't she ask him this question? Why did she assume otherwise? She was sure that she had asked him; maybe she assumed for some reason or other.

All she could do at that time was to nod her head. To make matters worse, he saw her reaction and said, "You didn't think that we were going to go anywhere with this, did you?" She was speechless. She couldn't say a word. After he was fully dressed, he walked over to the bed to kiss her goodbye. She raised her hand to stop him from doing so and asked him to please leave.

He said he was feeling badly that she had a different impression of him. All she wanted him to do was to get out and leave her alone with her stupidity. He finally left. She wasn't upset that they had sex and that was the end. She had engaged in many one-night stands in her life, but she knew from the beginning that they were only for one night. But this time, she let her guard down and did not listen to her logic. She was disappointed in herself, not the man with whom she had two fantastic hours of hot passionate sex.

After her divorce, she had changed herself and the way she went about dating, thinking that there was something wrong with her and the way she looked at relationships and love. She dumbed herself down by allowing herself to go with the flow against her better judgment and comfort level. She should have just tried to understand herself rather than to change herself. She believes this man came into her life to show her who she is and what makes her happy. The part that she is having a problem with is not the guy. But, rather, the problem is not knowing who she is. She needs to learn from scratch who she really is, what makes her happy, what she wants, and where she wants to be.

She told me, "This is the reason I am reading these books; I am trying to see if anyone else feels the way I do. After that night, I felt more alone and lost than ever. I couldn't think for few weeks. I didn't know whom to blame or if I even needed to blame anyone. I know that I am an extremely capable person, very successful and overall not bad looking. I just need to feel that I am not the only person feeling lonely and lost." I nodded. She concluded our conversation by telling me, "The people who come and go in our lives are just visitors."

LESSON LEARNED: Ask specifically whether someone is married before you date or sleep with him or her. Also, don't change the way you go about dating so that you are uncomfortable with yourself.

THE SLIPPERY SNAKE

She was good. She knew how to keep them all paying for her without finding out about one other. She and her friend had a scam going. She looked for rich guys and prioritized date nights according to wealth. Monday was least wealthy and Friday and Saturday were most wealthy. She would take the guys shopping at her friend's store to get them outfitted. While there, she would ask them to buy her something as well. As if that wasn't enough, the shop owner would add to the price of each piece, raising the total so that the woman could return later to shop for a few more items on the guy's dime. They had done this hundreds of times. She was a snake. Her closet had over 500 pairs of designer jeans in it, not one of which was purchased with her own money.

He met her in the bar. She was a looker. She was hot. He was interested in her; she had great physical appeal. He went up to her and told her, "You deserve to be with me." She laughed and agreed. After talking for the whole evening, she told him that she could go out with him on Tuesday evening. They went out to dinner and had a good time. She held back and gave him nothing physically. He was anxious to get into her pants. The next day she suggested that he needed to dress younger and she would be willing to help him do so. He was shocked that she didn't approve of his dress; he thought he always dressed well. He was very interested in dressing to look younger.

During the day on Friday, she took him to her friend's store and they picked out several outfits for him. She asked if it would be okay to pick something for herself after leaving the dressing room curtain gapped so he had a perfect view of her beautiful perky breasts. He eagerly agreed, telling her to pick a couple of items. She selected a pair of designer jeans and a few shirts; he got a couple of shirts and two pairs of slacks. The bill came to $2000, but he wasn't paying attention at that moment. She was hanging all over him when he was trying to sign the credit card slip and he was very distracted.

The next evening was his birthday and she agreed to spend Saturday night celebrating his birthday. He had arranged for a limo to pick them up and take them partying. After dropping everyone else off but the girl, he told the driver to keep driving until he tapped on the window. The limo rocked and rolled for a few hours. She liked the guy and his Tuesday evening spot was moved up to Sunday.

He spent and spent and spent and wondered why she wouldn't spend more time with him on Thursday through Sunday. She would come up with lame excuses as to why she couldn't see him. She was tired, but she didn't work. She had family obligations, but didn't have any family that he knew about. He became friendly with her girlfriends and they liked him. In fact, they were interested in him for themselves.

They saw him when he was out one Thursday night with his buddies. They told him that his new girlfriend was taking him for a ride. They told him that she was dating five guys at a time. They told him about the scam at the store that how the poor souls would get overcharged. He was pissed that he had allowed her to take advantage of him. This was his first dating experience after his divorce. It had been over 20 years since he had been in the dating scene and the learning curve was steep.

He confronted her with the stories and she denied them. She cried and he threw a napkin at her to wipe her eyes. He wasn't moved by her drama. He thanked her for teaching him the ropes and assured her that he would now be able to spot a gold-digging bitch from a mile away.

LESSON LEARNED: Don't buy expensive gifts until you really get to know a person. There are a lot of Takers out there.

THE ONLINE WIDOW

I grew up with one goal in mind. I wanted to be a wife and a mother. I met my husband in high school; we married right after high school graduation. I was eighteen. He was nineteen. Marrying young was not unusual back then. He went to college and I went to junior college for a couple of years until I became pregnant with our first child. We ultimately had three beautiful children. My husband worked hard and made his way up in the management of his company. We moved three times during our thirty-year marriage and our last house was our dream house.

My kids went off to college and were living their lives in other locations. My husband and I were wondering if our 3000 square foot house would be too large for the two of us. One night while watching Johnny Carson, he dropped dead of a sudden coronary arrest. I couldn't save him; he was gone. I was left alone. I was a forty-nine year old widow.

I sold the house and moved back home where my parents still lived. I found a job and bought a small house. I tried some widow groups at a church, but I couldn't stand it. They were wallowing in their grief, some four and five years after the death of their spouses. I found myself a private therapist and worked with her until I couldn't afford it anymore. She hooked me up with about six other girls and we had a group session for the rest of the year. I became very good friends with one of the girls in the group. She moved in with me; I am a very social person. I didn't like living alone and was thrilled to have a housemate.

I was ready to meet someone special. One night, we were home drinking wine. We had heard about on-line dating and weren't having much luck meeting anyone through the usual channels. I was fifty and she was fifty-two. We were vivacious and beautiful and we had a lot of life to live. We poured ourselves another glass of red wine, rolled up our sleeves, and pulled our credit cards out of our wallets. We sat at the computer and filled out the survey and questions for the on-line site. We rushed home the next day to find many emails on the account.

We read them; we laughed; we cried. Then, we had to decide if we were actually going to go out with any of them. There were a couple of cowboys; I was excited about that. We sifted through the possibilities and we each set up one date. It was a little scary out there. How were we going to keep ourselves safe?

We decided that we would only meet in a public, busy restaurant. We would always take our own cars. We would always back each other up. Sometimes, we would be in the place where the other's date was supposed to be. We would stay until the date was over. On other occasions, after about an hour, we would call the other and ask how everything was. If going well, we would say it was going great. If it was not going well, we would say something like, "What do you mean you were in an accident? I will be right there." One time, I met a guy who was not right for me. I thought he might be a better fit for my friend. I waived her over to our table and we sat and had a wonderful night with the three of us. She liked the guy so much that she is still dating him. She has been dating him for fourteen years now. They are happy and in love. They are not rushing to get married. They will never get married.

We couldn't believe how many bald men put in pictures that were fifteen years old, showing them to be fifty pounds lighter with hair and in shape. My friend and I were one hundred percent honest on our questionnaires and we expected everyone else to be. One man showed up for a date in a seventies style powder blue windbreaker, shorts and long white socks. My friend called and I immediately said, "What do you mean you were in an accident? I'll be right there!" I excused myself and ran to my car. I called her to thank her and laugh. She said, "No, I really was in an accident. Can you come to the emergency room?" She was fine, just needing a few stitches.

I ultimately met the nicest, kindest man through the site. He had been divorced for many years and also had grown children. We dated for a year and then married. I am still madly in love with him after twelve years. Our kids are happy for us both. I moved into his house and I rented mine to my friend and her companion.

LESSONS LEARNED: You can find love again. Honesty is the best policy in life, including your on-line dating profile. Always have an exit strategy for your dates.

FULLY COMMITTED TO TWO MEN

I was born into a dysfunctional immigrant family from Jamaica where I was abused by my father and other men throughout my childhood. My mother and I never bonded. I was left in the care of others from the time I was very small. I have been morbidly obese for most of my life. While visiting my aunt in Jamaica when I was sixteen, I met and fell in love with an East Indian man. We had a passionate romance and went back home to our respective countries. We have continued our communication throughout our lives. After that, my father never touched me again because he considered me to be "used" goods.

I married a man when I was 18. My family thought he would be a good match for me and that it would be good to get me away. That two-year marriage, however, was never consummated. He was gay. I met my next husband when I was 28. He was in a bad marriage. He was a good man, but I wanted more than he could give. He was still emotionally tied to his first marriage. So, we divorced and he introduced me to his cousin.

I had a relationship with the cousin, we lived together for a year, and then we married. I ignored the voice in my head telling me that I was making the biggest mistake of my life. I married him in spite of the voice. He had an alcohol problem. We were married for three years. I became pregnant and had a miscarriage. He was not supportive emotionally during that time. He left me at the hospital and went drinking. I had to take a cab home. I stayed with him because I was feeling desperate, lonely and needy. He used past information to torment me. He told me, "What do you expect from someone who used to fuck her father?" He tore down any self-esteem that I had managed to build. I felt that death would be better than living with him. When I was 32, I got pregnant again. He was jealous of the pregnancy. He argued that the baby wasn't his. He called me a whore. I felt so threatened by him that I slept with a hammer underneath my pillow. I had set up the phone to dial 911 directly.

When I was eight months pregnant, he said, "I could just leave you." I don't know how I mustered up the strength, but I said, "Stop threatening and just do." I went throughout the house and packed up all of his belongings. He left and I changed the locks the next morning. Within weeks, my position at work was cut and I had a complication with the pregnancy. I had to stay in the hospital and then had the baby early. She spent a while in the ICU.

I had no food or money to raise my child. When my child started eating solid food, I had to face the music and go onto public assistance. I am a proud woman and that was one of the most painful things I've ever had to do. A friend who was a social worker insisted that I do it or she was going to turn me in for not having any food to feed my child. Within six months, I had turned myself around. I found another data analyst job that paid $54,000 a year and I was on my way.

I started dating another man when my daughter was five. He started to wiggle his way into my world and, while I enjoyed the human contact and companionship, I recognized the signs that he was a taker. I wasn't going to get caught up in another bad relationship. We had one last hurrah in the hay and then I cut him off. I had stomach bypass surgery and decided to work on myself before bringing someone else into my family unit. I focused on my daughter and myself.

When I felt ready to try again, I decided to try to learn how to date. I looked into online dating. I decided to only look at gainfully employed men and was very specific about the lifestyle choices. I did not want a smoker, an alcoholic, or a recreational drug user. I wanted someone who was good with children. I had some on-line conversations with several men and learned to spot the dibble-dabblers.

Next, I decided that my self-improvement journey would include me doing something every week that I had never done before – I was going to enjoy new experiences. I tried escargot. One thing I had never tried was having a beer in an Irish pub. I went in a pub one afternoon while I waited for my daughter to finish her gymnastics class. It was dark and ominous. The bartender asked in a thick brogue, "What'll you be havin'?" I said, "I'll have a Guinness because I like my beer dark and my men white." You could hear a pin drop. I returned the following Sunday while I waited for my daughter to finish the gymnastics class. The bartender asked me what I was having and a pink-faced Irishman yelled from the back, "She'll be having a Guinness." I said, "No, I'll be having a Pearl Harbor." The bartender had to look that one up. The Irishman bought me another and we had a nice conversation. I was trying to disqualify him under my new criteria. He was gainfully employed. Granted the fact that I met him in a pub could indicate an alcohol problem. But, he gave me his business card and I called him a couple of days later.

I invited him to coffee and he accepted. After coffee, we went for a walk. I figured we would end up in the pub, but we walked for two hours. We went for ice cream. We went to the market. We went to a children's toy store where he needed to buy a gift for a niece. He opened the doors for me. He took the bags and carried them for me. Although I wasn't terribly physically attracted to him, we dated for a couple of months. The relationship gradually migrated into a sexual relationship. He would stay at my house four nights out of the seven. After we had dated for a year, we decided to buy a place together. My daughter and I have been living with him for three years.

However, once we moved in together, I noticed there was no longer any sexual activity. I thought maybe it was the pressure of the new mortgage. I looked into whether he had erectile dysfunction. He did not. He just wasn't interested. I went to the naughty shop to see if I could spice things up and peak an interest. I bought myself a vibrator and operated the thing for eight hours in a row. I started thinking I was a freak. I called the naughty shop and inquired whether there was something wrong with me. They assured me that it was normal. I used it and used it. I asked a friend of mine who was in the naughty business to help me get my relationship going. She sent me a set of Ben Wah balls.

I showed my boyfriend and I put them in and proceed to stand up. All of a sudden, I heard, "Plop, plop." Both balls dropped out of my vagina onto the Pergo floor. He laughed and thought it was funny. We continued going through life as usual. I work in Boston and my commute is three and a half hours a day.

Clearly, I wasn't getting what I wanted at home. I started to go out for a drink at different spots on the way home at night. It became a habit and a pattern. I kept pushing my boyfriend as to why we weren't having sex. He told me that he liked things the way they were and that he didn't want to change it. He told me that he loved me the way you would love a sibling or mother. He met 80% of what I wanted in a relationship; we were just missing the 20% sexual component. We were missing the sexual compatibility. He met all of his financial obligations.

At that point, I initiated communications with my sweet sixteen lover from Jamaica. We had stayed in touch over the last thirty years and over the long-distances – he lived in another country. I never stopped loving him. We lost contact when he became married because I did not want to interfere with his marriage. It turns out that he had begun looking for me as well. Although he was still married to the same woman, their marriage was on the rocks. We proceeded to pick up where we left off as if no time had passed. We talk to and text each other every day. My heart flutters every time we talk. Now, we are both at a place where we don't want to hurt our partners, but we both know we are not proper mates for our partners. There is a level of intimacy that I get with my old lover that I have never had with anyone else. He satisfies me in every way.

My live-in companion knows about my love. We have agreed to remain good friends and roommates, but that I will maintain a relationship with my old lover. I told him that I love my old lover and would like to have a sexual relationship with him. He told me to do what I need to do. I am now going to have them both. My lover is tired of being sick and tired with his current wife. They have been on a roller coaster of arguing for years. I envision myself as having a blended family. My family will be my current live-in companion, my lover when he is in the States, and my daughter. I am going to have the best of both worlds: a dynamic, sporadic, sexual fun relationship and my live-in as a responsible roommate. I have determined that it is all about getting your needs met and there are many ways to do it. This may not be traditional, but it works for me.

LESSON LEARNED: Stand up for yourself. Work on yourself so that you like yourself before you look to bring a man into the fray. Don't repeat your mistakes. Be open to the untraditional.

XI. Wisdom of the Ages –
A Breath of Fresh Air with the
Sixties & Seventies

As we prepare for our golden years, we realize that we reap what we sow. Some have left the baggage back in the middle years, realizing that it doesn't add value to carry it around; it only causes an aching back. It is at this point that people seem ready to look at their relationships with acceptance; if they have a partner, love is true and built on years of mutual experience. If they don't have a partner, they have what they have built throughout their life whether it be a family or a wealth of experience. This group more often accepts life for what it is; they know who they are and are no longer trying to prove they are someone else.

A. A Married Erudite

He is in his late sixties. He is married, but doesn't wear a ring. In fact, he never had a marriage ring. He has been married to the same woman for more than forty years. Together, they have traveled the globe. Their life has been fortunate in all areas. They have children and grandchildren. He is an atheist.

1. *What do you think about today's dating arena?* In many ways dating used to be more charming. Kids now are coming from more affluent areas and are tending to go out as groups. They play sports together. During my time you had to have steady dates. It is much healthier to have many friends and go out in groups.

    In my time there were many one-night stands after the college years. I met most of the women in singles' bars in NY City and at parties; the game was understood for both sexes. This was early in sixties. The sex act did not create a relationship obligation. There were no concerns about STD's. The only concern was pregnancy. You know the old saying: "Women are promiscuous, men are adventurous." After marriage, I have remained monogamous for 41 years.

2. *What are the problems for people dating today? And what makes it difficult to date today?* Generationally, young people have difficulty believing they are going to have a better life than their parents had. The uncertainty of today's world affects them post-college. Kids getting out of college today are not knowing if they can get a job. The in-

security and what-ifs and whether they can pay for their dates creates
anxiety and therefore adversely affects dating and relationships.
Women are now more capable of paying for things and taking care of
themselves. People will marry much later and don't have children. In
the developing world, you will have populations exploding and in the
industrial countries, there will be lower birth rates; therefore, the
younger generation will no longer be able to support the older in the
industrialized world. This will create a global problem.

This recession is pretty good for us getting back to families. There
are more extended families today as a result of the economy.

3. *What is attractive in women?* Past physical, most people like to mirror
themselves. Men in shape go for women in shape. The playboy image
of women is imaginary. If you want to cling onto your fantasy, you
better be rich, otherwise you'll be alone as a poor man.

I am attracted to women who are healthy and in good shape. I am
attracted to successful, happy, dancing people. They must be open-
minded. No baggage. I find the emotional crazy person to be a turn-
off. Anger and inner turmoil stuff drags down a relationship before it
can get started.

4. *What is sexy in women?* Breasts and bottoms. Dynamic, fun loving,
free, and full of energy. I find most women sexy. I like women.

5. *Is spirituality important in finding a mate?* Religion was never a topic
of conversation, as we didn't care. Who gave a shit?

6. *What is a turn-off in women?* Bad breath just kills. Less perfume is
better. Mean-spirited is bad; so is being demeaning and not being nice
to other people. Someone who knows everything and is judgmental. A
know-it-all is the worst. Unfortunately, times have changed in the dating world and I see a lot of gold-diggers out there. They have no values; they have nothing to offer but their vaginas or penises.

7. *What else do you see in the dating world?* You have a lot more exposure to pornography through the Internet today. Sport fucking is a
common occurrence. It is having sex without an emotional connection
and you are simply trying to see who is the fittest. The kids are hooking up these days without emotional attachment; they are basically
having a continuous stream of one-night stands. It is interesting to note
that a smart 18 year old ends up being a smart 40,50,60, or 70 year old.
People don't change; they evolve.

8. *How did you know your wife was the one?* We were set up by my
crazy roommate and married eight weeks later. She was supposed to

go out with him, but she ended up going out with me. Certain people make you feel good about yourself. You should marry those. Not the ones who create drama in your life or bring you down. That doesn't last. Timing is important. When you are at the right place at the right time, the right person comes along and it all falls in place. We genuinely liked each other.

9. *How old were you when you married her?* I was 26 years old.

10. *Thinking back on it, what would you change in your life, if anything?* I have been an extremely fortunate guy. My life is so much better than my parents' was and it has exceeded any imagined expectations and dreams.

11. *Is lingerie important to you?* I have no idea. Not particularly.

12. *What qualities did your wife have that made her attractive?* She is an exceedingly nice person. Artistic. Totally non-judgmental, almost no prejudice, kids like her immediately. Most men are more analytical. The way to know women is to think like a man with less logic and accountability.

13. *Did you date more than one woman at a time? If so, how did that work?* I never dated. I just went out with whomever I wanted. I had friends with benefits. We all went out with other people. Exclusive dating was rare and not expected.

14. *Do you believe there is a dating game? If so, what is it?* People play games according to their phase of life. There are people who are insecure who play the games and are afraid to be themselves. There are those who have bad values. They are the ones who cheated in school, and they manipulate the work force to get what they want. They also do it socially. They will continue cheating and manipulating and ending up alone inside and divorced. And there are people who just enjoy playing games.

In my opinion, 50% of married men and 35% of married women cheat. Women who stay in the cheating marriage stay for a variety of reasons. Most stay for the kids or because they are really in love. Others are abused emotionally and don't know how to get out. Still, other women want a meal ticket.

I don't think women or men should automatically divorce their spouses because of a slip, things can happen in the heat of the moment and it may be isolated from their love for the other person. People go through periods of life when they need validation for themselves; they might ask questions like, "How do I look?" Or "Am I desirable?" They do this to fill a void. But, if the cheating is chronic, then it is a different situation; they need help.

For women who have chronic cheating husbands, they turn the other eye because it is a lot to give up. If the woman stays with a poor man, she was probably emotionally and physically abused. If a woman stays with a rich man, she probably needs the financial support and status. The rich man's cheating wife stays due to being power hungry and liking the perks. If either spouse admits to it, they are out to hurt the other.

15. *Tell us about the most exotic places where you have had sex?* In Denmark with a nurse in the nursing school. On the deck of the cruise ship. On the beach in Shangri-la.

16. *How is sex as you get older?* Forty-year old men get horny. Fifty-year old men can have sex everyday, but not necessarily with their wives. I asked my wife to have sex back to back. She asked how. I said, "Bring over two other people and we would face them." We put too much emphasis on sex.

I don't think married people should tell each other about their affairs. It is a high-risk game. It is better to have fantasies and flirt.

B. A Captivating, Single Woman

We interviewed a 70-year old woman who was fit, limber, and one with herself. She was beautiful and full of life.

1. *How were you when you were young?* I was known to be ecstasy and disaster together. From a very young age, I defied authority, responsibility, acceptance and sameness. I was beautiful at the age of 18.

2. *Tell us your philosophy on life.* My life has been tumultuous and beautiful at the same time. My passion for life is endless. I have often thought that I was not from this world; I have been able to see beyond what most people were able to see in all aspects of life. Passion is the most important thing in life. I have passionately embraced life. Whatever I did, I did with passion and intense tenacity.

3. *Where did you learn most of life's lessons?* I was married and divorced, I lost a child when he was 21, I have had numerous affairs, I again married – this time to a true Prince Charming -- just because I could. I ultimately divorced him because I couldn't take perfect every day, day in and day out. He became boring; flowers and beautiful din-

ners every day. I was accustomed to turbulence and ups and downs. I needed excitement in my life. I broke his heart; he did everything for me and everything that he thought would make me happy. What he didn't realize and could not understand was that it didn't always have to be perfect. Life is not perfect. I needed variety and the unknown and the unexpected.

4. *What would you have done differently?* I would have loved more, laughed more and would have taken life much easier. I now believe that however you take life, it comes back to you. If you take it easy, it will be easy; if you take it hard, it will be hard.

When my Prince Charming entered my life, I was ecstatic. But after a while, he became boring and I needed to move on. I couldn't accept the fact that one more time life was bringing me ecstasy. I had to ruin it for myself one more time. Looking back, a little boring isn't so bad.

XII. The New Rules

First and foremost, there are no rules in dating. However, we can offer some guidelines. Be efficient; treat dating like a business. Unless you have all the time and money in the world, you must be efficient. Be aware, keep your eyes and ears open, and be real.

1. Love and know yourself to death.
2. Be real and true to yourself.
3. Go places where you'll meet people with common interests.
   a. For example, if you want to meet an alcoholic drunk, go to a bar to meet your future mate. Don't be surprised when you don't find an Einstein.
   b. If you want to date an active person, join a gym or sign up for a hiking club, join a USTA tennis team, or take some golf lessons and then go golfing.
   c. If you like a quiet reader, join a book club. Maybe the members of the club are not available, but they will have friends who share their common interests.
4. Ask for an activity date, not a dinner date. Save your dinner date for a time when you are comfortable being yourself with the other person; no need to be fake.
5. There is nothing wrong with splitting the bill. If you are a female, know that the guy will be relieved. The girl should be modern enough to split the bill without expecting a free ride. It is expected in today's society that each person is an equal and that means paying your fair share.
6. Politics and religion should not be avoided, but openly discussed with humor and no judgment. Don't take anything too seriously, but issues like these are very important to put on the table up front.
7. Don't take yourself too seriously, EVER. This will allow you to be free to laugh, love, live and make mistakes.
8. <u>Be humorous</u>. A sense of humor is your best marketing tool!
9. Life is too short to worry; enjoy the dating process. What will be will be if you don't force it.
10. Do not over-analyze tings. No one but you gives a SHIT about your past, your problems, or your issues. People steer away from negative, opinionated, and sarcastic people. It's almost better to be self-absorbed than one of the above. Get over your baggage. The past is

passed – it means nothing unless you make it everything. Don't forget that you may evolve over time – go ahead, reinvent yourself.

11. Be open and honest about your feelings – this makes you less emotional and sets everyone at ease. Honesty eliminates the game. It also eliminates ambiguity and shows your sensitivity. Show your sensitivity; it is okay. Always communicate. Be truthful about your expectations. If you enjoyed your first date, text the person and say, "I really enjoyed our outing. I hope to see you again." There is no reason to wait a certain number of hours or days to communicate. If such communication is not well received, do you really want to be with the person?

12. Don't over think things. Let it happen. Forget the game about wondering whether the other person liked you or will call you. Do what comes naturally to yourself. Be real and true to yourself. If you feel that you want to call, email, or text to set up another date, then do it.

The sooner you are rejected, the sooner you can move on and quit wasting your energy on someone who is not interested. Conversely, the sooner you find that the other is interested in another date, the sooner you can move forward.

The old rules of waiting for the phone to ring went out with the old landlines. Those rules are outdated, inefficient and emotionally distressing. There is simply no need to put yourself on a back shelf, hoping that someone will dust you off.

13. People don't change; they evolve. Your basic personality is set. If you're sunny, you are sunny. If you are an Eyeore, you are an Eyeore. What you can do is work on yourself to accentuate the positive and focus less on the less appealing aspects of your personality.

14. FLAWS, flaws, flaws. Remember, no one is perfect, including you. Soon the looks and the honeymoon period will end. Reality sets in when you realize the other has a flaw or two. The more people become comfortable, the more real they become.

15. Refer to #1 and #2. When reality sets in, it will be okay if you followed #1 and #2. If you did, there will be smooth sailing. If not, get out because people do not change on a dime – they are who they are. You cannot force someone to evolve into what you want; that is a natural process within themselves.

16. Do not have sex on the first date, even though it may be tempting. Resist with all your might. There is nothing wrong with having sex on a first date if you are looking for a one-night stand or a quick fling.

But this is no way to enter a long-term relationship because the relationship will be based upon physical attraction. One of the two of you may have a bad night (not perform up to your full potential) and you can never overcome that first impression. The foundation has not been set yet. Sometimes, the physical fades before the concrete in the foundation is dry.

XIII. Conclusion

Oprah also instructed the Stanford graduates in how to deal with "failures." She pointed out that:

> Nobody's journey is seamless or smooth. We all stumble. We all have setbacks. If things go wrong, you hit a dead end – as you will – it's just life's way of saying time to change course. So, ask every failure – this is what I do with every failure, every crisis, every difficult time – I say, what is this here to teach me? And as soon as you get the lesson, you get to move on. If you really get the lesson, you pass and you don't have to repeat the class. If you don't get the lesson, it shows up wearing another pair of pants – or skirt – to give you some remedial work. And what I've found is that difficulties come when you don't pay attention to life's whisper, because life always whispers to you first. And if you ignore the whisper, sooner or later you'll get a scream. Whatever you resist persists.[10]

She told them to ask the right question: "not why is this happening, but what is this here to teach me? – it puts you in the place and space to get the lesson you need."[11] She advised the graduates to live for the here and now when looking for happiness and to live for the moment and for today: "Whatever has happened to you in your past has no power over this present moment, because life is now." [12]

To date successfully, which means enjoying the process while looking for and finding whomever and whatever makes you happy, leave your baggage on the shelf and learn from the lessons provided in your past. Get to know who you are. In spite of labels and preconceived ideas about who and what you want, go into the dating market with an open mind and open heart. Trust your feelings. Desperation limits and repels, whereas confidence and contentment in yourself opens the door and provides a magnetic pull. The right person for you is out there. The harder you try, the more frustrated you'll become because the less you'll find. The less you look,

---

[10] http://news-service.stanford.edu/news/2008/june18/como-061808.html

[11] http://news-service.stanford.edu/news/2008/june18/como-061808.html

[12] http://news-service.stanford.edu/news/2008/june18/como-061808.html

the more you will find and the happier you will be. Spend your energy and time on the most important person in your life – you! Focus your energy on getting to know yourself – what do you really like? When you are happy with yourself and secure in who you are, others will be attracted to you and want to share in your life. Treat yourself to something good and fun once in a while and let life happen. Most importantly, know that in the dating scene, there is no concrete and finite game. If you're playing a game, make sure the other person knows that there is a game to be played and that they are playing the same game.

Enjoy the journey and each moment in the journey. Osho says it best in his book <u>Maturity: The Responsibility of Being Oneself</u> in a chapter involving climbing Mount Everest -- You have to take the journey to enjoy it and to reach your goal. On page 82 he writes:

> Hence my insistence not to renounce the world. Be in it, take its challenge, accept its dangers, its hurts, wounds. Go through it. Don't avoid it, don't try to find a shortcut because there is none. It is a struggle, it is arduous, it is an uphill task, but that is how one reaches the peak.

> And the joy will be more, far more than if you were dropped on the peak by a helicopter, because then you will have reached there ungrown; you will not be able to enjoy it. Just think of the difference. You try hard to reach Everest. It is so dangerous – every possibility of dying on the way, every possibility of never reaching to the peak; hazardous, dangerous. Death is waiting for you at each step, so many traps and so many possibilities of being defeated rather than being successful. Out of one hundred possibilities there is only one possibility that you may reach. But the closer you come to the peak, the higher the joy rises in you. Your spirit soars high. You earn it, it is not free. And the more you have paid for it, the more you will enjoy it. Then imagine – you can be dropped from a helicopter on the top. You will stand on the top and you will just look silly, stupid – what are you doing here? Within five minutes you will be finished, you will say, "So I have seen it! There is nothing much here!"

> The journey creates the goal. The goal is not sitting there at the end of the journey, the journey creates it at each step. The journey and the goal are not separate, they are not two things.

344

The end and the means are not two things. The end is spread over all the way; all the means contain the end in them.

Most importantly, when looking for happiness in the journey of dating and relationships, remember that, "*Seriously* . . . It's Not You; It's Me!" ™

APPENDIX

THE GRAVITY WHEEL – Depicts the magnetic pull toward certain characters.

We have found throughout our interviews that certain characters gravitate toward certain other characters in the dating world. While each of us hopes to find our version of Eve and Prince Charming, we are lucky to end up with our real Princess or Prince, who may be, in whole or in part, any one of the characters discussed in our book.

We created the Gravity Wheel to use as a tool when you meet a new character and want to test compatibility. Be careful, this is not scientific, but it is fun! You may find that you fit into several categories; maybe you are evenly distributed over several or you strongly identify with one. It is up to you to figure where you fit on the Gravity Wheel. Make your own deductions about your match, but see what you think of ours.

Use the Gravity Wheel as follows. Our twenty-six characters occupy the spaces on the left half of the Gravity Wheel. The characters are numbered and divided into sections of Takers, Give & Take, and Givers. Each character's "match" (the various characters that are most often found with that particular character – for better or worse) is found on the same numbered section on the right half of the Gravity Wheel. Note that the wheel is not a mirror image, what is good for one is not necessarily good for the other. You may then reference the book to learn about the potential matching characters.

Our twenty-six characters are briefly defined and described on the following page.

Takers

1. Diplomat: The ultimate Player who enriches others' lives.
2. Magnet: Player who has status and wealth, but no entitlement or self worth and who makes others feel badly after being with him.
3. Forever Bachelor: Player who is a smooth operator, but cannot commit for the long-term.
4. Sportsman: Player who has indiscriminate sex.
5. Gold-Digger: The ultimate user of others; climbing the ladder of wealth.
6. Smotherer: Quick to love and even quicker to demand commitment.
7. Home Wrecker: Partakes in the spoils of his or her friends.
8. Psycho Drama: Attention-seeking and scene-making.
9. Has-Been: Stuck in the success of the past; bruises the emotions of others for fun.
10. The Opportunist: The true chameleon.
11. Circumstantially Correct: Hiding behind the expectations of others.
12. Diva: A woman who plays by her own rules.

The Give & Take

13. Forbidden Fruit: Uses sex for power & energy.
14. Desperate Dater: Intensely wanting a relationship.
15. Trapped: Stuck in an emotionally abusive or loveless relationship.
16. Aggressively Awkward: Loudmouth jerk who is ignorant of social norms.
17. Passively Awkward: Shy and insecure.
18. Perpetual Kid: A fun-loving, impetuous person who has never emotionally grown up.

The Givers

19. Fantasizer: Likes a naughty diversion.
20. Responsible Adult: A loyal rule-follower who takes care of everything.
21. Nurturer: Takes care of others physically and emotionally.
22. Intellectual Professor: A loyal and responsible know-it-all.
23. Addict: Filling a void by clinging onto anyone or anything.
24. Put Upon Somebody [PUS]: A team player who has invested in the relationship and has a vested interest therein.
25. Stepped Upon Nobody [SUN]: Doormat with not much to offer; will accept whatever is offered in a relationship. SUN can be with any character; the issue is whether the other can deal with SUN.
26. The Lost Surfer: Confused and still learning about self.

The Gravity Wheel

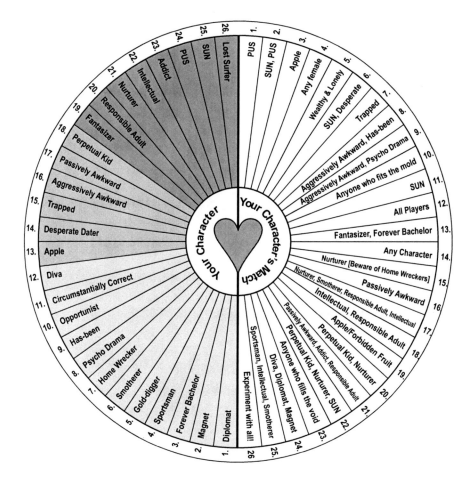

REFERENCES

Behrendt, Greg and Tuccillo, Liz. He's Just Not That Into You: The No-Excuses Truth to Understanding Guys. Simon Spotlight Entertainment, 2004.

Greene, Robert. The Art of Seduction. New York: Penguin (Non-Classics), 2003.

Osho. Maturity: The Responsibility of Being Oneself. USA: St. Martin's Griffin, 1999.

PBS. "Documentary on The Kennedys - A saga of ambition, wealth, familiy loyalty, and personal tragedy." [Online] Available http://video.PBS.org/video/1125268583/chapter/13/PBS. (July 1, 2009).

Stanford News. "Oprah talks to graduates about feelings, failure and finding happiness." [Online] Available http://news-service.stanford.edu/news/2008/june18/como-061808.html. (June 27, 2008).

Unknown. "Brainy Quote." [Online] Available http://www.brainyquote.com/quotes/quotes/j/jackiekenn126998.html. (9/1/09).

Unknown. "Brainy Quote." [Online] Available http://www.brainyquote.com/quotes/v/voltaire_133391.html. (11/4/09).

ABOUT THE AUTHORS

Marjan Fariba (right) and **Tiffany Lyon** (left) are two Saratoga women who have just completed their first book, _Seriously ... It's Not You; It's Me!_™ The dynamic energy between the two has resulted in an unbelievably creative and productive team that is at the heart of their production company, Impish Nymph Productions LLC. Through their current project, Marjan and Tiffany share their epiphany that the words in the old dating brush-off, "It's Not You; It's Me," actually ring true.

Marjan immigrated to the United States from Iran when she was eleven. She studied at Ohio State University where she met her husband. They moved to California and she completed her education in Public Relations and Marketing at San Jose State University. Since graduating, Marjan has established a thriving child development center, raised two sons, worked in high tech with start-up companies, served on many boards, chaired several campaigns and lead many successful fundraising drives in the areas of education, politics, entertainment, and business development. In addition, Marjan has been heavily involved with her community, serving in city and county offices.

Tiffany has a degree in Business Administration with emphases in Finance, Accounting, and Economic Analysis and Policy from the Haas School of Business at the University of California, Berkeley. She earned her law degree from Santa Clara University, School of Law. Immediately out of law school, Tiffany clerked for Justice Panelli on the California Supreme Court. She then practiced in various areas of law, including criminal prosecution, securities, and business litigation. However, her passion has always been writing. She has two children and is now pursuing her passion in life with her friend and writing partner, Marjan.

Breinigsville, PA USA
24 November 2009
228098BV00002B/2/P

9 781935 125624